GOETHE'S FAUST

Introduction

PART I: TEXT AND NOTES

R-M. S. HEFFNER
University of Wisconsin

HELMUT REHDER
University of Illinois

W. F. TWADDELL
Brown University

D. C. HEATH AND COMPANY
BOSTON

Printed in the United States of America

6 E 2

Library of Congress Catalog Card Number: 54-5658

FOREWORD

THIS EDITION has been made for the American student, not the Goethe scholar. We have kept in mind an American in his or her early twenties, who has a practical command of the fundamentals of German grammar and a vocabulary of a few thousand words in German, who is capable of reading and has some practice in reading adult literature, who already has some experience and still has some curiosity about the way this universe is put together and the way human beings get along with each other.

We have not tried to supply all the background and detailed information which such a student's teacher needs. We try instead to help that teacher by freeing his class time for the larger businesses of a FAUST course by giving the student the equipment needed to understand the actual text that lies before him.

These aims — positive and negative — have determined our editorial policy.

The text we print is aimed to reproduce the words which Goethe wrote or dictated. In this we have followed the authoritative tradition, which is unambiguous in nearly all points. The details of form (spelling, punctuation, compounding, capitalization, paragraphing), which represent the fashion of a time or the whim of a printer, have been subjected to critical scrutiny from the point of view of intelligibility.

The choice of Antiqua rather than Fraktur was easy.

Our spellings conform to current modern German usage (and coincide in large measure with Duden's formulations). Questions of compounding and hyphenization have been considered in the light of the *Wortindex zu Goethes Faust,* with an aim of achieving a consistency hitherto unattained in an edition of FAUST.

We have followed the increasingly common practice of using capital letters only for nominals and for the beginnings of sentences; see Duden, *Rechtschreibung* (13. Auflage, 1948), 19*.

Our most troublesome problem has been punctuation. We have found no predecessor and no tradition using the marks of punctuation as significant guides to meaning and the organization of ideas within the speech. Accordingly we have, in effect, reconsidered the punctuation throughout. We try to follow good German practice, with one special tendency: where German usage would *permit* a choice between two markings (e.g. comma or semicolon), and English would *require* or *favor* one of these (e.g. comma), we have selected that one. The result will occasionally strike a German reader as capricious (never, we hope, as incorrect); but it should help the American reader to follow the organization and development of ideas.

The longer speeches have been subjected to a similar pragmatic examination from the point of view of paragraphing. The printing tradition of FAUST makes some provision for major changes of theme, in the form of line break spaces in some of the long speeches. Most of these we have retained. We have added a few, where an important shift in thought occurs. We have also added indications of inner organization within a speech or a section of a speech by indenting the first line of a new sub-section.

We are well aware that our punctuations and paragraphings represent analytical interpretations; and in some few cases, no doubt, we have thereby led the reader to an interpretation at variance with the teacher's. We have preferred this disadvantage to the alternative: leaving the student with no guidepost to the organization of thoughts within a speech.

In three cases we have added stage directions, where Goethe did not specify an exit which is required by the subsequent action, and where this omission might trouble a careful reader. These additions are: SD 1525 *Ab.* SD 3715 *Faust und Mephistopheles ab.* SD 8159 *Thales und Homunculus* (*entfernen sich*).

The introduction is addressed to the student who is reading FAUST for the first time. In it we try to give him information about the poem which will add to his understanding and pleasure in reading it. We are more concerned with the poem FAUST itself than with FAUST as a milestone in German literature. Accordingly we give an account of its author insofar as a knowledge of his life and personality contributes to a reading of the poem, the content of the pre-Goethean Faust-tradition which influenced the composition of this work, the history of that composition itself, the social and intellectual background of Goethe's time as reflected in the FAUST poem, and a sketch of the rôle of FAUST in nineteenth and twentieth century thought.

Each chapter of the introduction is a more or less self-contained essay. The order in which the several chapters are here printed is not necessarily the order in which they must be read. Chapters I, VII, and VIII can be read at the beginning of the course. Chapters II–VI, which presuppose some knowledge of the poem, can be read during the course to supplement lectures and classroom discussion.

The notes are designed to further the understanding of the text. They offer assistance in the analysis of linguistically difficult phrases, clauses, and sentences. Only rarely is an individual word discussed in the notes for linguistic elucidation; the complete German-English vocabulary (Volume III of this edition) makes that unnecessary.

The chief purpose of the notes is to supply information which Goethe could presuppose in his immediate audience and which a modern American student cannot be expected to command: some knowledge of the period of the historical Faust; the European scene of 1770–1830, known to Goethe and his contemporary readers at first hand; the common knowledge of the educated reader of the time — the Bible, classical mythology, the current scientific and philosophical ideas of the period.

In the notes we aim to help the student understand a specific passage of the poem, not to increase his general knowledge or lead him into interesting excursions through German literature.

In the preparation of this Student's Edition, all three of the editors participated actively in every phase of the work.

The text was first scrutinized by R–MSH, with HR and WFT discussing R–MSH's proposals and making their own. After a dozen rounds of discussion, a mimeographed work-version was prepared. Thereafter WFT kept the books on text revisions, with proposals coming from R–MSH and HR and WFT.

For the introduction, R–MSH and WFT submitted sketch outlines of the desirable material. WFT drafted Chapters I and VIII, HR Chapters II–VI, R–MSH Chapter VII. Voluminous and vigorous discussion followed.

For the notes, WFT submitted a list of questions, referred to scenes, passages, lines, and words, which the notes should answer. R–MSH drafted notes to answer these questions, and others which occurred to all three of us. Discussions and counter-suggestions have led to the present form of the notes.

The vocabulary was prepared in three stages. HR first prepared A–K, and WFT prepared L–Z; two years later the rôles were reversed in a re-examination of the entries. (Or perhaps it was the other way around; none of us can remember confidently.) Then R–MSH examined the entire draft and raised questions and objections; R–MSH also kept the vocabulary entries abreast of early rounds of text and notes discussions. Some later revisions of text are not reflected in the vocabulary; we have introduced notes to protect the student from confusion in these cases.* We record here one misprint in the vocabulary: on page 176, in the entry *zustandekommen*, the past participle vowel should of course be **o**.

It goes without saying that when three persons with such different backgrounds, training, and interests as ours attack a job of this kind there are bound to be irreconcilable differences of opinion as to what to do and how to do it. The firmness of our friendship and our familiarity with each other's prejudices, based on a decade of close association and cooperation, made possible completely uninhibited discussion. Our more-than-average stubbornness insured that the discussion would be prolonged and vigorous.

Inevitably, there are points in this edition which were settled by a two-to-one vote, after full discussion. In some of these points, the minority of one is deeply convinced that the majority is wrong. No one of us regards this as being, from his individual point of view, the ideal Student's Edition of FAUST. But all of us are convinced in reason that the relatively few compromises and 2–1 decisions are less disadvantageous to the student user than the crotchets and personal idiosyncrasies which would have characterized any edition prepared exclusively by any one of us.

At any rate, the user can be assured that everything in this edition was carefully and repeatedly studied by all three editors. Whatever is here is here because either (a) two of us, at least, preferred it to an

* The advanced student of FAUST will find valuable supplementary material and illuminating discussion in Stuart Atkins: Some Lexicographical Notes on Goethe's FAUST (Mod. Lang. Qu. 14.82–97).

alternative, or (b) none of us was disturbed by it to the extent of making an objection.

We have used the major editions in our work of establishing the text; Hecker's has been particularly useful. The *Wortindex zu Goethes Faust* has been an invaluable tool.

Our colleagues have been generously helpful: we owe thanks to Roald Bergethon, Martin Joos, Walther Naumann, and Detlev Schumann for corrections and suggestions.

Even greater is our debt to the three loyal ladies who have endured almost five years of FAUST-widowhood.

R–M. S. Heffner
Helmut Rehder
W. F. Twaddell

June 1951

INTRODUCTION

INTRODUCTION

I. Goethe: A Biographical Sketch

Johann Wolfgang Goethe was born August 28, 1749 in Frankfurt-am-Main. His childhood was spent in circumstances of comfort and prosperity: his father had become a man of wealth and influence, largely by his own efforts; his mother was a member of a Frankfurt family which for generations had been prominent in the political, social, and commercial life of the city.

At the time of Goethe's birth, his father was nearly forty years old, his mother barely eighteen. In temperament, as well as in years, the parents differed — the father serious and severe, the mother imaginative and vivacious; throughout her life she remained close to her son through her wholesome and affectionate understanding. A gifted sister, Friederike Christiane Cornelia, the only sibling to survive infancy, who was one year younger than Johann Wolfgang, was the other member of the family to contribute significantly to the future poet's boyhood experiences.

His formal education was in the hands of his versatile and cultivated father, and of private tutors. The home had a good library and a large collection of paintings. And the Frankfurt of Goethe's childhood was the scene of exciting events. French troops were stationed there in 1759 (a high-ranking French officer was quartered upon the Goethe family); in 1764 the new Emperor of the Holy Roman Empire was crowned with great ceremony in the "Roemer," the medieval city building of Frankfurt.

Goethe's university education began when he was sixteen. In the autumn of 1765, he was sent to Leipzig, the metropolis of Saxony. Here the law courses in which he was enrolled interested him less than the social life in the city; but some courses in literature and the sciences and some extra-curricular studies in art, although outside his "major field," made an impression on the youth. He continued the experiments in verse which he had begun in his last years in Frankfurt; but now, in plays and lyrics, he aimed at a tone of conventional sophistication in the French manner, which was the mode of the time.

In the summer of 1768, Goethe became seriously ill. He was called home to Frankfurt to recuperate. For more than a year and a half it was considered unwise for him to attempt to return to university studies; at least once in this period (December 7, 1768) his life was despaired of. During this enforced leisure, the youth read extensively in ancient and contemporary literature; he also became absorbed in occult lore — notably the works of Theophrastus Paracelsus, Helmont, Swedenborg, and Welling's OPUS MAGO-CABBALISTICUM.

Still undecided between the orthodox beliefs in which he had been raised and the ways of freethinking he had acquired in Leipzig, the twenty-year-old Goethe was much influenced by an elderly friend of his family, Susanna von Klettenberg, who was devoted to pietistic doctrines and interested in spiritism and who induced him to engage extensively in introspection and to read widely in mystic and alchemistic writings.

By the spring of 1770, Goethe's recovery was so nearly complete that he could resume his university studies, this time in Strassburg. The young man who went to the Alsatian capital in April 1770 had outgrown the affectation of precocious cynicism which he had acquired in Leipzig, and was ready to meet emotion and idealism as realities. The first adult love of his life (Friederike Brion, the daughter of a country parson at Sesenheim) and the first close association with an intellect he had to respect as superior to his own (Johann Gottfried Herder, a young theologian) were both primary experiences, which Goethe underwent and reacted to without pose.

The love affair with Friederike resulted in deep-seated emotional turmoil and ultimate flight. Remorse over having deserted his love pursued Goethe for many years. His association with Herder brought him into contact with English literature, particularly with Shakespeare and Goldsmith, who were favorite subjects of Herder's inquiries into the nature of art and genius.

Goethe carried on his studies with enough diligence to receive his law license; but he also discussed art, philosophy, history of civilization with Herder and others; and he wrote lyrics of a directness and spontaneity hitherto unknown in Western literature, and planned dramas in which emotional violence was to break through the restraints of formal tradition.

The 22-year-old lawyer began his practice in Frankfurt in 1771, and spent some months of the following year at the Imperial Supreme Court in Wetzlar. In Frankfurt he found relief from the routine tedium of the law in talk with bright young critics and authors. In Wetzlar he barely escaped an ethical catastrophe: he fell in love with Charlotte Buff, a colleague's fiancée. Flight, and the writing of DIE LEIDEN DES JUNGEN WERTHERS — a novel (published 1774) which made Goethe known throughout Europe — saved him from disaster. Meanwhile, with the publication of GÖTZ VON BERLICHINGEN (a biographical drama of a Renaissance knight who dies maintaining ideals of individual freedom and justice), CLAVIGO (a drama of an ambitious but irresolute young man, who finds his career obstructed by his engagement to the girl he had once deeply adored), critical articles and reviews in the *Frankfurter Gelehrte Anzeigen*, and lyrics exalting genius and emotion, Goethe had won a leading place in the literary movement known as "Sturm und Drang," usually translated as "Storm and Stress." EGMONT (a tragedy of the revolt in the

Netherlands against Spanish rule), published in 1788, but planned and in large part written before 1775, and FAUST (see pages 32–36) are other enterprises of these busy years.

Love, too, was not absent in this Frankfurt period. Lili Schönemann, the daughter of a wealthy Frankfurt banking family, inspired some charming lyrics and became engaged to young Goethe. But the engagement was amicably broken after a few months.

By 1774, Goethe was sufficiently well-known to be sought out by the eighteen-year-old hereditary duke of Weimar, Karl August. On a trip to Paris in 1774, Karl August met the 25-year-old writer, and invited him to visit Weimar. The invitation was renewed in 1775. In November of that year, Goethe paid the visit to Weimar, a visit which lasted over fifty-six years.

At first, there was a period of gay enjoyment of the fun offered by a provincial court. Goethe and the young duke were each regarded as a bad influence on the other. But the duke saw more in Goethe than either the literary or the conventional faultfinders had been able to see: he found in Goethe an invaluable adviser and brought him more and more into positions of responsibility in the government. Goethe became a Geheimrat, later a Staatsminister; he threw himself into the planning-and-development administration of mining, forestry, and agriculture. By June 1782, when he was thirty-two, he had become Minister of Finance — the most powerful man in the government, after the duke himself. Yet he was constantly engaged in the management of the most trivial as well as the most important affairs. The poet suffered, for the time; but the man grew in assurance and maturity that was to enrich his poetry incomparably; the student of literature became a student of nature, and a student of ordinary humanity. The poet became a scientist with practical yet poetic understanding of the physical universe, an efficient man of affairs with both intuition and calculating experience, and — as a result — a poet who not only felt, but knew and calculated and appraised.

The maturing effects of responsibility for practical affairs were reinforced during Goethe's early years in Weimar by his love for a mature and inspiring woman. Frau von Stein, the wife of a fairly important official, was most nearly Goethe's equal of all the many women in his life. She was older than he, the mother of seven children, a woman of culture and discrimination, a stabilizing rather than a disruptive force. In more than a decade of intimate association with her the "Sturm und Drang" genius learned to respect discipline and taste, to acknowledge the claims of good form in life and classical restraint in literature.

The demands of practical day-by-day business, and the reappraisal of literary values, made this period, 1775–1786, one of the least productive in Goethe's literary life. A few superb lyrics, some sketches of masterpieces which were finished only later — these were the only visible products of a time in which a great man was attaining his stature. Some time in these years, a young noblewoman, Fräulein von Göchhausen, was allowed to copy a bundle of manuscript fragments of a FAUST, some scenes of which Goethe had read to a social gathering with great effect. This copy came to light in 1887; it is the so-called URFAUST. In these years, too, IPHIGENIE AUF TAURIS and WILHELM MEISTERS THEATRALISCHE SENDUNG were sketched and in part written out.

In the late summer of 1786, more than ten years after he had "come to visit" Weimar, Goethe was on vacation in Carlsbad, a Bohemian spa. The mysterious "daemon" which revealed to him what he must seek and what he must shun dictated his next move. Without a word to any of his friends in Weimar, Goethe left Carlsbad — traveling south, not west; instead of returning to his routine duties and routine social activities in the little German court, he journeyed to Italy — the land of ancient and Renaissance art, of antiquity, of the classics, and of Mediterranean acceptance of nature.

Whether Goethe's "daemon" drew him to Italy or drove him from Weimar, the year and a half in the South was a decisive rededication to his poetic calling. To be sure, Goethe in Italy was no longer the "Stürmer und Dränger" who had won international fame with GÖTZ and WERTHER. He was already a Goethe logically committed to form and discipline; in Italy he became a Goethe emotionally reconciled to and zealous for form and discipline, as the truest vehicles of truth. In his eager receptiveness, he found that the Mediterranean way of life about him gave him a better understanding of classical literature and art, and vice versa; forty years later, an aged Goethe was to remember his encounter with classical sculpture with almost youthful vividness:

> Vom frischen Geiste fühl' ich mich durchdrungen,
> Gestalten groß, groß die Erinnerungen.
>
> (FAUST 7190)

The Italian sojourn was by no means merely a passive, receptive experience. Goethe was working during these months in Italy, perhaps as he never worked again until those miraculous months when the octogenarian genius completed "the main business" — FAUST. Here, in Italy, between October 1786 and April 1788, he completed two major plays, made great progress with a third play, and composed two important scenes of FAUST. Significantly, revision of works of his earlier years busied him more than new undertakings: he was in his late thirties, the first "old age" of a genius. He set about reworking his youthful writings into the form which his judicious middle age could approve. In the terminology of literary historians, Goethe was no longer a "Stürmer und Dränger"; he was a classicist.

In Rome he drastically revised IPHIGENIE AUF TAURIS, a drama of the redeeming power of one individual's ethical integrity; the earlier prose IPHIGENIE was now recast into iambic verse which combines austerity and flexibility. EGMONT was prepared for the printer. The packet of FAUST-notes was studied and worked on: the chief product was the scene *Wald und Höhle,* much of which is in iambic pentameter, like IPHIGENIE. Yet his progress with FAUST was small, compared with what he accomplished with his other works. When FAUST: EIN FRAGMENT was published in 1790, it included some results of the revision in Italy, but omitted some scenes which — as we know from the URFAUST — already existed in the earlier version.

During the spring of 1788, in Italy and on the way back to Weimar, Goethe worked on his TASSO, the tragedy of a court poet whose intense imagination and sensitivity link him with the only woman who understands him, while their different social statuses separate them; at the same time, he is cut off from the practical man who is his intellectual counterpart by the difference between the mental processes of the poet and the practical man's calculating common sense.

In April 1788 Goethe traveled north to Weimar. He found himself, after nearly two years of absence, almost a visitor again. The old friends, seen from the end-point of Goethe's changed views, were almost unrecognizable. Frau von Stein was estranged; the literary associates were still echoing "Sturm und Drang." The next few years recall the restlessness — almost the planlessness — of youth. Goethe met and loved a girl in her early twenties — Christiane Vulpius, a worker in an artificial-flower factory. (She bore him a son in 1789, whereupon Goethe took her into his home as his common-law wife; he married her formally in 1806 to protect her and their son's legal interests; for almost thirty years, until her death in 1816, she was an anchor of domestic security and comfort.) Goethe undertook laboratory studies in botany, zoology, and physics, publishing researches of some importance. He spent several weeks in Venice; he accompanied the duke on journeys; he took part in two of the campaigns of the Napoleonic wars; he wrote poems, novels, plays; he resigned from most of his official posts, but began a 22-year term as director of the Weimar theater.

The decisive new human relationship which gave new impetus and direction to Goethe's genius in these post-Italian years was the friendship with Schiller, beginning in 1794, when Goethe was 45 and Schiller 35. The younger man had followed in the path Goethe had traveled. In 1794, after several years of rather impersonal association, the two geniuses became close friends, on terms of mutual admiration. The older man could respect the younger's intellectual power; Schiller could defer to Goethe's versatility and intuition. The decade of their association, from

1794 to Schiller's death in May 1805, enriched literature as well as their personal lives, for each stimulated the other to works which would scarcely have been undertaken, let alone completed, without the counsel and criticism which flowed back and forth in letters and discussions in Weimar and Jena.

Goethe's response to this friendship was a renewed dedication of his talents to literature. By 1794 he had begun to rework earlier sketches of WILHELM MEISTERS LEHRJAHRE — originally a novel of the theater, now broadened in scope to portray a young man's apprenticeship to life rather than the stage. To Schiller's influence can be traced the completion of the LEHRJAHRE (1796), the composition of HERMANN UND DOROTHEA (an epic, with a happy ending, of displaced persons fleeing the French Revolution), ballads, and the resumption of work on FAUST. It was not until after Schiller's death, however, that the next FAUST publication appeared: in 1808 FAUST: DER TRAGÖDIE ERSTER TEIL was published in the form in which we now know it. This "completion" was only a partial victory over the stubborn subject matter which had fascinated and foiled Goethe for a third of a century; he had to win "completion" by relegating to a future Second Part that mass of themes and actions with which he still felt unable to cope.

From 1808 on, FAUST was but one of many literary enterprises of the poet. DIE WAHLVERWANDTSCHAFTEN, a novel of subtle psychological analysis, appeared in 1809, when Goethe was 60; in 1810 his FARBENLEHRE, a formidable monograph on optics, was published; and in 1811 the first book of his autobiography, DICHTUNG UND WAHRHEIT, came from the press, the second and third books following in 1812 and 1814.

In 1819, the 70-year-old poet published a collection of lyrics, WESTÖSTLICHER DIWAN, reflecting his love for Marianne von Willemer. These lyrics, within an Oriental (Persian) framework, fuse the ever-young ardor of love with the discipline of maturity, communicating the complex wisdom of the old Goethe in images of the utmost simplicity and directness.

Meanwhile, scientific treatises, critical reviews, and the continuation of WILHELM MEISTER were being sketched, revised, polished, and published. Goethe's prodigious correspondence with the leaders of literature, art, and science in Germany, France, England, Scandinavia, Russia, and Italy would have taxed the full energy of most men.

The last revitalizing emotional upheaval was the septuagenarian's love for a teen-age girl, Ulrike von Levetzow, which stopped at the point of a formal proposal of marriage. Goethe's renunciation — the last great "Entbehren sollst du, sollst entbehren" — is reflected directly in the magnificent TRILOGIE DER LEIDENSCHAFT ("Marienbader Elegie," 1823–1824) and indirectly in the energy which led to the completion of FAUST, as an inescapable duty.

As early as 1800, Goethe had sketched a HELENA scene in classical verse forms. In 1816 he outlined in prose a résumé of Acts I, III, and IV of the Second Part. In 1825 the work on a HELENA episode began in earnest. Goethe studied Greek history, geography, mythology; in 1827 he published HELENA. KLASSISCH-ROMANTISCHE PHANTASMAGORIE. ZWISCHENSPIEL ZU FAUST. This is Act III of the Second Part as we now have it.

Bit by bit, Acts I, II, and IV were drafted and worked over. Parts of Act V (Faust's death) had been undertaken thirty years earlier. The revision of such earlier sketches and the filling in of the gaps between them became the "main business" of the poet. When the 12th volume of Goethe's collected works appeared in 1828, it included lines 4613–6036 of FAUST, Part II.

The remainder of Part II (6037–8487, 10 039–12 111) was the work of Goethe's last years. By his 82nd birthday, he had finished it; it appeared late in 1832, the first of Goethe's posthumous publications.

For the student of FAUST, these are the crucial dates:

1749, August 28: Born.
1770–75: First sketches of FAUST (Goethe in his early twenties).
177?: URFAUST copied by Fräulein von Göchhausen.
1790: FAUST: EIN FRAGMENT (Goethe 41 years old).
1800: First draft of part of HELENA scene (Goethe 51 years old).
1808: FAUST: DER TRAGÖDIE ERSTER TEIL (Goethe 59 years old).
1816: Prose sketch of Part II, Acts I, III, IV (Goethe 67).
1827: HELENA published (Goethe 78).
1828: Lines 4613–6036 published (Goethe 79).
1831, August: Part II completed, copied, sealed (Goethe 82).
1832, March 22: Died.

II. Goethe and the Legend of Doctor Faust

The Theme of Goethe's FAUST — Goethe and the Poetic Tradition — Goethe Encounters Faust — The Legend of Doctor Faust — The Literary Faust Tradition.

1. THE THEME OF GOETHE'S FAUST

FAUST: EINE TRAGÖDIE — the most respected dramatic poem in the German language — occupied Goethe's creative imagination for sixty years. When Goethe first conceived the idea of writing a Faust drama, Thomas Jefferson was just entering on a brilliant political career. By the time Goethe was preparing for print the last portions of his FAUST, Andrew Jackson was in the White House, and the young Abraham Lincoln was waiting on customers in a little country store in Illinois. In 1768, when Goethe possibly wrote the first sketch of a scene dealing with Faust in academic surroundings, the young poet-student was scarcely aware of the world tensions which eight years later were to lead to the American Declaration of Independence. When in 1831 the poet noted in his diary, "The main business accomplished," he had witnessed two revolutions in France (1789 and 1830) and the Napoleonic wars — events which marked the beginning of the transformation of Western culture into a rapidly progressing, technological, democratic civilization.

Still, Goethe's FAUST, though it owes much to the spiritual climate of the age, is not a direct outgrowth of these upheavals and developments. Nor is it merely a dramatization of the private experiences of a poet, nor merely the artistic treatment of a historical theme: the life and the death of the arch-magician Doctor Faustus. In its poetic message, which at times is concealed in cryptic symbolism, FAUST may be considered the drama of modern Man — a poem portraying events, characters, and problems of human life in terms of the cultural and intellectual history of modern times since the days of the Renaissance.

Faust: Modern Man. To recognize the theme of FAUST as peculiarly "modern" is one thing; whether it was so meant by its author is another. Like any great work of art, FAUST is rich enough to satisfy many tastes and permit many interpretations. The words of the Stage Manager, "Wer vieles bringt, wird manchem etwas bringen" (97), indeed apply to FAUST. The thoughtful reader will find more here than the mere "story" of Faust and Margaret, or of a wretched "adept's" servitude to the Devil. Such a thoughtful reader, if he is interested in history, may be able to identify in the play reflections of the French Revolution (1789), or of the War of Greek Liberation (1821–1829); but he will also be able to recognize any war or any revolution when he realizes that the historical background of this play is not limited to the late Middle Ages or early Renaissance but spans three thousand years, from the days of Helen of Troy to relatively recent political and cultural events. If the thoughtful reader should happen to be a scientist, he will find that many a problem in the fields of physics and biology, familiar to modern research, may have been not entirely unknown to Goethe's poetic vision. If the reader is a philosopher, he will be impressed with the wealth of abstract thought in Goethe's poem; but all of these abstract thoughts are infused into the richness of human experience which is here unfolded.

Much of the play is laid in scenes remote from modern life; yet none of the characters, none of the thinking or feeling, is "obsolete" or "old-fashioned." What these characters have to say concerns us today as much as it concerned Goethe when he created them. FAUST is relevant, not because it sets forth a particular doctrine, but because it inquires into the purposes and values of human existence, as these appear in many kinds of deliberate and constructive, or desultory and destructive human activities. In reading FAUST the student of the human mind will discern some of the desires and drives which account for suffering or happiness, hope or despair among men. The student of human society will discover some of the tensions which make for war, and some of the stability which brings about peace. The creative intellectual, when he reads FAUST, will become aware of the factors which may allow him to succeed or may cause him to fail. The lover will find a mirror of his passion, the cynic a challenge to his wit, the believer a challenge to his faith. Fathers will read lines in FAUST which will remind them of the inadequacies of their sons, and sons may begin to understand the shortcomings of their fathers. FAUST is human in its scope, and neither the remote historical scene nor the scholarly paraphernalia of the play interfere with its strong human appeal to the reader in modern times.

"Progress" and the individual. Viewed in this perspective of universal human significance, FAUST is the first symbolic drama in world literature to appraise the role of the individual — his liberty, initiative, and integrity — within a society that is bent on material and spiritual progress. Faust's nature is characterized by the words he speaks in his old age:

> Im Weiterschreiten find' er Qual und Glück, —
> er, unbefriedigt jeden Augenblick! (11 452)

These words exemplify a concept of limitless progress. They apply to a type of man particularly adapted to a world of "practical" considerations: the active man, the efficient man, "der Tüchtige" (11 446), who has not even begun to exhaust the resources of this planet and who is therefore spurred on to ever greater discoveries, achievements — and disappointments. There may be moments in the life of such an individual in which he finds himself in conflict with his community. Organized society may either stimulate or stifle individual initiative; and powerful individual initiative, if it is not properly balanced and controlled, may produce, not a genius, but a criminal.

Faust possesses the potentialities of both the genius and the criminal. In this play Faust is not presented as an individual consistently advancing to ever higher levels of intellect and morality. On the contrary, as the play unfolds, Faust's development seems to be the very opposite of such "progress." Nevertheless, as he is held back, or sometimes even driven forward, by his own failings, he represents in his activities a crusade much greater than his career: the upward course of the human race. The evolution of human culture is comparable to that of organisms — except that man's progress is contingent upon the development of moral freedom and therefore upon an increase of "wisdom" and a limitation of individual license and selfishness. The words of the Lord in the 'Prolog' apply equally to Faust and to Man in general:

> Ein guter Mensch, in seinem dunklen Drange,
> ist sich des rechten Weges wohl bewußt. (329)

Not until the reader has realized this, will he become aware that he is observing Faust on a path of action that leads, not from imperfection to perfection, nor from guilt to atonement, but from a state of "dull confusion" to a state of increasing clarity which is, after all, the natural progress of individual as well as general human culture in the course of history.

Two drives of Man. Still, with all its symbolism and mysteries, the FAUST poem is not sugar-coated philosophy. It is rather the colorful poetic portrayal of two very real and powerful impulses which at all times have distinguished the human race in its evolutionary progress and have been at the root of many a human enterprise: the drive of love and the drive for knowledge.

Love is not limited to any particular cultural level or period. Figures like Gretchen or Helen of Troy have lived at all times. The drive for knowledge, on the other hand, organized into a consistent and systematic endeavor, is characteristic of more "rational" modern times. But it is a perennial human trait which has found expression in the literature of all ages. The Old Testament pictured the desire for ultimate knowledge as the beginning of man's fall into sin. The Greek world celebrated this drive in such figures as Ulysses and Empedocles. Ever since antiquity such figures as the sage, the explorer, the scholar have been objects of admiration and respect — because their motives seemed new and extraordinary, and because often they sacrificed personal comfort to the spirit of inquiry. Even the modern folklore — science fiction — is in awe of the "scientist" who builds space ships and robots, only to have his ambition and curiosity rewarded by fear for his life when the products of his constructive imagination turn against him.

In the FAUST poem, which derives from popular fiction, the drive of love and the drive for knowledge are intimately connected with and modified by the precepts of the Christian tradition. Although Western civilization, in the nearly two thousand years of the Christian tradition, has sublimated love to *Caritas* — Charity, the love of one's neighbor — it has at the same time tolerated the fixing of some stigma of sinfulness upon the drive for knowledge. The Christian Middle Ages attached the label of "magician" to the lone scholar who ventured to explore the realm of nature at his own risk. For centuries the story of Doctor Faustus and his sinister companion, Mephistopheles, served as a striking example of the "godless" pursuit of magic art.

Magic. The inclusion of "magic" in the FAUST poem poses a difficult problem for the modern reader. Surely he cannot be expected — as readers of the 16th century Faust story could be expected — to believe in the miraculous effectiveness of mere words or in the performance of supernatural deeds. And yet in his own world, a modern reader of FAUST is faced with a complexity of social and technological processes of which he possesses no detailed and accurate knowledge. In fact, he must often accept effects which to his reasoning may appear miraculous. He has placed his trust in the expert and he assumes that the expert has obtained his results by mysterious but natural and rational means. Faust's use of magic must be viewed in this perspective. Faust is no longer the "miracle man" of primitive tribes — who may be either an uncommonly gifted person or a fake. Faust is the individual whose objective is insight into the cause-and-effect relationships in his experience.

Thus, the FAUST poem is not concerned with the performance of miraculous feats, but rather with the exploration of "new spheres of pure activity" (705) which, like any first exploration, contains an element of daring, risk, and uncompromising desire to know. In Goethe's work, the legendary magician Faustus who signed his "soul" over to the devil in order to "penetrate the unknown" has become the searcher for truth who is eager to find it in any province of human experience. The heretical wizard of the 16th century was assigned to eternal perdition; the Faust of Goethe's poem is vindicated because in his life he exemplifies the "will of God": the search for truth and for ever-increasing clarity.

The Faust theme. The theme of the FAUST poem, then, may be summarized thus: What is the role of personal initiative and merit in the progress of the human race? Ever since the days of the Renaissance the relative significance of personal merit has entered into the speculations on the attainment of human happiness. By the time Goethe came to write the first scenes of his FAUST, the discussion of this theme was in full swing; in fact, it had a distinct bearing on the intellectual development of the young poet.

2. GOETHE AND THE POETIC TRADITION

The academic view of literature which Goethe had encountered in Leipzig regarded the essential feature of poetry to be the skillful application of traditional classical rhetoric to writing in the national tongue. In this view, there were two criteria of great poetry: style and subject matter. With the ornamentation of a delicate or pompous style even inane generalizations, fanciful abstractions, or trivial observations could pass for genuine poetry. On the other hand, also the moral magnitude of a noble and elevating subject was held to establish the aesthetic value of literature, whether in a dignified tragedy or a heroic epic. Poetry was expected to instruct as well as to delight. The student of poetry and rhetoric was reminded by Opitz (BUCH VON DER DEUTSCHEN POETEREY, 1624, ed. Witkowski, p. 131) that "Poetry is the most ancient philosophy, a guide for life from youth on, which should teach the morals, the emotions, the conduct of man." A poet was free to follow his inspiration — provided he stayed within the limits of "nature"; and since the ancients, according to general assumption, had been closer to "nature," the more a poet imitated the ancients, the greater naturalness he would achieve.

Goethe's early poetic endeavors were not long guided by this rationalistic aesthetic theory. He felt that performances of this sort might be brilliant; but they might also be tiresome and barren. What they lacked was the convincing tone of personal experience. In his association with Herder, Goethe made the first great discovery of his life, a discovery which gave him and modern German poetry a new direction: the works of Shakespeare, where Goethe felt the authentic creative power of the word, the ability to express and communicate that which is alive and genuinely felt in every human being.

Literary historians have become accustomed to attach the label of "Storm and Stress" to the literary movement which took its keynote from the writings of Goethe, Hamann, Herder, Gerstenberg, and others. In 18th century France the process of intellectual enlightenment joined forces with the emotions of the populace and was carried into the streets in the enterprise of the French Revolution. In Germany, the revolutionary spirit remained the private endowment of a few enlightened or temperamental youths who refused to acknowledge any form of domination by an absolute principle — whether by absolute monarchy or by the rule of reason. They protested against the subordination of personal liberty to general or abstract considerations. Still, Storm and Stress betrays its close kinship to the movement of the Enlightenment. The same desire for abstract "truth" which dominated philosophical reasoning can be recognized in the desire for "originality" that animated the literary effusions of the younger generation. To possess "creative genius" was surely a mark of distinction and at least as desirable as the patient search for abstract "truth." Moreover, was not a creative "genius" better qualified to attain "truth" than the philosopher who follows reason? For if reason is a universal gift to all men, how could it suffice to express the personal and characteristic differences among individuals? And was not the individual the only "real" man, whereas "mankind" and its gift of "reason" were mere abstractions? Thus the writers of Storm and Stress emphasized just these personal and characteristic differences, exalted "genuineness" of experience rather than reasonableness, and gave expression to their intuitive and emotional "originality" rather than to abstract reflections and traditional standards of taste. Intelligent, self-assertive, freedom-loving, the writers of Storm and Stress refused to accept ethical clichés and social conventions. They desired to live intensively rather than prudently. Hence, they never organized into a political spearhead; they remained writers of dramas or literary satires and never became authors of political manifestoes or constitutions. In the Germany of the eighteenth century the Revolution remained an intellectual, an artistic enterprise, and lively discussions about the significance of Rousseau's call for a "return to nature," about Spinoza's pantheism, or about the simplicity and calm of Greek heroism, took the place of barricades and political assemblies.

Such was the literary scene in which Goethe assumed the position of leadership when he wrote his GÖTZ VON BERLICHINGEN and his WERTHER, and when he discovered the poetic symbol that expresses genuineness of experience, which he most completely formulated in his Faust figure.

3. GOETHE ENCOUNTERS FAUST

An author in search of a theme. A young man of twenty-four and a practicing lawyer of several years' experience, Goethe still had not found his real calling. Presumably he was devoting a passable minimum of his time to the study of his cases or of legal literature. A far greater portion was being spent in reading and reviewing the latest publications in literature and the fine arts. For a while he was an enthusiastic contributor to a review journal. But even this occupation did not satisfy his restless mind.

An attractive bachelor, Johann Wolfgang Goethe was not at all disliked by the young ladies of Frankfurt and Darmstadt society, and he was not always rebuffed by those whose fiancés were busy elsewhere earning a basis for future marriage. When he was left to himself Goethe sought comfort in nature — and nature was not easily accessible in those days without wading through the bottomless mud of footpaths and highways — or he tried his hand at painting and drawing (a hobby he never abandoned), or he read great books which filled him with a feeling for the glory and the misery of man — the works of Homer, Pindar, Cicero, Plutarch, "Ossian," Shakespeare, Rousseau.

Satires. Often a young poet feels compelled to test his powers in a satire directed against his own age. But Goethe's Storm and Stress satires express more than such capricious disapproval. They reveal a sincere faith in man, even though they censure what Goethe considered fundamental deceptions — the basic selfishness of pantheists (persiflage of Herder in "Satyros"), of over-sentimental pietists (Leuchsenring in "Pater Brey"), and sophisticated cynics ("Götter, Helden und Wieland"). Or they present the human world on the colorful stage of a country fair, as in the "Jahrmarktsfest von Plundersweilern," where grand and petty passions are displayed in grotesque confusion.

Hero-worship. These satires, casual as they may seem, form a counterpart to Goethe's more grandiose plans to portray or to dramatize the lives of the heroes of mankind, the bringers of culture and founders of religion — Prometheus, Mahomet, Socrates, and Christ. Of these, only the first two matured, and even they remained fragmentary. Like the unfinished epic, "Der ewige Jude," they were inspired by an almost mystical love of mankind, a profound awe for solitary greatness, and an equally profound melancholy over the inadequacy of all ages.

For Goethe, the years of "Sturm und Drang" were a period of restless tension and irrational productivity. Often his writings were "hingewühlt," as he said, almost without his will; but, though they may reflect incoherent frenzy, all of them present a fairly consistent picture of the young poet — a man who in his associations, in his letters, conversations, actions appeared unpredictable and possessed by a daemonic force.

It is not surprising that under these circumstances many of Goethe's poetic plans remained mere sketches. Only GÖTZ VON BERLICHINGEN, a play in the style of a Shakespearean "History" about a "rohen wohlmeinenden Selbsthelfer in wilder anarchischer Zeit," grew to imperfect completion (1773). It turned out to be rather a polemic aimed at the pedantic and timid spirit of security of Goethe's own age than a portrait of the age of the Reformation which it purported to paint.

The Renaissance. Goethe must have realized that Germany had never really shared in the splendor of the Renaissance which gave the European nations of the South and the West their Golden Age in world trade and politics, art and literature. Instead, the German century of the Reformation, dynamic as it was, was distinguished by such contradictory characters as Maximilian, the melancholy emperor and the "Last of the Knights," and Martin Luther, the steadfast reformer who feared both God and the Devil, by searching artists, such as Dürer, and speculative alchemists, such as Paracelsus. Germany produced no such celebrated poets as Italy (Ariosto), France (Ronsard), or England (Sir Philip Sidney), but pedantic master-singers (Hans Sachs) or gloomy satirists (Thomas Murner) and chroniclers (Sebastian Franck). Even Erasmus of Rotterdam, perhaps the most cosmopolitan mind north of the Alps, was not altogether free of the inner conflicts which characterized the spiritual heritage of the Germans.

Doctor Faust. In his studies of the Reformation era, Goethe encountered the figure of Doctor Johann Faust, world-famous magician and wayward scholar, who had forfeited his soul to the Devil in return for a period of pleasure, power, and magic accomplishments. Goethe had run across this mysterious character before, as a student in Leipzig, when he must have seen wall paintings in the cellar of 'Auerbachs Hof,' which depicted astonishing tricks performed by the sixteenth-century pseudo-scientist, whose story was already known to him from the performance of puppet plays in Frankfurt.

It is probable that Goethe was first attracted by the satirical possibilities in the story of this unfortunate victim of misguided learning. As with Götz von Berlichingen, Goethe may have been tempted to conjure up the memory of another desperate 'individualist in times of anarchy' in order to castigate the unjustified claims of learning and justice of his own time. The Imperial Court of Justice at Wetzlar, where Goethe practiced law in 1772, was but a shell surviving from former times, a slow-moving institution perpetuating shallowness and formalism and of little usefulness in the administration of justice. Also, the schools of higher learning in Goethe's time perpetuated a great deal of empty formalism. Goethe had attended two of them; both possessed excellent reputations and high standards, as schools went in those days. He had obtained a professional law degree at one of them, which at least qualified him for a job and pacified his father. But these schools had not furnished him the knowledge and understanding which seemed essential to him — insight into nature and man, into the origins and purposes of a complex human society, and into the concepts and habits which this society had come to adopt as "laws" governing its conduct, tastes, and beliefs.

So Goethe looked elsewhere to satisfy his needs, to books and to friends and mentors, to whom he was devoted as long as he could learn from them, and whom he left behind once he had absorbed whatever they had to offer. Behrisch in Leipzig, Herder in Strassburg, Merck in Darmstadt were such friends; their penetrating and cynical wit sometimes stimulated, and often punctured, the sentimental conceit of the young poet. Each of the three has variously been suspected of having contributed toward the portrait which Goethe later drew of Faust's associate, Mephistopheles. Only from his friendship with Herder in Strassburg did Goethe derive a lasting intellectual stimulation which has left a mark in many of his writings.

It is generally believed that during his university years Goethe not only became acquainted with the story of Doctor Faust, but that he toyed with the idea of writing a Faust drama which would reflect satirically, or perhaps even cynically, his own discontent and disillusion. That such a Faust play might have revealed much of its author's intellectual and emotional situation may be concluded from Goethe's confession, in retrospect, that he had carefully hidden these sketches from Herder's criticism, although he generally permitted Herder to participate in almost everything else that concerned him while they were together in Strassburg. In 1811, when he was a man of sixty (it is plausible that his memory was confusing facts with fiction), Goethe admitted a kinship between Faust's situation and his own, a similarity which, he said, had struck him when he was a young writer, groping for a way out of a serious intellectual predicament:

Die bedeutende Puppenspielfabel (Faust) klang und summte gar vieltönig in mir wider. Auch ich hatte mich in allem Wissen umhergetrieben und war früh genug auf die Eitelkeit desselben hingewiesen worden. Ich hatte es auch im Leben auf allerlei Weise versucht und war immer unbefriedigter und gequälter zurückgekommen. Nun trug ich diese Dinge, sowie manche andre, mit mir herum und ergötzte mich daran in einsamen Stunden, ohne jedoch etwas davon aufzuschreiben.

(DICHTUNG UND WAHRHEIT, 10. Buch)

The writing of FAUST was to progress through six decades and many involved stages. And the poetic transformation of a relatively simple story into one of the most profound books about humanity was not completed until many obstacles and inhibitions had been conquered. The FAUST poem has about as much in common with the Faust legends of the sixteenth and seventeenth centuries as the cathedral of St. Peter in Rome has with the marble quarries which furnished its building materials. Still, without the quarries, there would be no St. Peter's.

4. THE LEGEND OF DOCTOR FAUST

The historical Faust. The Doctor Faust of the sixteenth century, whose life ended around the year 1540 under mysterious circumstances, cannot have been merely a notorious swindler and mountebank. The persistent recurrence of reports dealing with his alchemistic exploits, his pact with the Devil, and his horrible demise indicate that he must have been a person of unusual character who excelled his more cautious and conventional contemporaries in daring and in the practical application of his knowledge.

These reports concern a vagrant scholar whose name appears sometimes as Johann Faust, sometimes as Georg Faust, also called Sabellicus. His name alone poses many riddles. Like many another learned man of the time he may have latinized his German name (Zabel?) to that of Sabellicus, suggesting the tribe of the Sabellians in ancient Italy who were held to be experts in magic, just as the people of ancient Thessaly were thought to possess magic powers (see lines 7920 ff). We do not know where Faust was born. Some believed that he came from the Swabian city of Knittlingen and, with peculiar etymological irony, had derived his name from that of his native town (*Knittel* "club, stick" = Lat. *fūstis:* Ger. *Faust*). A similar practice resulted in grotesque names for some of his more famous compatriots (Königsberger = *Regiomontanus*, Pickel = *Celtis*, Schwarzerdt = *Melanchthon*). Or he may have been boasting of his successful experiments in the black arts by adopting a Latin name for advertising purposes: the Fortunate, *Faustus*, "der Glückliche genannt" (cf. note to line

10 305). In this case, Faust's name suggests a meaning similar to that of Prospero, the sage in Shakespeare's TEMPEST.

Johann Faust's activities are reported in various cities in southwestern and central Germany during the first half of the sixteenth century. In Gelnhausen he boasted of being able to restore the lost writings of Plato and Aristotle. In Würzburg he made bold to imitate the miracles of Christ. He was driven out of Kreuznach as an untrustworthy teacher of the young. He associated with students at Heidelberg, Ingolstadt, Erfurt, Leipzig, and Wittenberg. Though he was never admitted to the faculty at any of these universities, his influence outside the classrooms appears to have been considerable; at any rate, in all of these places scholars and administrative authorities alike felt compelled to intervene and expel the corrupter of youth from their communities.

Not all of these stories deal with academic surroundings. True, Faust was alleged to have entertained students with an aërial flight to a princely wedding or with the supernatural appearance of Homeric characters before his frightened audience. Most of the tales show him deceiving peasants, innkeepers, friars, and other simple folk, performing spectacularly at imperial courts and furnishing horoscopes to persons of dignity and rank. Not all of these stories are of the farcical character which satisfied the crude taste of the sixteenth century. Some of the accounts indicate that Faust was a man of principle and character, even though this meant keeping his word to the Devil or facing the horrors of eternal damnation. It may have been secret respect for, and sympathy with, this mysterious outcast, as much as the horror at his wretched end, which kept his fame alive for more than two centuries. For, soon after his death, documents were circulated, first in Latin, then in German, which celebrated his talents and his adventures; and often the imagination of later chroniclers outweighed their respect for historical facts.

Growth of a legend. In these early literary documents, which are evidence of a lively oral tradition, the figure of Faust seems to have merged with older legends of sorcerers and necromancers in which the beliefs, fears, and desires of former ages had expressed themselves. Numerous are the legends built up around the personalities of men who defied the taboos of their times and sought to probe the unknown nature of man and the universe. Their strength lay in their "magic," their power over the "right" word; their weakness lay in their isolation, which invited distrust and condemnation. In ancient times there was thought to be something of a "magician" in all artists or scientists who succeeded in convincing their public of the reality of the make-believe which they produced. As violators of the conventions of their society they were regarded with both curiosity and indignation. Popular reasoning attributed their successes to a pact with the Devil, their frustration to their immorality and sin.

Many legends of such men of magic were told in Biblical, Latin, Greek, or oriental literature — among them the story of Simon Magus (see Acts 8), and similar legends about the potent sorcerer Cyprianus of Antiochia and about the pious bishop Theophilus of Cilicia, who became a victim of a pact with the Devil but was ultimately granted absolution by the Pope.

As the Church expanded and became established, these stories assumed a standard pattern. Seekers of knowledge outside the Church were suspected of traffic with the minions of Hell. These were believed to render service only upon the definite promise of the sorcerer's soul, confirmed by a contract valid for a specific period of time and validated, with all primitive rites of legality, by a signature in the victim's blood. It was an age with few scruples about the extermination of human lives upon the mere suspicion of witchcraft. As the belief in the power of the Devil over man shows, little confidence was placed in the strength of the human mind. In such an age, a physician who succeeded in saving lives where others had abandoned hope was not altogether free from suspicion of having employed devilish helpers. When even such recognized scholars as Albertus Magnus (1206–1280), Agrippa von Nettesheim (1486–1535), and Paracelsus (1493–1541) were not exempt from persecution, a vagrant alchemist like Faust was scarcely able to escape it.

5. THE LITERARY FAUST TRADITION

The cumulative Faust tradition is a good example of the growth of popular hearsay. About 1570, thirty years after Faust's death, an unknown writer in Nürnberg compiled an account of most astonishing feats performed by a notorious Doctor Faust. The subject, it appears, was of such interest to students that within a decade a semi-educated writer presented the story, adequately inflated, in their Latin. No copy of this Latin version has been preserved.

The first Faust Book. Interest in this story seems to have grown rapidly. In 1587 there appeared (in Frankfurt) the first printed account of the Faust legend, generally known as the "Volksbuch" (published by Spiess). Within five years at least sixteen different printings, legitimate or pirated, are recorded, to say nothing of those which have not been preserved. During the same period translations from the "Volksbuch" carried the fame of Doctor Faustus to England (1587), to France (1598), and to Holland (1592).

The "Volksbuch" did not attempt to give an "objective" account of Faust's amazing abilities. Rather, it had an axe to grind: with evangelistic zeal it held up the fate of the "weitbeschreyter Zauberer und Schwartzkünstler" as a warning to those who might be tempted to abandon God and ally themselves with the Devil, i.e., to tread the devious paths of alchemistic inquiry. Though the narrative, meanwhile grown to sixty-nine chapters, was obviously composed in a spirit of righteous indignation and as a frightening deterrent, the anonymous author could not fully conceal his attraction to the coarser and more sensational details of the story. He based his account on the preceding manuscript tradition; in fact, he alleged that he had at his disposal some papers left behind by Faust himself! However, out of concern for the salvation of his readers, he withheld the precise formula with which Faust had succeeded in conjuring up the Devil! The author must have been close to theological circles, since he liberally adorned his account with quotations from the Bible and with other pious admonitions; and he must have adhered to an orthodox Lutheran point of view, for he displayed strong anti-papal sentiments throughout (the Devil appears disguised as a monk) and localized the story at Wittenberg, the Saxon university town where the Reformation had started. This gave him the opportunity to contrast Doctor Faust, the associate of the Devil, with Doctor Luther, the man of God.

One of the significant features of the "Volksbuch" of 1587 is the emphasis on Faust's "speculative" ambition. This speculative interest has nothing in common with the higher intellectual aspirations which mark the eighteenth century and Goethe's Faust. "Speculation" in the "Volksbuch" is directed toward finding ways to enjoy with impunity those pleasures and acts which medieval ethics had branded as stemming from cardinal sins: pride, greed, voluptuousness, anger, gluttony, envy, and spiritual sloth. To the moralizing author, Faust's fate is a striking example of what happens when man forgets God; the effort of the narrator is to make his story whet the appetite of the uncritical reader to eagerly witness, with horror and contrition, the miserable end of an unrepentant sinner.

There is such a notable difference, in purpose and meaning, between the first surviving print of the Faust legend and Goethe's poem, that there is little profit in searching for agreement in detail. Suffice it to say that the earliest legend associates Faust with an ambassador from Hell, Mephostophiles (a name still not satisfactorily explained), and with an academic assistant, Wagner; that Faust lives with, and has a son by, fair Helen of Greece, both of whom, mother and son, vanish from sight on the same day on which Faust goes to his just reward.

New edition. A new and augmented edition of the Faust Book, printed in 1590, mentions Faust as performing impressive but not particularly significant tricks: he seats himself astride a barrel and rides it out of a wine cellar in Leipzig. On another occasion, he supplies a party at Erfurt with precious wines after equipping the tables with the appropriate taps. — More significant is the note on which the original Faust Book closes: "Be sober, be vigilant: because your adversary, the Devil, as a roaring lion, walketh about, seeking whom he may devour: whom resist, steadfast in your faith" (I Peter 5.8).

Other Faust Books. Whereas the Faust Book of 1587 seems to have been inspired by genuine theological concern, the Faust Book by Georg R. Widman (1599) was largely motivated by a demand for the sensational, the miraculous, the dreadful. Widman suppressed the few remaining scientific interests in the "History" of the famous magician and greatly inflated the demonological elements of the book, diluting them with extensive moralizing reflections. Widman's book was thoroughly revised in 1674 by Dr. Nicolaus Pfitzer of Nürnberg, who restored the erotic passages which Widman omitted, and thereby enhanced the popular character of the book. Pfitzer's version went through seven editions during the next fifty years. In 1725 it was supplanted by a streamlined version by an unknown author who, writing under the pen name of "Der Christlich-Meynende," favored the sensational over the moralizing element and, with an eye to sales, reduced Widman's compendium to a booklet which flooded the market in numerous editions until well toward the end of the century.

During his youth Goethe must have become acquainted with one or the other of these Faust Books, probably with that of the "Christlich-Meynende," the most accessible. Here he may have found the spelling of the name *Mephistopheles.* Other details which found a place in Goethe's FAUST, such as Faust's love for a simple country maiden and his infatuation with Helen of Troy, suggest an acquaintance with Pfitzer and Widman. By the time Goethe read these books, he had been reached by a different channel of the Faust tradition — one which may have appealed to the imagination of the young boy much more forcefully — the drama.

Folk Play. The stage of the mid-eighteenth century was colorful and spectacular. The actors were members of traveling companies who were accustomed more to failure and to the miseries of the road than to security in the pay of a few affluent patrons. Dependent upon the applause of a public of mediocre tastes and education, these companies sacrificed artistic quality to considerations of the box office. As a result, theatrical success was dubious, determined often by the glitter of stage properties, the excitement of the spectacle, and — rarely — by brilliance of the performance or the literary merit of the play.

Marlowe's FAUSTUS. The Faust legend was eminently suited for this baroque tradition of the theater, particularly insofar as the story of the impious, adventurous magician offered possibilities for staging the miraculous, the supernatural, and the horrendous. Shortly after the publication of the Faust Book of 1587, the legend became known in England (the English Faust Book of 1592 was an amended printing of an earlier English account of the story). It is not certain when Christopher Marlowe, the most "Faustian" of the early Elizabethan playwrights, composed his

TRAGICAL HISTORY OF DOCTOR FAUSTUS; it may have been as early as 1588. In Marlowe's hands the wretched "Doctor" of the Faust Book became a daring superman who expected from science a more than partial insight into the nature of human life. Marlowe's Faustus demands increase in personal powers, powers of action as well as enjoyment; he is not content with tricking peasants or students, but aims at directing world politics by influencing the Pope and the Emperor. Even the sensational circumstances of his death have grown in proportion with his tragic personality: not the horror of these circumstances alone, but the inward struggle in his anticipation of death puts Marlowe's Faustus in the ranks of those great characters with which the Elizabethan drama abounds.

Marlowe's play follows the account of the Faust Book fairly closely. But the rather monotonous sequence of the German prose report has been molded into an astonishingly compact composition of dramatic action and character. Obviously, the dramatist was fascinated by the tragic involvements of character, whereas the prose narrator had been more concerned with the feats than with the personality of his hero.

There is a peculiar resemblance between the structure of Marlowe's tragedy and Goethe's dramatic poem, at least in regard to what appears to have been Goethe's original plan. Marlowe's drama introduces its hero in his study in a grand soliloquy, in which the four "faculties" of the medieval university are examined and rejected, and the scholar succumbs to the enticements of magic. In Marlowe's FAUSTUS, as in Goethe's FAUST, the pact with the Devil is the result of two discussion scenes in the study. In Marlowe, the reason for the second scene is evident: Mephistophilis has to obtain the permission of his superior, Lucifer; in Goethe's play the reason for the second scene is not immediately transparent. Marlowe's Faustus demands power over the treasures of this earth and is willing to forego the prospects of eternal salvation in order to realize this desire. The drive for knowledge, the experience of love and beauty, the ambitions of an active life in the sphere of worldly power suggest a more than accidental similarity in the dramatic patterns.

Yet it is almost certain that Goethe was not even aware of Marlowe's play at the time of the earliest conception of his own poem (Goethe did not become acquainted with Marlowe's DOCTOR FAUSTUS until 1818, when it was translated into German). There may have been a German Faust drama at the end of the sixteenth century which shared with Marlowe's drama the same source and a similar structure. If there was, no trace of it has been preserved. On the other hand, when English comedians, touring the European continent in the following century, brought Marlowe's tragedy to Germany, a tradition of stage adaptations was started in which the English dramatist's masterpiece was only faintly recognizable. At any rate, throughout the next hundred and fifty years, the Faust fable remained alive in the repertory of popular stage presentations, of companies visiting large cities and small towns, princely courts and rural centers, country fairs and city festivals, in the pretentious performances of "machine comedies" and in the simple programs of puppet shows. When by popular demand the role of the harlequin ("Hanswurst," a clever little fool who alone managed to elude the sinister Mephistopheles) was emphasized and expanded, the Faust play became a favorite without which no repertory could claim completeness.

Around 1750 several German stages prided themselves on their extensive "machinery," which facilitated swift changes in scenery or the appearance of ghosts. It is established that such a "machine comedy," entitled "Das lastervolle Leben und erschröckliche Ende des . . . Erzzauberers Doctoris Joannis Fausti," was performed in Frankfurt in 1768. In such a comedy sublime and ridiculous elements were crudely joined. Possibly Goethe witnessed this performance shortly after his return from Leipzig. He may also have seen performances by other companies in Leipzig or in Strassburg. Susceptible as he was to any kind of popular art, he must have been deeply impressed with the tragic fate of Faust, with the satirical potentialities of Mephisto and Wagner, and with the daemonic charms of Helen of Troy. Thus he could claim, when he wrote his autobiography, that the ancient and mysterious fable of the puppet play of Doctor Faust "reverberated within him in manifold tunes."

Lessing's FAUST. We know that Goethe did not see the sketches of a Faust drama which Lessing, the great reformer of the German stage, was planning to write in the third quarter of the eighteenth century.* Still, Lessing's plan deserves mentioning because it appears to have been the first poetic treatment of the Faust legend in which the ancient magician did not meet the fate of eternal damnation. In this sense, Lessing's sketch was imbued with the same optimistic view of the human desire for knowledge which later was to characterize Goethe's dramatic poem. As a man of the Age of Reason, Lessing was not impressed by the orthodox view which condemned, as a disciple of Satan, the scholar who dared to seek the truth by means of his own powers. Goethe's Faust was more than a mere scholar. He experienced the world of practical affairs with all its emotional and spiritual tensions and crises. — However, Goethe was to wrestle with this great theme for many years before he arrived at a solution according to which Faust was no longer destined to end in Hell, but to earn spiritual salvation and justification.

Other Faust Books in Goethe's time. But before the Faust theme received

* Our knowledge of these sketches comes from a fragmentary scene printed in Lessing's 17th "Literaturbrief," from scattered notes found among his papers, and from reports by some of Lessing's friends. On the basis of these reports, the manuscript is believed either to have been lost with a piece of Lessing's baggage or to have been destroyed by Lessing himself.

its lasting formulation in Goethe's poem, it acquired, through lesser writers, a popularity seldom attained by other literary themes. The spectacle of Faust's tragic death continued to exert a grim fascination for some writers, who remained close to the tradition of the chapbook and popular plays. For other writers, touched by the cynicism of a more "enlightened" age, the story had lost much of its original significance and only offered possibilities for comedy, parody, or farce. On the stages in Catholic South Germany the theme underwent still further modification: the anti-papal jibes of the "Volksbuch" were eliminated or replaced, and sometimes even the prospect of divine forgiveness was held out to a properly repentant Faust. This ecclesiastical bias recalls the story of Cyprianus of Antiochia (see p. 20), which the Spaniard Calderón de la Barca (1600–1681) had dramatized in his EL MÁGICO PRODIGIOSO more than a century earlier.

Some of these plays have been lost — only the playbills attest to their existence; others exemplified the tastes of the times in which they were written, and have survived. Two Faust plays achieved passing fame: that of Paul Weidmann, whose allegorical drama JOHANN FAUST (1775) — at one time suspected of being Lessing's lost Faust play — maintained its place in German repertories for a number of years, expressing the sentimentalism of the age; and that of Friedrich Müller, known as "Maler Müller," whose spirited SITUATION AUS FAUSTS LEBEN (1776) and FAUSTS LEBEN I. TEIL (1778) deserve a place among the outstanding literary products of the "Sturm und Drang" movement.

According to Maler Müller, who dedicated his SITUATION to "Shakespeare's Spirit," Faust was to be an example of unfettered genius:

Es gibt Momente im Leben, — wer erfährt das nicht, hat's nicht schon tausendmal erfahren? — wo das Herz sich selbst überspringt, wo der herrlichste, beste Kerl, trotz Gerechtigkeit und Gesetze, absolut über sich selbst hinaus begehrt. — Von dieser Seite griff ich meinen Faust.

(*Dedication to* FAUSTS LEBEN)

As Maler Müller wrote this he knew that Goethe was engaged in writing a Faust poem; but no literary connections between the two poets can be established. Nor does Ferdinand Maximilian Klinger's novel of 1791, FAUSTS LEBEN, TATEN UND HÖLLENFAHRT, have anything in common with Goethe's FAUST, although the two writers — both natives of Frankfurt — had been temporarily associated in the early days of "Storm and Stress." Planned within the ambitious framework of ten novels, each of which, as a variation of the same theme, condemned the shortcomings of human society, Klinger's FAUST was a disguised philosophical inquiry into the origin of Evil; but its idealism turned into vociferous polemics, its compassion for mankind into expressions of solitary despair. It was a belated manifestation of ecstatic Rousseauism.

Even during the years when Goethe's FAUST was slowly growing into its present form, popular interest continued to encourage dramatizations of the legend. Among them the DOCTOR FAUST by Julius Heinrich von Soden (1797), Johann Friedrich Schink's JOHANN FAUST (1804), and Ernst Klingemann's DOCTOR FAUST (1814) achieved more than ephemeral recognition.

III. The Writing of FAUST

A Poet's Progress — History of Composition and Publication.

1. A POET'S PROGRESS

The six decades which Goethe spent writing FAUST were filled with many different activities that would have been full-time occupations for as many people. During these years, progress in the composition of FAUST was anything but steady. There were periods of intense concentration, impatience, and even haste, alternating with periods of indifference and repugnance. FAUST grew in two unequal stages: a relatively brief period characterized by Goethe's emotional instability and fitful creativeness (1770–1775) and a lengthy span of time (1775–1831) during which Goethe developed from a hotly-debated young author into the most respected literary figure of Europe.

Goethe in Weimar. On November 7, 1775, a little over a year after DIE LEIDEN DES JUNGEN WERTHERS had made Goethe famous, the young poet arrived at Weimar, the seat of the small provincial court in Central Germany with which his name was to be associated ever after. In Weimar, Goethe swiftly became the young duke's most intimate companion and councilor; here he grew from an unruly Storm-and-Stress genius into the sage to whom the educated travelers of the next half century made their pilgrimages. Here Goethe found the active life which his nature demanded, in the discharge of public duties and private responsibilities — as the administrator of mines, forests, theaters, and other institutions, and in the study of the natural sciences and humanities which challenged his mind and his imagination.

Weimar was the secure base from which he embarked on his many fruitful journeys — to South Germany and Switzerland, to the central German and Bohemian resorts, to Italy, to the Rhine, to northeastern France, to Berlin. In Weimar, and in the neighboring university community of Jena, friendship united him with many of the outstanding minds of the age: the poet and dramatist Schiller, the philosopher Schelling, the explorer and scientist Alexander von Humboldt, the diplomat Wilhelm von Humboldt. From Weimar he fled when he found no other way out of an unhappy passion for Frau von Stein (1786); to Weimar he withdrew when, in his old age, renunciation was the only solution for his love for Marianne von Willemer (1815) or Ulrike von Levetzow (1823).

Interests of an author. The twenty-six-year-old writer Goethe came to Weimar as a visitor with no more than his necessary baggage, and he had no expectation of a permanent association. His first home was a romantic garden house under the trees of the Duke's park. Fifty-seven years later, when Geheimrat von Goethe died, a Minister of State, he left a comfortable and rambling house, furnished in a dignified and balanced European taste, with an excellent library and one of the finest museum collections of his time in the fields of science and the arts. His collections were the cumulative result of hobby and methodical inquiry, the outward evidence of the astonishing range of Goethe's intellectual interests.

FAUST was probably not much more than a bundle of dramatic sketches when Goethe came to Weimar. Some promising beginnings existed, but if Goethe had any clearly defined plan for FAUST, we do not know what it was.

At first, his new obligations, the new associations, and the distracting life at the court allowed him time for little more than writing in a lighter vein. But when it came to more serious writing, he did not continue his work on FAUST, but turned to other works which dealt, in a limited fashion, with those fundamental problems which, as we now know, were to find their fullest expression in FAUST.

Major dramatic and narrative works. Such projects were EGMONT, the tragedy of the Flemish champion of liberty; IPHIGENIE AUF TAURIS, the legend of the priestess of early Greek antiquity who showed the way to "pure humanity" and inner freedom through determined self-discipline and the will for truth; TORQUATO TASSO, the drama of the Renaissance poet who had to learn how to place adjustment to others above his own God-given talents.

There were also plans for a biographical novel whose hero, like Tasso (and Goethe himself), had to find out that the detours in life were often more worth-while and exciting than the direct routes he had mapped for himself. WILHELM MEISTER, first conceived as a short novel dealing with a dilettante's "call to the ministry of the theater," turned out to be a much more complex theme than the author had realized; like FAUST, it occupied his creative imagination intermittently for more than fifty years. Its first part, the LEHRJAHRE, appeared in print in 1795–1796, but only after the first draft (which was begun as far back as the early Weimar years) had been thoroughly recast. The WANDERJAHRE, the second part of the novel, began to appear as late as 1821 and was not available in complete form until it was printed in the "Ausgabe letzter Hand" (1829), the last complete edition of Goethe's works made under his supervision.

The manner in which WILHELM MEISTER was written resembles to some degree the composition of FAUST. In both instances we observe the gradual completion of a "first part" which traces the growth of an individual under the influence of outward circumstances. Meanwhile, the more remote material, reflecting this individual's growth as a process of more universal significance, is reserved for the "second part," slowly accumulating, as it were, in an immense reservoir, which feeds the streams of poetic intuition during the last thirty years of the poet's life. Many of the shorter prose narratives which Goethe wrote after the completion of the LEHRJAHRE were later fitted into the mysterious mosaic of the WANDERJAHRE, and only the WAHLVERWANDTSCHAFTEN (1809) appeared as a separate novel, a mature counterpart to the youthfully sentimental LEIDEN DES JUNGEN WERTHERS (1774).

Lyrics. In Weimar Goethe became one of the foremost lyrical poets of his time (certainly one of the most articulate), who knew how to express human emotion and personal experience in meaningful language comprehensible to all. The less a poem appears "made," the more a reader feels that the experience it expresses may be his own. Goethe's poems possess a quality of directness and conciseness and human appeal which makes the reader accept them without wishing to inquire into the identity of their author or the particular occasion of their origin. The aspects of life which they present are the potential adventures of any reader: they reflect occasions of highest emotional tension ("An den Mond," 1778, "Marienbader Elegie," 1823) or serenity after turmoil ("Wandrers Nachtlied," 1780, "Urworte Orphisch," 1817); they show the sombre mood of a ballad ("Erlkönig," 1780, "Die Braut von Korinth," 1797) or the animated brightness of lyrical cycles ("Römische Elegien," 1795, "Westöstlicher Diwan," 1819).

These poems display an astonishing variety of form and structure, of rhythm and rime-pattern. Rarely did Goethe permit any fortunate pattern to become stereotyped, as any lesser lyrical poet might do who has "found his style." Almost all of Goethe's lyric poems are "occasional" poems, growing from personal experience rather than from meditation, with no other justification than that of a "lebendiges Gefühl der Zustände und Fähigkeit es auszudrücken." Each poem, in its own way, reflects an aspect of the continuity of change which, Goethe believed, is the nature of all existence.

Autobiographical writings. There are poets who prize intensity of personal experience as the indispensable content of poetry, even though this intensity involves a sacrifice of objective detachment in the poetic expression of that experience. The work of such a poet is likely to be autobiographical in nature. Of all of Goethe's writings, his lyrics reveal their "confession" character most clearly; and Goethe himself did not hesitate to admit that his novels and dramas, too, were "fragments of a great confession." Moreover, a considerable portion of Goethe's prose is devoted to an account of his own intellectual and artistic development, even when he is ostensibly describing the brilliant background of the times of his youth and the cultural currents of those times. Goethe's DICHTUNG UND WAHRHEIT (1811–1814) and his minor autobiographical writings, such as the ITALIENISCHE REISE (1816–1817) and CAMPAGNE IN FRANKREICH (1822), have a double function for the modern reader: as the portrait of a historical epoch of great significance, and as a poet's self-vindication. At a time when all of Europe was undergoing decisive changes at the hands of the ruthless conqueror Napoleon (Emperor of France 1804–1815) — when the United States and Great Britain were at war and the British occupied Washington (1814) — when nevertheless the young nation was vigorously expanding westward (Louisiana acquiring statehood in 1812, Indiana in 1816, Missouri in 1821) — Goethe was revealing the image of Europe during the years 1750–1792, as it presented itself to the eyes of one of its most receptive and universal spirits. He did so in a manner neither magnifying nor disparaging. He took stock of the existing realities, of the driving and restraining forces of his age. He scrutinized and weighed those spiritual, social, and political factors which in the growth of his own personality had been a gain, and those which had been a loss.

Moreover, the writing of his autobiography gave Goethe the opportunity to justify and, so to say, to atone for his conduct when, as a young man, he flitted from one love to another, unstable and unpredictable. DICHTUNG UND WAHRHEIT is not an accurate biography; it is the story of a genius who must pursue his course, however swiftly, along the path prescribed for ordinary men; a genius whom time and destiny have assigned to the role of a charioteer:

Wie von unsichtbaren Geistern gepeitscht, gehen die Sonnenpferde der Zeit mit unsers Schicksals leichtem Wagen durch, und uns bleibt nichts als, mutig gefaßt, die Zügel festzuhalten und bald rechts, bald links, vom Steine hier, vom Sturze da, die Räder wegzulenken. Wohin es geht, wer weiß es? Erinnert er sich doch kaum, woher er kam.

(*Conclusion of* DICHTUNG UND WAHRHEIT)

Scientific interests. There is a remarkable gap in Goethe's autobiographical narrative. The period between 1775 — his arrival in Weimar — and 1786 — his departure for Italy — is covered very inadequately in his biographical writings. It is precisely during this period of about ten years that Goethe went through what he considered the decisive educational experience of any individual: the process of limitation, the disciplining of will-power, the exercise of self-control. Like Torquato Tasso, the hero of his austere play, Goethe went through a painful school of self-discipline which made him a better citizen and a greater artist.

The trend toward objectivity and aloofness which marks Goethe's works from about 1778 on is paralleled by an ever-increasing interest in natural science. New responsibilities in the administration of the duchy forced Goethe to consolidate his knowledge in such fields as botany, geology, zoology, meteorology.

This was not Goethe's first contact with the natural sciences. In 1768–1770, after Goethe had returned sick from Leipzig, he read widely in alchemy and even undertook some experiments — studies which may have intensified his early interest in the Faust legend, since they made him acquainted with mystical and theosophical literature. His experiments in alchemy were a boyish hobby rather than a serious study of nature. They were short in observation and long on theory, if not mythology. Practitioners of this dubious art of alchemy ascribed certain "qualities" to certain "elements" and hoped to arrive at the "essence" of nature by synthesis, since they did not possess the proper equipment for analysis.

Goethe's more serious nature studies — begun at Weimar, earnestly pursued during his sojourn in Italy, and carried on methodically and in close consultation with scientists near and far ever after — followed a quite different principle. The mature Goethe insisted on observation; his manifold collections, his careful studies, his extended excursions and field trips were devoted to this purpose. His method of observation did not lead to dissection, the analysis of small and ever smaller particles of matter — the objective of specialized science. He did not aim at abstract classification of natural phenomena, as the botanical system of Linnaeus did; nor did he accept, or even approve of, the mathematical formulation of a natural law, which has been the basis of natural science since the days of Newton. Not unlike the nature studies of Benjamin Franklin, Goethe's "observation" was thoroughly descriptive; but it relied on intuition rather than on measurement. Preoccupied with the characteristic distinguishing features of a thing, Goethe sought to determine its underlying purposes and functions which, themselves inaccessible to direct observation, are manifested in the shape, form, configuration a natural object "happens" to assume. As a creative artist Goethe was concerned with the forms and configurations of the visible world around him which he called "Nature." As a philosopher (rather than a scientist) he believed that he could trace these forms to a "formative energy" which he also called "Nature." In his metaphysical speculation and theory, this "Nature" was not a domain of material phenomena, held together by an unbroken nexus of cause-and-effect and governed by laws that can be abstracted in mathematical formulas, like those of Newtonian physics; — it was rather a reality of matter *and* mind, a synthesis of substance and energy, in which the "geprägte Form" of any existing being was the necessary result of its intrinsic purpose.

Goethe considered "Life" to be such a synthesis of substance and energy: existence in any and all possible forms, held together by an unbroken nexus of continuous change ("Werden"). Consequently, Goethe's interest in the observation of individual "forms" was secondary to his desire to detect the "archetypes," or "basic forms," which he considered present and manifest in the disparate phases of development of any individual organism, class, or species; and since man, living being and observer, is included in this comprehensive image of Nature, any claim to perceive such "basic forms" presupposes appropriate qualifications, education, "Bildung," within the observer himself. Transformation, or metamorphosis, became the keyword of Goethe's philosophy of nature. "Metamorphosis" — a concept derived from intuition rather than borrowed from biological science and much less communicable than a mathematical formula — assumed for Goethe the significance of an artistic or even religious creed:

> Die Gottheit . . . ist wirksam im Lebendigen, aber nicht im Toten; sie ist im Werdenden und sich Verwandelnden, aber nicht im Gewordenen und Erstarrten. Deshalb hat auch die Vernunft in ihrer Tendenz zum Göttlichen es nur mit dem Werdenden, Lebendigen zu tun; der Verstand mit dem Gewordenen, Erstarrten, daß er es nutze.
>
> (Eckermann, GESPRÄCHE MIT GOETHE, February 13, 1829)

It is evident that Goethe's interest in a universal philosophy of Life, coupled with his desire for personal experience and a unique talent for lyrical expression, had to resort to a medium of symbolic presentation which conveyed explicitly the rational and intimated the intuitive aspects of his creed.

Such a medium he found in FAUST. In its various stages of composition the play reveals the history of Goethe's progress as a poet; and on the different levels of meaning which are accessible to the modern reader, FAUST reveals Goethe's philosophy of "Werden."

2. HISTORY OF COMPOSITION AND PUBLICATION

Stages of publication. The FAUST poem as a whole first appeared in two separate book publications:

1) FAUST: EINE TRAGÖDIE appeared as the eighth volume of Goethe's works in 1808. It contained the First Part (lines 1–4612).

2) FAUST: DER TRAGÖDIE ZWEITER TEIL IN FÜNF AKTEN was published in 1832, shortly after Goethe's death (March 22, 1832) in the forty-first volume of the "Ausgabe letzter Hand." (In a reprint of 1833, this volume bore the subtitle: "Goethes Nachgelassene Werke. Erster Band.") It contained the Second Part (lines 4613–12 111).

In other publications, larger or smaller portions of the poem appeared for the first time. They are:

3) FAUST: EIN FRAGMENT. The first FAUST text made public by the poet, issued in 1790, in the seventh volume of an edition of Goethe's "Schriften."

4) HELENA. KLASSISCH-ROMANTISCHE PHANTASMAGORIE. ZWISCHENSPIEL ZU FAUST. Published in the fourth volume of the "Ausgabe letzter Hand" (1827). It contained the text that was later incorporated into the Second Part as Act III (lines 8488–10 038).

5) The first scenes of the first act of Part II. They were printed, following a complete reprint of Part I, in the twelfth volume of the same edition (1828). Concluding with the laconic remark, "Ist fortzusetzen," they carried the action of the play to the "Lustgarten" scene (lines 4613–6036).

Our interest in these partial publications lies in the foundation they provide for comparisons with the completed FAUST and for conjectures concerning its genesis. For the reading public of Goethe's day these publications, from the "Fragment" to the "Second Part," marked the stages in which the entire poem gradually became known. For the scholar, however, who is interested in establishing an "authentic text" of the FAUST poem, they have to be supplemented with several additional prints of Part I made during Goethe's lifetime and containing minor alterations sanctioned by the author, and — above all — with numerous manuscripts (particularly of Part II) which range from first sketches to the finished clean copy of the "main manuscript."

By far the greatest new impetus to FAUST research was the discovery in 1887 of a manuscript — not in Goethe's hand but in that of a lady at the Weimar court, Luise von Göchhausen. This manuscript (about 1830 lines in all) contained in very fragmentary form many of the scenes of Part I. It was published (1887) by Erich Schmidt, under the title

6) GOETHES FAUST IN URSPRÜNGLICHER GESTALT, and is generally referred to as the "Urfaust." This publication, along with numerous sketches, plans, notations in Goethe's hand, generally known as the

7) PARALIPOMENA, represents the basic and most necessary material to be taken into account in the attempt to reconstruct the stages in which the FAUST poem was composed.

URFAUST. Although the "Urfaust" (No. 6 above) contains the oldest FAUST material known, it can scarcely be said that it reflects the *first* version which Goethe gave his play. The exact form and content of the FAUST manuscript which the young poet brought with him to Weimar are not known. Some friends who saw Goethe during the latter half of 1775 gave contradictory reports: that FAUST was almost finished; that it consisted of many scraps of paper stuffed into a bag; that Goethe pulled the sketches from every corner of his room. Goethe's own statement in his old age — that he wrote FAUST without a plan and without a break — cannot be substantiated. It may be assumed that the earliest version of the FAUST play was a satire on university life; this sentiment is still reflected in such scenes of the URFAUST as that between the student and Mephistopheles, in Faust's opening soliloquy, and in "Auerbachs Keller." Also, these scenes deal with the milieu traditionally associated with the Faust legend.

The Gretchen Tragedy. But then, at a relatively early stage (1772–1773?), Goethe introduced a new element into his FAUST scenes: the tragedy of Gretchen. Not only did this element demand a new kind of FAUST plot; it may also have contributed toward the delay in the completion of the play. To let Faust, the disillusioned scholar, become infatuated with a simple, small-town, middle-class maiden, to have his intellectual pursuits upset by a deep-reaching emotional experience and even by guilt — that was an extraordinary theme which no writer attracted by the Faust legend had tried before. At once this inclusion transformed the profligate of the "Volksbuch" into a lover whom we can understand, the sixteenth century magician into the timeless prototype of human striving and sinning and suffering.

We may never know to what extent the Gretchen episode, in terms of biography, rests on Goethe's unhappy flight from Friederike Brion (1771), or to what extent it was occasioned by the execution in Frankfurt, almost under Goethe's eyes, of an unfortunate unwed mother, Susanna Margaretha Brandt, who in her desperation had killed her child (1772). At any rate, roughly two-thirds of the FAUST poem, as it had come to exist in the early Weimar days, was devoted to the tragedy of Margaret — from the scene of the lovers' first meeting in front of the cathedral to their tragic parting in the dungeon. In a sequence of seventeen clear-cut scenes (of the twenty-one scenes in the URFAUST), charged with grandeur and misery, Goethe presented his version of one of the favorite themes of the time — the story of the girl abandoned by her lover.

The Gretchen theme must have forced itself upon the young poet at an early time. This is indicated by one of the earliest scenes written, "Trüber Tag," which includes references to Margaret and which shows Faust and Mephistopheles in a relationship not compatible with the final version of Part I. In this early stage of composition the Gretchen theme was the central interest of Goethe to the almost complete exclusion of the traditional magician Doctor Faustus.

The traditional Doctor Faustus. In the URFAUST there are indeed only two scenes that can be properly linked with the traditional Faust story ("Nacht," "Auerbachs Keller") and of them only the impassioned and melancholy soliloquy of the first reveals Faust as the restless and disappointed disciple of magic art, comparable to Marlowe's Doctor Faustus. As Goethe here depicts him, Faust is a lonely scholar who is ready to risk his life in order to attain the secret of an ever active and changing nature and universe, and who is deeply repelled by the "drab existence" around him. Half a century later (1826) Goethe described this "modern" Faust as a man

> welcher, in den allgemeinen Erdeschranken sich ungeduldig und unbehaglich fühlend, den Besitz des höchsten Wissens, den Genuß der schönsten Güter für unzulänglich achtet, seine Sehnsucht auch nur im mindesten zu befriedigen, einen Geist, welcher deshalb nach allen Seiten hin sich wendend immer unglücklicher zurückkehrt.
>
> (Paralipomenon 123)

From the very beginning, Goethe treated Faust as a tragic character whose involvement was brought about neither by obstinate "godlessness" nor by an unfortunate commitment made in a moment of moral weakness. Faust's tragedy was not to result from his "immoral" deeds but to grow out of his character, his peculiar nature. FAUST was not to be a mere dramatic "History" like GÖTZ VON BERLICHINGEN. Goethe was not attracted by the sensationalism of the Faust Book; his FAUST tragedy was conceived as the necessary result of character and situation. In fact, the poet was undecided about two major points in Faust's career: his pact with the Devil, and his death — precisely the two motifs which had been the main attraction of the old Faust story.

Mephistopheles. It is impossible to ascertain how Goethe had originally conceived the association between Faust and Mephistopheles. There is a gap in the sequence of scenes in the manuscript copy made by Luise von Göchhausen sometime between 1775 and 1786 (which is improperly called the "Urfaust"). From the beginning of the Gretchen episode, indeed even from the scene in Auerbachs Keller, Mephistopheles appears as Faust's companion and helper, and their conversations reveal nothing about the exact nature of their first meeting. This "great gap" (lines 606–1867) in the Faust drama was not satisfactorily filled until 1808, with the completion of Part I.

In one of the oldest scenes, "Trüber Tag," Mephistopheles still possesses plainly bestial qualities such as marked the devil in the "Volksbuch" and in many fifteenth and sixteenth century pictures, e.g., in Dürer's famous etching of the Knight riding past Death and the Devil. Still, this scene does not shed any light on the circumstances in which they met, or concluded a pact, or otherwise were tied to each other. In all other scenes of the URFAUST where he appears, Mephistopheles is a modernized devil, a cynic of the Age of Enlightenment who enjoys breaking down the simple beliefs of a student or perverting the natural impulses of an enamoured scholar. In the URFAUST, Mephistopheles is simply the source of "magic," such as is employed there in order to bring about the seduction of Gretchen and the moral decline of Faust. In other words, Mephistopheles is the outward instigator of Faust's guilt, insofar as this guilt may be considered to consist in transgressing the laws of God and man. At the end of the URFAUST there is little doubt that Gretchen may expect vindication, whereas there is every reason to expect that Faust will be carried to his doom by Mephistopheles. Only with the publication of the Second Part (1832) could the problem of the "tragedy" — the question of Faust's damnation or salvation — be considered solved.

Faust and Helena. The inclusion of the Gretchen episode in the early FAUST plan required another departure from the traditional Faust legend. According to the latter, Faust, in the pursuit of the supreme pleasure, spent the last year of his life with Helen of Troy, the highest embodiment of beauty and passion imaginable to the late medieval writer. Such a union with the ghost of one dead for more than three thousand years was *prima facie* evidence of Faust's use of devilish arts, and feminine beauty which once had wrought destruction on many deserving men might conceivably be considered a daemonic quality and a passport to Hell.

In 1826 Goethe asserted that a dramatized HELENA was "eine meiner ältesten Konzeptionen; sie ruht auf der Puppenspiel-Überlieferung, daß Faust den Mephistopheles genötigt, ihm die Helena zum Beilager heranzuschaffen" (Letter to W. von Humboldt, October 22, 1826). We have no definite indication of what the character of this early Helena figure might have been, had Goethe included it in his play in 1773–1775. It has been suggested by some that she would have resembled Adelheid, the daemonic temptress in GÖTZ VON BERLICHINGEN (1773) rather than the exalted Helena of Part II. A daemonic Helena would have contributed to Faust's perdition. But this became impossible once she had been replaced, in the URFAUST, by the figure of Gretchen; here Helena's "Sinnenschönheit" is replaced by Gretchen's "Seelenschönheit," the shade of the departed Greek Queen, who had been selfish and ruthless, by the charm of the living German girl, whose existence was synonymous with devotion and self-sacrifice. Faust's ultimate salvation became possible as soon as his fate was linked with Gretchen's. In spite of her failing in the eyes of society, Gretchen is a symbol of completeness, harmony, purity, and love — that is, of those qualities which Faust himself does not possess. In the Second Part, indeed, her love becomes an instrument of Faust's salvation.

We must remember that the URFAUST does not represent a version specifically sanctioned by Goethe. We cannot be sure whether or not it contains everything which was in the FAUST manuscript Goethe sent to his mother in December 1777, or in the manuscript which he took with him to Italy in 1786 as a basis of further composition. Since these manuscripts are lost, the URFAUST is our only indication of the stage from which Goethe proceeded when, early in 1788, he returned to a revision of FAUST to be included in the first edition of his "Schriften."

FAUST: EIN FRAGMENT. (No. 3 above) During the Italian journey (1786–1788) Goethe was again, after more than ten years, master of his own time. Now he devoted himself to a penetrating study of art and nature; he also subjected some of his older dramatic works to searching scrutiny and revision. Thus IPHIGENIE AUF TAURIS, TORQUATO TASSO, and EGMONT were cast in the form in which they are now known. Goethe was less successful with FAUST. It was not easy to pick up the old threads and to continue where he had left off more than fifteen years earlier. If the poem was to be the tragedy of Faust, then it had to be freed from domination by the Gretchen tragedy, and Faust's psychological situation had to have greater prominence. Such a shift could be accomplished by rewriting older scenes or by composing new scenes. Goethe did both. The prose in "Auerbachs Keller" was turned into terse and sprightly verse, and the magician's tricks in this scene were shifted from Faust to Mephistopheles. Faust himself was changed to a bystander showing cool and bored aloofness. The same aloofness distinguishes him in the two new scenes which Goethe composed under the brilliant southern skies — both scenes particularly reminiscent of northern gloom, "Hexenküche" and "Wald und Höhle." These scenes represent important steps: Faust's rejuvenation, and his decision to return to Gretchen. Goethe was certain that these scenes, though offering an entirely new aspect of Faust's personality, could easily be fitted into the old manuscript — indeed, of one of these scenes he said: "... wenn ich das Papier räuchere, so dächt' ich, sollte sie mir niemand aus den alten heraus finden" (ITALIENISCHE REISE, letter of March 1, 1788). Besides, Goethe somewhat revised the satirical, almost farcical, dialogue between Mephistopheles and the student — which had very little in common with the Faust theme — and sharpened it into a fundamental criticism of the traditional university curriculum. Moreover, he prefaced this scene with roughly a hundred lines (1770–1867) of dialogue between Faust and Mephistopheles, expressing Faust's new distrust of "Vernunft und Wissenschaft." By so doing, Goethe indicated that he had decided how to settle at least one dilemma of the play — the basis of the association between Faust and Mephistopheles.

When Goethe sent the manuscript of FAUST: EIN FRAGMENT to his publisher, Goeschen, on January 10, 1790, he was fully aware of its shortcomings. Nevertheless, he broke off "for the time being" his work on FAUST, hinting that at some future time he might tell the whole story.

Actually, the FRAGMENT offered more and offered less than the URFAUST. For one thing, it was longer than URFAUST (with 2137 lines as compared with 1830 lines), due to the insertion of "Hexenküche," "Wald und

Höhle," and other additions. On the other hand, it ended abruptly after the Cathedral Scene and left not only the fate of Faust but also that of Gretchen utterly undecided.

Nor did it tell how the pact between Faust and Mephistopheles had come about — the "great gap" was still there, though somewhat narrowed down (lines 606–1769). Thus the Fragment gave even less indication of the final solution of the Faust problems than did the Urfaust.

The reason may be seen in the ambiguous position and function of "Wald und Höhle." When Goethe inserted this scene after "Am Brunnen," he concluded it with passages originally found in the 18th scene (unnamed) of Urfaust. Moreover, he omitted this scene as such from the Fragment, and suppressed the four scenes "Nacht. Vor Gretgens Tür," "Trüber Tag," "Nacht. Offen Feld," and "Kercker" (which we know existed in his manuscript, for we have them in the Urfaust) and thus left in abeyance the whole problem of Faust and Gretchen's destiny.

A comparison between Fragment and Urfaust discloses that the most significant change was not that of altering the sequence or structure of plot, but that of intensifying the characters of Faust and of Mephistopheles. Faust in the Fragment differs from the Faust of the first version by his intense desire for experience rather than for knowledge. In the Urfaust there was an unbridged gap between the scholar who wanted to know the laws and secrets of nature, and the suitor, who plunged blindly into his passion for Gretchen. This Faust was living on two different levels, if indeed he *was* the same Faust throughout the poem. All of the new materials in the Fragment indicate that the new Faust was driven by thirst for Life more than by thirst for Knowledge, and that even his scholarly inquiries were inspired by the titanic desires of one who wants to identify his own experience with all humanly possible experience. The first lines, added in the Fragment, express this new emphasis:

> und was der ganzen Menschheit zugeteilt ist,
> will ich in meinem innern Selbst genießen,
> mit meinem Geist das Höchst' und Tiefste greifen,
> ihr Wohl und Weh auf meinen Busen häufen
> und so mein eigen Selbst zu ihrem Selbst erweitern —
> und, wie sie selbst, am End' auch ich zerscheitern.
>
> (Faust, 1770–75; Fragment, 249–254)

Mephistopheles, leading Faust into "die kleine, dann die große Welt," congratulates his disciple "zum neuen Lebenslauf." The scene "Hexenküche" had to be written because it provided an explanation for the physical rejuvenation which made Faust's new "Lebenslauf" possible. The other new scene, "Wald und Höhle," was to point up even more the dominance of erotic desire over "der Betrachtung strenge Lust." This rejuvenated Faust is more amenable to Mephistopheles' schemes; Mephistopheles himself has become more purposeful, more cynical, more diabolical. It was chance that Faust met Gretchen; but it was one of Mephistopheles' plans that Faust should have a love affair. And Faust's return to Gretchen indicates that, under the incitement of Mephistopheles, Faust's insatiable appetites, expressed in the concluding lines of his soliloquy in "Wald und Höhle" (lines 3247–3250), have got the better of his intellectual ambition. The Faust of the FRAGMENT has become more "human," more susceptible to temptations, and more amenable to the wiles of Mephistopheles. It is doubtful whether this Faust — had the FRAGMENT been completed — could have been vindicated. The mood of the FRAGMENT, compared with that of the URFAUST, is infinitely more pessimistic. In the FRAGMENT, Faust's last words are an expression of despair:

> Mag ihr Geschick auf mich zusammenstürzen
> und sie mit mir zugrunde gehn!
> (FAUST, 3364–65; FRAGMENT, 2037–38)

Completion of FAUST, *Part I.* (No. 1 above) After the publication of the FRAGMENT in 1790, the literary world in Germany, deeply impressed with this new style of poetry, was astir with speculations about the poet's plans in regard to a conclusion of the poem. In German universities students discussed and professors lectured on the eventual outcome of Faust's fate, and though opinions differed, almost everyone agreed that this FAUST was, or promised to be, one of the most stimulating and meaningful works ever produced in the German language. In June 1808, when the eighth volume of Goethe's new edition of Collected Works was published by Cotta in Tübingen, FAUST, Part I, was presented to the reader as "Eine Tragödie," but still the final solution was not revealed.

During the eighteen years which had passed since the publication of the FRAGMENT, Goethe had spent some of the most trying hours of his literary career on the completion — or, at least, the tentative completion — of the poem, which by now had become the most problematical of his works. These eighteen years included the decade of his intimate association with Schiller (1794–1805) — years which Goethe later fondly recalled as "his best."

Literary history can scarcely point to another meeting of minds comparable to that which occurred in Germany in the summer of 1794, when Schiller invited Goethe to participate in the editing of the periodical "Die Horen." This collaboration turned into a most fruitful friendship which afforded the two famous writers the opportunity not only to discuss and judge their productions, but also to inspire and encourage each other in the conception of new works. Thus Goethe's experienced and humanly understanding counsel made itself felt in the realistic aspects of Schiller's great ballads and dramas, whereas Schiller's dialectical manner of thinking imparted itself to many of Goethe's works, which had been slow in crystallizing themselves into clear compositions.

Fired by the reading of the FRAGMENT, Schiller urged his new friend to make known the still unpublished parts of his FAUST. Goethe did not have the courage to untie the old package, lest, like the sorcerer's apprentice in his "Zauberlehrling," he succumb to the spell of the "barbaric composition." But finally he gave in, and by midsummer 1797 he was again at work on FAUST. Late in June the "Zueignung" was written, capturing the recollections of his youth and anticipating the writing of the scenes which had been dormant in him for more than seven years. A prologue, originally written by Goethe for performance with Mozart's MAGIC FLUTE, seemed to describe the theatrical requirements of FAUST; it was incorporated in the new work as the "Vorspiel auf dem Theater."

By May 1798 Goethe had numbered and arranged not only the scenes of the FRAGMENT but the unpublished drafts and sketches as well, and he had organized the entire Faust material into a well-considered plan ("Schema") which was susceptible of further development. After some reflection, Goethe wrote (1797–1800) the "Prolog im Himmel," indicating that meanwhile the entire FAUST poem had assumed symbolical significance on a grand scale — that it was for him no longer the tragedy of the individual, Faust, but had grown to be a drama of man, his nature and fate.

Like Milton's PARADISE LOST (which Goethe re-read at this time) and Dante's DIVINE COMEDY, FAUST was to deal with the problem of the meaning of human life, a drama evolving on a stage much wider than that of the earth. Now the term "tragedy" — a drama of serious and lofty intent — had become applicable, in much the same manner as the term "comedy" — drama with hopeful and happy resolution — had been applied to Dante's sublime cantos. When the action of the FAUST play was elevated to a level where divine interference in earthly matters could be made visible, the last doubt of the ultimate salvation of Faust was removed; for now Faust, once the representative of intellectual man, had become a fitting symbol of all men striving and erring in their upward course. With the addition of the "Prolog," the pessimistic atmosphere which had prevailed in the FRAGMENT gave way to a considerably more conciliatory mood.

The immediate tasks which Goethe faced at this time were (1) the filling of the "great gap" (lines 606–1769) and (2) the continuation of Faust's adventures beyond the point at which progress had been thwarted for more than twenty years: Faust's departure from Gretchen's dungeon. Was Faust to proceed to the association with Helena, as the Faust tradition demanded and as had been planned in the earliest stages of the composition? And was not Faust's surrender to magic — the necessary premise of his pact with Mephistopheles and of his infatuation with Helena -- incompatible with the character of Faust which had just received sanction in the "Prolog im Himmel"?

The more Goethe pondered over the completion of the poem, the more difficult progress became. By 1798 the "Kerker" scene had been versified; the scene "Trüber Tag" refused to yield — it remains the only scene which still shows the stylistic traits of early composition. Indeed, in its ultimate form, Goethe found it desirable to recast very little even of the wording of this scene; in content he made no change at all from the original scene of the URFAUST. By 1800 a set of satirical epigrams, originally composed (1797) to censure contemporary literary personages and practices, had been added to the "Walpurgisnacht" (on which Goethe happened to be working) under the title of "Walpurgisnachtstraum oder Oberons und Titanias goldene Hochzeit" — a step which revealed, if nothing else, sovereign poetic whim and irony and an effort of the poet to detach himself from the spell of his creation.

In 1800 the writing of the two poems "Abkündigung" and "Abschied" indicated — insofar as these poems are counterparts to the "Vorspiel" and the "Zueignung" of FAUST — that Goethe was occupied with the conclusion of his work. About the same time Goethe wrote to Schiller (April 16) that the devil he had conjured up was acting quite strangely — probably an indication that the first of the two "Study" scenes (lines 1178–1529) was under construction. (This remark has also been taken to refer to the concluding passages of the scene "Vor dem Tor.") In September of the same year Goethe was intensely occupied with the introduction of Helena into the play. After considerable reflection concerning the structure and style of ancient tragedy, Goethe could joyfully report that his Helena "had really appeared on the stage" (letter to Schiller, September 12, 1800).

It is at this point that we hear for the first time about plans for a Second Part of the poem, although they must have been present in Goethe's mind for some time. In his play WALLENSTEIN, Schiller, too, had divided an unwieldy material into two parts with a short prologue.

The following months find Goethe at work on various parts of the play; now it is the "Walpurgisnacht," now certain passages of the "Valentin Scene," now the "Disputation Scene." (In the end this "Disputation" scene did not materialize.) Meanwhile, numerous other interests, particularly in the field of natural sciences, were capturing Goethe's attention. His work on FAUST became sporadic, halting, came to a standstill in April 1801. For the next five years nothing seems to have been done with FAUST. Then, under pressure from his publisher, Goethe resumed work on the play, and in the short period between February and April 1806 the First Part of FAUST: EINE TRAGÖDIE received the form in which it appeared in 1808.

The progress beyond the FRAGMENT of 1790 was indeed considerable. With its 4612 lines (to which must be added the prose of "Trüber Tag"), Part I had grown 2475 lines beyond the FRAGMENT's 2137. Apart from "Zueignung," "Vorspiel," and "Prolog," this increase consists primarily of the second soliloquy of Faust (606–807), the scene "Vor dem Tor," the two "Studierzimmer" scenes, "Walpurgisnacht," "Walpurgisnachtstraum," and the concluding scenes which had existed in the URFAUST but had been missing from the FRAGMENT.

The structure of the First Part was largely that of the earlier versions; but there were some important changes, primarily the transposition of "Wald und Höhle" to a place immediately following the first garden and arbor scenes. This change was the direct result of another, even more significant modification — the dramatic intensification of the characters of Faust and Mephistopheles.

For the first time, Goethe represented Faust as a man caught between the influences of two fundamentally opposite forces. Mephistopheles is no longer merely a devil, engaged in trying to win Faust to his ways; he has become the representative of the forces of chaos, of the negation of organization in nature. Faust, as God's servant, now strives toward the affirmation of life, of organized existence. Mephistopheles, as the force of negation, seeks to destroy this bond between Faust and God and thus to reduce Faust's world to chaos. No doubt Goethe's studies of nature (of the phenomena of growth in particular) had had a decisive bearing on this new interpretation. Just as Goethe had described the process of plant growth as a perennial succession of "contraction and expansion," or the process of human growth, physical and intellectual, as an analogous succession of "systole and diastole," so he represented the influence of Mephistopheles as an alternation of "attraction and repulsion," which in constant tension produces higher and more complex forms of experience for Faust. According to the words of the Lord, Mephistopheles has become Faust's associate "der reizt und wirkt und muß als Teufel schaffen" (343).

Thus Goethe's Faust differs profoundly from the Faust of the legend. The pact which Goethe's Faust concludes with the Devil is no simple contract providing enjoyment of earthly pleasures and use of supernatural powers in return for Faust's soul — as the legend had told. In Goethe's work, Faust enters into an agreement with Mephistopheles according to which the latter, in return for services rendered, may try to induce Faust to give up his striving. If he succeeds, he may do whatever he wishes with Faust. As to Faust, he knows that he will lose his wager should he ever abandon the very drives which define his nature — his striving, his thirst for ever more complete forms of life and experience — and succumb to the allurement of absolute inactivity or inertia. Faust's tragedy consists in the fact that by virtue of his human nature, the moment he enjoys an experience, he must desire to transcend it.

Beginning with the "Prolog im Himmel," the reader is permitted to view the human "tragedy," the struggle of man caught between the polar opposites of positive expansion and organization and negative limitation and chaos, to witness from a high vantage point the spectacle of man's evolving progress between error and clarity.

Completion of Part II. (No. 2 above) The fact that the edition of 1808 carried the subtitle "Der Tragödie erster Teil," following the "Prolog im Himmel," was a clear indication that Goethe planned a continuation. Accordingly, "Zueignung," "Vorspiel," and "Prolog," though published in 1808, were intended to preface the work complete in two parts, and not the First Part alone.

However, almost seventeen years passed in which Goethe's attention to FAUST was very slight. The First Part had been published shortly after Napoleon had brought disaster (at Jena and Auerstädt, 1806) to Prussia, to which Saxe-Weimar had been tied by a military alliance. Goethe had been summoned to appear before the French Emperor, who wanted a close look at "the other" genius of his time; and Goethe had gone to Erfurt to pay his respects.

A much less exciting political atmosphere prevailed when Part II of FAUST was written. Europe had settled down into the monotony of a post-war depression. Napoleon was long since defeated, banished, dead and buried; and the German states had returned to the lethargy of a conservative system. In the extreme southeast of Europe, on the Greek peninsula, young idealists like Lord Byron were rallying to the cause of Greek liberation from Turkish domination, and distant America was echoing with debates on the Monroe doctrine and abolitionism. Liberals and conservatives were contending in various quarters of Europe, scientific materialism and economic imperialism began to spread in the west-European nations; and in the German middle class, frugality and a spirit of righteousness found their expression in the sober style of "Biedermeier" art.

The Second Part of FAUST was to reflect little of the political reality of these years. Instead, its author withdrew to a realm of timelessness and symbolism. At first it had been Goethe's intention to follow up the First Part with an early publication of the Second. After all, the Helena theme of Act III, based on the "oldest conceptions" of Goethe's youth, was worked on with great enthusiasm in 1800; and certain scenes of Acts I and V may even have been sketched in the late nineties. But again other interests interfered; the WAHLVERWANDTSCHAFTEN, the FARBENLEHRE, the monumental autobiography DICHTUNG UND WAHRHEIT crowded the FAUST enterprise into the background. There exists a fairly detailed résumé of Goethe's FAUST plans, dating from the year 1816. As it was a sketch intended for an account of FAUST in DICHTUNG UND WAHRHEIT, we do not know whether it contained more "fiction" than "truth." In any event, it fails to indicate the ultimate solution of the play.

Goethe's serious occupation with Part II falls between the years 1825 and 1831, when his friend and literary aide, Johann Peter Eckermann, did his utmost to encourage and support the aged poet in bringing his FAUST to completion. Within the economy of the drama only two basic problems remained to be solved — the introduction of the Helena episode, and the resolution of the whole in Faust's death. However, the fascinating subject matter again seemed to grow under the poet's hands.

Early in 1825 Goethe proceeded to revise the Helena scene of 1800. This material consisted essentially of lines 8489–8802 of the play as it now stands, though some of the choruses were not yet written and some verbal changes still had to be made to obtain greater metrical smoothness. When Goethe decided to set the scene of his Helena episode in the Peloponnesus, instead of Faust's castle in Germany (as he had planned in his sketch of December 16, 1816), he created for himself the interesting problem of introducing a medieval, northern character, Faust, into the classical, southern milieu. It also provided the occasion for attempting a synthesis of medieval and classical cultures. After considerable study of geographical and archaeological detail, accompanied by warm interest in the Greek War of Liberation, Goethe finished the third act by the summer of 1826. In the next spring it was published by Cotta as a separate work: HELENA. KLASSISCH-ROMANTISCHE PHANTASMAGORIE. ZWISCHENSPIEL ZU FAUST (No. 4 above).

During the remainder of that year the beginning of Act IV was considered but soon abandoned in favor of the scenes at the Imperial Court intended for Act I. These scenes, ending with the present line 6036, were published in the twelfth volume of the "Ausgabe letzter Hand," in April 1828. They followed the full text of FAUST, Part I, and were headed by the simple title page "FAUST, Zweyter Teil." They were the last FAUST scenes published during Goethe's lifetime (No. 5 above). Thus, only lines 4613–6036 and 8488–10 038 of Part II were published while Goethe was still living; everything else was printed posthumously.

The remaining scenes were written slowly and often with painfully little progress; the closing scenes of Act I, the conjuring of the shades of Paris and Helena, were read to Eckermann on December 30, 1829; Act II came into being during the first half of 1830. Immediately after recovering from a pulmonary hemorrhage late in 1830, Goethe was again at work on Act IV during the winter of 1830–1831; the opening scenes of Act V followed in the summer of 1831 and were linked to the scenes of Faust's death written some thirty years earlier. By August 1831, the entire

Second Part was completely dictated, copied, bound, wrapped up, and sealed; and the poet vowed never to touch FAUST again.

Yet, in January 1832, we find Goethe before the opened package again, reading the entire work to his daughter-in-law. New restlessness came over him; he found that too many passages had been treated "too laconically." But there is no evidence that Goethe ever resumed work on the poem.

FAUST: DER TRAGÖDIE ZWEITER TEIL appeared in print in 1832, as the first volume of Goethe's posthumous works, the forty-first volume of the "Ausgabe letzter Hand." Goethe's sketches and scattered notes, "Paralipomena," were published in part by Eckermann and Riemer in 1836. In their entirety they were made public in 1887–1888, in the first comprehensive and carefully prepared edition of Goethe's Complete Works, the "Weimarer Ausgabe" (No. 7 above).

Even though the Second Part, with its 7499 lines, appears to be a well-rounded opus, tracing and motivating Faust's course through the "große Welt," it lacks continuity and smoothness of transition in more than one place. On the other hand, it is less sketchy and fragmentary than Part I and reveals, above all, the master-plan of a cosmic poem which in the end returns to the point of its origin, Heaven. While Part I derives its powerful appeal to the reader from the intensity of physical experience, Part II gains its forcefulness from the depth of intellectual experience of the poet who, by reading and contemplation, by keen observation and mature understanding, had absorbed the heritage of cultural history.

Part II and the Faust tradition. The Faust of Part II appears at the court of the Emperor, as the Renaissance legend requires; but this court is no longer the court of Charles V, as the "Volksbuch" relates; it represents now the world of politics — the struggle for power — with all its revelation of human ambitions and human foibles. The Faust of Part II also achieves a magic conquest of time by realizing a union with Helena — as the legend demands. In fact, more than half of the Second Part dwells on the preparation, accomplishment, and recollection of this memorable adventure. But this Helena is not the daemonic ghost which the chapbooks and puppet plays made her, but the embodiment of all the charm and happiness which beautiful form can convey.

In addition to these two adventures, the Second Part transports Faust through many another colorful experience not prescribed by the Faust tradition. The number of characters with whom Faust comes into contact grows to astonishing proportions. The involvements of Faust and Mephistopheles likewise increase in symbolic complexity. In the figures of the Emperor and Helena and their retinues, the reader may at least recognize known historical or mythological characters. But when the Three Mighty Men or Philemon and Baucis appear, when Dame Care moves across the stage, the reader begins to realize that he is witnessing a play of immense complexity and symbolic significance — the tragedy of man who, symbolized in Faust, wills greater experience and achievements and who strives, errs, and fails — and continues to strive.

In contrast to the "Prolog," no words of the Lord are heard in the last scene of FAUST, even though Goethe drew extensively on traditional Christian legends when he wrote that scene. To Eckermann he said in regard to the conclusion of FAUST:

Übrigens werden Sie zugeben, daß der Schluß, wo es mit der geretteten Seele nach oben geht, sehr schwer zu machen war und daß ich, bei so übersinnlichen, kaum zu ahnenden Dingen, mich sehr leicht im Vagen hätte verlieren können, wenn ich nicht meinen poetischen Intentionen, durch die scharf umrissenen christlich-kirchlichen Figuren und Vorstellungen, eine wohltätig beschränkende Form und Festigkeit gegeben hätte. (*June 6, 1831*)

The Christian symbolism at the end of FAUST contains as much religious creed as it contains experiences of a lifetime. Goethe's ultimate views on life, his studies of nature and art, his concepts of spirit and man found joint expression in the grandiose image of "Werden" which concludes, as it began, the FAUST poem. His Faust has come a long way from the Faust of the "Volksbuch" and the puppet play, who was the object of evangelistic zeal and abomination. With all his ambitions and shortcomings, his defeats and his victories, this Faust has become a symbol of all mankind, and of "Steigerung" — dynamic improvement of man's innate powers.

Still, this Christian symbolism does not indicate a return to the narrow orthodoxy out of which the Faust theme grew at the end of the Middle Ages. Not wrath, not damnation, but *Caritas*, God's Love of Man, vindicates Faust's existence. The figure of Gretchen, interceding in Faust's behalf, is the symbol of Love, of "das Ewig-Weibliche," the force which gives all other forces meaning and without which all of man's efforts are of no avail.

Now it becomes clear what the Gretchen theme may have meant to Goethe when he introduced it into the FAUST poem in 1772–1773. This Gretchen, who promised the departing Faust, "Wir werden uns wiedersehn," was thought of by Goethe as the instrument of Faust's salvation, though he may not have foreseen the manner in which this plan was to be carried out.

In a letter in early spring, 1832, Goethe recalled to his old friend, Wilhelm von Humboldt, the earliest plans for the poem:

Es sind über sechzig Jahre, daß die Konzeption des Faust bei mir jugendlich von vorne herein klar, die ganze Reihenfolge hin weniger ausführlich vorlag. Nun hab' ich die Absicht immer sachte neben mir hergehn lassen und nur die mir gerade interessantesten Stellen einzeln durchgearbeitet, so daß im zweiten Teil Lücken blieben, durch ein gleichmäßiges Interesse mit dem Übrigen zu verbinden. Hier trat nun freilich die große Schwierigkeit ein, dasjenige durch Vorsatz und Charakter zu erreichen, was eigentlich der freiwillig tätigen Natur allein zukommen sollte. Es wäre aber nicht gut, wenn es nicht auch nach einem so langen, tätig nachdenkenden Leben möglich geworden wäre, und ich lasse mich keine Furcht angehen: man werde das Ältere vom Neueren, das Spätere vom Früheren unterscheiden können; — welches wir denn den künftigen Lesern zu geneigter Einsicht übergeben wollen.

Ganz ohne Frage würd' es mir unendliche Freude machen, meinen werten, durchaus dankbar anerkannten, weitverteilten Freunden auch bei Lebzeiten diese sehr ernsten Scherze zu widmen, mitzuteilen und ihre Erwiderung zu vernehmen. Der Tag aber ist wirklich so absurd und konfus, daß ich mich überzeuge, meine redlichen, lange verfolgten Bemühungen um dieses seltsame Gebäu würden schlecht belohnt und an den Strand getrieben, wie ein Wrack in Trümmern daliegen und von dem Dünenschutt der Stunden zunächst überschüttet werden. Verwirrende Lehre zu verwirrtem Handel waltet über die Welt, und ich habe nichts angelegentlicher zu tun, als dasjenige, was an mir ist und geblieben ist, womöglich zu steigern und meine Eigentümlichkeiten zu kohobieren . . .

This was the last letter Goethe wrote. Five days later, on March 22, 1832, he died.

IV. Analysis and Interpretation of Faust

Analysis of the Play — Interpretation of the Characters.

1. ANALYSIS OF THE PLAY

As a piece of artistic workmanship, Goethe's Faust may be compared with one of the most venerable buildings on the European continent, the ancient cathedral in the Rhenish city of Aachen (Aix-la-Chapelle), once the coronation city of the Holy Roman Empire. Built over the tomb of Charlemagne (d. A.D. 814), this cathedral reflects the variety of stages and styles in which it was constructed: — at its core the simple basilica dating back to the years when Christianity first spread to Northern Europe; in its dome the Romanesque dignity of the Hohenstaufen period; in its nave and apse the Gothic gracefulness of the late Middle Ages; and in some of its portals the charm of the Renaissance. Goethe's Faust, as we have seen, was completed slowly through six decades of intermittent writing. For this reason the component parts are marked by notable differences in poetic style. Yet, with all this stylistic variety, the poem manifests a basic pattern of composition, just as the ancient coronation church at Aachen — in spite of its bewildering detail — displays a fairly harmonious and compact fundamental design.

The reader who knows only the first part of the poem is likely to remember the Gretchen episode, or Faust's tortured soliloquy at the opening of the play, or the eerie scenes of the Walpurgis Night and the Witch's Kitchen. The fairly harmonious and compact fundamental design of the FAUST poem as a whole becomes apparent when the Second Part also is read and re-read. Then one discerns that, through all the diverse stages of its construction, a basic plan, or blueprint, has directed the writing of each of the parts.

The poem as a whole. When Goethe was engaged in writing the Carnival scenes of Part II, he guided his friend Knebel toward an understanding of FAUST with these words:

> . . . die Hauptintention ist klar und das Ganze deutlich; auch das Einzelne wird es sein und werden, wenn man die Teile nicht an sich betrachten und erklären, sondern in Beziehung auf das Ganze sich verdeutlichen mag. (*November 14, 1827*)

On the other hand, Goethe was also able to say to Eckermann:

> Auch kommt es bei einer solchen Komposition bloß darauf an, daß die einzelnen Massen bedeutend und klar seien, während es als ein Ganzes immer inkommensurabel bleibt. (*February 13, 1831*)

To understand both statements we must remember that, in writing the Second Part, Goethe showed a tendency which he also followed in the writing of other works during his advancing age (e.g., WESTÖSTLICHER DIWAN and WILHELM MEISTERS WANDERJAHRE) — the tendency to plan a work as a "cycle" into which he could fit even such elements as seemed to have only slight connection with the main theme. In order to force himself to view the entire Second Part as a whole, Goethe (in February 1831) had the manuscript bound, leaving vacant pages for the still unwritten fourth act, quite confident that the completed portions would somehow suggest the substance and shape of that which was still to be done.

As we read the entire poem, the First Part appears as a more homogeneous creation than the Second Part, whereas the latter clearly reflects the older author's broader wisdom and greater experience in human affairs. The drama of Faust, Mephistopheles, and Gretchen is the work of youth, intuition, and genius. The drama of the "große Welt," of the Emperor's Court, of Faust's union with Helena — this panorama is the product of the wisdom of old age, of reflection, of deliberate composition.

The conception of FAUST as a poem in two parts dates back to the closing years of the 18th century when, at Schiller's insistence, Goethe subjected to the authority of an "idea" the colorful, diffuse, and even chaotic FAUST material, as it had developed under his hands until 1790. In June 1797, Schiller wrote to Goethe:

> Kurz, die Anforderungen an den FAUST sind zugleich philosophisch und poetisch, und Sie mögen sich wenden, wie Sie wollen, so wird Ihnen die Natur des Gegenstandes eine philosophische Behandlung auflegen, und

die Einbildungskraft wird sich zum Dienst einer Vernunftidee bequemen müssen.

Goethe, to be sure, was not quite so rigorous as his philosophical friend; he did not marshal his imaginative talents in the service of a philosophical "idea." Indeed, throughout his life, Goethe was reluctant to confess to any philosophical "idea" behind his poem. But he went so far as to sketch — apparently in great haste — a plan in which he indicated for the first time that there were to be two parts of the poem, and assigned to each a guiding theme. According to this preliminary sketch (which is undated and was probably written in June 1797, though it might also be a sketch connected with the FRAGMENT of 1790), the First Part was to deal with "Lebensgenuß der Person von außen gesehn; . . . in der Dumpfheit Leidenschaft," whereas the Second Part was to portray "Tatengenuß nach außen . . . und Genuß mit Bewußtsein. Schönheit." It is impossible to recognize in these words anything more than the attempt to distinguish between two modes of operation of the same basic 'love of life' (*Genuß*).

Two cycles of action. More important was the step which Goethe took (1798? 1800?) when he wrote the "Prolog im Himmel." In the light of the complete play, this scene indicates an intention to divide the drama into two separate levels and, indeed, two separate cycles of action, of which the first determines, regulates, and finally absorbs the second.

There is one action which takes place in "higher spheres," at the beginning and at the end of the play — in the "Prolog im Himmel" and in the scene "Bergschluchten." Both times the action consists of the interplay of transcendental characters or voices; Faust himself is not present. He is discussed and acted upon rather than active. The central theme of this action is the wager which Mephistopheles offers to the Lord (312) and which the Lord counters by permitting Mephistopheles to try to lead Faust astray from God's ways, as long as he shall live on earth (315–316). The final scenes show that Mephistopheles has been unsuccessful. Mephistopheles' wager was motivated by the Lord's statement:

> Wenn er mir jetzt auch nur verworren dient,
> so werd' ich ihn bald in die Klarheit führen. (309)

The last scene reveals that the Lord's intention has been carried out.

The other, the earthly action proceeds within this framework of celestial scenes. It extends from the moment we meet Faust in his study in his first soliloquy to the moment in which his soul is carried away by the angels. This action is the story of Faust's striving and erring, his resort to the art of magic and his attempts to free himself from it, his course through "die kleine, dann die große Welt." It is held together structurally by the pact which Faust concludes with Mephistopheles and the final outcome of this pact at Faust's death. Though our attention is focused throughout most of the play on the earthly action of the FAUST theme proper, it is from the realm of the transcendental that these earthly events receive significance. The agreement in Heaven and the agreement on Earth are correlated, not as cause and effect, but as terse statement and detailed elaboration of the same theme. Thus the real world of Faust's actions and meditations, of his physical experiences and spiritual endeavors, is surrounded by another and "higher" reality. At the end of Part I, when Gretchen is dismissed by Mephistopheles with a curt "Sie ist gerichtet!", this other reality appears in the "Voice (from above)": "Ist gerettet!" — thereby indicating that the supernatural, "heavenly" world may at any time assert its judgment in the empirical world of human affairs.

The earthly action may be divided into three main parts: — an exposition, comprising the scenes from Faust's solitary despair to his pact with Mephistopheles; — a main part, comprising Faust's "journey" through the world in the company of Mephistopheles, i.e., all scenes leading up to and including the Gretchen episode, the Helena adventure, the experience of great power in war and in peacetime construction, and the final crisis involving the destruction of Philemon and Baucis; — and a conclusion, comprising Faust's encounter with Dame Care and his death. The supernatural, "heavenly," action, since it is a frame, consists merely of an exposition and a conclusion.

In briefest outline the dramatic structure of the FAUST play shows this pattern:

VORSPIEL		(33–242)
SUPERNATURAL ACTION	Exposition: *Prolog im Himmel*	(243–353)
EARTHLY ACTION		
I. Exposition:	From Faust's soliloquy to conclusion of pact	(354–2072)
II. "Kleine Welt":	*Auerbachs Keller*, *Hexenküche*, Gretchen episode	(2073–4612)
III. "Große Welt":	*Kaiserliche Pfalz*, *Klassische Walpurgisnacht*, Helena episode, "Große Politik," Philemon and Baucis	(4613–11 383)
IV. Conclusion:	"Sorge," Faust's death, *Grablegung*	(11 384–11 843)
SUPERNATURAL ACTION	Conclusion: *Bergschluchten*	(11 844–12 111)

For purposes of analysis and interpretation, the reader may further subdivide the "earthly" action of the play, and various ways of dividing this action have been proposed. According to the conventional standards of a five-act play the following division could be made: I. Faust's pact with

Mephistopheles (354–2604); II. Faust and Gretchen (2605–4612); III. Faust at the Emperor's Court (4613–6565); IV. Faust wins and loses Helena (6566–10 038); V. Faust's tragedy of power (10 039–11 843). The only division which we know to have had Goethe's approval is that made in the "Ausgabe letzter Hand," which presents the play in the two parts with the subdivisions as we now know them.

Dramatic time and space. Evidently, there can be no unity of time or of place in the conventional sense in a poem which follows its hero from early manhood to his death at the age of a hundred years. The freedom with which the poet treats time and space is one of the striking features of FAUST.

After the "Vorspiel auf dem Theater," which is not an integral part of the FAUST action, we find ourselves transported to "Heaven," where neither time nor space has any meaning. At the end of the "earthly action" we are transported out of this world to a realm somewhere "on the way" to Heaven once more. Clearly, the conventional ideas of time and space have no validity here, either.

On the other hand, the first scenes of FAUST (exposition, lines 354–2072) take place in a fairly definite historical period and place. In keeping with the traditional legend, Faust is presented as living in a free imperial city in 16th century Germany, a city protected by wall and gate, priding itself on the possession of a university, a garrison, a cathedral. After the transitional scenes in Auerbach's Keller in Leipzig and in the Witch's Kitchen (2073–2604), Faust is transferred by Mephistopheles to a city different from his own residence but not much distinguished from it in regard to milieu and surroundings except for the lack of a university. In the first city, Faust is known and respected as "Herr Doktor"; in the second, Gretchen's city, he is a complete stranger. For the most part, the scenes of Part I follow one another in fairly regular order. The excursion to the Harz Mountains during the Walpurgis Night represents but an interlude in the regular sequence of events. After this interlude Faust is found in Gretchen's city again, where the First Part is concluded. The action of Part I seems to extend from the night before Easter to well into the spring or summer of the next year.

With the opening of Part II we are transferred to a quite different scene. Faust, awakening from the slumber which has soothed his heart and mind after the racking experience of Gretchen's tragedy, finds himself in an "anmutige Gegend," facing the grandeur of a summer dawn in an Alpine region.

Chronologically and logically this scene connects with the end of Part I without difficulty. But from here on, the rational cohesion of space and time begins to give way to a more and more "poetic," i.e. imaginative, coherence. Faust appears next at the Imperial Court, whose pageantry suggests the era of the Renaissance, of Emperor Maximilian (reigned 1493–1519), the "Last Knight", a contemporary of the historical Faust. Since Faust's appearance at court occurs in February, at the beginning of the carnival season, it poses an unsolved problem as to the lapse of time.

Temporal boundaries break down altogether from here on. With Faust's brief return to the laboratory of former days we learn that at least three or four years have passed since the beginning of the play; for the student of Part I, then an entering freshman, now appears as a graduate.

When Faust is conveyed to the Classical Walpurgis Night (7040) to find Helen of Troy and bring her back to life, the action of the drama expands to include characters from ancient mythology and scenes from legendary geography. A scene showing Faust descending into the nether world, a second Orpheus, imploring Persephoneia to release the shade of his beloved, was never written. When Goethe omitted it, he left untold the manner of Helena's return to life. The limits of time are completely abrogated in the Helena action. A magic, dreamlike timelessness envelops the entire act. After all, the discovery of the Beautiful, ever-present and timeless, is an act of poetic imagination, and — "den Poeten bindet keine Zeit."

In Act IV, when Faust returns from Greece, he re-enters the Renaissance milieu which he left in Act I, although no indication is given as to the time which has since elapsed. Nor is any such indication given at the opening of Act V, which tells of Faust's old age, his last enterprise, and his death. In a discussion with Eckermann (June 6, 1831), Goethe described this aged Faust as "a hundred years" old; and we accept this statement in its symbolic significance. It is useless and probably impossible anyway to set up chronological tables for this play. Moreover, time is turned back by the effect of the magic potion in the Witch's Kitchen, by virtue of which Faust is thought to have been made thirty years younger.

The concluding scenes are timeless and ethereal. Time and space become meaningless in the clear light of eternity, and our interest centers wholly on the final verdict passed on Faust's earthly existence.

FAUST *as a pageant.* The projection of the FAUST play onto two stages, an earthly and a supernatural stage, accounts for the peculiar structure of this unique drama.

In plays such as Sophocles' ANTIGONE or Shakespeare's HAMLET, the dramatic action is developed from an individual event expanding into a definite plot, contingent upon the nature of a specific character or characters, in a given social or historical situation. Hence it was possible for Aristotle and Lessing (the leading dramatic critic of Goethe's day) to demand unity of dramatic action (and to presuppose, accordingly, a reasonable unity of time and place) in a dramatic production.

FAUST does not meet these classic requirements of unity. Its plot is not based on a single event but on a number of events, and is held together by an evolving character rather than by "unity of action."

In many of his works Goethe showed a fondness for the poetic image of the "wanderer." Faust can be considered such a "wanderer," and the play portraying his fate presents a "journey" through life by a human being who is compelled by his character and set of values to make certain decisions which have a lasting effect upon his mode of living. The FAUST play is the work of a poet who is first and foremost a lyric poet — one who perceives the reality around him in relation to himself, and to whom the symbol of the "wanderer" is a most meaningful form of self-expression.

Structurally, a play portraying a "journey" resembles a pageant rather than a closely knit drama. Thus FAUST has more in common with the medieval miracle play, which was of the "pageant" type, than with the classical five-act tragedy. In FAUST, as in a miracle play, we witness no plotting and counterplotting, no clash between hostile factions, no "climax" in the traditional sense, no culminating catastrophe. The action of FAUST proceeds in a simple succession of scenes; only rarely (e.g., in "Wald und Höhle" and "Gretchens Stube," or in the scenes of the Classical Walpurgis Night) are we to think of two successive scenes as taking place at approximately the same time.

This "serial" arrangement of scenes is plainly manifest in the First Part, while in the Second Part it appears to be concealed under the traditional five-act structure of tragedy. But fundamentally the Second Part, too, exhibits a "serial" structure; its "acts" are not much more than an outward device for grouping together scenes which, for the sake of logical and chronological continuity, should be read in one sitting. To be sure, there are "bridge" scenes, like the scene "Anmutige Gegend" or "Hochgewölbtes gotisches Zimmer" and "Laboratorium," which link a major episode with preceding or following episodes, and thus serve as prelude or postlude.

Transitional scenes. The transitional character of these three scenes is clear at first sight. This leads one to look for other "bridge" scenes whose transitional character is not quite so apparent; and indeed they are there. In the First Part they are: "Hexenküche," "Wald und Höhle," and "Walpurgisnacht." In the Second Part the entire "Klassische Walpurgisnacht" reveals itself as being of a transitional character; and the scene "Hochgebirg" at the beginning of Act IV is likewise a "bridge" which gets the Faust of the preceding Helena adventure back into the world of Emperor, war, and conquest. In each of these transitional scenes Faust makes an important decision which deeply affects his further action. (It is noteworthy that these scenes also coincide with those points in the action where, in the long process of composition, Goethe's imagination appears to have been temporarily arrested.)

Dramatically, each of these scenes fulfills a specific function: Faust's rejuvenation, Faust's decision to return to Gretchen, and Faust's inward depravation and complete psychological confusion mark three important stages in the First Part, preparatory to, or intimately connected with, the tragedy of Gretchen. Faust's search for Helena, and his resolution to curb the destructive power of the sea, mark equally important stages of the Second Part, before and after the Helena episode.

The significance of these transitional scenes becomes even more evident when it is realized that they constitute a parallelism between the two parts both in their sequence and in their dramatic function — a parallelism which can scarcely be considered accidental. There appears to be an outward correlation between the Northern and the Classical Walpurgis Night; but there is an even more fundamental correspondence between "Hexenküche" and "Classical Walpurgis Night." Both represent a descent to the level of the subconscious, both are preparations for the appearance, in the following scenes, of two different aspects of womanhood: passion (Gretchen) and beauty (Helena). In both scenes Faust is rejuvenated — in the "Hexenküche" physically, in the "Klassische Walpurgisnacht" spiritually. However, in these two transitional scenes Faust and Mephistopheles are shown in reversed order of authority and dependence: in the "Hexenküche," Mephistopheles is in command and Faust finds it difficult to adjust himself; in the Classical Walpurgis Night, Faust is growing in self-assertion and self-confidence, while Mephistopheles is increasingly bewildered by the creatures of ancient mythology. The Mephistopheles of the Classical Walpurgis Night is not a likely conqueror of Faust's soul.

There is a similar parallelism between "Wald und Höhle" and "Hochgebirg." In both scenes, a soliloquy of Faust, in a mood of self-reflection and contemplation, is followed by the arrival of the tempter, Mephistopheles. But while in the First Part Mephistopheles finds Faust an easy prey to his seductive wiles, the situation is quite different in the Second Part: Mephistopheles, up to this point an *instigator* of Faust's enterprises, finds himself reduced to the role of a mere *implementer* of Faust's plan, and Faust — not attracted by Mephistopheles' portrayal of busy city life or Sardanapalian luxury (10 136–10 176) — insists upon his project of attack upon the tyranny of the sea. The Mephistopheles of this scene has little prospect of conquering Faust's soul.

The organic relationship of the Northern "Walpurgisnacht" remains somewhat obscure. Unlike "Hexenküche" and "Wald und Höhle," it lacks any immediately corresponding scene in the Second Part, unless it is the scene "Mitternacht" — the meeting between Faust and "Sorge."

Still, the two scenes are related. To be sure, "Walpurgisnacht" interrupts the action of the Gretchen tragedy; however, as an adumbration of a stage in the disintegration of Gretchen's world, it has its proper place in the sequence: "Am Brunnen," "Zwinger," "Nacht," "Dom," "Walpurgisnacht," "Kerker." Also, it portrays the deepest humiliation and agony of Faust, who, under the domination of Mephistopheles, has committed murder and become a fugitive from justice. The appearance of the Gretchen effigy in the Witches' Sabbath, against the will of Mephistopheles, causes in Faust a stirring of sympathy, love, concern which, in the following scene, "Trüber Tag," makes him return to Gretchen's dungeon. In the scene "Mitternacht" — following the destruction of Philemon's and Baucis' "kleine Welt" (as the Walpurgis Night followed the destruction of Gretchen's world) — Faust is confronted with Care; but he has to face her alone, without the presence or support of Mephistopheles. As in the Northern "Walpurgisnacht," Faust is again in deepest inward confusion and darkness. But at this point, when Faust holds his own, the reader senses that Mephistopheles has no prospect of conquering Faust's soul.

Goethe never hinted at any fundamental correspondence between scenes of the First and the Second Parts. In fact, he denied that the poet should be his own interpreter:

> . . . Damit würde er aufhören, Dichter zu sein. Der Dichter stellt seine Schöpfung in die Welt hinaus; es ist die Sache des Lesers, des Ästhetikers, des Kritikers, zu untersuchen, was er mit seiner Schöpfung gewollt hat.
> (*Conversation with the historian Luden, August 19, 1806*)

In view of the obvious correspondence between the "Prolog im Himmel" and the concluding scene, and in view of the correspondence between lines 1699–1700 and lines 11 581–11 582, it is left to the reader to recognize significant parallelisms in the structure of FAUST which may aid in the understanding of the entire work. Within this implied wider unity of form — which is, as it were, a growth rather than a design — the reader is able to reconcile such contrasts as that between the "Sturm und Drang" and the "classical" style, between the short, impassioned scenes of Part I and the lengthy, reserved processions ("Mummenschanz" and "Klassische Walpurgisnacht") of Part II, between the lyrical intensity of the youthful poet and the philosophical calm of old age.

Poetic style. Unlike his friend Schiller, Goethe did not usually compose his works according to an integrated program or a central idea. Fascinated more by immediate impressions than by abstractions, Goethe would often record his observations in breathless haste, writing a scene or a group of scenes before he conceived the plan of a well-rounded composition. We have Goethe's word for the fact that the URFAUST was composed in this

way, and the URFAUST furnished the basic pattern of the FRAGMENT and of the First Part. Individual scenes, vibrating with the pulse beat of experience and creative imagination, were written before an overall plan forged them into a whole.

Evidence of this mode of composition is found in the characteristic features of poetic language in FAUST. Almost every scene has its own poetic style. To be sure, there exists what might be called a "Faust verse," a loose rhythmical line of four iambic feet, often rimed, though not always in couplets (see Chapter VII, Rhythm and Rime). We know that Goethe freely adapted this form from the simple, quaint, but still popular and appealing writings of Hans Sachs, the Nürnberg shoemaker-poet (1494–1576). But this verse is hardly more representative of the style of FAUST than any of the other verse-patterns which were introduced whenever the mood of a scene demanded a change.

Thus we find such extremes as free rhythms and plain prose, quatrains and blank verse, as the situation or the character of the speaker may require. For these were the realities of paramount poetic importance. When the stilted and formal court ceremonies of Act IV get under way, the imperial dignitaries speak in stately Alexandrines, the verse which is representative of seventeenth century courtly drama. But sometimes, in Part I, we hear Frau Marthe or Gretchen and even Faust or Mephistopheles utter an Alexandrine verse, and in that case the young author seems to be making use of the polished style of the Leipzig Rococo of his early university days, which he had tried his best to outgrow in the Storm and Stress of Strassburg and Wetzlar.

The solemn restraint of classical antiquity is reflected in *sostenuto* trimeters in which Helena recounts her heroic experiences as she enters her Spartan palace. Her attendants express themselves in the intricate pattern of the Greek tragic chorus.

Even a casual glance at the first soliloquy or the conjuring scene of Part I (1178–1321) reveals a rich variety of poetic verse — melancholy, ecstatic, rebellious, soothing. The successive groups of allegorical figures in the "Mummenschanz," the grotesque spectres of the Northern and the Classical Walpurgis Night, the groups in the Arcadian Idyll — which first appear festive and later mournful — are characterized with the same virtuosity of lyrical variety. Throughout the drama, in a magnificent display of continual variety, every level of human thought and sentiment finds poetic expression — from the despondent to the self-assured, from the farcical to the sublime.

Imagery and symbolism. The richness of Goethe's lyric style is not confined to the ingenious use of metrical forms; it is revealed even more strikingly in Goethe's imagery, his choice of words, his use of metaphors and other devices of figurative language. It is in this medium that the

subtlest charms of characterization make themselves felt; and often repeated reading may be necessary before quite simple, self-evident passages yield their deeper significance. Sometimes familiarity with the imagery in other works of Goethe — in his WERTHER, his lyrics, his IPHIGENIE or his WILHELM MEISTER — will make a word or a phrase peculiarly significant for the reader of FAUST. Conversely, an acquaintance with the imagery in FAUST may furnish a key to the comprehension of other works.

In a play like FAUST, whose innermost meaning signifies a firm belief in "Life," the sovereign omniscience of the Lord could scarcely be more appropriately expressed than by the symbol of the gardener, confident in his growing tree:

> Weiß doch der Gärtner, wenn das Bäumchen grünt,
> daß Blüt' und Frucht die künft'gen Jahre zieren. (311)

Compared with this, the symbol of cat-and-mouse (322) not only expresses the nature of Mephistopheles, but it also suggests the difference in intellectual levels and interests between the Lord and the Devil in the "Prolog im Himmel." Life and growth — evolution upwards and on — contrasts with the tendency to level off and paralyze all forces. While the last words of the play are reserved for a characterization of the realm of God in the Chorus mysticus, the domain of Mephistopheles is indicated in the "Prolog":

> Und führ ihn, kannst du ihn erfassen,
> auf deinem Wege mit herab. (326)

The destructiveness, the rigid barrenness, which is exemplified in Mephistopheles, repeatedly finds its way into Mephistopheles' words. Of the Faust who has signed his contract with the Devil he says:

> Er soll mir zappeln, starren, kleben,
> und seiner Unersättlichkeit
> soll Speis' und Trank vor gier'gen Lippen schweben. (1864)

Mephistopheles is delighted to give an account of chaotic primeval volcanic revolutions (10 105 ff); they have given him his freedom and they correspond to his character. In the Classical Walpurgis Night, Faust is searching for Helena in a region suggesting organic fertility, growth, and heroic figures of the past:

> . . . O laßt sie walten,
> die unvergleichlichen Gestalten,
> wie sie dorthin mein Auge schickt.
> So wunderbar bin ich durchdrungen!
> Sind's Träume? Sind's Erinnerungen?
> Schon einmal warst du so beglückt.
> Gewässer schleichen durch die Frische
> der dichten, sanft bewegten Büsche,
> nicht rauschen sie, sie rieseln kaum. (7279)

Meanwhile, Mephistopheles is associating with sphinxes, griffons, and lamiae in an area of barren desolation, finding his counterparts, the Phorkyads, only after he has lost his way among the rocks:

> Da muß ich mich durch steile Felsentreppen,
> durch alter Eichen starre Wurzeln schleppen! (7952)

While the mode of Mephistopheles' speech is often staccato and violent and often smooth and unctuous — as the situation requires — it reveals a character which is basically uniform, a principle of which Faust can say:

> So setzest du der ewig regen,
> der heilsam schaffenden Gewalt
> die kalte Teufelsfaust entgegen,
> die sich vergebens tückisch ballt! (1382)

Compared with Mephistopheles' speech, that of Faust expresses a character deeply at odds with himself. In terms of poetic diction, Faust's words reveal a man who is equally attracted to the realm of God, Whose love lifts him "hinan," and to the realm of the Devil, which pulls him "herab." In the "Prolog," Mephistopheles describes Faust's twofold desires:

> Vom Himmel fordert er die schönsten Sterne
> und von der Erde jede höchste Lust. (305)

A similar dualism of feeling is expressed by Faust himself in the imagery of the two souls and their different drives:

> Zwei Seelen wohnen, ach, in meiner Brust,
> die eine will sich von der andern trennen:
> die eine hält in derber Liebeslust
> sich an die Welt mit klammernden Organen;
> die andre hebt gewaltsam sich vom Dust
> zu den Gefilden hoher Ahnen. (1117)

"Hoch" and "tief" are among the words most frequently occurring in FAUST; their influence upon the expressiveness of imagery is considerable.

Young Werther, in Goethe's novel, ponders

> . . . über die Begier im Menschen, sich auszubreiten, neue Entdeckungen zu machen, herumzuschweifen; und dann wieder über den innern Trieb, sich der Einschränkung willig zu ergeben, in dem Gleise der Gewohnheit so hinzufahren und sich weder um rechts noch um links zu bekümmern — (Am 21. Junius).

Faust's nature is dominated by two similar drives, even though the second, "sich der Einschränkung willig zu ergeben," is almost never realized. Still, the possibility of self-limitation is considered by Faust at various times. When it is, it is reflected in the setting of the garden (Gretchen, Philemon and Baucis) and contrasted with that of wilderness ("Wald und Höhle") — or with that of the palace which is not safe from the visits of Dame Care ("Mitternacht"). Or it is reflected in the imagery of the peaceful hut, which is denied to the restless fugitive, the wanderer:

Bin ich der Flüchtling nicht, der Unbehauste,
der Unmensch ohne Zweck und Ruh,
der wie ein Wassersturz von Fels' zu Felsen brauste,
begierig wütend, nach dem Abgrund zu?
Und seitwärts sie, mit kindlich dumpfen Sinnen,
im Hüttchen auf dem kleinen Alpenfeld,
und all ihr häusliches Beginnen
umfangen in der kleinen Welt. (3355)

Much of this poetic imagery — while in itself brilliant and fascinating — becomes really significant to the reader only when he discovers that it is governed by the same principle of contrast on which the entire play is built. Gretchen's existence is symbolized in the image of the hut (3353, 2708), and Faust's is suggested in that of the rushing cataract which destroys the cottage (3359). And while Gretchen is symbolized in the flowers of her garden (3179, 3611), Faust's subconscious fear of destroying is adumbrated in the fall of the giant fir in "Wald und Höhle" (3228 ff). The world of "Staub" (653 ff) to which Faust feels himself condemned becomes even more depressing when contrasted with the thought of the "sources of life":

Man sehnt sich nach des Lebens Bächen,
ach, nach des Lebens Quelle hin. (1201)

The occurrence of the "water" symbol throughout the play, and its frequent association with the idea of growth and development, makes it one of the more significant poetic devices — particularly when it is set off against the imagery of barrenness, stones, rocks, and similar inorganic objects. In the argument between Thales and Anaxagoras in the Classical Walpurgis Night it is even employed in order to indicate — almost humorously — where the poet stood in a controversy between two schools of geological theory of his time — namely, on the side of those who believed that the shape of the earth's surface and the origin of organic life on earth had resulted from the consistent beneficial influence of water. But the water symbol does not always suggest fruitful productivity in Faust. Clearly the image of the waterfall shows that its significance can vary, and that it can symbolize destructiveness in one place (3350) and sheer vitality in another (4716). In one instance water symbolizes destructiveness in an almost Mephistophelian manner: the sea which causes Faust to conceive his last plan, a plan involving courageous, creative activity against infertility and waste:

Sie schleicht heran, an abertausend Enden,
unfruchtbar selbst, Unfruchtbarkeit zu spenden.
Nun schwillt's und wächst und rollt und überzieht
der wüsten Strecke widerlich Gebiet. (10 215)

Still, this waste can be converted to productiveness: in the end, Faust is almost fanatically devoted to his task of defeating stagnation:

Ein Sumpf zieht am Gebirge hin,
verpestet alles schon Errungene;
den faulen Pfuhl auch abzuziehn,
das Letzte wär' das Höchsterrungene. (11 562)

Mephistopheles may even here have a last triumph. For the sea may at any time break into the reclaimed land, devastating the spaces that have been opened up to millions of free and active settlers, and obliterating their work. Among the last words Mephistopheles addresses to Faust, the image of destruction stands out as a symbol of the most significant aspect of Mephistopheles' character:

Du bist doch nur für uns bemüht
mit deinen Dämmen, deinen Buhnen;
denn du bereitest schon Neptunen,
dem Wasserteufel, großen Schmaus.—
In jeder Art seid ihr verloren:
die Elemente sind mit uns verschworen,
und auf Vernichtung läuft's hinaus. (11 550)

The poetic symbolism in FAUST does not always betray such specifically "pointed" intentions as in this scene of the last encounter between Faust and the Devil. On the whole, Goethe shielded his symbolism — one of the most delicate means of his art — from an oversimple interpretation on the part of his reader. But on occasions he must have been aware that only the suggestive power of symbolism would make the innermost depths of some of his characters comprehensible.

The emotions, the desires, the anxieties which occupy the subconscious of any individual are formless and inexpressible until they are cast into the definite form of meaningful symbols. As we have seen, in the early years of his "Sturm und Drang," Goethe was fond of expressing his obsession by poetry in the image of the charioteer. Symbols chosen by an author permit a glance into the realm of his subconscious, where creative imagination is at work; at the same time, they show him as an artist of superior consciousness and power of observation. It is in this sphere that Goethe's imagery achieves its most magnificent creations — when he elucidates Faust's character in the repeated visionary flights into space (699 ff, 1074 ff), in Mephistopheles' symbolization of libido (3282 ff), or in Homunculus' description of Faust's dream (6903 ff).

In the last analysis, the entire Second Part of FAUST is projected into the realm of pure imagination, pure poetry, pure "magic." In terms of the traditional drama, there is very little dramatic action going on in this part, and the few events which do take place are often connected with one another by whims of imagination rather than strict causality. But in terms of "poetry," i.e., of "creativeness" (in the original sense of the Greek term, "poiētḗs" = maker, creator), the "action" of the Second

Part amounts to a symbolic self-revelation of the art of poetry — from the antics of Knabe Lenker (5573–5708) and the mysteries of the Mothers (6216 ff, 6427 ff), through the realm of ancient creative imagination (= mythology) and the symbolic rise and fall of Euphorion — to the poetic vision of the future (11 559–11 586) and the solemn chant of the *Chorus mysticus*.

Dialogues and monologues. The prevalent form of dramatic presentation in FAUST is the dialogue between two speakers; rarely are more than two persons shown engaged in discourse at any given time. This fact would not be noteworthy if it did not indicate a fundamental and characteristic feature of Goethe's poetic art: an interest in the interaction of opposites, "polarity." At times his handling of dialogue is impressively skillful, as in the delicate intertwining of two simultaneous conversations between Faust and Gretchen and between Mephistopheles and Marthe (3073–3204). The several scenes of the Classical Walpurgis Night, depicting the various ambitions of Faust, Mephistopheles, and Homunculus, reveal a similar structure of dialogue intertwined.

A variation of the dialogue is found in such scenes as "Auerbachs Keller," "Hexenküche," "Walpurgisnacht," and the court scenes, where the contrast between the main speakers in the foreground is effectively heightened by the presence of colorful supporting figures in the background.

Even the monologue, so unforgettably associated with the character of Faust himself and of Gretchen, often reveals the significant features of dramatic *dialogue:* changes of pitch or mood, of tempo or intensity. There are soliloquies in which the speaker is portrayed as engaged not merely in rational deliberation or in lyrical effusion, but in a truly dramatic conflict with himself.

The monodrama. In the 1770's, when he was first occupied with the FAUST poem, Goethe was especially fond of the monodrama, an operatic type of soliloquy then fashionable. A monodrama was often composed to provide some noted tragic actor or actress with the opportunity to display his or her talents, to concentrate the usual features of the drama (contrast, intrigue, complication, conflict, catastrophe, etc.) in the reflections of *one* character, thus making the psychological conflict of this character unusually impressive. Rousseau, the French philosopher, was among the first to write such monodramas.

The structure of Goethe's first novel, WERTHER, suggests monodramatic tendencies. Faust, as the agonies of his first soliloquy indicate, was a character likewise suitable for monodramatic presentation.

As performed, a monodrama was a soliloquy recited with an orchestra playing appropriate music in the background. Sometimes, toward the end of the monologue, when an emotional crisis was reached and a fateful decision was to be made, the voices of an invisible chorus or solo singer responded off-stage. Certain portions of FAUST — the opening soliloquies of Faust (354–521, 606–807) and the Gretchen soliloquies (3374–3413, 3587–3619) — show a close kinship in structure and mood with PROSERPINA, a monodrama Goethe wrote a few years after his arrival in Weimar (1777). During the same period he composed several "Singspiele" — librettos for light operas, to be performed before the court at Weimar.

Musical elements. The musical elements in FAUST indicate how much of the poetic language of FAUST is lyrical in nature and calls for the most direct — musical — means of self-expression. The scale of human emotions on which this drama is played runs from the utter dejection and desolation of a lost soul to the highest elation in the immensities and grandeurs of cosmic space. Gretchen's misery in her dungeon is underscored by the pathetic simplicity and insanity of her song. The opening and closing scenes of the play ring with the hymnic praise of Creation and Heavenly Love. Again and again the dramatic dialogue is accentuated by a song — now expressing the naive sensuousness of peasants celebrating the return of spring (949 ff), now the vulgarity of carousing students (2090 ff), now the innocent purity of Gretchen in her simple appraisal of loyalty (2759 ff), and now the lascivious cynicism of Mephistopheles (3682 ff).

Such musical "numbers" are more than a romantic intrusion of music into a dramatic text. They are part of a fundamentally lyrical mode of composition without which the high emotional pitch of the action, particularly in the First Part, could scarcely be sustained. At times these musical devices assume the importance of dramatic agents: the ringing of church bells and singing of Easter hymns (737 SD) and the tolling of the bell in the little chapel of Philemon and Baucis (11 151) are reminders of a transcendental world.

Without the Easter music in the neighboring church (783) Faust would have succumbed to his plans of suicide; without the chapel bell he would not have been whipped into that frantic impatience which drives him to his last deed of violence: the removal of Philemon and Baucis (11 258). Without the musical charm of the spirits (1447 ff) Mephistopheles would not have escaped from Faust's study. Gretchen breaks down under the combined force of the Evil Spirit's whisperings and the reverberating tones of the *Dies irae* in the cathedral. The witches' revel of the Walpurgis Night, symbolical of Faust's deepest emotional confusion, is inseparable from its infernal din. And the "Walpurgisnachtstraum," whatever its dramatic function, presents the interesting attempt to express in words the intricacies of a witches' orchestra or — on the level of symbolism — to express the fading away of exhausting hallucinations into a fatiguing dream. When the dream is spent in a breeze-like pianissimo, the harshness of the tragedy goes on in the violent tirades of the prose scene "Trüber

Tag." One of the striking acoustic effects of the play occurs at the end of Part I when Faust is dragged away by Mephistopheles and Gretchen's voice calls his name in heartrending lament — "von innen, verhallend."

In the Second Part entire scenes follow an operatic pattern, even though musical accompaniment may not always be specifically prescribed in the stage directions. At the beginning of Act I, when Faust is shown recovering from his paralyzing experience under the healing influence of music, the transition from a subconscious to a conscious state of mind is symbolized by a similar transition from music to word, from the chanting of spirits to Faust's soliloquy — one of the most magnificent lyrical passages of the entire poem. Other scenes show the reverse process. The Classical Walpurgis Night, at first resounding with the snarling and croaking of mythological monsters, finally resolves itself into a festival of music in praise of creative Eros. Above all, the Arcadian Idyll — Faust's union with Helena and the birth and death of Euphorion — was composed by Goethe along operatic lines, and constant musical accompaniment is prescribed (cf. 9679, 9938). Goethe wished to see this part of Helena's role performed by a grand-opera singer; and his suggestion that Mozart should have written the music for FAUST (conversation with Eckermann, February 12, 1829) indicates that music was to take over where words failed to describe the indescribable.

Allusions to the fine arts. Like many of Goethe's lyric poems, certain portions of FAUST owe their poetic effect to the force and clarity of the poet's intuition. These portions of FAUST impress themselves upon the reader's imagination as art works impress the spectator.

At the turn of the century, when Goethe followed Schiller's counsel and resumed his work on FAUST, he was guided by a new conception of feminine beauty which was quite different from his first visions of Helena, the daemonic temptress. This new Helena, as she appeared in the sketch of 1800, embodied the idealism of Greek art, the Platonic concept of perennial beauty which had been the subject of several of Schiller's essays and of many conversations and letters between the two poets. The beauty of Helena, the "Gestalt aller Gestalten" (8907), suggests the dignified beauty of ancient masterpieces which Goethe had seen in Italy and whose replicas he had begun to acquire for his collections — that beauty which, according to Schiller, is free from all earthly attachments, relieved of the "Angst des Irdischen," and is untouched by the passage of time:

> Aber frei von jeder Zeitgewalt,
> die Gespielin ewiger Naturen,
> wandelt oben in des Lichtes Fluren
> göttlich unter Göttern die G e s t a l t.
>
> (Schiller, "Das Ideal und das Leben")

The statue-like beauty of Helena cannot be fully imagined without the contrasting effect of extreme ugliness in the grotesque shape of Phorkyas-Mephistopheles, of whom Helena says:

> . . . das Wort bemüht
> sich nur umsonst, Gestalten schöpferisch aufzubaun.
> Da seht sie selbst! (8693)

A contrast of visual elements distinguishes some of the main portions of the play, the northern nd the classical scenes. The Gothic vaults of Faust's laboratory, of the cathedral, and of the Hall of the Knights are effectively contrasted with the monumental dignity of the Greek temple (6403–6408) in which the pantomime "The Rape of Helena" is performed, and the ancient Mycenaean palace at Sparta before which Helena makes her appearance (8488 SD).

The beginning scenes of Act I and Act V are seen with the eye of a painter: they suggest the sweeping perspective of landscape painting, one of Goethe's favorite avocations. The reader's pictorial imagination is called upon to visualize, from the detail described, the Masquerade Procession in the "Mummenschanz" and the succession of grotesque figures in the two Walpurgis Nights.

The ends of Act II and Act V — the praises of Eros and of spiritual Love — develop the visual appeal of a grand, concluding "tableau" to a maximum of stage effect. And we remember that Goethe's own experience in the arrangement of pantomimes and masques for court festivals at Weimar provided him with frequent occasions to fuse the poetic and the pictorial arts in the service of allegory.

The imagery of Faust, as we have seen, reveals the emotion of the lyric poet who is deeply affected by the fleeting sequence of moods, and for whom visual perceptions readily pass into meaningful visions. A moonrise, depicted in detail, sets the stage for the spooks of the two Walpurgis Nights (3851 ff, 7031 ff), just as the weak glimmer of a lonely vestry lamp presages the gloom of the "Valentin" scene (3650 ff). The detailed descriptions of withdrawing winter and approaching spring (903 ff) create the mood for that peculiar restlessness and mental discontent which makes Faust accept the "harmless" poodle, half playfully, half suspiciously. In an image of magnificent clarity and animation — sunrise, Alpine grandeur, waterfall — Faust gains deeper insight into the meaning of life: "Am farbigen Abglanz haben wir das Leben" (4727).

Faust's receptiveness for visual stimuli demonstrates that by nature Faust is a poet who wants to behold the "Reihe der Lebendigen" (3225) or possess a "Luginsland . . . , um ins Unendliche zu schaun" (11 345), rather than the scholar or the scientist in whose role he finds himself in the beginning. And in this respect, Faust mirrors Goethe, the poet, to whom "intuition" — *Anschauung* of life in its totality — was the fundamental ambition, no matter how much he was tempted by "scientific" pursuits.

FAUST *on the stage.* Goethe, a theater expert, envisaged his drama as a stage performance. This is indicated not only by the "Vorspiel" but also by the many, often detailed, stage directions scattered throughout the text.

For the reader of FAUST, the fusion of many scenes into an organic and meaningful whole will not be complete until he has seen the play enacted on the stage. When the action of the play is projected into the spatial dimensions suggested by the stage, when the poetry comes to life in the spoken word, and when an imagined reality merges with symbolism, then the spectator may perhaps experience what the reader is called upon to imagine: to view the FAUST play in its totality.

Still, any performance will be confronted with almost unsurmountable difficulties. There are few glorious chapters in the stage history of FAUST. The reasons for the many failures may be the technical inadequacies of German stages in the nineteenth and twentieth centuries, or the temptation to present merely the "sensational" elements of the play, such as the Gretchen episode.

Between 1812 and 1817 the staging of FAUST (Part I) was considered several times at the Weimar theater, and Goethe himself sketched a few of the stage settings. Ultimately these plans were abandoned and Goethe shifted his interest to a private performance, at the Prussian court in Berlin, of a few scenes for which an aristocratic dilettante, Prince Radziwill, had written acceptable music. The first performance of the complete First Part was staged in Braunschweig by Klingemann on January 19, 1829. The text used in this performance, though it was a mutilated version of Goethe's text, set the pattern for several other presentations in Germany. Goethe himself first saw his play enacted when he was eighty years old, in a performance at Weimar on August 29, 1829, to which he himself contributed much time and effort.

It was not until almost half a century later (May 1876) that the entire tragedy was presented on the stage. Under the direction of Otto Devrient it was given in Weimar on two evenings. Encouraged by Devrient's success, other German stages undertook similar experiments which divided the play into two, three, or four evenings, or were even so ambitious as to compress it into the eight hours between 5:00 P.M. and 1:00 A.M.

The introduction of the revolving stage made it possible to present the two parts comfortably and adequately in two evenings. With this device the pioneering enterprise of Max Reinhardt (Deutsches Theater, Berlin, 1909) set the example for many successful performances throughout Germany. With the coming of the film, further difficulties were overcome; and although the silent film of the twenties exploited the Faust theme in a mixture of legendary and Goethean motifs, its success gave reason to hope that eventually even Goethe's FAUST, the masterpiece of poetic language, might yield to the technical skill and artistic conscience of the modern sound film.

Max Reinhardt's staging of FAUST took its cue from the spirit rather than the letter of Goethe's theatrical directions. Addressing himself to the imagination of intelligent spectators, he reduced the detail of stage paraphernalia to a minimum, and exploited the suggestiveness of Darkness and Light to a maximum. Above all, under his direction the significance of the spoken word, the main concern of the poet, received the attention which it deserved.

Much of the success of a stage performance of FAUST depends, of course, on the personality and artistic skill of the actors. The role of Faust demands a talent which an actor either does or does not possess. For Mephistopheles the histrionic requirements are even more difficult to meet, since not only a person who is a cynic, but the spirit of cynicism and negation itself, is to be impersonated — and the part of the Devil is one of the oldest mimic ambitions of men. The roles of Gretchen and Helena presuppose a high order of grace and beauty to do justice to the "Seelenschönheit" and "Sinnenschönheit" which make Faust act the way he does. In comparison with these characters, all other figures of the drama recede into the background where they become mere types, if they are human, or mere qualities, if they are supernatural.

As a whole, the appeal of FAUST is lyrical rather than dramatic. We have the impression that a most serious festival play, a profound allegory, is passing before our eyes "und spiegelt blendend flücht'ger Tage großen Sinn." Symbolic as to space and time, creating the illusion of immense depth, such a play invites theatrical experimentation. That is particularly true of the scenes which involve a constantly changing background. Faust and Wagner wandering from the city to the country on Easter Day, Faust and Mephistopheles wending their way through the confusing throngs of the Northern Walpurgis Night, and Faust and Chiron roaming through the Peneios Valley in the Classical Walpurgis Night demand a freedom of movement that no stage can fully satisfy. As they proceed, the scenery changes, and with the scenery their moods. Unknown creatures emerge before them and lure them into unforeseen adventures. All Nature seems to be drawn into a spell of motion, of restlessness. Thus it is on the stage that a few scenes suggest the fundamental design of the entire FAUST play: that it is not merely a drama dealing with the doings and sufferings of a dramatic "hero" in the traditional sense, but a drama presenting Faust's "journey" through life.

Unwritten scenes. Despite its twelve thousand and more lines a reader of FAUST soon discerns that this play was not really completed. A few weeks before his death, Goethe felt urged to unseal and re-examine the manuscript and noted in his diary (January 24, 1832) that he had treated some of the main themes too "laconically." In the present version, the existence of such scenes seems to be betrayed at a number of places by stage directions which state what might have been expressed in poetic dialogue. We find these stage directions in the Carnival scenes of Act II, and also in several places in Act IV of Part II.

In addition, there are still some gaps in the dramatic continuity which Goethe might have filled in with poetic speech, characterization, and action. The "Walpurgisnachtstraum" is still no "intermezzo," as its title indicates it was intended to be, for it is not followed by a concluding scene of the Walpurgis Night, which was to contain the homage to Satan. There is no proper transition between "Anmutige Gegend" and the scenes at the Imperial Court, to explain the introduction of the magician Faust into "die große Welt." Similarly, the scene at the end of Act IV, which was to depict the granting of the seashore as a fief to Faust, was never written. A few lines describing the investiture did not mature into the dignified scene which is demanded. Finally, the grandiose plan for a scene depicting Faust's descent into the nether world, his plea before Persephoneia for the release of Helena, did not materialize. Goethe was deterred from this undertaking by the immensity of the poetic task involved: to write a plea which would stir to tears even the goddess of death.

2. INTERPRETATION OF THE CHARACTERS

In FAUST, as in any work of imaginative literature, there are many details which form a meaningful pattern when they are related to a fundamental belief, a philosophical system, a specific artistic intention, a "typical" mode of behavior. Many a reader will read his own "pattern" into FAUST. These patterns may be different, though they need not be mutually exclusive. In fact, the variety and divergence of the patterns which have been and may be applied to FAUST testify to the immense experience and wisdom which Goethe embodied in his work. As the structure of the play indicates, Goethe invites his readers to look at human life, as it were, "from within" and "from without" — from an earthly and from a supernatural point of view, to see the characters that make the play on two levels: he can observe them in the life they lead, and he can interpret them according to a fundamental pattern of meaning.

Faust

Two views of Faust's character. The reader who looks for unity of character and purpose in the figure of Faust soon realizes that Faust must be considered from two points of view — as an individual human being and as a representative of man, of human endeavor and activity.

As an individual human being Faust is a man whose destiny it is to waver between God and the Devil. In his flight from one experience to another, Faust is never completely clear about this basic dualism in his character, but the reader is. For the reader knows that Faust is the subject of an agreement between the Lord and Mephistopheles whereby the latter is granted permission to try to divert this human being from his true path as a servant of the Lord. God relies entirely upon the human nature of Faust, the "good" man, whereas Mephistopheles brings to bear upon Faust all manner of "temptations" and inducements to abandon God's ways. Faust is susceptible to these temptations and inducements because he is as yet "confused" (308) in his service of God. Presumably the Lord frees Faust from divine control for the duration of the experiment (315). For the reader, therefore, the question is whether this human being, Faust, will use his innate "freedom" in such a manner that he will not succumb to the blandishments of Mephistopheles, and will thereby justify the trust which the Lord has placed in him.

As a representative of human endeavor and activity Faust is a man whose nature is characterized by his "striving." Yet, in his varying experiences, Faust shows no consistency in his "strivings" and apparently no fundamental improvement in any single experience. But the reader, considering the upward course of human civilization, knows that mankind, too, has shown little consistency in the individual stages of cultural evolution; however, from an overall point of view, and in the light of its history, mankind promises progress toward greater spiritual and intellectual perfection. For the reader the question is whether Faust, as a representative of this human endeavor, will, by his innate "striving," be protected against the wiles of Mephistopheles, and thereby justify the trust which the Lord has placed in man's human nature.

As an individual character, Faust must be appraised on the basis of his personal nature, his actions, his morality — in terms of Good or Evil. But in regard to his universal significance, Faust must be judged in terms of "striving" or "rest," of Life or Destruction. It is not on the strength of "good deeds" but of his human striving that Faust is granted ultimate salvation.

This twofold significance of Faust's character is illustrated by a striking analogy to two Biblical themes employed by Goethe at the beginning and at the end of the FAUST play: (1) the situation in the "Prolog im Himmel" resembles that described in the Book of Job, where Satan appears before the Lord and is given permission to try to lead Job astray from his God-fearing ways (Job 1.6–12). (2) The situation at Faust's death, with Faust's vision of human and social freedom, resembles that at the death of Moses, who viewed the Promised Land without being allowed to enter it (Deut. 34.1–6); this theme is elaborated by a Hebrew legend according to which angels defeated devils in a battle for the possession of Moses' soul.

Like Job, Faust is the individual who is given the freedom to prove himself "conscious of the right path." Like Moses, Faust is the embodiment of human endeavor to strive toward higher forms of human existence.

Faust's dual nature. Within the play, Faust interests us first and foremost as an individual character. Faust is essentially of a dual nature. What he describes as the "two souls" in his breast (1112) appears in manifold variations throughout the play — now as a conflict between his material desires and his spiritual demands, now as a conflict between a life of action and one of contemplation. Faust is torn by two forces: the dictates of his nature and the demands of his reason. This theme is stated for the first time when Mephistopheles remarks that man would lead a much happier life, had he not been endowed with "heavenly light":

> Er nennt's Vernunft und braucht's allein,
> nur tierischer als jedes Tier zu sein. (286)

The target of Mephistopheles' sardonic remark is the fact of human freedom: man, who is free to use his reason to make his existence more perfectly the realization of his innate capacities, perverts it into a tool for the satisfaction of his baser desires. Possessing "freedom" as well as "nature," Faust exemplifies an unfortunate cleavage in man. Reason, which was meant by the Creator as an endowment of Heavenly Love, has turned in man's hand into an instrument of egotism. Thus Faust is vulnerable to Mephistopheles' designs — particularly when he wavers between faith and despair, patience and impatience, moments of clarity and moments of utter confusion. The words of the Lord in the "Prolog" (328–329) prepare the reader to view Faust as a "guter Mensch"; but throughout the play Faust remains "off balance," and his own decisions do not bring about his mental or moral equilibrium. Freedom of choice and action alone does not decide Faust's fate; as long as there is no other determining factor, Faust's actions do not keep him from falling a prey to Mephistopheles.

Nor is there any lofty "intention" behind Faust's activities that insures his "salvation." Faust is not a representative of that naively optimistic individualism which conceives of a "hero" who, through dissatisfaction and in spite of error and guilt, rises from step to step until in his old age he reaches the summit of humanitarian activity — and self-perfection. Such a Faust would be the author of his own salvation, the maker of his own fate, comparable to Prometheus who — in Goethe's youthfully exuberant ode — can ask himself:

Hast du nicht alles selbst vollendet,
heilig glühend Herz?

and who in stubborn defiance of a tyrannical Zeus prides himself on his own achievements:

Hier sitz' ich, forme Menschen
nach meinem Bilde,
ein Geschlecht, das mir gleich sei,
zu leiden, zu weinen,
zu genießen und zu freuen sich
und dein nicht zu achten, —
wie ich!

On the contrary, the Faust play reflects the presence in earthly life of an element of reason, of "das Göttliche," as Goethe expressed it in his ode of more mature years (1783):

Nach ewigen, ehrnen,
großen Gesetzen
müssen wir alle
unseres Daseins
Kreise vollenden.

The first and the last scenes of the play indicate that Faust's life proceeds according to these "eternal laws," and the question remains to what extent Faust's striving and erring symbolizes them.

"*Streben.*" Nine months before his death Goethe interpreted to Eckermann (June 6, 1831) the meaning of the lines

Wer immer strebend sich bemüht,
den können wir erlösen. (11 937)

in the following words:

In diesen Versen ist der Schlüssel zu Fausts Rettung enthalten: in Faust selber eine immer höhere und reinere Tätigkeit bis ans Ende, und von oben die ihm zu Hülfe kommende ewige Liebe. Es steht dieses mit unserer religiösen Vorstellung durchaus in Harmonie, nach welcher wir nicht bloß durch eigene Kraft selig werden, sondern durch die hinzukommende göttliche Gnade.

Throughout the play "Streben" represents Faust's mode of existence; it is the most characteristic trait of his nature. At the beginning of the Second Part, Faust professes it as the guiding maxim of his life:

Zum höchsten Dasein immerfort zu streben. (4685)

Even in the moment of his greatest alienation from God — when he concludes his pact with Mephistopheles — Faust pledges the full strength of his endeavor:

Das Streben meiner ganzen Kraft
ist grade das, was ich verspreche. (1743)

In a feeling of overconfidence Faust questions Mephistopheles' ability to comprehend the basic nature of man, his "striving":

Ward eines Menschen Geist, in seinem hohen Streben,
von deinesgleichen je gefaßt? (1677)

And Mephistopheles himself acknowledges this nature of Faust:

Ihm hat das Schicksal einen Geist gegeben,
der ungebändigt immer vorwärts dringt,
und dessen übereiltes Streben
der Erde Freuden überspringt. (1859)

Mephistopheles' first comment on Faust's death recognizes the strength of this fundamental drive in Faust's character:

Ihn sättigt keine Lust, ihm g'nügt kein Glück,
so buhlt er fort nach wechselnden Gestalten. (11 588)

There is nothing particularly purposeful, clear-sighted, or rational about this "striving" as the fundamental form of Faust's character. On the contrary, it is often no more than a mere feeling of restlessness and a desire for change. Sometimes it is the source of Faust's feeling of greatness, individuality, and independence, sometimes of thwarted ambition and frustration; as such it is strikingly portrayed in the second soliloquy (606–736) of Faust, placed between two extremes — the Erdgeist, who may be considered a symbolization of pure "Streben," and Wagner, who possesses limited objectives but no "Streben" as Faust knows it. "Striving" is that force in man's existence in which Faust feels most himself, now elated and now dejected, but always unwilling to accept stagnation. In a feeling of superiority he challenges Mephistopheles to a wager (1698); but this feeling of superiority is at the same time one of desperation, for Faust, although he knows he cannot reach his ambitious goals by his own unaided efforts, is also sure that no arts of the Devil can help him achieve his aim. Yet he cannot give up; alone, or with the Devil's help if need be, he must strive as long as he lives.

This is only one of the two indispensable conditions of Faust's salvation (11 936–11 939). Faust is saved not merely because he strives, but also because Divine Love intervenes in his behalf. The mystery of such "intervention" is never fully revealed. At the end of the play we are told that Gretchen intercedes in Faust's behalf and that her prayer is granted; but the exact relationship between Faust's striving and Divine Love does not become immediately manifest.

The answer to this problem may be sought partly in FAUST itself; partly it is suggested by analogous problems in the philosophy of Goethe's time. When it is recognized there, it is not difficult to discover it in FAUST as well.

"Streben und Liebe." While the action of the earthly FAUST play acquaints us with the manifestations of "Streben" in Faust's life, the first and the last scenes give us a hint as to the origin and the aim of "striving." To use an analogy: only the visible frequencies of light are

displayed in the colors, while the infrared and ultraviolet parts of the spectrum are invisible. The same source of radiant energy emits the rays which are visible and those which are invisible to the human eye. In terms of Spinozistic philosophy, the same force which manifests itself visibly in the various forms of Faust's earthly "Streben" has shaped his nature before, and will determine his fate after, he is shown on the earthly scene.

In keeping with the philosophy of pantheism which is implicit in the FAUST poem, particularly the First Part, Faust regards Nature as permeated with the energy of God; it is this pantheism — characteristic of "Sturm und Drang" — which inspires Faust with the desire to participate in Nature and all of its manifestations. In Nature, Faust senses the same "Streben" which animates him. In the idiom of Schopenhauer, the "lust for existence" which appears in Faust as personal will, appears in Nature as "Wille in der Natur." That some notion of this kind must have been in Goethe's mind becomes evident from the use of the term "Streben" in connection with Nature. The sign of the macrocosm reveals to Faust a similar "mysterious drive" (437), and the words of the Earth Spirit likewise suggest it: (501–9)

In Lebensfluten, im Tatensturm
wall' ich auf und ab,
webe hin und her!
Geburt und Grab,
ein ewiges Meer,
ein wechselnd Weben,
ein glühend Leben:
so schaff' ich am sausenden Webstuhl der Zeit
und wirke der Gottheit lebendiges Kleid.

These words describe a physical life whose essence is change, growth and decay and new growth, and nowhere is there any notion of purposeful evolution: that is left to the will of the godhead. Faust soon abandons the desire to recognize such a purposeful plan of the universe; but in his life he does not cease to exemplify it.

"Streben," then, appears in the FAUST poem as the manifestation of a fundamental force governing all existence: in the process of growth, transformation, "becoming" ("Werden"), it is the natural drive animating everything alive. The fundamental force is that of Divine Love, the cause and the end of all creation, which must intervene if "Becoming" is to be transformed into everlasting "Being." At the end of FAUST, in the union of "striving" and "Love" (11 936–11 941), the task is completed which the Lord stated in the "Prolog" in words reading like the philosophical keynote of the FAUST poem:

Das Werdende, das ewig wirkt und lebt,
umfass' euch mit der Liebe holden Schranken,

und was in schwankender Erscheinung schwebt,
befestiget mit dauernden Gedanken! (349)

The outcome of the great drama seems to say that the forces of negation cannot stop or destroy the development of the human spirit if this spirit persists in its striving to become what, by its nature, it is destined to be. The implication is clear that the forces of negation can only destroy that human spirit which fails to persist in this striving. Hence, it is not merely "das Werdende" which is important, but "das Werdende, das ewig wirkt und lebt"; not merely "wer strebt," but "wer immer strebend sich bemüht."

Faust himself soon discovers that he is far from being the "Ebenbild der Gottheit"; he follows his "dunkler Drang," and his striving involves him in error and imperfection. He desires to participate in the "Werden" that pervades the universe (447 ff); but he has to learn patience until that "Werden" can work in him. Himself a "Werdender," Faust wavers in "schwankender Erscheinung" until his desire for knowledge and his drive of love, his "Streben," have been sanctioned by God's will.

The mere fact that Faust "strives" to participate in the "Werden" of the universe does not make him either a scholar or a philosopher. For both of these callings he lacks the objectivity and sense of proportion and the necessary degree of personal detachment. When he expresses dissatisfaction with the four academic disciplines (354 ff), he passes sentence not so much on these disciplines as on his own weaknesses. Faust is a man of feeling, of sensitivity, of changing emotions — like the youthful Goethe, who would write poetry when he ought to be practicing law, and engage in nature studies when he intended to write poetry. Faust possesses high intelligence; but his intelligence is at the mercy of his feelings — feelings now demanding immediate satisfaction, now dissolving into awe, devotion, "Schauer," and "heil'ges Grauen" (1180). He is occupied with "life" in every possible aspect, but he follows no specific trade or profession. He leads one life respected by the multitude, and then again another as a clandestine lover. As the play begins, Faust is a university professor. As a scholar he seeks to discover ". . . was die Welt im Innersten zusammenhält"; he is vexed by the prosaic views of his companion Wagner whose erudition may satisfy antiquarian interests but scarcely penetrate into "nature's innermost core." The deep-seated conflict within Faust's personality imparts itself to his intellectual activities: he cannot recognize any condition in nature without desiring to experience it. Thus his intellect is confounded by his will, his insight by the desire for action and consummation.

The "daemonic." A character as diverse and contradictory as Faust's becomes more easily intelligible from a consideration of a passage in Goethe's autobiography (Book 20), where the poet describes himself as a young man striving to achieve a satisfactory attitude toward the supernatural. He had, he says, successively embraced natural religion, positive religion, and pantheistic philosophy. But in passing from one to the other of these beliefs he had observed something which seemed to belong to none of them — the "inscrutable," the "tremendous" — and he became more and more convinced that he had better abandon hope of ever understanding it.

Speaking of his own observation, Goethe describes this inscrutable element as follows:

Er [Goethe] glaubte, in der Natur, der belebten und unbelebten, der beseelten und unbeseelten, etwas zu entdecken, das sich nur in Widersprüchen manifestierte und deshalb unter keinen Begriff, noch viel weniger unter ein Wort gefaßt werden könnte. Es war nicht göttlich, denn es schien unvernünftig; nicht menschlich, denn es hatte keinen Verstand; nicht teuflisch, denn es war wohltätig; nicht englisch, denn es ließ oft Schadenfreude merken. Es glich dem Zufall, denn es bewies keine Folge; es ähnelte der Vorsehung, denn es deutete auf Zusammenhang. Alles, was uns begrenzt, schien für dasselbe durchdringbar; es schien mit den notwendigen Elementen unsres Daseins willkürlich zu schalten; es zog die Zeit zusammen und dehnte den Raum aus. Nur im Unmöglichen schien es sich zu gefallen und das Mögliche mit Verachtung von sich zu stoßen.

Dieses Wesen, das zwischen alle übrigen hineinzutreten, sie zu sondern, sie zu verbinden schien, nannte ich *dämonisch*, nach dem Beispiel der Alten und derer, die etwas Ähnliches gewahrt hatten. Ich suchte mich vor diesem furchtbaren Wesen zu retten, indem ich mich nach meiner Gewohnheit hinter ein Bild flüchtete.

(Dichtung und Wahrheit, 20. Buch)

The poetic image which was to shield Goethe at this time and in which he sought to objectify his feeling of alarm was the figure of Egmont. And thus Goethe finally created a character who is distinguished by his love of life, his unshakable self-confidence, his gift for attracting people — a man who sees no danger and blindly walks into the arms of those who destroy him.

The "daemonic" was variously interpreted by Goethe: It manifests itself in nature and in human life; it expresses itself in moments that hold the possibility of productivity or destruction. Reason and practical understanding are helpless before it (to Eckermann, March 2, 1831). Often it manifests itself in outstanding individuals; indeed, the more highly gifted a man, the more he is under the influence of the "daemons," and therefore the more necessary it is for such a man to exercise his will in order to keep to his proper course (March 24, 1829). The "daemonic" is akin to creativeness of the highest kind (March 11, 1828); above all it is to be found in every passion, particularly in love (March 5, 1830).

Am furchtbarsten aber erscheint dieses Dämonische, wenn es in irgendeinem Menschen überwiegend hervortritt ... Es sind nicht immer die vorzüglichsten Menschen, weder an Geist noch an Talenten, selten durch Herzensgüte sich empfehlend; aber eine ungeheure Kraft geht von ihnen aus, und sie üben eine unglaubliche Gewalt über alle Geschöpfe, ja sogar über die Elemente, und wer kann sagen, wie weit sich eine solche Wirkung erstrecken wird? Alle vereinten sittlichen Kräfte vermögen nichts gegen sie; vergebens, daß der hellere Teil der Menschen sie als Betrogene oder als Betrüger verdächtig machen will, die Masse wird von ihnen angezogen. Selten oder nie finden sich Gleichzeitige ihresgleichen, und sie sind durch nichts zu überwinden als durch das Universum selbst, mit dem sie den Kampf begonnen; und aus solchen Bemerkungen mag wohl jener sonderbare, aber ungeheure Spruch entstanden sein: *Nemo contra deum nisi deus ipse* [No one against God except God Himself].

(DICHTUNG UND WAHRHEIT, 20. Buch)

These words from the last part of Goethe's autobiography were written when Goethe was eighty years old, that is, at a time when he was intent upon completing his "Hauptgeschäft," FAUST. They are meant to characterize one of the most distraught periods in Goethe's life — the months of his love for Lili Schönemann, the days before his departure for Weimar, 1775. While the conception of "das Dämonische" was intended to convey to the reader a notion of Goethe's own inner unrest, it furnishes a key to the understanding of Faust's character.

Renaissance features. Faust's character resembles a type of character which since the times of the Renaissance has been the subject of many psychological investigations: the melancholy individual who isolates himself, sacrifices happy association with his fellow men, abandons God, all in the hope of penetrating the mystery of the universe. This man is a lonely ponderer. "Hier saß ich oft gedankenvoll allein" (1024), Faust tells Wagner during their Easter Sunday walk. The figure of the contemplative man, rapt in thoughts of the sufferings of his fellow men — as Faust was during the great plague — belongs to a tradition of literary and artistic imagery which, long before Goethe, had been established by such masterpieces as Milton's "Il Penseroso," Michelangelo's "Jeremiah" and "Lorenzo de' Medici," and Dürer's "Melancholia." It was during the Renaissance that the melancholy temperament, denounced in the Middle Ages, began to be extolled in the writings of the Humanists; and numerous psychological essays were devoted to the type of man who by virtue of his "complexion" was considered capable of deeper insight, deeper experience than men of other "complexions." Thus the Renaissance created a position apart for the man of the intellect, the "poeta," the "creative man," who dared to defy God and challenge the Devil, and whom the inner conflicts of his personality carried alternately to heights of enthusiasm and depths of despair.

Goethe's Faust reveals a distant kinship with this melancholy man of the Renaissance who is characterized by his oscillating between excited and depressive states of mind and by his penchant for contemplation and mentally creative activity. Almost in one breath Faust can aspire "zu neuen Sphären reiner Tätigkeit" (705) and be ready "ins Nichts dahinzufließen" (719). Within him "wilde Triebe" (1182) and "Liebe Gottes" (1185) dwell side by side. Frustrated in his excessive desires, Faust can renounce life altogether (1571) and accept an alliance with Mephistopheles, because daily life with its pettinesses suffocates his aspirations —

> die Schöpfung meiner regen Brust
> mit tausend Lebensfratzen hindert. (1561)

The pact with the Devil. When Faust is ready for a pact with the Devil, he is utterly estranged from everything that once revealed to him a divine origin of all creation: he has lost his faith and the security that faith once gave him. The belief in an afterlife has become meaningless to him — especially if imagined as a mere continuation of earthly existence. His frantic ambition to sense and control life as God would sense and control it (1566 ff) has given way to frustration; and in a final expression of desperate egotism he denounces life and all the "illusions" that generally make life worth living (1583 ff). Yet, even in his rebellion against his fate, Faust is no nihilist or aloof cynic; even in his rebellion against God, he is fulfilling a condition imposed upon human existence — that of "striving," exerting himself; to Mephistopheles he says:

> Ich habe mich nicht freventlich vermessen:
> wie ich beharre, bin ich Knecht,
> ob dein, was frag' ich, oder wessen. (1711)

What Faust demands from the Devil is not knowledge, practical or transcendental, but universal human experience. He demands to learn every pain, every joy, the highest and the deepest, so that his own experience may be commensurate with that of all humanity. The conditions on which Faust and the Devil conclude their pact are unequivocal; still, it seems as if the two were not speaking quite the same language. Mephistopheles seeks to capture Faust's individual human soul (1674); but Faust's words imply that he is thinking in terms of mankind, seeking to transcend the limitations of his own individual self. For that reason he feels contempt for "a poor devil" who cannot comprehend such a desire (1675 ff). Mephistopheles readily promises even impossible pleasures to satisfy the individual (1689); but Faust wagers that no such pleasure will ever induce him to be "pleased with himself" (1695). The terms of their agreement are indisputable, but the implications are different for the two contracting parties: Mephistopheles offers delightful personal enjoyment, Faust wants to undergo the totality of all human experience:

> Und was der ganzen Menschheit zugeteilt ist,
> will ich in meinem innern Selbst genießen,

mit meinem Geist das Höchst' und Tiefste greifen,
ihr Wohl und Weh auf meinen Busen häufen
und so mein eigen Selbst zu ihrem Selbst erweitern —
und, wie sie selbst, am End' auch ich zerscheitern. (1775)

This demand of Faust is more than mere personal "selfishness"; and it is more than mere boisterous language. For Faust knows that to experience the sufferings and joys of "all mankind" is impossible for any one individual, unless he be God Himself. As Mephistopheles reminds Faust: "dieses Ganze ist nur für einen Gott gemacht! . . . und euch taugt einzig Tag und Nacht" (1784). In the face of these human limitations Faust has only one answer: "Allein ich will!" (1785) — the answer of the "daemonic" man, whose will is absolute, and who knows no limitations. His desire to "be mankind," even to the point of death (1774–5), is an almost blasphemous echo of Christ's sacrificial death, and his ambition to win "der Menschheit Krone" (1804) reflects the pride of his limitless will. Faust's motive is his love of life; but it is a confused love, for nearly all of his experiences spring from his egotistic desire for self-realization: he values people and things and ideals in relation to himself and himself alone.

To be human — and thus to become really representative of humanity — Faust must be brought to acknowledge human limitations and still retain the most valuable asset of his nature — his "striving." To his very end Faust is never satisfied with any achievement; nor does he show any readiness to accept limitations. Even in his last moments he permits destruction and murder to be committed, and his last project, which has seemingly democratic purposes, is carried out with slave labor. Indeed, Faust sees this project chiefly as a reflection of his own greatness, his personal merit (11 509 f, 11 583 f).

There is only one occasion on which Faust has to accept limitation and become aware of his human, finite existence — the approach of his death. For him this moment has an outward as well as an inner implication. For Faust, who has defied nature in many ways, nature has ceased to be an obstacle or a burden. The old impatience is still there (11 233), but he does not despair. Death prevents him from participating in the enjoyment of what he considers his greatest achievement (11 581 f); but he does not rebel. Like Moses viewing the Promised Land, Faust beholds a vision of a community of free men where freedom and life are won by vigorous and competent (tüchtig) endeavor; he now confesses to the enjoyment of his greatest moment. — The other form of limitation is even more significant; it is a decision of his free will and therefore more truly an expression of his "humanity." He realizes that, in order to be wholly free, he has to rid himself of his dependence on magic:

Könnt' ich Magie von meinem Pfad entfernen,
die Zaubersprüche ganz und gar verlernen,

stünd' ich, Natur, vor dir ein Mann allein,
da wär's der Mühe wert, ein Mensch zu sein! (11 407)

In this spirit he recalls the situation in which he denounced the world and his own existence and, in extreme despair, entered upon his pact with the Devil. A comparable situation confronts him now: gloom, disaster, superstition are in the air. But now Faust seeks no supernatural assistance; he no longer craves to identify himself with the "self" of mankind (1774); now he desires to be merely "a man, alone." With this decision he is able to face *Sorge*, Dame Care, in whom all the constraining features of human existence — toil, worry, indecision, frustration, apathy, insensibility — are personified. And *Sorge*, though defied to the last, makes Faust "human" again in his considerations. She blinds him, saying that all men are "blind" in their lives — which means that they are incapable of seeing beyond the reach of their earthly experience. Faust's next thought is how he can free himself from the "daemons," the spectres that beset mankind, and how he can liberate himself from Mephistopheles:

Dämonen, weiß ich, wird man schwerlich los,
das geistig-strenge Band ist nicht zu trennen;
doch deine Macht, o Sorge, schleichend groß,
ich werde sie nicht anerkennen! (11 494)

Freedom. The crucial problem in the interpretation of Faust's character is the question whether Faust, by himself, is able to free himself from the influence of Mephistopheles. This problem is touched upon in a preliminary plan which Goethe sketched on December 16, 1816, for an account of the continuation of FAUST, to be used in the 18th book of Goethe's autobiography, DICHTUNG UND WAHRHEIT. This plan contains a scene in whose general outlines we can recognize the first sketch for the Helena and Euphorion episode. The scene of this episode is laid in an abandoned medieval castle, protected by a magic circle. After an account of the disappearance of mother and son, the sketch concludes as follows:

Mephistopheles, der bisher unter der Gestalt einer alten Schaffnerin von allem Zeuge gewesen, sucht seinen Freund zu trösten und ihm Lust zum Besitz einzuflößen. Der Schloßherr ist in Palästina umgekommen, Mönche wollen sich der Güter bemächtigen, ihre Segensprüche heben den Zauberkreis auf. Mephistopheles rät zur physischen Gewalt und stellt Fausten drei Helfershelfer, mit Namen: Raufebold, Habebald, Haltefest. Faust glaubt sich nun genug ausgestattet und entläßt den Mephistopheles und Kastellan, führt Krieg mit den Mönchen, rächt den Tod seines Sohnes und gewinnt große Güter. Indessen altert er, und wie es weiter ergangen, wird sich zeigen, wenn wir künftig die Fragmente, oder vielmehr die zerstreut gearbeiteten Stellen dieses zweiten Teils zusammen räumen und dadurch einiges retten, was den Lesern interessant sein wird.

This sketch does not make it clear whether a temporary or permanent "dismissal" of Mephistopheles was here intended, and the scene, as it was sketched, was never written. The scene with *Sorge* comes closest to its realization: as Faust once associated himself with Mephistopheles and the world of magic by an act of free will, so he has to end this association by a free decision, if he wants to preserve himself; the renunciation of magic amounts to voluntary self-limitation and in a real sense a "return to the earth," and to humanity. In his first decision, Faust, "in seinem dunklen Drange," used his freedom to make a pact with the Devil. In his second decision, Faust freely renounces magic and thus indicates that he may be "sich des rechten Weges wohl bewußt." Expressly Faust disclaims any desire for knowledge of any world but his own; he recognizes that his problem is to "follow his own way" (11 450), always driving forward, never content with his present situation. In his final moments, Faust arrives at the insight:

> Nur der verdient sich Freiheit wie das Leben,
> der täglich sie erobern muß. (11 576)

Although an actual separation from Mephistopheles is not dramatized, these words indicate that in Faust's mind it has taken on the shape of an irrevocable decision.

There is a peculiar correspondence between the lives and activities of Faust and of Wilhelm Meister, his spiritual counterpart in Goethe's work. Both move through a life filled with failure and error; but while Wilhelm Meister is taught to practice consideration of others and responsibility, an undercurrent of irresponsible willfulness runs through Faust's actions. However, the most remarkable correspondence between the two characters is revealed in the fact that their careers appear to be guided by invisible forces: in the novel, WILHELM MEISTER, which seldom leaves the world of everyday reality, this invisible force in the end turns out to be the active, benevolent influence of the "Society of the Tower." In the symbolic play, FAUST, which reaches far beyond the boundaries of reality, this force is revealed in the end as that of Divine Grace and Love which, we hear, has "von oben teilgenommen" in the striving and erring of Faust. In the final scenes it becomes apparent that the force from which Faust became estranged throughout his life has, in reality, sustained his existence all along, even while through his alliance with the Devil his ultimate fate was in the balance.

Mephistopheles

Spirit of negation. When Goethe resumed work on his FAUST in 1797, he made one of the most significant changes in the manner in which he conceived of the figure of Mephistopheles. The devil, who had formerly been a mere spirit, an elemental demon from the subterranean realm, an emissary of the Erdgeist, now became a more humanized devil, a "man of the world," who in experience and wit was far superior to the scholar in the study. This Mephistopheles is distinguished by the agility of his mind, the subtlety of his designs — in brief, by his mobility and resourcefulness. Faust's feelings are dissolved into sentimentalities and his ideals into illusions as soon as Mephistopheles subjects them to his reasoning. Whereas Faust thinks in terms of absolutes, Mephistopheles is the practical opportunist who is constantly changing his position and method of attack. He is a servant — but one who seeks to trap his master; a guide, who deliberately leads in the opposite direction of where his client wants to go.

Mephistopheles' function as an instrument in the work of creation is described in the Prologue (343). Activity is his nature; the living, not the dead, are his targets,

> . . . denn mit den Toten
> hab' ich mich niemals gern befangen. (319)

To Faust, Mephistopheles identifies himself as "der Geist, der stets verneint" (1338), but his negative activity is not mere contrariness of opinion or logical contradiction. In the "Prolog im Himmel," the Lord numbers Mephistopheles among the "Geister, die verneinen," and compares him to a "Schalk" — a jester — whom He is glad to permit to associate with men, because by his irritation of them and the trouble he makes them, this kind of "Devil" contributes in spite of himself to the work of creation. But Mephistopheles proves to be much more than a "jester": he feels a deep-seated hatred against all creation. He rejoices at the death of Faust, the exponent of creative forces; he loves "das Nicht," "das Einerlei," "das Ewig-Leere" (11 597 ff). But he confesses that he is unable to interfere seriously with the creative evolution of life on earth:

> Wie viele hab' ich schon begraben,
> und immer zirkuliert ein neues, frisches Blut!
> So geht es fort, man möchte rasend werden! (1373)

His purpose is destruction; his principle, the leveling-out of the works of creation:

> . . . denn alles, was entsteht,
> ist wert, daß es zugrunde geht;
> drum besser wär's, daß nichts entstünde. (1341)

In principle, then, Mephistopheles may be considered the antagonist of God, and in this function he appears in the framework of the supernatural action of the play.

The companion of Faust. To achieve his purpose, Mephistopheles must seek to annihilate "life," not merely "living beings": he must paralyze that force which makes things grow — the force which makes the plant rise toward the light, and that which makes Faust strive for ever deeper experience. But the Lord has quite a different task in mind for him; He assigns him to Faust in the role of a tempter because

Des Menschen Tätigkeit kann allzuleicht erschlaffen,
er liebt sich bald die unbedingte Ruh. (341)

Thus the tension develops on which the FAUST play is built: when Mephistopheles attaches himself to Faust, he singles out the moment in which Faust, in a mood of deepest consternation, is most susceptible to the lure of absolute rest. Absolute rest would mean the destruction of Faust's whole being, as it would mean the cessation of life if it were imposed upon the physical universe. In Faust, however, the alliance with the Devil awakens a new vitality. Thus the function of Mephistopheles' companionship is twofold: while Mephistopheles is free to pursue his own aims, he cannot help but fulfill his part in a universal design. He must ever challenge Faust to new enterprises when, at the same time, he is seeking to draw Faust deeper into the bondage of his sensual nature (3251–3367). The "Prince of Lies" is telling the truth when he identifies himself as

Ein Teil von jener Kraft,
die stets das Böse will und stets das Gute schafft. (1336)

Friendless, like Faust — but eminently more practical — Mephistopheles is a symbol of egotism, ruthless and skeptical, unscrupulous and vindictive. As Faust's companion, Mephistopheles is a seducer, deceiver, destroyer throughout the play. He gives the impetus and lends encouragement to Faust's infractions of moral and social order in the "kleine" and the "große Welt." From the chant of the spirits (1447 ff) to the colonization project (11 123 ff), Mephistopheles is able to direct Faust's actions with the help of his blandishments. He perverts Faust's will into libido and license (3282 ff, 4118 ff), and tries his best to silence the voice of his conscience (4189, 11 273). Feeding Faust's egotism, he attempts to keep him from transcending himself by learning consideration for others.

However, as the play progresses, Mephistopheles appears to lose influence over his intended victim. After the Gretchen episode, Faust is helplessly whisked away by his companion; after the debacle at the Emperor's Court, Mephistopheles even hoists the unconscious Faust onto his shoulder to carry him away. The transfer to the setting of ancient Greece is the result of Mephistopheles' machinations, and the Helena episode is his "phantasmagoria." But in the Classical Walpurgis Night we see Faust for the first time pursue his own aim without interference on the part of Mephistopheles: in the origin and development of beauty the spirit of negation has little influence. In his cloud-borne return from Greece, Faust is inspired with the recollection of beauty and the reflection of nobility, and in this mood he far outdistances Mephistopheles, who cannot keep pace, even in seven-league boots. At the beginning of Act IV it is Faust who seizes the initiative and himself selects the next adventure, which is left to Mephistopheles to implement. In Act V Faust's mastery over Mephistopheles becomes even more apparent. Finally, Faust's encounter with *Sorge* indicates that he is ready to dispense with magic, and to accept — actively — the real challenge of his "humanity": the daily struggle for freedom.

Faust's evil self. Mephistopheles may also be regarded as the representative of Faust's own evil self, at odds with his better self. He may be said to embody the unconscious desires and apprehensions governing Faust's emotional nature. When Faust doubts Mephistopheles' ability to comprehend "the higher nature of man" (1676), we know that it is Faust himself who is in darkness. When Gretchen feels dread in the presence of Mephistopheles, it is fundamentally an unholy spirit and sentiment in Faust himself that she senses and fears (3471–3500). When Faust's and Helena's love idyll is disrupted by Mephistopheles, Faust's own inner restlessness has a share in the destruction of the perfect moment. Philosophically, Mephistopheles corresponds to the element of "negativity" — "Für-sich-Sein" — in Hegel's system of dialectics. But Mephistopheles is not merely the poetic representative of an abstract idea, any more than Faust is. He is in a real sense Faust's antagonist: when Faust is all love, Mephistopheles is all lust; when Faust is generous Wealth, dispensing treasures, Mephistopheles is Avarice; when Faust seeks Helena, Mephistopheles seeks the acme of ugliness, the Phorkyads.

Spirit of contradiction. The most persistent trait of Mephistopheles' nature is his predisposition toward irony. As the Devil he is a spirit of contradiction, "ein Geist des Widerspruchs" (4030) whose very nature represents the opposite of that of Faust. Where Faust is idealistic, Mephistopheles is cynical and materialistic; and where Faust is given to enthusiasm, Mephistopheles takes a fiendish delight in puncturing it.

Mephistopheles' versatile spirit of contradiction is reflected in the many garbs in which he appears. He is the same cynical, smart fiend, whether he is in the gown of a student, or in the apparel of a cavalier, the robes of a professor, in the terrifying shape of Phorkyas, or in the colorful costume of a court-jester, the uniform of a military aide, the attire of a fashionable traveller, or — finally — the trappings of the conventional Satan. He lies, though often his lies are "true" on the basis of his specific assumptions. Endowed with keenest intellect, Mephistopheles is ever ready to employ it for perverse purposes: lasciviously, he sings a moralizing song (3680 ff); ironically he even exhorts Faust to cling to the pathetic souvenirs of an ennobling experience (9945 ff).

There is a necessary, if ironical, conflict in Mephistopheles' nature in that he, who hates activity and motion and who seeks to reduce all life of creation to absolute rest, must restlessly exert himself to attain that end. That is why Mephistopheles, like Faust, displays restlessness of mind and behavior. But he is erratic in his motions, and his restlessness almost becomes an end in itself. Faust's restlessness is serious and often melancholy; at no time does a flash of humor lighten his life. Mephistopheles' restlessness is mercurial and often leavened with mockery; he is always alert to espy his advantage, make a thrust, parry, and change his position. But knowing no sentiment, he does not become personally involved. His sense of humor allows him to adjust himself quickly to any situation. He makes his way through the confusion of the Witch's Kitchen and the two Walpurgis Nights with puns, insinuating remarks, glib rejoinders; where they fail, clever self-irony keeps him aloof. Sophisticated, he knows how to manage people according to their stations and to put himself into their good graces — whether he is dealing with a lecherous widow, a sensual, wavering Emperor, or a blasé court society. Indeed, it is in this society of political intrigue that Mephistopheles appears most perfectly at home; clever, witty, unscrupulous, he reflects their basically selfish and unproductive interests.

Mephistopheles possesses a part of what Faust lacks: that sense of proportion which often expresses itself in humor, in the ability to view one's own shortcomings — and sometimes expresses itself in freedom, the ability to accept limitations. From his age-old experience he has learned how to accept defeat; and his failures have taught him patience and detachment.

These features make Mephistopheles an appropriate vehicle for Goethe's poetic irony. Mephistopheles, not Faust, becomes the poet's mouthpiece when, at the close of many scenes, the poetic illusion of the play is briefly broken and the poet addresses his reader (or his audience) in a bit of moral wisdom or pertinent commentary (cf. 3373, 6815 ff, 10 038 SD). In the figure of Mephistopheles, Goethe created a representative of realism, common sense, and objective detachment — human attitudes which characterize a "Spirit of Contradiction," but scarcely befit the "Spirit of Negation." On the other hand, Mephistopheles, not Faust, is repeatedly singled out as a target for mockery, and provides incongruities of situation which only poetic imagination could conceive. As the play ends, the Devil, who has been free to lead Faust down "the Devil's path," has in spite of himself contributed toward the confirmation of Faust's better self. It is an ironical realization of his own nature when in his struggle with the messengers of Divine Love the "Spirit of Negation" is not only deprived of his prize but irresistibly drawn into a perverted form of love.

The Mephistophelian element lends an atmosphere of humor and objectivity, even of lightness, to the FAUST play, particularly where the incongruity between Mephistopheles' expenditure of energy and the results achieved becomes visible (2805, 11 837). A humanly understandable Devil, a "Spirit of Contradiction" — who displays inner conflicts and weaknesses and suffers defeats — provides the appropriate balance for a "daemonic" Faust, who aspires to universal experiences. Such a Mephistopheles, applying himself methodically and efficiently to his business, is the necessary complement to a clamorous superman. But the Mephistopheles who reveals himself as the "Spirit of Negation" and of Chaos is beyond the level of the humorous — the irreconcilable destroyer of all existence.

Gretchen

Love. Goethe overcame the greatest obstacle to the completion of his FAUST when he clearly visualized the function which Gretchen was to play in the ultimate redemption of Faust. It was the inclusion of the Gretchen episode (see Chapter III) which directed the development of the drama away from the course indicated by the legend. Part I contains only one mysterious hint in regard to Faust's fate: the words of Gretchen, "Wir werden uns wiedersehn" (4585) — words which are peculiarly clear and prophetic in her half-demented anticipation of death. At the end of Part II, when Faust's soul has been rescued from the hosts of Hell and is carried into the regions of Heaven, two chants of "Una poenitentium, sonst Gretchen genannt" reveal her hidden share in Faust's redemption. One of the two chants is a hymn of jubilation, echoing Gretchen's song of heartbroken misery in the "Zwinger" scene of Part I; the other is reminiscent of the austere hymn of the archangels in the "Prolog im Himmel." Gretchen, now accepted by the *Mater Gloriosa,* has a definite function in Faust's preparation for a life in "higher spheres":

Komm! Hebe dich zu höhern Sphären!
Wenn er dich ahnet, folgt er nach. (12 095)

And, accompanied by the chant of the *Doctor Marianus,* Faust's immortal soul is carried out of sight while the *Chorus mysticus* is heard — in whose praise of "das Ewig-Weibliche" we must believe Gretchen to be included.

In another passage of Part II the recollection of Gretchen impresses itself upon Faust's mind, though her name is not mentioned. The cloud which has carried Faust from Greece deposits him, moves on, and in changing forms reflects the figure of majestic Helena. Then, out of a wisp of mist there rises another, gentle shape:

Täuscht mich ein entzückend Bild,
als jugenderstes, längstentbehrtes höchstes Gut?
Des tiefsten Herzens frühste Schätze quellen auf:
Aurorens Liebe, leichten Schwung bezeichnet's mir,
den schnellempfundnen, ersten, kaum verstandnen Blick,
der, festgehalten, überglänzte jeden Schatz.
Wie Seelenschönheit steigert sich die holde Form,
löst sich nicht auf, erhebt sich in den Äther hin
und zieht das Beste meines Innern mit sich fort. (10 066)

The preference for Gretchen over Helena in Faust's memories should be noted. The brief scene in which this vision occurs, at the opening of

Act IV, resembles in function and atmosphere two other mountain scenes ("Wald und Höhle," "Anmutige Gegend") in which Faust scrutinizes his own situation. Now Mephistopheles is not slow in catching up with Faust, inciting him to new adventures, and thereby preventing him from seeking, in the recollection of Gretchen, the foundations of his true and permanent self. Implicitly, the simple maiden, who at first seemed to represent merely one of the many stages of experience through which Faust has to pass, has become an instrument in the divine plan for Faust's redemption.

By character and experience Gretchen is qualified for her role as an instrument of Faust's redemption. Unpretentious and without self-consciousness, she has devoted her existence to the service of others. Their lives are her life, their welfare is hers. After her father's death she assumed many responsibilities for the family; her little house breathes an air of contentment. She is a model of the bourgeois virtue, moderation; she is neither irresponsible and presumptuous, like her neighbor, Frau Marthe, nor conventional and security-minded, like some of the citizens in "Vor dem Tor." She is devout, and her faith is a most personal concern, not mere participation in public religious practices; hence, she is concerned about the fate of the man she loves and the questionable character of his companion. She fulfills "the demands of the day"; she is most herself in the fulfillment of her duties. In the care for her infant sister she displays the inborn traits of motherhood; at the same time she is attached to the memory of her ancestors. Devotion and loyalty are the keynotes of her existence. Her innermost nature is expressed in the sombre ballad of the King of Thule, of the strength of faithfulness unto death.

Self-sacrifice. Devotion to activity links Gretchen to Faust, though she is his opposite in everything that she represents and undertakes. He is detached from spiritual security, from his origin, from the past, from the people surrounding him, and he seeks to escape beyond himself. She is secure within herself, and her existence is a loyal continuation of the traditions of her ancestors. From the beginning, the Love and the Grace of God are upon Gretchen; and she has earned what Faust feels he is lacking when he exclaims: "Die Hütte wird durch dich ein Himmelreich" (2708).

Gretchen's love is self-surrender and self-sacrifice, wholly devoid of that self-centered passion which Faust eloquently expresses (3188 ff). Her tragedy proceeds from clarity to confusion — the opposite of Faust's fate. Confusion involves her in guilt, for which she atones in accordance with the laws of society; but she makes her real atonement when she surrenders herself to the judgment of God. In complete confusion — out of her mind — she goes to her death. At one point, at which he comes close to a separation from Mephistopheles, Faust seems to be aware of the magnitude of Gretchen's sacrifice:

Jammer! Jammer! Von keiner Menschenseele zu fassen, daß mehr als ein Geschöpf in die Tiefe dieses Elendes versank, daß nicht das erste genug tat für die Schuld aller übrigen in seiner windenden Todesnot vor den Augen des ewig Verzeihenden! (TT 22–26)

And for once Faust appears ready to risk his life for someone else. But when he fails to save her, he does not seem to be aware of the fact that Gretchen's last thoughts, in the hour of her death, are devoted, not to herself, but to him and his salvation. Gretchen's sacrifice of herself makes her a participant in *Caritas*, unselfish Love, intervening at the end of the play to save Faust. Gretchen is among those whose names are remembered: "Nicht nur Verdienst, auch Treue wahrt uns die Person" (9984).

When Goethe added to the concluding lines of Part I the words of the Voice from above, "(Sie) ist gerettet," he must have seen his way clear to a final solution of the play, with Gretchen as an instrument of Love, "das Ewig-Weibliche" which draws Faust upwards and on.

Helena

Beauty. The Gretchen episode of Part I and the Helena episode of Part II represent fascinating and mysterious stages in Faust's career. When Goethe was writing the first draft of the Helena act (1800), he was interested in the philosophy of aesthetic idealism — represented by Schiller and Schelling — which considered beauty the end of all creative activity, the union of nature and art. During this period of "classicism" Goethe shared Schiller's conviction that the ideal of the beautiful was identical with the ideal of moral perfection, and that man could be led to the state of moral perfection ("freedom") only through a state of "creative," artistic activity ("beauty"). For this ideal of beauty, the figure of Helena became an appropriate symbol.

Whereas the Faust legend had presented Helena as the siren who provided the final sensuous temptation leading to the fall and damnation of Faust, Goethe's conception was one in which the classical heritage had replaced medieval narrowness and darkness, and a pagan glorification of life had replaced the Christian cult of the spirit. This new Helena was to play an important part in the further development of Faust, if not in his deliverance. The Second Part which Goethe planned in 1797 was to show Faust in a state of "Tatengenuß nach außen," a state in which he was to experience "Genuß mit Bewußtsein. Schönheit" (Paralip. 1). These cryptic remarks indicate Helena's function: she was to lead Faust out of the "Leidenschaft" of the First Part, and prepare him for "Schöpfungsgenuß von innen." Thus, the two leading female characters of the play were placed in sharp contrast: the simple innocence of Gretchen and the brilliance of Helena's mature womanhood; the confused passion which possessed Faust in his love for the medieval middle-class maiden and his determined and single-minded search for the Greek demi-goddess.

Gretchen had entered into Faust's life suddenly, without warning, and his love for her had sprung up and overwhelmed him on the spur of the moment. On the other hand, the appearance of Helena is dramatically prepared in several stages, and Faust's love for her is intensified in each stage.

The magic mirror. The first time Helena is suggested is in the Witch's Kitchen, when Faust is transformed into an ardent lover at the sight of the image in the magic mirror and the witch's brew is beginning to make him see

> . . . mit diesem Trank im Leibe,
> bald Helenen in jedem Weibe. (2604)

Mephistopheles' gloating cynicism may be no more than a passing reference to Helena as the ideal of feminine beauty; we do not know for certain what enticing figure Faust sees in the magic mirror. But we do know that Mephistopheles will ceaselessly try to pervert Faust's love into lascivious passion, and we suspect that Helena, like any other medieval "Teufelsliebchen," is a part of his design.

Helena's shade. The second time Helena is mentioned she belongs to the atmosphere of medieval superstition; as in the "Volksbuch," the Emperor wants to have her apparition conjured up for his entertainment. Helena's appearance, as a shade from the realm of the Mothers, is made possible by the assistance of Mephistopheles, but he feigns reluctance and professes to have no authority in the realm of the Mothers. This phantom of Helena is intended to lure Faust into a state where he might be deceived with enjoyment and brought closer to the loss of his wager. But soon Mephistopheles is farther than ever from the realization of his designs: The pantomime of *Paris and Helena*, a play within a play, ends in disaster for Faust; as he attempts to seize Helena from the arms of Paris, he is knocked unconscious by an explosion.

So far this Helena adventure has had the same results as Faust's first meeting with Gretchen; Mephistopheles has provided the occasion for a new passion, but he cannot control its effects upon Faust. The sight of Helena's beauty evokes in Faust a yearning which in the following scenes — first, unconsciously in his dreams, then, consciously in his search through the Classical Walpurgis Night — governs him and inspires his striving. Beauty may reflect the divine; a beautiful woman may symbolize "das Ewig-Weibliche" which once again, in the form of Helena, prevents Faust from falling a prey to Mephistopheles.

But Beauty may also be the instrument of the Devil, a temptation to moral irresponsibility and confusion. That is why Mephistopheles helps Faust win Helena, as he had helped him win Gretchen — even though he said about Gretchen: "Über die hab' ich keine Gewalt," and feigned inability to conjure up Helena's shade.

The "real" Helena. This Helena is quite different from what the reader may have expected her to be after the earlier occurrences of the Helena theme. Confused and apprehensive, she returns to her palace in Sparta, coming out of a darkness of terror and depressing recollections. She has escaped death when Troy was destroyed, but she still fears the revenge of her glowering husband, Menelas. She knows that she may still be sacrificed for her breach of loyalty. Bewildered by the threatening talk of Phorkyas, who recalls the oldest and most dreadful monsters of Hades to her mind, she begins to lose her hold on herself, and her past collapses upon her. A curse has been attached to her beauty: never in her life has she belonged to herself. She has gone through her life unsettled and restless, and her fate has been to belong to others rather than to choose for herself. Phorkyas is deliberately breaking down what little emotional stability is left in her. In deepest confusion — "Selbst jetzo, welche denn ich sei, ich weiß es nicht" (8875) — she faints; and her swoon is a loss of her identity: "Ich schwinde hin und werde selbst mir ein Idol" (8881).

The spirit of Chaos has gotten hold of her personality. When she, recovered, "decides" to seek refuge in Faust's castle, she is being dominated by Phorkyas. When Phorkyas succeeds in luring Helena away from Homeric Sparta and into the splendor of Faust's medieval castle, she (Phorkyas-Mephistopheles) is indeed bringing about a situation in which the Devil may hope to win his wager. Yet, Faust being what he is, the meeting between Faust and Helena does not lead to "absolute rest" but, on the contrary, "zu neuem, buntem Leben."

Helena is quickly conducted "through the ages" — from prehistoric times and the confusion of myths to the threshold of modern history, rational thinking and "beautiful" speech. The highlights of centuries are traversed in fleeting allusions to the Teutonic migrations of the early Middle Ages and the events of the Chivalric Era.

Helena and Faust. When Faust and Helena meet, Faust has indeed matured. His words of welcome are dignified and composed; he is not beside himself as he was in the Witch's Kitchen or at the Emperor's court — or as Lynkeus is now — at the sight of Helena. He is willing to pardon Lynkeus, as if to indicate that the experience of beauty has humanized him. He is even willing to place his power at Helena's feet, as if love had made him humble and unselfish for the first time in his life. His orders to his army leaders express assurance and self-discipline. The Faust of Act III is no longer confused. He knows how to re-establish Helena's self-confidence and satisfaction in life. Indeed, even Helena "grows" in her union with Faust. When she asks, "Wie sprech' ich auch so schön?" (9377), he "instructs" her in the language of love, the rimed language of poetry where the second word comes "dem ersten liebzukosen" (9371), and where one person knows what the other feels and wants to say. Faust becomes "creative" in giving Helena, as it were, a new personality; in return, he receives from her a new satisfaction in life, a new appreciation of existence.

Helena as an aesthetic experience. In the Helena episode, Faust does not become a poet; but his experience of the beautiful comes to symbolize the creative process of poetic art. It may be remembered that, at the court masque, Plutus (Faust) had described to Knabe Lenker the domain of poetry:

> Nur wo du klar ins holde Klare schaust,
> dir angehörst und dir allein vertraust,
> dorthin, wo Schönes, Gutes nur gefällt, —
> zur Einsamkeit! — Da schaffe deine Welt! (5696)

The Helena episode is a realization of this. According to the philosophy of aesthetic idealism, only the beautiful can convey the image of an existence which is in balance between nature and mind, between sensation and thought. It is in aesthetic experiences that the two domains meet, and that man, as creative artist, may become a reflection of the supreme Creator. As Schiller put it: in a mood of sovereign freedom, the artist takes hold of the matter presented by nature, and bestows on it the form presented by mind. In such a creative moment, the experience of existence has quieted all desires, and time dissolves in the illusion of an everlasting moment.

As a person, Helena is "real" to Faust, as the content of his creative imagination is real to a poet. As a symbol, Helena represents the transitory appearance in life of a transcendent idea, though in the medium of "Schein," in the imagined "reality" of art.

In order to bring this symbol into existence, the poet must "descend" into the realm of archetypes, as Faust descended into the realm of the Mothers. And he must pass through the oldest forms of human imagination, through mythology and dreams, as Faust passed through the Classical Walpurgis Night. In the events leading up to Helena's appearance — Goethe called them "Helenas Antecedenzien" — the dream image of her creation impresses itself on Faust's mind with increasing intensity (6911 ff, 7275 ff, 9518 ff). According to mythology, Helena is the offspring of Leda, the mortal, and Jupiter, the god. When Faust and Helena are united, two forms of existence — the mortal and the divine — meet, and Faust conceives of this union in the image of another Golden Age: nature and culture become one, garden and wilderness merge, men become like unto gods, and gods assume the shape of men in Arcadian happiness (9538–9573).

But this moment of the aesthetic experience affords only a reflection of an existence beyond good and evil; only in imagination, not in reality, can the past and the present be permanently united. Helena departs, leaving her garment and veil in Faust's hands; they dissolve into clouds and envelop and conceal Faust — whereupon Mephistopheles, who has been disguised in the mask and the veil of Phorkyas, now reveals himself. Again Mephistopheles has been foiled; the "klassisch-romantische Phantasmagorie" has ended in a synthesis of form (classical) and content (romantic), rather than in chaos. Indeed, even Mephistopheles has to admit the ennobling effect of this experience on Faust:

> Es trägt dich über alles Gemeine rasch
> am Äther hin, solange du dauern kannst. (9953)

Helena remains a splendid, melancholy recollection in Faust's mind, superseded only by another recollection, that of Gretchen, whose love is accompanying him, unknown, as the guardian of his striving.

Symbolical and Allegorical Characters

Faust, Mephistopheles, Gretchen, and Helena occupy the foreground in the dramatic action of the FAUST play. They are surrounded by colorful supporting figures who dwell either in the real world of human society or in the transcendental world of the spirits. Through these secondary characters, often symbolical or allegorical, the action gains in depth, and the mysterious and indeed bewildering effect of the play as a whole is enhanced. If one includes also the phantoms which sometimes participate in the action, sometimes are merely suggested in the text, then the number of *dramatis personae* grows into the hundreds, particularly in Part II. But in all this crowd of dramatic figures, as in a Breughel painting, a hidden order, a deeper meaning prevails. These secondary characters not only offer contrast and supplementation, a sense of proportion; they also serve a purpose of higher symbolism, bringing into relief significant aspects of the four main characters and suggesting what their words and their actions leave untold.

Faust's academic surroundings are represented by two extremes in the university community — Wagner, the famulus and later scholar who manages to achieve a convenient compromise between his intellectual ambitions and his need for security, and the freshman who in the four years of his undergraduate course succeeds in replacing his initial timidity with the arrogance which limited knowledge sometimes brings.

Faust is set apart from his middle-class surroundings by his tendency to seclusion and his melancholy aloofness. This middle-class world, too, is sketched in two contrasting minor characters: the stern and loyal Valentin, defender of the order and honor of "Bürgertum," and the amoral Frau Marthe, who is just as oblivious of an ethical code as Valentin is aware of it.

Finally there is the world of state and government, represented by a wavering Emperor, a corrupt, arrogant cabinet, and a decadent aristocracy.

Besides these subordinate human characters Faust is associated from time to time with supernatural or symbolic figures, each of which is peculiarly appropriate to Faust's striving at a particular stage of his "journey."

Erdgeist. One of the most impressive scenes of the play is the meeting between Faust and the Spirit of the Earth, which results in Faust's utter desolation. Whatever the philosophical motives which induced Goethe to include this grandiose vision in his play, the dramatic tension it creates, and the spectacular stage effect it presents, make it one of the most significant scenes in FAUST. Without the rejection which Faust has to accept from this spirit of activity and physical energy ("Tatengenius"), he would scarcely be ready for the pact with Mephistopheles. Faust is terrified: he faces, in this "Flammenbildung" (499), a kindred force — but one which rejects him. Only once is there another situation in the play where Faust comes face to face with the source of life and energy — the sun; and again a "Flammenübermaß" (4708) overwhelms him. But by that time he has learned his human limitations: he knows that only the "Abglanz," not the reality of "Life," can be revealed to him (4725 ff).

The references later in the play to the apparition of the Earth Spirit ("Wald und Höhle," "Trüber Tag") have caused some uncertainty as to the true relation of this frightening spirit to Mephistopheles and to the Lord, respectively. The "Erdgeist," as the symbol of continuity and productiveness of all life, was part of the earliest conception of the play, which made Mephistopheles the emissary of a daemonic being. The image of the Earth Spirit reflects the poet's early plans, which put Faust in an atmosphere of Renaissance demonology and Paracelsean philosophy of nature. But when, in 1797, Goethe resumed his work on FAUST and introduced, in the "Prolog," the Christian dualism of a heavenly and an earthly plane of action, the Spirit of the Earth had no real function in the new metaphysical system, but it still possessed a striking symbolical force and the author did not remove it, despite the inconsistency involved.

The Mothers. At the Emperor's court, Mephistopheles is quite loath to reveal to Faust the means by which the phantom of Helena could be conjured up. Faust is given a magic key and told to follow it down to the realm of the "Mothers"; there he is to touch a tripod which will then follow him and serve him in the incantation by which the phantom of Helena will be forced to appear. Faust is struck with terror and awe.

The Mothers, he is told, are enthroned in solitude, with no space and no time surrounding them, with no path leading to them. But Faust is ready to risk his existence and undertakes the most daring expedition of his life.

On the basis of Goethe's known reading in Plutarch it has been concluded that the author allowed himself a bit of poetic mystification and had Faust pay a visit to the realm of Platonic ideas, the prototypes of all existing things. With considerable magic hocus-pocus, Faust performs the conjuring scene of the *Raub der Helena.* But in view of the intensely serious atmosphere of this scene it seems wrong to assume that Faust is merely traveling to some distant vacuum in order to discover spectres which no one can see. Goethe may indeed have permitted himself some "solemn fooling"; but the scene may also be interpreted as a symbolic presentation of the act of creating poetry. Faust is not departing for any locality in space. Rather, he is experiencing inner processes of creative imagination. It is into the solitude of his own thought that the poet must descend if he is to comprehend the cryptic formula of metamorphosis:

Gestaltung, Umgestaltung,
des ewigen Sinnes ewige Unterhaltung. (6288)

The Mothers, a grandiose poetic image of Goethe's invention, thus become a symbol of poetic creation. Formative forces — at work in the imagination as in nature — will prevent a poet from clinging to "flache Unbedeutenheit" and will elevate him to a spirit of wonderment, the stimulus to inquiry:

Doch im Erstarren such' ich nicht mein Heil,
das Schaudern ist der Menschheit bestes Teil. (6272)

Homunculus. Originally, the fantastic scenes comprising the Classical Walpurgis Night were planned by Goethe to include Faust's pleading in Hades for Helena's release from the realm of the dead. As the act was written, it turned out to be a threefold adventure and search: Faust seeking Helena, Mephistopheles seeking the archetype of ugliness (Phorkyas), Homunculus seeking corporeal existence.

Of the three, only Mephistopheles seems to reach his goal. When we last see Faust in this act, he is preparing to descend to Persephoneia, queen of the nether world. Homunculus is last seen shattering his vial at the feet of Galatea, a goddess of Love. When Helena appears on the scene (Act III), we do not know whether it is Faust's plea which has brought her back to life. And when Homunculus hurls himself into the ocean, we do not know whether his "herrisches Sehnen" has found its realization. These uncertainties have led some critics to believe that Helena, appearing at the castle in Sparta, owes her renewed existence to the self-sacrifice of Homunculus.

The story of Homunculus' origin in Wagner's vial is a masterpiece of Goethe's poetic irony. We do not know whether this ethereal "little man" crystallizes as a result of Wagner's unaided labors or with Mephistopheles' sympathetic assistance. At any rate, even though Homunculus appears to be a spirit akin to Mephistopheles, gifted with cynicism and clairvoyance, he is also indebted to the chemical laboratory for his existence.

Goethe's purpose in introducing Homunculus as a significant minor character in the second act of Part II is not immediately clear. The concept of a *spiritus familiaris*, who is enclosed in a bottle, or in a crystal, and renders advice to its owner, is known in occult literature. In this light, Homunculus might even be considered a product of "black magic." But, though he is a little "daemon," there is nothing devilish about him. In fact, it appears that Goethe wanted him considered favorably, sympathetically. His name is descriptive and satirical at the same time; his function is both serious and parodistic: at a time when even Mephistopheles is at his wits' end, Homunculus — a "distilled" intellect, the product of the efforts of mechanistic science — prescribes a visit to classical antiquity. As Goethe admitted, there is "a sort of relationship" between Mephistopheles and Homunculus; but the "little man" excels his "cousin" in several ways: he possesses a drive of productive activity, a yearning for the beautiful, which are foreign to the Spirit of Negation. These are features of Faust's character, and it is in relation to Faust that Homunculus' function becomes intelligible.

Homunculus comes into being at a time when Faust lies unconscious as a result of his audacious attempt to seize Helena by force. Homunculus is able to see what is occupying Faust's mind and to comprehend the desires that govern Faust's dreamings; Mephistopheles has never been able to understand Faust in his striving. When finally Homunculus shatters his crystal prison in the sea, the life-giving element, Faust is on his way to Hades, the realm of death, in order to beg for the release of Helena. Homunculus leaves as Faust sets foot on Grecian soil and regains consciousness, and they never meet. In fact, Faust never addresses a word to Homunculus, and is entirely unaware that Homunculus ever existed.

Homunculus and Faust are similar, and mutually complementary; both are driven by "imperious yearning." But Homunculus is driven in a reversed sense: whereas Faust rebels against the limitations of his physical nature, Homunculus aspires to gain a physical nature, a corporeal existence. The one seeks to transcend what the other longs to possess. And Homunculus has a gift of comprehension and knowledge which precedes, and is independent of, experience. Before he is "born," Homunculus possesses an understanding which human beings can acquire only through experience, and which Faust will have acquired only after he has completed his course through human experience. Many times in his conversations with Eckermann, Goethe described this kind of knowledge as an intuitive knowledge, as innate awareness and comprehension by "*Antizipation.*" Faust achieves it in his vision of a future, free community of men:

> Im Vorgefühl von solchem hohen Glück
> genieß' ich jetzt den höchsten Augenblick. (11 586)

Throughout the Classical Walpurgis Night, Faust and Homunculus represent two aspects of the same "Sehnen" in the nature of men, of whom the wise Nereus says in morose disappointment:

> Gebilde, strebsam, Götter zu erreichen,
> und doch verdammt, sich immer selbst zu gleichen! (8097)

There is one situation in the play in which the *form* of Faust's existence resembles — though it does not correspond to — the form of Homunculus' existence. At the end of the play, the angels appear in the heavenly regions "schwebend in der höheren Atmosphäre, Faustens Unsterbliches tragend" (SD 11 934). As "pure intellect," free at last from corporeal limitations, Faust is received and carried on into the reaches of the spirit. In a manuscript version of this last scene Goethe used the term "Entelechie" in the place of "Unsterbliches." This Aristotelean term gives us a hint as to Goethe's idea of the ultimate stage of Faust's nature. As an "entelechy," as an individual "realizing" its purpose or aim, Faust enters into immortality. As an "entelechy," as a realization of form-giving energy, Homunculus enters into the world of physical existence. In an act of transformation, or metamorphosis, in which the "force of spirit" merges with the elements in order to achieve reality, Homunculus hurls himself into the sea. In a higher act of transformation, in which Eternal Love alone is capable of abstracting the spiritual from the elemental ("Erdenrest"), Faust is carried into the reaches of the spirit. This is expressed in the chorus of the angels rejoicing at Faust's transformation:

> Wenn starke Geisteskraft
> die Elemente
> an sich herangerafft,
> kein Engel trennte
> geeinte Zwienatur
> der innigen beiden:
> die ewige Liebe nur
> vermag's zu scheiden. (11 965)

Thus the disappearance of Homunculus, portrayed in the festival of Eros at the end of the Classical Walpurgis Night, is paralleled by Faust's ascension in the play's concluding scene. In neither case is "death" involved, but a transition to "higher spheres of creative activity."

Three festivals of love form the culminating points of three almost equal parts of the FAUST poem. The Northern Walpurgis Night (3835–4222), symbolizing deepest confusion in Faust's mind, is carnal debauchery. The Classical Walpurgis Night (7005–8487), fantastic and weird in its beginnings, ends in a celebration of creative Eros. The conclusion of the FAUST poem is a *Magnificat* to Divine Love. At each of these points a higher and clearer state of existence is foreshadowed. Thus the action of the FAUST play, in its implicit symbolism, proceeds upward following the course of a spiral — a concept which Goethe had cherished because it helped him visualize the physiology of plant growth. He said: "Das neue Aperçu der Spiraltendenz ist meiner Metamorphosenlehre durchaus gemäß" (cf. Conversations with Eckermann, October 6, 1828).

Euphorion. The impulse that led Goethe to adapt the figure of Euphorion to suit the brilliant life of Lord Byron, when he heard of the latter's death, has not impaired Euphorion's allegorical significance within the FAUST play. Euphorion is still to be interpreted as the creative power of poetry:

> Heilige Poesie,
> himmelan steige sie! (9864)

Euphorion, striving from the idyllic toward the heroic form of existence, basically symbolizes the force of metamorphosis, like Faust. The allegorical character of this figure is evident, and it is understandable that it requires music in order to relieve the rational barrenness which goes with all allegory. As one realization of Faust's own inner desires, however, Euphorion demonstrates the necessity of self-transcending which remains to the end Faust's challenge. This Spirit of Poetry, who is beyond limitations of empirical reality, who leaps heavenward like a flame, knows no energy other than will; and in supreme willfulness he seizes anything in the world about him that strikes his fancy. It is ironic that Faust himself cautions Euphorion to use moderation.

In his preliminary plan for the completion of FAUST, Goethe wrote of "Schöpfungsgenuß von innen (gesehn)." In the Euphorion scene we have the execution of this plan. What we see before us is not merely an idyllic and (ultimately) martial scene in Arcadia. It is the symbolization of poetic creativeness "seen from within": first Phorkyas describes "unerforschte Tiefen" (9596) in which this impetuous "Genius ohne Flügel, faunenartig ohne Tierheit" (9603) comes to life. Then the Chorus of Trojan Women observe that this mercurial "favorable daemon" (9665) reminds them of the creative fancifulness of ancient mythology — "liebliche Lüge, glaubhaftiger als Wahrheit" (9643). And finally it is enacted before our eyes by Euphorion himself — first as a charming, then a fascinating, then a frightening spectacle. In one respect the Euphorion scene is comparable to Faust's visit to the Mothers: then he was to penetrate into the depth of creative imagination; now he sees in the antics of his own son the joy and the sorrows of his own desires (9903–9904).

Philemon and Baucis. Philemon and Baucis, the venerable old couple whom Faust's ambition destroys, are models of civic peacefulness and contentment. Loving one another with deep devotion, ready to help the distressed, clinging to their faith even when outward circumstances seem to disprove it, they have lived their lives true to their own purpose. Although they have not figured before in the play, their appearance in the last act is entirely appropriate; they represent the same kind of human activity as Gretchen. Their kind of existence has never been respected by Faust; now it causes him to act like an ill-tempered, impatient old man. They are in Faust's way, and their insistence on their own individual independence makes them the victims of his ambition. When they are destroyed, the violence, injustice, inadequacy of the Faustian will is evident.

No matter how "high" Faust may have risen — and this is underscored in the scene "Tiefe Nacht" — he is still accessible to *Sorge,* whom no one can shut out and who, like other baleful spectres, can turn ordinary days into "garstigen Wirrwarr netzumstrickter Qualen" (11 490). Philemon and Baucis become the occasion for Faust's last significant earthly experience: in the encounter with *Sorge,* Faust is made to feel sympathy for mankind (11 488), and yet he refuses to admit defeat by the daemonic (11 494).

Mephistophelian characters. Mephistopheles, like Faust, is surrounded by a number of minor characters which emphasize striking aspects of his nature and of his dramatic function in the play as a whole.

These characters are to be found in the ghost scenes of the play, such as the Witch's Kitchen and the Walpurgis Nights. Significantly, almost all of these "Mephistophelian" figures are libidinous and infertile females, the opposite of the productive, the motherly, the "Ewig-Weibliche." The "Hexe" of the Witch's Kitchen and the witches' sabbath, Lilith, "Adams erste Frau" (4119), the Sphinxes and the Lamiae, Empusa and, above all, the Phorkyads, are composite in nature and appearance, a grotesque parody of the human body. When they are pursued for their attractiveness, like the Lamiae, they turn into a broom, or slip away like a lizard, or burst like a puffball (7784). In contrast to Helena, the acme of beauty, the Phorkyads represent the perfection of ugliness. Their appearance is a mockery of human form: not complete eyelessness or toothlessness makes them abhorrent, but one eye and one tooth between them! And to complete this parody, Mephistopheles (7999) compares the Phorkyads with Juno, Pallas, and Venus, the three goddesses of whom Paris had to choose the most beautiful, receiving as his reward the permission to abduct Helena.

Whereas the Phorkyads reflect Mephistopheles' profound dislike of any organic form, some other characters symbolize a correspondingly Mephistophelian fondness for senseless motion (Giant Ants, Griffins), of blind, purposeless, unorganized force (Seismos), and of stolid immobility (Sphinxes). In the dispute between the two philosophers, Anaxagoras takes the side of violent, unpredictable, eruptive forces, while Thales speaks for orderly regular processes. On a small scale, a similar contrast is presented in the court masque of Act I, where the Faustian side is revealed in the figures of Wealth and Poetry (Plutus, Knabe Wagenlenker), while Mephistopheles' negative tendencies become apparent in the lewd actions of Avarice and the hateful words of Zoilo-Thersites.

* * *

To the attentive reader, the multitude of these supporting figures (particularly in Part II) will not be distracting. As he reads and re-reads FAUST, they will harmonize with the main characters of the play and the problems of human concern which they express. Then he will realize that he is reading a play about Man and his place in the universe. Perhaps he will enjoy the "story" of the play — a peculiarly fantastic story, involving a man who dared the Devil in order to derive the fullest and deepest experience from existence. But he may also remember more than the tragedy of Gretchen or the grand illusion of the Helena adventure. Perhaps he will recognize behind Faust's struggle with Mephistopheles the battle of Man against the forces that threaten Man's existence: inertia, chaos, the "Nichts." Faust's enemy is the enemy of Man. In Man's world — the physical and moral world — there is change and continuous "Werden." Whatever Man builds and produces is threatened by the possibility of destruction — by time, wear, and decay, whose force equals the force of his endeavor and even exceeds it. His expenditure in constructive energy is outweighed by an even greater amount of blind resistance and waste. But Man is not only contending with the physical universe; he is equally at war with his own tendencies to bog down, to be inactive, to yield to rest — to the idleness of enjoyment or the monotony of waste. Once he surrenders, the chaotic, leveling force will begin to destroy what he once created.

Der Herr — Mater Gloriosa. Although the FAUST play ends in "higher spheres," it does not conclude on the same "level" as that from which it started. In terms of the cosmology of the FAUST poem, the sphere of everlasting Being, which is beyond that of change, has not been reached: the Lord is not present to receive and to judge His "Knecht." Rather, Faust's immortal soul is received by *Mater Gloriosa* — the symbol of "das Ewig-Weibliche" — who by suffering, sacrifice, unselfish love has become an instrument of divine "Caritas." Human will alone does not redeem Faust; his activity remains in "dunklem Drang" until he is received by "Liebe von oben." That which on earth presented itself as "vergänglich" continues its metamorphosis in the Heaven of the spirit until it realizes its purpose in the peace of the Absolute Being. In a short poem Goethe expressed what he left unsaid in the conclusion of FAUST:

Wenn im Unendlichen dasselbe
sich wiederholend ewig fließt,
das tausendfältige Gewölbe
sich kräftig aneinander schließt, —
strömt Lebenslust aus allen Dingen,
dem kleinsten wie dem größten Stern:
und alles Drängen, alles Ringen
ist ewige Ruh in Gott, dem Herrn.
(*Zahme Xenien*, VI)

V. FAUST, a Mirror of Goethe's Times

Society — The Age of Reason — Worship of Nature.

The poetic and philosophical problems of FAUST are not only rooted in Goethe's own personal experiences; they also reflect the spirit of the age in which it was written. To the political historian this age represents one of the most significant epochs in modern history; for many of the factors that have shaped modern living were then in the making. It was the age in which the institutions of medieval feudalism crumbled and gave way, constitutions were written, and a new political ideal — the democratic ideal — made its appearance in public life. It was the time when British armies fought on American soil (1776), when Napoleon's armies swept across Europe (1798–1815), when Russian soldiers, as allies of the Prussians and Austrians, marched victoriously through the streets of Paris (1814), and when liberty, on an individual and national scale, finally became a reality in several parts of the Western world.

1. SOCIETY

The bourgeois. If any particular group or class in Europe was repaid for the suffering it had endured in many years of continuous warfare (Seven Years' War, Wars of Coalition, Napoleonic Wars), it was the class which had made greater sacrifices in material possessions and human lives than ever before — the bourgeois class, the "Bürgertum." By the end of the 18th century the common man, the citizen, had risen to assume leadership in government for the first time, as e.g., in France and in the United States. The struggle for liberty was the citizen's struggle. Wherever the slogan of "freedom" was heard — political, economic, educational, ethical — it proclaimed the realization of new standards in cultural life:

the standards of an enlightened, disciplined, dignified "Bürgertum." In terms of the social background of its author, FAUST is the product of an enlightened German middle class.

But the "Bürgertum" of Goethe's time was slow in attaining these standards. In most regions of Germany citizens lived under despotisms, and had no choice but to recognize their monarchs as embodiments of God's order on earth. Pointedly, Schiller gave his first play, DIE RÄUBER (2d. ed., 1782), a motto "Against tyrants!" and in his third play, KABALE UND LIEBE (1784), he followed the direction indicated by Lessing's EMILIA GALOTTI (1772), and presented the German "Bürger" as a victim of whim and exploitation at the hands of a more privileged aristocracy. But the fact that these dramas found theaters to perform them and enthusiastic audiences indicates that in some parts of Germany freedom and tolerance were winning out over censorship and persecution, and that the example of enlightened government which Frederick II (1712–1786) had set in Prussia was being accepted in other German states. Goethe was, like his father, "fritzisch gesinnt," and throughout his life retained his sympathies for the Prussian monarch.

Wherever limited freedom was established, the German "Bürger" was an individualist whose strength lay in the fruits of his labors, his savings, his learning, his frugality, and his social virtues of patience, moderation and mutual consideration. He was a practical man and believed in progress and self-improvement, though within the limitations of reasonableness and a (God-given) order. In this social setting, "Streben" could be readily conceived and understood. The bourgeois of the late 18th century was devoted to the pursuit of his own and other people's happiness; but he had to realize that "freedom for all" was more than mere social or political emancipation — that it could hardly be a mere possession and be taken for granted — and that, in order to be beneficial for all, freedom must be guarded and earned in every day's activities (11 574–11 576).

Faust, as an individualist, is essentially unsocial and "unbürgerlich" in thoughts and actions. He is not an example of the free citizen. On the contrary, he is a "Freigeist," who has arrogated freedom to himself and who, using it, would endanger the welfare of human society. Still, it is significant that Faust's parting words express the ideal of the perfect democratic society: a community of free individuals that is guided by "Gemeindrang," tested by common danger, and inspired by a social consciousness of "active freedom" (11 564 ff).

Goethe, a "Bürger" at heart, satirized the shortcomings of the bourgeoisie surrounding him. For the German "Bürgertum" of the late 18th century did not yet seem mature for life in a truly free community. It was too respectful of traditional authority to take up arms for democracy, and too fond of orderliness to risk a revolution. Its citizens were provincial in spirit, content with "Fried' und Friedenszeiten" (867), and happy when war was remote, "hinten, weit, in der Türkei" (862). There were, to be sure, some outward signs of progress in Germany: in rural regions serfdom began to be abolished toward the end of the century; but a benevolent paternalism took its place. Sons of commoners succeeded in becoming ministers of state; but they could not afford to refuse tokens of princely favor — even Johann Wolfgang von Goethe was no exception. In 1806, amidst the Napoleonic Wars, the venerable "Holy Roman Empire of the German Nation" was dissolved; but the "Holy Alliance" of continental princes (1815) indicated that the feudal conservatism of old was powerfully restored.

Under these circumstances the ideals of a "Bürgertum," indeed of a "Weltbürgertum," were clear to relatively few individuals in Europe. They were men who felt "oppressed by the fetters of daily social reality" and sought to escape them. Lessing wrote his NATHAN DER WEISE (1779), his manifesto of a universal brotherhood of man, while he was constrained by theological censorship. And Goethe's IPHIGENIE (1787), Schiller's DON CARLOS (1787), and Herder's BRIEFE ZUR BEFÖRDERUNG DER HUMANITÄT (1793–1797) were expressions of an educated and idealistic bourgeoisie which had taken over the cultural leadership in Germany but was still impotent against the political leadership.

Meanwhile the bourgeoisie at large lived its life of practical efficiency and righteousness. For the first time in history, German cities began to spread beyond their medieval walls, but in their centers they still displayed

> Bürger-Nahrungs-Graus,
> krummenge Gäßchen, spitze Giebeln,
> beschränkten Markt, Kohl, Rüben, Zwiebeln,
> Fleischbänke, wo die Schmeißen hausen,
> die fetten Braten anzuschmausen. (10 141)

By and large the Germans remained — as the title of Kotzebue's comedy suggests — "Kleinstädter," and obeyed like the citizens of Berlin when, after the defeat at Jena in 1806, the commanding general issued the order of the day: "Der König hat eine Bataille verloren. Ruhe ist die erste Bürgerpflicht." Their kings had lost battles before, perhaps because they had, at the expense of their citizens, built charming castles with pleasure grounds and parks, grottoes and cascades — "schlecht und modern! Sardanapal!" (10 176) — and had whiled away their time with court masques, while anarchy and mismanagement threatened to disrupt their states (Act I, Part II). If under such circumstances citizens dreamt of "freedom," they were likely to be like the boisterous students in "Auerbachs Keller" who sing a toast to freedom because they do not possess it. Realistic and conscientious, the bourgeoisie was made to practice moderation and self-abnegation.

And still, this same dignified bourgeoisie, seeking escape from the boredom of daily routine and the strain of duties, produced an intellectual movement which is as characteristic of the 18th century as the bourgeois realism itself — the Romantic Movement.

Romanticism. Goethe's life (1749–1832) covered a span of time in which the rationalist interest in speculative philosophy faded away and the scientific interest in reality became manifest. Literary historians usually designate this period of cultural transition, bounded roughly by the emergence of Rousseauistic thought (1749) and the socialist revolution in France (1830), as the Romantic period. The European literatures of the time reveal "romantic" tendencies: the desire to escape from the world of every-day reality; the preference for far-away times and places — the exotic, the oriental, the ancient, the medieval — pastoral scenes where a mode of existence was believed to prevail which was essentially "natural," simple, naive, "good" and not distraught by modern haste, doubt, greed, and sophistication. It appeared to be "romantic" to flee into the darkness of the unconscious, the dream, the night; for the true nature of man, unadulterated and uninhibited, was thought to emerge in its genuine essence in such surroundings. The refusal to accept the dictum of reason was likewise considered "romantic"; for reason was held to be cold and impartial, allowing little freedom to the imagination and lacking sympathy with the delicate and irreplaceable originality of artistic minds.

Goethe's FAUST has but little in common with this kind of romanticism, although Goethe himself was not unfriendly toward the members of romantic literary circles in Jena and Heidelberg.

But there is another kind of romanticism which seeks to preserve a place for keen, sensitive, creative minds in a world of political ruthlessness and impersonal technology. Although it is contemplative by nature and origin, this romanticism desires no escape. It shows high regard for, and even envy of, Life itself and contempt for the sterility of mere erudition. This romanticism links the present with the past by keeping alive the memory of the "hohe Ahnen" (1117), the creative benefactors of mankind, whose works reveal insight into the relations of man and nature — Homer, Dante, Leonardo da Vinci, Albrecht Dürer, Giordano Bruno, Shakespeare. Many of these men first received universal recognition during the age of romanticism, which was marked by intellectual alertness and by a feeling of historical indebtedness. With this form of romantic thinking Goethe's FAUST is indeed intimately associated.

An element of superior irony distinguishes Goethe's FAUST from the movement of systematic Enlightenment with which it would otherwise have much in common. For no one could be a more adequate protagonist of the age of reason than Faust himself, the searcher for truth, whose entire being is initially inspired by the desire to know the nature of the universe.

But ultimately it is not Knowledge but Love which promises to gain for Faust the end he seeks — Love in its widest scope, which includes love of life as well as love of truth.

2. THE AGE OF REASON

Enlightenment. Goethe injected into his play the salient characteristics of the age of rationalism. Rationalism had shaped the thinking of his father, who directed the youthful Goethe's early education and later selected the appropriate tutors. Rationalism governed the minds of the men with whom Goethe came in contact at the age of seventeen, when he left for Leipzig, the center of the Enlightenment in Germany. The critic Gottsched and the moralist Gellert were among the guides who led the young Goethe into the areas in which he was most receptive and talented: poetry and philosophy. In particular, rationalism held sway in the field of jurisprudence in which, according to his father's demands, he was to attain his degree. Small wonder, then, that at the universities of Leipzig and Strassburg he absorbed the principles of the rationalism which he was soon to question.

By temperament Goethe was disposed to give free expression to forces of human nature which in the age of reason had been neglected or even repressed. The Enlightenment had scorned intuition and feeling, passion and will; Goethe considered them essential to the full experience of human existence. But when he expounded them in his FAUST, even this poem was not entirely free from an undercurrent of that rationalism to which he had been exposed in the early years of his training.

Eighteenth-century Enlightenment was fundamentally connected with the movement of the Reformation. The Reformation had broken up the harmony of the medieval world view, based upon a theory of supernatural revelation, but it had retained its belief in that supernatural revelation itself. The Enlightenment undertook what the Reformation had hesitated to do in regard to the emancipation of the individual. In a spirit of doubt and criticism it acknowledged no authority other than human reason. In science and philosophy it insisted on clarity, demonstrability, and proof; in practical ethics it demanded realistic reasoning as a prerequisite to moral action. Rationalism proceeded from the assumption that the universe reveals a logical, or "natural," system of cause and effect, and that human reason — operating with this concept of causality — is the appropriate instrument with which the mechanism of the universe could be comprehended. Hence rationalism found it necessary to rely on logical demonstration and conclusion, rather than on observation and experience, since only reason was considered able to muster compelling evidence. Reason, then, demanded emancipation of a thinking individual from moral and religious traditions and prejudices. And since reason was thought to be the same in all men, its consistent application meant freedom and intellectual enlightenment and progress for all "mankind." It was no longer a universal *faith*, but universal *reason*, the same spirit of skepticism and inquiry, which was held to unite men and to possess sole jurisdiction in human affairs.

Although the Enlightenment, in its fundamentally optimistic attitude, thus proved applicable to scientific research or to practical, everyday conduct, it was inadequate to cope with ultimate questions of philosophy — questions concerning the purpose of knowledge, of values, and the moral conduct of life. Few people ever attained that degree of true "Enlightenment" of which Socrates had been a guiding example — that attitude of stoic self-discipline and detached contemplation which would enable a thinker to detect the fallacies of common reasoning and to expose the selfish motives in such reasoning. This kind of enlightenment demanded an almost superhuman faculty for detachment, wisdom, and tolerance. Whoever possessed these, enjoyed "freedom," whether he occupied a throne, like Frederick the Great, or lived in an attic room, like Spinoza, or confined himself to his library, like Lessing.

The Enlightenment in Germany was a predominantly bourgeois movement. And the "Bürger" was content when, with the help of reason, he could enjoy the apparent order and purposefulness of his existence. While this kind of enlightenment was often the source of considerable imagined freedom (as the case of Famulus Wagner exemplifies), it might also lead to contentment with the *status quo*, with the "Faulbett" (1692) which Faust denounces as his gravest danger. If the striving for "Glückseligkeit" — happiness — was taught as an ultimate goal (as it was by Leibnitz and Shaftesbury and other leading philosophers of the time), any form of enjoyment or comfort could easily be accepted in the place of mere "striving," where, after all, success was not necessarily certain.

The inadequacy of the Enlightenment was even more obvious where the question of ultimate causes was raised, the question of the origin and the purpose of all life — a question which occupies Faust, as it did Spinoza, Leibnitz, Wolff, philosophers who built philosophical *systems*. In this province the metaphysician competed with the theologian, with the result that both often got themselves enmeshed in a network of abstractions that resembled medieval scholasticism. But although rationalistic speculation had broken down the belief in positive religion, it was unable to offer a universally and permanently satisfactory substitute.

Goethe was not interested in the disputes between the theologians and the metaphysicians, although he was not entirely unaffected by these disputes. Brought up in the conservative traditions of his family, he developed a belief which satisfied his spiritual needs — an enlightened eclecticism which owed as much to the Bible as to the philosophers. Thus he was able to present Faust as a "free thinker" who can no longer believe in the content of the Easter message (765), who denies the possibility of transcendental knowledge (1660 ff), and to his very end limits his interest to this earth (11 442 ff). But in regard to the ultimate problems of cosmology and the origin of evil, FAUST definitely shows a close relationship to the leading philosophical theories of rationalism — Spinoza's pantheism and Leibnitz' Theory of Monads.

Although FAUST expresses certain tenets of Enlightenment, it was not written in the spirit of the Enlightenment. Rationalism was in many ways a form of narrow utilitarianism. With its emphasis on "normal" and "reasonable" behavior it had no room for "Faustian" characters; and with its insistence on methodical procedure it was unable to satisfy the spiritual and emotional needs of the individual. Many of those who were in need of spiritual comfort found it in the movement of Pietism. And those who felt that life meant more than methods of classification, found it in an emotional worship of "Nature" which is reflected in the literary movement of Storm and Stress. Both of these movements converged in the Romantic Movement which sought to give free expression to those sides of human nature which had found little or no consideration during the age of the Enlightenment.

Pietism. Pietism resulted from a feeling of disillusionment. The century of religious wars that followed the Reformation had scarcely furthered the practice of Christian ethics. By the end of the 17th century many Protestants believed that only a determined application of Christian principles in the life of each individual might offer some hope for society. Thus a movement arose within the Lutheran and Calvinistic churches — a movement which was not primarily interested in questions of dogma and theoretical discussions, but in personal edification through faith and humane works. The ideal of the "Imitation of Christ" which once had inspired the work of the medieval friar Thomas a Kempis (c. 1380–1471) gained wide favor in these "pious" circles. Some even envisaged the possibility of a peaceful understanding with the Roman Catholic Church.

Originally, the movement was connected with such men as Labadie (1610–1674), Spener (1635–1705), and Francke (1663–1727), who were responsible for the establishment of private circles of worshippers or of charitable institutions — for example, the orphanage and hospital at Halle. Then it spread throughout Germany, and by the time young Goethe became aware of it, many "conventicles" had sprung up. Under the initiative of Count Zinzendorf (1700–1760), who, disregarding social privileges, opened his manor to a communal brotherhood ("Moravian Brethren") in the spirit of the original church of the first Christians, the movement gained momentum and became a social force through its practicing spiritual and, sometimes, economic equality.

Goethe came into personal contact with Pietism in Frankfurt upon his return from Leipzig in 1768. He became a member of a devotional circle which had gathered around a gentle elderly lady, Susanna von Klettenberg. The association with the members of this conventicle seems to have induced in Goethe intense self-examination and self-analysis, activities quite in agreement with the devotional fervor of the pietists. In many respects Pietism was akin to medieval mysticism which had preached the individual's union with God through self-abasement, introspection, contemplation, and had developed psychological and devotional techniques for such communion.

Just as mysticism had formed a counterpart to medieval scholasticism and had borrowed its method of dialectics, so the pietists borrowed the deductive method of rationalism and applied it to their practice of introspection. Thus the pietists succeeded in developing methods of observing themselves in the moments of their highest exaltation and their deepest contrition. The Enlightenment was favorable for the development of natural sciences, Pietism for the development of psychology.

Pietism also exerted a decisive influence upon 18th-century German literature. Many of Goethe's forerunners had come under its sway, and their writings were among the books read by the young Goethe: Klopstock, Wieland, Hamann, and Herder. Likewise many of his friends and contemporaries — Lavater, Moritz, the Stolberg brothers, Novalis, Schleiermacher — derived many of their basic attitudes from this spiritual atmosphere. Part of the singular appeal of Pietism consisted in the attention it gave to individual observation and characterization, part in the peculiar poetic charm of its hymns; at all events, one of the strongest attractions lay in the form of communication itself: its poetic language.

In contrast to the language of rationalism which served to convey abstract notions and logical relationships, the language of Pietism possessed personal depth and sentiment. When it was expressing grief, or joy, or the glory of divine love, or the ever-present activity of divine grace, every image of nature was pressed into service to lend substance to the expression.

Many of Goethe's works betray the influence of Pietistic thinking and feeling, as, for example, GANYMED and MAHOMETS GESANG, WERTHER, and, above all, the monument to Susanna von Klettenberg, the "Confessions of a Beautiful Soul," which Goethe inserted as Book VI in his novel WILHELM MEISTERS LEHRJAHRE.

The traces in FAUST are less obvious. They are scarcely to be identified with the theme of any particular scene or the emotions of any particular character. Here and there they can be recognized in a detail of poetic style, as in the imagery of the wilderness (3279), in the frantic cries of self-accusation (3348 ff), or in the ever-recurring image of the source, the brook, the river, symbolizing life. They are most impressive in the motif of all-redeeming Heavenly Love, from the "Prolog" to the praise of "das Ewig-Weibliche" in the concluding Mystical Chorus.

Pietism emphasized the sinfulness of human nature. It must have been this fundamental assumption, which Goethe could not share, that made him turn his back on the movement altogether. For, in spite of its declared ideal of spiritual activity, many members became exemplars of quietism, of intellectual passivity — a state of mind in which they waited for divine illumination to descend on them. For Pietism was exposed to the same limitations and dangers as its counterpart, the Enlightenment: what was originally the humility of striving and questioning could easily deteriorate into narrow-minded pride of believing that the goal had been achieved.

In its two extremes of spiritual fervor and lachrymose self-humiliation, Pietism lacked naturalness no less than the Enlightenment. The self-righteousness of both movements banned any free expression of intuitions or emotions which were contrary to their own rational and ethical code. The literary history of the century abounds with tragic or pathetic figures who dared to reveal their genuine convictions at the risk of being labeled zealots, "Schwärmer." Neither the Enlightenment nor Pietism satisfied the ultimate need for a natural expression of what Famulus Wagner calls "des Menschen Herz und Geist"; and Faust is aware of this unfulfilled need when he exclaims:

> Die wenigen, die was davon erkannt,
> die, töricht g'nug, ihr volles Herz nicht wahrten,
> dem Pöbel ihr Gefühl, ihr Schauen offenbarten,
> hat man von je gekreuzigt und verbrannt. (593)

3. WORSHIP OF NATURE

It is significant that Goethe, when he took up the study of law at Strassburg, was more susceptible to nature on a grand scale than to the formalism which prevailed in the university of this medieval German (politically French) city. For the first time, he felt, he was experiencing "Life" itself and no longer an artificial set of social conventions. But almost at once he found himself in that conflict between experience and desire which is so characteristic of the romantic mind, and for which FAUST was to become a poetic symbol. It was at Strassburg that the foundations of a world view were laid which may be called "Faustian." Coming from an environment demanding observance of a thousand and one little social amenities, Goethe found himself in the midst of a life that seemed genuinely simple and "whole" to him. But the more he came to know it, the more he realized that this apparent simplicity was itself the product of a venerable historical tradition. And since Goethe was accustomed not merely to accept what his environment had to offer, but to try to comprehend it as a part of a greater nexus of relationships, even simple experiences could assume universal significance for him.

In the rise of individualism no factor has been of greater importance than the exploration of nature. In FAUST this process of exploration is reflected in various forms: (a) direct experience, (b) scientific pursuits, (c) artistic perception, (d) philosophical reflection. Toward each of these, Goethe and his century displayed an attitude of profound interest.

Experience. After concluding his pact with Mephistopheles, Faust is impatient to put the pact into operation. He says:

Stürzen wir uns in das Rauschen der Zeit,
ins Rollen der Begebenheit!
Da mag denn Schmerz und Genuß,
Gelingen und Verdruß
miteinander wechseln, wie es kann;
nur rastlos betätigt sich der Mann. (1759)

Faust, it seems, has abandoned that desire for abstract knowledge which had dominated him, and has resolved to follow Mephistopheles "grad mit in die Welt hinein" (1829). After this, Faust is led through a series of experiences which might fascinate the emotional man, but scarcely the rational scholar. On the surface, these experiences may not seem to follow any logical pattern. Still, their sequence represents a rising degree of reliance by Faust on his own powers, as he understands them. What Mephistopheles had planned as "das wilde Leben" (1860) or as "flache Unbedeutenheit" (1861) — in which he hopes to eventually trap Faust — turns out to be a series of experiences which bring out the peculiarly "Faustian" qualities in Faust.

"Experience" was a battle cry of the 18th century. According to Kant, experience is the touchstone of knowledge and truth. According to the pietist, experience is the assurance of divine intervention. In FAUST, experience is the only means through which man can be assured of his existence as an independent individuality. The element of certainty is common to all of these modes of "experience," whether it is objective experience, "Erfahrung," or subjective experience, "Erlebnis." It is a certainty which is granted by life, not by reflection, not by books. In the words of the "Vorspiel," experience is the proper subject of poetic presentation:

Greift nur hinein ins volle Menschenleben!
Ein jeder lebt's, nicht vielen ist's bekannt,
und wo Ihr's packt, da ist's interessant.

In bunten Bildern wenig Klarheit,
viel Irrtum und ein Fünkchen Wahrheit:
so wird der beste Trank gebraut,
der alle Welt erquickt und auferbaut. (173)

Experience, to supplement formal instruction, was the purpose of the "grand tour" which every young nobleman of the 18th century was expected to make through Europe. Similarly, an interest in experience is shown by the popularity of the numerous biographies, autobiographies, and travel descriptions which dominated the 18th-century book market. This popularity indicates a strong individualistic interest in the objective world. Experience is personal, direct, and unreflected: one must see things oneself — or at least read about someone's seeing them. Each new situation may present a surprise or a challenge in which the individual has to prove himself or his "philosophy." Thus, experience, which may be exciting or drab, introduces an irrational element of the unpredictable. When Faust dedicates himself to a life of experience, he accepts this challenge of the unpredictable, and of chance; and Mephistopheles' mockery of Faust's contempt of reason and science only emphasizes the gap which Faust has created between himself and the tenets of the Enlightenment.

The age of Goethe had begun to ring with a clamor for experience, for nature — for life. Men were no longer satisfied with sentimentality in lieu of feeling, or with the artificiality of Rococo shepherds and shepherdesses in elaborate gardens and parks. They sought the open country which was not yet touched by the "Kultur, die alle Welt beleckt" (2495), and ventured into regions which had not yet been explored, described, or cultivated. Traveling became a fashionable and profitable pastime, even though highways and footpaths were often impassable and not always safe from robbers. By the end of the 18th century regular passenger service by mail coach had connected even remote provincial towns with metropolitan centers. Numerous guidebooks and travel accounts testify to the immense variety of experience that had become generally accessible through the development of travel facilities. Goethe was an inveterate traveler; even during his last years, old age did not reduce his interest in travel.

The literature of the late 18th century, in-so-far as it reflects this discovery of nature, was marked by two favorite topics: the preference for scenes of natural grandeur and, inversely, of idyllic smallness. In a natural setting of either greatness or smallness, the individual was likely to feel the value of his own personality. Travelers marvelled at the "sublime" impressions they received upon crossing towering mountains or watching rushing waterfalls — as Faust does in Act I (4679 ff) and Act IV (10 039 ff) of Part II. Horace Bénédict Saussure, one of the first to scale Mont Blanc (1787) was struck with awe rather than with fear, at the view of the icy solitude which presented itself to him. The idea of the sublimity of the individual human being was often experienced, particularly in comparison with the idea of space; for it is in the thought of infiniteness, as Kant remarked, that man imagines himself "der Natur in uns selbst, mithin auch der außer uns . . . überlegen zu sein" (KRITIK DER URTEILSKRAFT [1790], Par. 29). Klopstock, the poet of transcendental enthusiasm, felt happiest when he could dissolve into the limitless universe; and many of Schiller's philosophical poems invite their reader to ascend into infinite space. Kant concluded his KRITIK DER PRAKTISCHEN VERNUNFT (1788) with the famous words about the two sublimities:

Zwei Dinge erfüllen das Gemüt mit immer neuer und zunehmender Bewunderung und Ehrfurcht, je öfter und anhaltender sich das Nachdenken damit beschäftigt: der bestirnte Himmel über mir, und das moralische Gesetz in mir.

On the other hand, the enjoyment of the small and idyllic world was considered equally thought-provoking; for it caused the individual to discover his "true" greatness in the acceptance of restrictions imposed from without. The idylls of Gessner and Voss and many other writers of the time thus expressed the ideals of a bourgeois society.

The origins of such an emotional or aesthetic experience are difficult to detect. Doubtless the expeditions into hitherto unclimbed heights or into newly discovered continents (Australia was explored late in the 18th century) were both cause and effect of this new spirit of adventure. The discovery of boundless space, of the "infinite," was reflected in lyric poetry and in mathematics, in treatises on aesthetics and in landscape painting. The experience of the sublime, and the experience of solitude which is often connected with it, are also expressed in the many heroic tragedies for which this century showed a marked preference; both solitude and the sense of the sublime were assigned an important function in the current theories of education, since both offered powerful incentives for "freedom." A physician, J. G. Zimmermann, wrote a voluminous work ÜBER DIE EINSAMKEIT (1784), praising the merits of solitude but warning of its social and psychological dangers.

In FAUST it is not difficult to discover the traces of the experience the sublime and of solitude. The Faust of the first soliloquy expresses when he addresses the moon:

> Ach, könnt' ich doch auf Bergeshöh'n
> in deinem lieben Lichte gehn,
> um Bergeshöhle mit Geistern schweben,
> auf Wiesen in deinem Dämmer weben,
> von allem Wissensqualm entladen
> in deinem Tau gesund mich baden! (397)

The same feeling is alive in Faust as he speaks to the "Erhabener Geist" in the solitary wilderness of "Wald und Höhle," and even the Faust of

Act V (11 345) lives in a feeling of solitary greatness derived from his view of the infinite, a feeling in which life is a fundamental fact which admits no analysis.

Sciences. While the element of "experience" in FAUST may be described in terms of confused "Gefühl" or "Gewühl" (3060, 3456), the discovery of nature through science is reflected with relative clarity. To be sure, experience is so much a part of the entire action of FAUST that it almost constitutes the integrating idea of the play, whereas scientific considerations are suggested only in sporadic allusions. However, these allusions are no less significant than the portrayal of experience for an understanding of the poem. It was inevitable that Goethe's active interest in the natural sciences, his extensive observations, his collecting and experimenting, should be reflected in a work which is so deeply devoted to the understanding of nature.

But such passages would be little more than evidence of scientific dilettantism if we did not know that Goethe participated most seriously in the progress of science, that he was an avid and intelligent reader, and that he kept in touch with many leading scientists of his time through personal contact or correspondence. Thus, echoes of his work on optics, his FARBENLEHRE, which was written in open opposition to the accepted theory of Isaac Newton, eventually found their way into FAUST, as, for example, in the scenes "Vor dem Tor" (910 ff, 1154 ff) and "Anmutige Gegend" (4692, 4722). His morphological interests in such problems as the metamorphosis of plants or the theory of cloud formations can be recognized in such passages as the transformation of some of Helena's attendants into trees (9992 ff) and in the atmospheric conditions pictured in lines 6440 ff and 10 044 ff. There are many such references. As in any poetic image, it is often difficult to determine where the allusion to the natural object ends and the poetic metaphor begins. The creative artist freely exploits a scientific system; he does not blueprint one.

The situation is different in the Classical Walpurgis Night. Here Goethe, ironically and as a poet, took sides in a current dispute regarding the geological history of the earth, and he decided in favor of the school of "Neptunism," which assumed gradual change of the earth's surface through sedimentary processes, as against the school of "Vulcanism," which believed in change through violent upheavals (cf. also lines 10 095–10 123). This choice, which has only historical interest today, reveals one aspect of Goethe's philosophy: he would accept only such scientific theories as stress consistent development and not random chance.

Goethe was fundamentally in accord with the scientific precepts of the Enlightenment when he declared that "one does not possess that which one does not understand." But he differed from rationalism when he demanded that observation should deal with objects "according to their nature." On the surface such a view would seem to agree with the precepts of 16th-century mysticism and the intuitive approach of "natural magic," cultivated by men like Paracelsus (1493–1541), Jeronimo Cardano (1501–1576), Bernardino Telesio (1508–1588), or Johannes Kepler (1571–1630). At an early age Goethe was familiar with the writings of many of these "extraordinary" men of the Renaissance. He included an account of them in the historical chapters of his FARBENLEHRE; indeed, he seems to have blended their various metaphysical beliefs into Faust's passionate outburst:

> Geheimnisvoll am lichten Tag,
> läßt sich Natur des Schleiers nicht berauben;
> und was sie deinem Geist nicht offenbaren mag,
> das zwingst du ihr nicht ab mit Hebeln und mit Schrauben. (675)

What attracted Goethe to the theories of a Paracelsus or a Kepler was their compelling awareness of the organic unity of nature — an awareness to which Goethe had educated himself. He wrote:

> Alles ist in der Natur aufs innigste verknüpft und verbunden, und selbst was in der Natur getrennt ist, mag der Mensch gern zusammenbringen und zusammenhalten.
>
> (MATERIALIEN ZUR GESCHICHTE DER FARBENLEHRE, 4. Abteilung)

That is why on the one hand he was an attentive student of the leading scientists of his own age, of Buffon (1707–1788), Blumenbach (1752–1840), Soemmering (1755–1830), Alexander von Humboldt (1769–1859), and Cuvier (1769–1832), and why on the other he could at times sharply disagree with them (as with Cuvier) when he felt that their morphological hypotheses ignored the organic unity of nature.

In chemistry he was aware of the current trend toward quantitative, rather than qualitative, investigations, and he gave less credence to Stahl's phlogiston theory than many of his contemporaries; he accepted Lavoisier's (1743–1794) and Priestley's (1733–1804) findings on oxygen and other chemical elements, and Dalton's (1766–1844) theory of the atom. Nevertheless, he viewed the essentially materialistic analysis of nature with some suspicion and reserve, since it deprived him of the opportunity to apply his favorite distinction between reason and understanding, theory and observation:

> Die Vernunft ist auf das Werdende, der Verstand auf das Gewordene angewiesen; jene bekümmert sich nicht: wozu? dieser fragt nicht: woher? — Sie erfreut sich am Entwickeln; er wünscht alles festzuhalten, damit er es nutzen könne.
>
> (Maxime No. 555. *Schriften der Goethe-Gesellschaft*, Vol. 21 [1907])

Analysis and synthesis were to go hand in hand. And by "synthesis" Goethe understood, not chemical experiments in a laboratory, but an individual's intuitive integration of the parts into an organic whole. Thus the 18th century appeared to him as a century of analysis; he expected the 19th to be a century of "synthesis." But when he looked for a way to achieve such a "synthesis" within the prevailing specialization of the sciences, he distrusted instruments, and relied on the individual scholar's gift of "integrating intuition." Nevertheless, he did not ignore the progress of the experimental physical sciences, and even in his old age he faithfully consulted Gay-Lussac's ANNALS OF CHEMISTRY and Gilbert's ANNALS OF PHYSICS.

Physics held far more attraction for Goethe than chemistry, especially since the startling discoveries of Galvani (1737–1798), Volta (1745–1827), and Ampère (1775–1836) about electricity had thrown 18th-century thinking into a state of unrest — much as the atomic theory has done in the 20th century. The discovery of thermoelectricity by Seebeck (1770–1831) took place at Jena, almost under Goethe's eyes, and the formulation of an electrodynamic theory by Ampère was announced during the last decade of Goethe's life.

Certainly Goethe was not among those who hastened to incorporate vague notions concerning these discoveries into a personal philosophy. Still, nothing prevented him, as a creative artist, from taking a position as to these advances of science — even though it might be an ironical position — in his FAUST poem. Since he was concerned with the problem of presenting poetically his own notions of a "divine" energy permeating all natural life — for which Faust or even Homunculus could be used as a fitting symbol — he was free to make imaginative use of scientific truths, which, as he saw it, were bound to have a specific and therefore limited application. He was deeply impressed when he discovered in the physiological writings of the Dresden scholar Carl Gustav Carus (1789–1869) a view of evolutionary theory which corresponded to his own: "daß nichts entspringt, als was schon angekündigt ist und daß die Ankündigung erst durch das Angekündigte klar wird." And he expressed his acknowledgment and appreciation in poetic words, in which the Faust monologue of "Anmutige Gegend" (written in 1798) came to his mind again:

Wenn ich das neuste Vorschreiten der Naturwissenschaften betrachte, so komm ich mir vor wie ein Wandrer, der in der Morgendämmerung gegen Osten ging, das heranwachsende Licht mit Freuden anschaute und die Erscheinung des großen Feuerballens mit Sehnsucht erwartete, aber doch bei dem Hervortreten desselben die Augen wegwenden mußte, welche den gewünschten gehofften Glanz nicht ertragen konnten.

(*Letter of January 7, 1826*)

Goethe did not hesitate to draw upon the researches of Luke Howard (1772–1864), the first to apply a system of classification to clouds — as Linnaeus had done for plants — or upon the work of Abraham Gottlob Werner (1749–1817), founder of crystallography and methodical geology, who had made the Saxon Institute of Mining at Freiberg the leading school in the field. Goethe also looked with favor on the then popular technique of "geognosy" — a method by which the inner geological structure or "history" of a mountain is read out of its outer form. It appealed to his morphological way of thinking, according to which the outer configuration of a natural object reveals, or should reveal, the inner processes which have contributed to its making.

Goethe conceived the function of science in a sense much wider than that accepted by the scientists of his age. He complained that the sciences, on the whole, lead away from life and return to it only in a roundabout way (Maxim No. 691); and he considered it the greatest shortcoming of physics that it had, as it were, separated its experiments from man and claimed to recognize, limit, and "prove" nature merely through readings from instruments — whereas man, in the wholesome use of his senses, is the greatest and most exact physical apparatus there is (Maxim No. 706).

Obviously, Goethe faced the same problem to which Kant had given most adequate expression when, in his KRITIK DER REINEN VERNUNFT (1781), he undertook to point out the limitations of human knowledge in order "to open up the way toward faith." According to Kant, knowledge is possible wherever experience proves the conclusions of reason; but beyond the boundaries of experience, the ideas of reason have only "regulative" value, that is to say, thinking alone can only give the direction in which man may seek further knowledge. Goethe expressed it in different words — words which reflect a deeper challenge to the individual. True, he considered his century an "enlightened" century; yet every individual — like Faust — has to start from the beginning. The same striving, the tendency to "outdo oneself" ("Steigerung") which prevails in all "experience," also governs that specific form of experience known as "scientific research": "Der Mensch muß bei dem Glauben verharren, daß das Unbegreifliche begreiflich sei; er würde sonst nicht forschen" (Maxim No. 563). FAUST is the poetic presentation of such a belief.

The arts. One of the most conspicuous ways in which the 18th century demonstrated its cultural superiority and cosmopolitan spirit was its esteem of the fine arts and the artist. In imitation of the brilliant example of the Italian Renaissance princes, patronage of the arts — as much a matter of prestige as of genuine appreciation — spread throughout the German courts during the ensuing centuries. Splendid art collections (Berlin, Cassel, Dresden, Düsseldorf) were established in many principalities. By the middle of the 18th century this custom was being emulated by the bourgeoisie; and in Goethe's own childhood home, works of art were as familiar as a collection of well-bound books. After all, a "man of the world" was a person who had seen foreign countries, had learned their languages, and acquired — through the experience of their arts — resources of manners and taste of which he could not be deprived.

Throughout his life, Goethe was an enthusiastic student and patron of art, of painting in particular. In Leipzig he interested himself in the arts in a fashionable way; he even took lessons from A. F. Oeser, a noted painter, sculptor, engraver, and director of the art collections at the court in Dresden. The cathedral at Strassburg attracted Goethe to the architecture of the Gothic Middle Ages, so that for a time this affection was uppermost in his mind and wiped out his liking for the superficialities of the Leipzig and Dresden Rococo.

The dominating artistic experience of his life, however, was his journey to Italy, the Mecca of all artists. There he attempted to develop his own artistic talents. But he soon found them inadequate compared with the works of Greek antiquity and Italian Renaissance which his eyes met at every turn. This experience of art determined the pattern of his taste; only rarely did he later acknowledge other standards than those of ancient architecture and sculpture. They guided him as he built up his own collection in Weimar; they dominated him when — with an artist-friend, Heinrich Meyer — he founded a small art association, the "Weimarer Kunstfreunde," and when, at various times, he edited short-lived periodicals which were devoted to the criticism of art (*Die Propyläen*, *Kunst und Altertum*) and attempted to direct young artists toward the classical ideal. "Unter allen Völkerschaften haben die Griechen den Traum des Lebens am schönsten geträumt," he wrote (Maxime No. 298).

This domination of the German mind by the Greek ideal of classicism during the age of Goethe has been the object of much discussion. However, except in the field of architecture, the enthusiasm for what was "Greek" scarcely produced great art in Germany, in spite of the pioneering efforts of Goethe, Schiller, and Wilhelm von Humboldt, the most ardent follower of this ideal. On the other hand, German literature, philosophy, and education have been consistently attracted to Greek thought, because it appeared to be the first formulation of a fully integrated humanistic culture.

Classicism was proclaimed to Germany in 1755 by the publication of Johann Joachim Winckelmann's GEDANKEN ÜBER DIE NACHAHMUNG DER GRIECHISCHEN WERKE. According to Winckelmann, no conflict existed between living and thinking among the ancient Greeks; they lived as if in the lap of nature, and beauty was their everyday milieu. Hence, their art reflected "noble simplicity and quiet grandeur"; and the only way for modern men "to become great and — possibly — inimitable is to imitate the ancients." Such a statement was dogmatic and could not be verified except by broken statues unearthed in Italy — for Greece, at the time, was inaccessible under Turkish domination.

The salient feature of this classicism was that it attributed to art a moral incentive, presupposing restraint and personal limitation as necessary if art is to be "natural." This classicism reduces the aesthetic qualities of art to a secondary role; for, in this way of thinking, art is instructive and presupposes the use of allegory, for which a knowledge of mythology and archaeology is necessary.

Although Winckelmann belonged to the era of the Enlightenment, his doctrines brought about a fundamental revision of the rationalistic view that art is "imitation of nature." If the genius of Greek art was to be emulated *because* it was and expressed "Nature," then the implied assumption must be that "Nature" itself is the innate creative force in the artist, and the artist indeed must be a "creator," a "poet," a "second Maker, a just Prometheus under Jove."

Such reflections, first voiced by the English philosopher, Shaftesbury (1671–1713), were imported into Germany by the writings of Herder (1744–1803). With the translation into German of Edward Young's CONJECTURES ON ORIGINAL COMPOSITION (1759), these ideas became the basis of a worship of the artist's creative activity, an attitude which has remained characteristic of German criticism to the present day. Goethe's own participation in this "cult of genius" lent strong support to the practice. Many of his Storm and Stress poems tell of the independence, the pride, the suffering, the joy of creativeness, best expressed in his famous ode on Prometheus.

From this vantage point we can understand Faust's exalted mood in which he feels akin to divine, creative forces in the universe (490 ff, 614 ff). But we can also understand how an individual, claiming the prerogatives of an artist, can place himself outside the jurisdiction of ordinary mortals, show contempt for accepted artistic, social, and religious practices, and extol "originality" at any cost.

Goethe was one of the first to foresee the danger of confusion and formlessness arising from the subjectivism of the Storm and Stress and its cult of the genius. From his Italian journey on, indeed even earlier, he changed his course and sought to cultivate a sense of proportion, balance, and harmonious form.

In his post-Italian years, Goethe was given to reflections on the nature of artistic "form." He observed: "Den Stoff sieht jedermann vor sich; den Gehalt findet nur der, der etwas dazu zu tun hat; und die Form ist ein Geheimnis den meisten" (Maxime No. 289). In his efforts to determine the nature of art Goethe found strong support in Schiller's two essays BRIEFE ÜBER DIE AESTHETISCHE ERZIEHUNG DES MENSCHEN (1795) and ÜBER NAIVE UND SENTIMENTALISCHE DICHTUNG (1795–96). According to Schiller, art is the activity of the human mind which finds the "right" form for the "right" subject matter. An object of nature can be presented in many different forms, depending on the artist's ability or the purposes he may be pursuing. But there is only one form which is fully appropriate to the object's own inner purpose. In order to discover this form the artist must reject all those which only reveal his personal intentions. He must objectify himself. And the more he subordinates himself, the more he will succeed in discovering the "law," the "intrinsic pattern" which every object "carries within itself." The more objective and detached his observation, the more he can hope to penetrate into the "spirit of nature" and into the "freedom" which nature exhibited in the choice of its "laws." As Goethe expresses it:

> In der Beschränkung zeigt sich erst der Meister,
> und das Gesetz nur kann uns Freiheit geben.
> ("Natur und Kunst")

In Schiller's view, the work of art is a "schöner Schein" — the mere *appearance* of freedom in a state of beauty in which all striving has been quieted. The artist, however, must search for the essence of nature, for "freedom"; nature *in its essence* never becomes visible except in those artistic creations in which matter and form, the physical and the spiritual, are harmoniously blended. That is why the Arcadian Idyll in Act III of Part II can only be a temporary solution of the FAUST play. The poet must go on to an ever deeper fathoming of nature, just as Faust must. Unceasing effort must go into what Goethe called the "artistic conception": "Bei jedem Kunstwerk, groß oder klein, bis ins Kleinste kommt alles auf die Konzeption an" (Maxim No. 224). Compared with the imagined freedom of the Storm and Stress artist, who scorned objectivity, Goethe's ideal "classical" artist is charged with a cultural, educational function. For through his acquaintance with the "formative" principles of nature he has become a guide in the education of man.

While such general aesthetic reflections on the function of art appear to underlie certain scenes dealing with the Helena theme ("Mothers," Classical Walpurgis Night, Arcadian Idyll), there are numerous instances in which specific works of art seem to have served as "models" in the solution of specific poetic problems in FAUST. Goethe himself permitted an etching done by his friend Lips after a well-known engraving of Rembrandt's to be printed as a frontispiece to the edition of the FRAGMENT in 1790. The figures of Paris and Helena which suggest to a lady of the court "Endymion und Luna, wie gemalt" (6509) do not suggest any particular painting; but the subject of the ancient fable of Endymion and Luna was a favorite topic of 17th-century baroque art. Guido Reni's famous "Aurora" may have been in Goethe's mind when he described the dawn in "Anmutige Gegend" (4666 ff), and Correggio's "Leda" when he described what Homunculus sees in the dreaming Faust's mind (6903 ff).

It is often assumed that one of Titian's or Giorgione's "Venus" paintings may have inspired the description of what Faust sees in the magic mirror in the "Hexenküche" (2429 ff). The stage settings of the "Prolog" and the "Grablegung" may have been suggested by certain early Italian frescoes in the Campo Santo at Pisa.

Once the reader begins to search for such "allusions," his efforts will be rewarded. Scholarship has established a long list of works of art which may throw light on certain details in the "Mummenschanz," in the Northern and in the Classical Walpurgis Nights, and in many other scenes. If one considers that Goethe did permit himself to be inspired by impressions from the fine arts, the large number of such allusions is not surprising. More significant is the observation that Goethe was not prejudiced in favor of certain "styles" when he made his selections. For in the array of such "sources" the reader will find the medieval as much represented as the classical, the Northern as much as the Greek, Dürer as much as Raphael, Hieronymus Bosch and Teniers as much as Titian and Luca Signorelli. There seems to be no particular preference for the "Classical" in the sense of Winckelmann; on the contrary, often it appears as if the weird, the unharmonious, the fantastic were equally attractive and fascinating to Goethe, judging by the many primitive woodcut illustrations from books on witchcraft and demonology and the equally primitive ornamentations from ancient vases and graves which stimulated Goethe's imagination.

One need not stop here. Literary reminiscences must have been in Goethe's mind with equal frequency. Detailed examination of the poem reveals that in the writing of many passages specific motifs from Homer and Euripides, Virgil and Dante, Shakespeare and Milton, Haller and Klopstock and many other writers lingered in Goethe's mind. These reminiscences do not detract from the originality of the work; rather, they enhance the reader's impression of Goethe's immense versatility as a poet. Goethe himself defended the originality of an artist who uses such motifs when he admitted to Eckermann that he had been baffled by those scholars "who believe that the writing of poetry takes place from book to poem, and not from life to poem."

Philosophy. The 18th century was a century of philosophers. In Germany an unbroken tradition of metaphysical speculation extended from Leibnitz (1646–1716) to Kant (1724–1804) and the schools of "German Idealism." Goethe was no systematic philosopher, but he read philosophical books with keen interest and formed his own philosophy of life, as any thinking individual does, without subscribing to a particular philosophical system. In FAUST he posed a question about the experience of reality and its ultimate value — and this is a philosophical question.

As we have seen, Goethe was affected by the Enlightenment and by

Pietism, the intellectual and spiritual movements of his own day. He was no less exposed to the philosophical thought of many other ages — the idealism of Plato, the naturalism of Aristotle, the pantheism of Giordano Bruno, the symbolism of Paracelsus and his followers. Ancient and modern thinkers alike contributed to Goethe's early reading: Pliny and Quintilian, Plutarch and Cicero, Voltaire and Rousseau, Berkeley and Mendelssohn were equally familiar to him — though not as familiar as the Bible. Goethe was an eclectic who chose his basic concepts from any philosopher who convinced him or was to his liking; and he managed to avoid being either encyclopedic or dogmatic.

The philosophical keynote of Goethe's time was sounded by the publication of Kant's KRITIK DER REINEN VERNUNFT (1781), an event of the first magnitude in the history of philosophical thought. Not only did it put an end to metaphysical dogmatism and self-contained rationalistic speculation, but it made "knowledge" dependent on the evidence of experience. Thereby it encouraged science and technology to take the lead in making this world over and rendering it more suitable to human needs.

Goethe was only partially on Kant's side. To be sure, he approved of the emphasis on experience, and he accepted the leading precept of Kantian ethics (according to which any individual action is justified which is applicable to every human being with equal justice). But Kant's way of thinking was too abstract and systematic for the creative artist Goethe; nevertheless, Goethe thanked Kant for having popularized the useful term "objective thinking." As the "Prolog" shows, Goethe still preferred to draw on such metaphysical systems as Leibnitz' Theory of Monads when he wanted to suggest poetically the idea of an unbroken, living series of beings in nature — from the lowest, unreflecting, inorganic Thing to the highest, spiritual, all-embracing Being. It was more than a vague recollection of Leibnitz' doctrine of the difference between "confused" and "clear" cognition when Goethe described Faust's way through life in the Lord's words of the "Prolog":

> Wenn er mir jetzt auch nur verworren dient,
> so werd' ich ihn bald in die Klarheit führen. (309)

Or he remembered, as he did in writing "Wald und Höhle," the placid pantheism of Spinoza, for whom God and Nature (*Deus sive Natura*) had become interchangeable terms. But he chose according to his artistic purposes; he did not review his differential calculus in order to understand Leibnitz, nor his geometry in order to do justice to Spinoza's carefully deduced system.

Much of the poetic application of these older metaphysical theories w- suggested to Goethe by his friend Herder's IDEEN ZU EINER PHILOSOPHIE

DER GESCHICHTE DER MENSCHHEIT (1784). Herder's book was a brilliant attempt to conceive of the origin and the evolution of the physical world — from cosmic nebulae to the emergence of man — as a grand history of self-development of an organic force. Herder asserted that the "unity of an organic force" was responsible for the infinite variety of existing forms and species. Herder's purpose was not to present scientific "truth" or factual "insight," but to express a confession of pantheistic faith which for many, including Goethe, had taken the place of philosophical deduction and orthodox beliefs. Therefore it mattered little whether Kant denounced this "unity of organic force" as "an idea entirely outside the field of empirical observation and belonging to the area of speculation, where it would, indeed — if it were generally adopted — create the greatest confusion." For, *mutatis mutandis*, it was adopted in FAUST. Faust's difficulty in translating the beginning of the Gospel according to Saint John, his passing from the notion of "Wort" to "Sinn" to "Kraft" and to "Tat" (1224 ff), indicates the impossibility of verbalizing this pantheism for which form and content, "outside" and "inside," effect and cause, matter and mind have become identical — merely different aspects of the same thing. Such pantheism availed itself of literary support wherever it could find it: in the idealism of Plato and Cicero, in the materialism of Democritus and Lucretius, in the writings of the British philosophers Shaftesbury and Hobbes, as in those of the Frenchmen Voltaire and La Mettrie. Spinoza's detached contemplation became as significant as the mystical fervor of the ancient Orphic Hymns, which were becoming available in new editions in Germany at this time. And it is significant, perhaps, that one of the major philosophical disputes of the time, the argument between Goethe's philosopher-friend Friedrich Heinrich Jacobi and Moses Mendelssohn over whether Lessing had been a "pantheist" (for pantheism was considered synonymous with atheism), was set off by an unsigned manuscript in Jacobi's possession — Goethe's *Prometheus*.

It is evident that pantheism, as it was expressed in Herder's work, represented an emancipation from orthodox theology. Still, this pantheism sprang from a fundamentally religious experience, and it was merely the scope, not the aim of such thinking, that had undergone a change. Theology, in the strict sense, had been occupied with the exegesis of Scripture; pantheism, as Herder saw it, aimed at the interpretation of all literature. Both followed the same purpose — to read the "spirit" from the "word."

Pantheism was basically eclectic; but behind its vast amount of reading from the great thinkers of all times there was an exuberant worship of "life," presupposing the existence and operation of a universal, all-pervading "spirit." To discover this "spirit" required a searching and yet reserved attitude of the mind — a mind willing to operate with hypotheses and yet skeptical of its own findings. This had been the attitude of Socrates — his irony, his admission of ignorance — that had qualified him to break down the traditional beliefs of his contemporaries. Socrates' irony made him the ideal of 18th-century philosophers.

Thus a concept became dominant in 18th-century Germany which has been of fundamental importance in German thinking ever since: the concept of objective *irony* — of "Geist." This concept found expression in Herder's historical approach to the problem of organic evolution. It found support in Kant's definition of "intuitive judgment" in the appreciation of art and of nature (cf. KRITIK DER URTEILSKRAFT, Par. 49).

"Geist," rather than reason, became the standard slogan in the vocabulary of aesthetic pantheism which characterized German thought in post-Kantian days, and a key word in the philosophies of Fichte (1762–1814), Hegel (1770–1831), and Schelling (1775–1854).

Without the word "Geist," Schiller's poetry would lack much of its exaltation. In FAUST, "Geist" is one of the most frequently occurring nouns. "Geist" became the word for the faculty of the mind which seeks to integrate parts into a whole, or which perceives "organic" entities in objects of nature and art. It was considered the principle determining the pattern of personality and character, as well as that of entire nations, ages, or institutions. Besides, "Geist" was a very useful word, for it included within its meaning allusions to any spiritual being, from primitive folklore and mythology ("ghost"), to medieval occultism ("Erdgeist") and to Christian theology ("Heiliger Geist"). Famulus Wagner speaks of the "Geist der Zeiten" (571) as Herder had spoken of a spirit of the people — "Volksgeist" — or as Montesquieu had spoken about the "Spirit of the Laws" (L'ESPRIT DES LOIS).

Schelling's IDEEN ZU EINER PHILOSOPHIE DER NATUR (1797), written as a counterpart to Herder's main work, postulated that "Natur soll der sichtbare Geist, der Geist die unsichtbare Natur sein." Around the turn of the century Goethe was planning to write a nature poem in collaboration with Schelling. Nothing came of it. Instead, Goethe withdrew more and more from the contact with formal philosophy. When he wrote the Baccalaureus Scene of the Second Part of FAUST, he was suspected of having satirized Fichtean idealism, according to which the absolute Ego (Mind, or "Geist") determines the absolute Non-Ego (Nature). And it was satire, not merely of orthodox theology, but of Schelling's school of speculative philosophy, when Goethe had the Archbishop say in the scene at the Imperial Court (Act I):

> "Natur und Geist"! So spricht man nicht zu Christen;
> deshalb verbrennt man Atheisten,
> weil solche Reden höchst gefährlich sind.
> Natur ist Sünde, Geist ist Teufel!

Sie hegen zwischen sich den Zweifel,
ihr mißgestaltet Zwitterkind. (4902)

With advancing age, Goethe became increasingly skeptical of any philosophical system, although his relations to some philosophers (Schelling, Jacobi, Schopenhauer) continued to be friendly, though reserved. When the romantic writers of the early 19th century made it their program to present "Geist in der Natur," Goethe found not clarity, but confusion and concealed subjectivism in their writings. His own philosophy of life became one of "resignation" in matters of theory and universal truths, and one of optimism in matters of observation and faith. The objective of his philosophy was the reality of life itself which, in a mystical fashion, he called "Gott-Natur." For him "Gott-Natur" included the highest principle as well as the smallest detail of life:

Das Höchste, was wir von Gott und der Natur erhalten haben, ist das Leben, die rotierende Bewegung der Monas um sich selbst, welche weder Rast noch Ruhe kennt; der Trieb, das Leben zu hegen und zu pflegen, ist einem jeden unverwüstlich eingeboren, die Eigentümlichkeit desselben jedoch bleibt uns und andern ein Geheimnis.

Die zweite Gunst der von oben wirkenden Wesen ist das Erlebte, das Gewahrwerden, das Eingreifen der lebendig-beweglichen Monas in die Umgebungen der Außenwelt, wodurch sie sich erst selbst als innerlich Grenzenloses, als äußerlich Begrenztes gewahr wird. Über dieses Erlebte können wir, obgleich Anlage, Aufmerksamkeit und Glück dazu gehört, in uns selbst klar werden; andern bleibt aber auch dies immer ein Geheimnis.

Als Drittes entwickelt sich nun dasjenige, was wir als Handlung und Tat, als Wort und Schrift gegen die Außenwelt richten; dieses gehört derselben mehr an als uns selbst, so wie sie sich darüber auch eher verständigen kann, als wir es selbst vermögen; jedoch fühlt sie, daß sie, um recht klar darüber zu werden, auch von unserm Erlebten so viel als möglich zu erfahren habe. Weshalb man auch auf Jugendanfänge, Stufen der Bildung, Lebenseinzelnheiten, Anekdoten und dergleichen höchst begierig ist.

(Maximen, No. 391–393)

Goethe's philosophy of life was built on the foundations of his century. He shared its desire for ultimate principles; but he did not engage in speculations about the nature of these principles. He participated in the scientific discovery of the physical world; but he did not lose sight of the human beings for whom these discoveries were supposed to be beneficial. He was interested in the development of the individual human being; but he did not permit himself to be carried away by general political theories, idealistic or materialistic, since either was bound to ignore the unique pattern which each individual carries within himself from the time of his birth.

VI. The Reception of FAUST

Early Reception of FAUST — Beginnings of a Critical Reception of FAUST — Faust in Music and Literature — Faust in Modern Times — Faust Renaissance.

Ever since the publication of FAUST: EIN FRAGMENT (1790), the poem has been the subject of vigorous discussion and controversy. After the appearance of the First Part (1808) and the posthumous Second Part (1832), opinions naturally became more definite and began to range from enthusiastic approval to more or less polite embarrassment. Despite the trend toward social and economic collectivism, the 19th century was an age of individualism and hero worship; in such a century, a figure like Faust was bound to attract and hold attention. Literary criticism, while it attempts to achieve a deeper and deeper understanding of a work of literature, must do so in terms of the standards and prejudices of its time. The history of the reception of FAUST during the 19th and 20th centuries reflects this fact; and often FAUST criticism has revealed less about Goethe's poem than about the ambitions or the shortcomings of a critic or his public.

1. EARLY RECEPTION OF FAUST

The first readers of FAUST were those to whom Goethe seems to have addressed his work in the first place: students, writers, art lovers, theater-goers, teachers — the young generation in the universities who had an interest in the cultural and intellectual life of the immediate future. After all, Faust was a university man by profession; his first associates came from the university milieu, and this milieu determined his initial outlook on life. The same problems that Goethe had faced at Leipzig and Strassburg were still faced — and perhaps with increased intensity — by the more alert students at Jena and Göttingen, then the leading universities in Germany, and at Heidelberg and Berlin which, by 1810, had become strong competitors.

It was in these university towns that FAUST was first read, discussed, lectured on and written about. With only the FRAGMENT available, writers began to look for the deeper implications of the poem. To August Wilhelm Schlegel, leader of the "romantic" group of writers, FAUST seemed "an unsolved riddle at which one can only marvel, without being able to comprehend the poet's intentions" (1802). Nevertheless, Schlegel discerned that the subject had not been chosen primarily for its historical interest; indeed, he believed he recognized "modern times" in its treatment of philosophical, scientific, and moral problems. Schelling, the romantic philosopher, was even more outspoken. In 1802 he called FAUST a "really philosophical poem," "the typical poem of the Germans," original, contained within itself, and comparable only to itself. If it was to be compared with anything, then it must be with Dante's poem, although FAUST, Schelling said, was far more a "Comedy" and far more poetically "Divine" than Dante's work. In FAUST he recognized an intention which was more "Aristophanic" than tragic; for there is the spirit of comedy in the acknowledgment of man's limitations — limitations which make it impossible for him "to partake of the infinite in knowledge or in experience."

Literature and the social realities. Such statements reveal a tendency of interpretation which is metaphysical and not particularly concerned with everyday realities. Meanwhile, it should be remembered, the first two decades of the 19th century were a period of turmoil: war and national restoration, struggles for constitutions and political franchise — events which brought friction, unrest, and sacrifice, and made a citizen very much conscious of the "finite" world he lived in. FAUST I was printed only two years after Prussia and its allies had suffered complete defeat at the hands of Napoleon, and it is understandable that Fichte's REDEN AN DIE DEUTSCHE NATION (1808) aroused greater attention than a play dealing with the emotional and spiritual sufferings of a Renaissance university professor.

Goethe and the public. When the battles of Leipzig (1813) and Waterloo (1815) were fought, Goethe held himself aloof from the events of the day. He did, upon request, write a play commemorating the liberation of Germany; but he wrote DES EPIMENIDES ERWACHEN in the austere form of classical antiquity, not in an antiquarian, medieval style, as he had perhaps been expected to do.

The last twenty years of his life Goethe spent in virtual isolation from the affairs of the day. Not that he was a misanthrope; he had many friends and disciples, and his counsel was sought by many minds throughout Europe. But his attention was not vitally centered on the trivia that filled the journals, rather on the mysterious ways in which nature develops forms and organisms. And while others became excited about social reforms, such as the establishment of constitutional government, Goethe studied stones and plants, or the manner in which, centuries ago, the Persian poet Hafiz had developed a serene art, or the way in which an individual can be most successfully integrated into a community.

The writings of the romantic poets — who had grown up under the protection and in the shadow of Goethe's prestige — were now in the public limelight; and the "neudeutsch-religiös-patriotische Kunst" of Tieck and Wackenroder, Arnim and Brentano, Kleist, Werner, and Eichendorff seemed to satisfy the public taste more than the old master's WESTÖSTLICHER DIWAN or WILHELM MEISTERS WANDERJAHRE. While the day-by-day affairs of the state were being administered by a bureaucratic machinery, sanctioned by the rationalist system of Hegel's philosophy,

Goethe's own life and work seemed to be guided by the ideal of a free and detached artist whose actions are inspired by deep reverence for eternal nature.

Criticisms and protests. FAUST II (1832) was presented to a public which was anything but prepared for it. A bourgeois reading public, accustomed to realistic and even trivial plots, was bewildered by the grand allegories of a medieval court festival and by the dream flights into ancient mythology. Orthodox citizens, accustomed to literary censorship, were embarrassed and uncomfortable at the satirical undertone of Act IV or the theatrical display of Faust's ascension into a Christian heaven. Although some critics had already argued on the basis of Part I that Gretchen and Faust might ultimately be expected to attain "salvation," the manner in which this was carried out was something of a shock to many readers. Protests against the "theological" ending of FAUST were raised in many quarters, Catholic and Protestant alike. Such protests were based on considerations of practical ethics: for the seducer of virtue, the ally of Satan, and the autocratic destroyer of human rights was represented as receiving ultimate pardon.

Allegorical interpretations. While Goethe's unconventional treatment of human relationships was thus frowned upon by the defenders of bourgeois morality, the hidden philosophical implications, which are abundant, especially in Part II, became the happy hunting ground of philosophical interpreters who proceeded to explain FAUST "allegorically," that is to say, according to the esoteric system of Hegelian dialectics. In the end, the critics from both camps — those representing the standards of the German middle class and those speaking for the "initiate" circles of academic life — succeeded in raising barriers which stood in the way of an unprejudiced appreciation of FAUST. Around the middle of the century, younger writers (for example, Mörike and Keller) tried in vain to find a deeper understanding of the Second Part of Goethe's poem. But even the lectures of the witty Swabian philosopher, Friedrich Theodor Vischer, and his high-spirited parody, FAUST, DRITTER TEIL (1862) (published under the pseudonym of Deutobold Symbolizetti Allegoriowitsch Mystifizinsky), merely contributed toward discrediting the excessively allegorical (Hegelian) mode of interpretation, but scarcely created an unbiased appreciation of Goethe's FAUST itself.

Polite respect. To many, the Second Part appeared an unsolved mystery, far more so than the FRAGMENT had been for the Romanticists. To a writer like Grillparzer, it was a failure, showing the signs of senility. It did not seem to fulfill the expectations which the titanic character of Faust, even in his despair at the end of Part I, had warranted; and the more the readers of the First Part had been fascinated by the personality that had risked its own existence in the quest for truth, the more those readers were baffled by the mass of allegorical, historical, mythological, archaeological, and scientific detail which they found in the Second. That is why they showed, at most, respectful admiration for FAUST, whereas they had shown unreserved enthusiasm for Goethe's lyric creations, which had meanwhile indeed become a lasting and universal cultural heritage in homes and concert halls through the compositions of Schubert, Schumann, and Zelter.

In general popularity on the stage, in the homes, in the schools, Schiller far surpassed his older friend. Schiller seemed to have a more clearly defined political ideal and a more generally acceptable morality of optimism and universal progress. Goethe, on the other hand, did not offer such simple solutions; he worshipped nature as well as abstract ideals, and one could never be quite sure whether the characters of his poetry and novels were meant as models to be emulated or as warnings to be heeded. Thus the stereotype of Goethe "the great pagan," "the Olympian," came into being, which testified to both the respect and the envy which the poet inspired in his own nation. The reading — and understanding — of FAUST, Part II became equivalent to a certificate of rare "Bildung" among the Germans.

2. BEGINNINGS OF A CRITICAL RECEPTION OF FAUST

Heine. Nevertheless, a keen observer like Heinrich Heine (1797–1856) did not accept the popular discrediting of Goethe in comparison with Schiller. For one thing, Goethe appeared to him to be the more perfect, the more original artist, whose creations could be imitated less easily than Schiller's life-size "altar panels of virtue and morality." As an artist, Heine observed that it required less artistic skill to construct ("verfertigen") the serene, idealistic figures in Schiller's works than the beings from a "sinful and impure world of human imperfection" which Goethe had presented in his works. In FAUST, particularly, Heine recognized a higher degree of realism and completeness. For an "absolute" poet — and in his realm, Heine remarked, Goethe was like an absolute monarch by God's grace — nothing is ever of secondary importance; whatever he has under his pen at a given moment is most important; that is why even the smallest figures in Goethe's works are so admirably "complete," like the creations of Homer and Shakespeare.

But it was not the fascination of the work of art as such which made FAUST, as Heine said, "the secular Bible of the Germans." Rather, it was its significance in the history of ideas. For with the figure of Faust the period of medieval faith had come to an end and the period of modern scientific inquiry had begun. Thus Goethe's FAUST became for Heine the symbol of modern realism which believes in the attainment of human happiness, equality, and brotherhood on this earth, and professes indifference toward the spiritual brotherhood taught by medieval, Christian transcendentalism:

Das Wissen, die Erkenntnis der Dinge durch die Vernunft, die Wissenschaft, gibt uns endlich die Genüsse, um die uns der Glaube . . . so lange geprellt hat.

Applying this symbolism of Faust to the political and intellectual reality of his own day, Heine continued:

Das deutsche Volk ist selber jener gelehrte Doktor Faust, es ist selber jener Spiritualist, der mit dem Geiste endlich die Ungenügbarkeit des Geistes begriffen, und nach materiellen Genüssen verlangt und dem Fleische seine Rechte wiedergibt. Doch noch befangen in der Symbolik der katholischen Poesie, wo Gott als der Repräsentant des Geistes und der Teufel als der Repräsentant des Fleisches gilt, bezeichnete man jene Rehabilitation des Fleisches als einen Abfall von Gott, als ein Bündnis mit dem Teufel.

But, Heine added prophetically, it would be a long time before the German nation would see fulfilled what it anticipated so profoundly in Goethe's poem — and that would be the revolution, "the great daughter of the Reformation" (Die romantische Schule [1833], Buch I).

It must be remembered that Heine was writing these lines to introduce the spirit of German literature to the French public. In a way, he was only repeating what Lessing, the great 18th-century critic, had said more than two generations before him: "How much has Germany been in love — and in part still is — with her Doctor Faustus!"

Faust *criticism abroad.* Heine was not the only critic who undertook to interpret the significance of Faust to readers abroad. Writers such as Carlyle and Ruskin, Emerson and Margaret Fuller adopted and proclaimed Goethean ideas in England and in America. It was a situation which often occurs in the history of ideas: an intellectual movement within a nation may be witnessed and felt by the people of that nation themselves, but it is not recognized in its fuller significance until it is diagnosed from outside, by an objective observer. These writers felt that Goethe was not an isolated phenomenon, not merely the remainder of a "Golden Age" of literature that had visited Germany later than other countries in Europe, but rather that he was the true exponent of humanistic thought in an age of technical and scientific expansion of human capacities.

By the middle of the 19th century the atmosphere of confusion and indifference in which Faust had first been received had cleared away, and the stimulating force of the poem had become manifest and was clearly recognized. This is indicated by the increasing number of Faust translations into other languages, among them that into French by Gérard de Nerval (1828), and those into English by Shelley (selected scenes, 1815–1824), Hayward (1834), Anster (1835), Anna Swanwick (1850–1878), and particularly that of Bayard Taylor (1870–1871). These, as well as many critical discussions of FAUST — such as those by Madame de Staël (DE L'ALLEMAGNE, 1810), Henry Crabb Robinson (1832), Thomas Carlyle (1822), Sarah Austin (1833) — demonstrated that Goethe and his FAUST no longer belonged to Germany and the Germans alone.

3. FAUST IN MUSIC AND LITERATURE

Romantic music. The rise of romantic literature and philosophy in Germany was accompanied by an extraordinary development of operatic and symphonic music. The musical compositions of Gluck and Mozart, Haydn and Beethoven were a new achievement in art, for they lent expression to a hitherto untold intensity of human experience. Likewise, FAUST was an enormous advance of poetry, for it opened up depths of emotions which had seldom been expressed before. What Goethe said upon another occasion may be applied to FAUST:

> Und wenn der Mensch in seiner Qual verstummt,
> gab mir ein Gott zu sagen, was ich leide. ("Elegie")

We know that Goethe conceived of FAUST, particularly the Second Part, as a work of poetic art depending extensively upon the support of music. It is immaterial whether in this connection Goethe was aware that music had been an integral part of ancient tragedy, or whether he was merely sharing the "romantic" fashion of his age — enhancing the emotional effect of the word by the supplementary use of music in the form of melody or song. In his "Trilogie der Leidenschaft" (1823) Goethe had shown how much the "Doppelglück der Töne und der Liebe" meant to him. If anywhere, it is in music that the "daemonic" power of human passion finds an adequate medium of expression; and Mozart's DON GIOVANNI (1787) and MAGIC FLUTE (1791) were more than merely "charming" presentations of favorite topics of the time: they were striking examples of love's destructive and constructive effects upon human society. Much of Beethoven's seriousness became comprehensible in the light of his preoccupation with the thought that "daemonic," irrational forces can at any time intervene in the existence of man. In a more popular, though by no means superficial manner, the same thought found expression in the operas of Carl Maria von Weber — in the theme of a pact with the Devil (FREISCHÜTZ, 1821), or of the immanence of spiritual beings in the material world (OBERON, 1826). In the works of Ernst Theodor Amadeus Hoffmann, author of the *Tales* and himself a striking example of a "daemonic" personality, these tendencies achieved their fullest realization, as, for example, in his weird novel, DIE ELIXIERE DES TEUFELS (1815–1816).

Faust and Don Juan. Goethe had kept himself meticulously aloof from the romantic materialization of the spiritual — from the "Nacht- und

Grabdichter," as he called them in his FAUST (SD 5298). But the theme of a pact with the Devil constituted for romantic composers a temptation which could not easily be ignored. In 1818 Louis Spohr adapted the story of a devil-ridden Faust to an opera in the Viennese, romantic, Catholic tradition, in a manner reminiscent of DON GIOVANNI. Faust, the scholar, driven by his passionate desires, indeed showed a similarity to the famous insatiable lover. In 1829 (ten years after Lord Byron had published the first canto of his monumental epic DON JUAN, 1819–1824), Christian Dietrich Grabbe chose the theme of DON JUAN UND FAUST with its suggestive ambiguity as the subject of a play; here, the "sinnliche" and the "übersinnliche Freier" were confronted with one another in uncompromising competition. But Grabbe's drama, though spectacular in composition, offered to the reader a calculated experiment with human "types" rather than a plausible solution.

Once Goethe had set the pattern, it was difficult for younger authors to escape comparison or to discover a point of view which was not at least hinted at in Goethe's poem. Such a situation is discouraging and irksome for any young writer; and much of the unenthusiastic respect for Goethe's FAUST that marked its reception during the first half of the 19th century came from younger dramatists who felt frustrated in the shadow of greatness. At any rate, such writers as Hebbel and Büchner never tried their hands at a FAUST play, although by temperament and philosophical interest they might have been tempted to do so. Other writers did; but their treatments of the theme reveal less about the actual popularity of the subject than about the personal intentions and tastes of the authors. Many of these creations indicate a shift of interest away from the personal, or philosophical, appeal which a Faust drama would have aroused earlier in the century, and toward a calmer, more objective contemplation of the historical Faust and his century.

FAUST *poems after Goethe.* Between such extremes as the self-torturing reflections of Lenau's FAUST (1833–1835) and the unpretentious popular rendition of the Faust chapbook by Gustav Schwab (1838) the literary historian will find many different variations of the Faust theme: in 1847 Karl Simrock revived the old Faust puppet-play; his book inspired the editing of many similar survivals in other parts of Central Europe. There appeared a FAUSTUS poem by Bechstein and a FAUST drama by Braunthal; and it became evident that even in such figures as Immermann's MERLIN (1832) and Mosen's AHASVERUS (1838) spiritual kinsmen of Faustus were concealed. Corresponding figures in the works of Byron and Eugene Sue indicated that the Faustian type had found its way into European literature on a broad scale, later to appear in such diverse forms as Ibsen's Peer Gynt and Shaw's Don Juan in MAN AND SUPERMAN.

When Heinrich Heine wrote his "Tanzpoem" DOKTOR FAUST (1847) in response to a request from London for a ballet to be performed in great splendor at the Royal Theatre, he seized upon the historical tradition of the Faust theme with complete subjectivity and artistic freedom. This enabled him to transform the Faust figure, which had once been a warning symbol of melancholy man, into a free, and indeed irresponsible, intellectual — a symbol of art existing for its own sake.

Heine's FAUST was not performed. Yet the circumstances and the haste in which it was written, and the concessions that had to be made in composing it, indicate that the Faust theme did not have for Heine the force of a compelling challenge it had had for Goethe. As a reflection of its time, Heine's FAUST contains a note of tired resignation: it ends in a witches' sabbath, and thus is in strong contrast to the message of activity and vital intensification ("Steigerung") expressed in Goethe's FAUST. On the other hand, Heine's emphasis on a basically lyrical mood and his keen sensitivity for techniques to express this mood, showed Heine to be closely akin to the world of music which — about the middle of the century — began to take over the theme of Faust.

Faust symphonies. In 1845, Richard Wagner wrote his FAUST OVERTURE. In the following year Hector Berlioz, the French composer, revised his youthful "Scenes from Faust" (written on the basis of de Nerval's translation) and created his famous DAMNATION DE FAUST. In 1850 Robert Schumann completed his FAUST SCENES, directly suggested by the Gretchen scenes of Part I, and the opening and concluding scenes of Part II of Goethe's poem. In 1857 Franz Liszt followed with his FAUST Symphony, an experiment with new means of orchestration largely suggested by the works of Berlioz and Richard Wagner. The TRAGIC OVERTURE of Johannes Brahms (1881), sometimes referred to as his "Faust Overture," might be mentioned in this connection. As in all program music, it is often only the title which suggests the source of the composer's inspiration; it is left to the imagination of the listener to recognize the "Faust" theme, the conflict between restlessness and repose, between will and reason, between chaos and order — or whatever life may offer in the way of fundamental contradictions.

Gounod's FAUST. Far more comprehensible for the general public was the opera FAUST ("Marguerite") which Charles François Gounod composed in 1859. Based on a libretto by Barbier and Carré, this opera restricted itself to the tragedy of Gretchen and thus revealed its direct dependence on Goethe's poem. Through its charm of melody, the striking effect of its arias and other musical "numbers," Gounod's opera has enjoyed undiminished popularity. Besides, it has been the main source of popular acquaintance with the Faust theme. Although its subject matter reflects a social situation of the 18th century, the opera expresses a human element of tragic sympathy, of sentimentality, and even of moderate irony and thus has achieved a difficult task: it has made Faust acceptable to the bourgeois world.

4. Faust in modern times

Gounod's Faust represents a significant milestone in the reception of Goethe's Faust: it was the last time that the *subject matter* of Goethe's poem proved stimulating and productive to other creative artists. During the century thereafter the influence of the poem became less obvious and direct, but by no means less effective. In fact, the more the influence of Faust proceeded "below the surface" of popular attention, the more subtle, the more urgent, and the more inescapable it seems to have become. It is true that since Gounod there have been innumerable "Faust" publications in literature, music, the arts, and especially in the fields of philology and criticism. This indicates not merely an increase in popularity of the subject matter; it also reflects an enormous effort to comprehend and expound the "spirit" of Goethe's work — particularly in a cultural situation which seemed hostile to the message which Goethe was believed to have put into his Faust.

A striking example is the opera Mefistofele of the Italian composer Arrigo Boito (1868), who by the choice of his title seemed to indicate that it was the daemonic element rather than the Faust problem as such that had inspired his subtle and effective music. Nevertheless, he borrowed extensively from Goethe's Faust: in nine terse scenes he touched not only on the Gretchen and the Helena adventures, but on the Witch's Kitchen and the Northern and Classical Walpurgis Nights as well; even the "Prologue in Heaven" and the rescue of Faust's soul through the Heavenly "Phalanxes" are included. Thus his work presents a Faust figure wavering between earthly and heavenly love.

Faust *and 19th-century materialism.* The modern acceptance of a materialistic mode of living, the general spread of a pragmatic view of things, the keen skepticism toward all "ideologies," the necessary and desirable promotion of technological, social, and communal "progress" — these seemed to have little in common with a work of literary art which, on the whole, is occupied with "esoteric" problems. And yet, to their mutual benefit, the poem could very well be fitted into, and indeed dignify, a philosophy of material expansion and progress.

There were interpreters of Faust who, in cheerful optimism, could look past the more obscure passages of Faust's suffering and limitations, and recognize the poem as an unreserved praise of progress — "ein Weiterschreiten" from self-centered motives to humanitarian principles.

Particularly in Germany, after the Franco-Prussian War of 1870–1871 and the establishment of a flourishing German Reich, the real problems in life seemed to lie in a sphere different from that of an individual scholar in search of truth. Now the building of machines and factories, the founding of a colonial empire, the expansion of business, coupled with the ever-present question of how to attain and to retain public prosperity and security, demanded ever-alert activity and practical competence. Perhaps such activity was poetically envisaged in Act V of FAUST; if it was, that activity had now to become part of a community program rather than be left to the chance of personal initiative. Such a demand could be satisfied by the establishment of technical schools and colleges and commercially oriented laboratories. The Germany of the late 19th and the early 20th centuries could boast of two outstanding features: the advance of the physical sciences and the emergence of a thoroughly organized school system in which scarcely any field of knowledge was neglected. It is in these two areas that we must look for traces that might reveal a more than superficial reception of FAUST.

FAUST *and 19th-century science.* We have seen that Goethe's scientific interests had a philosophical bias, in that he concentrated on the totality of an organism and its functioning, rather than on analyzing the organism. His ideas of "Werden" and of "Steigerung" brought an intuitive factor into the process of observation which was not seriously objected to by the scientists of his own age, many of whom proceeded along similar lines. Among Goethe's friends were Alexander von Humboldt, natural historian and traveler in the New World, whose KOSMOS (1848) represented a harmonious blending of observation and intuition, and Carl Gustav Carus, anatomist, physiologist, and psychologist, who was also a skillful and sympathetic interpreter of Goethe and his FAUST (BRIEFE ÜBER GOETHES *Faust,* 1835. — GOETHE. ZU DESSEN NÄHEREM VERSTÄNDNIS, 1843. — GOETHE UND SEINE BEDEUTUNG FÜR DIESE UND DIE KÜNFTIGE ZEIT, 1849).

What these men admired in Goethe's nature studies was the manner in which he had combined observation with the observer. In Goethe's view, it seemed, the natural sciences possessed a humanistic purpose: their findings revealed the wisdom of the finder.

In contrast to this view, only a strict detachment from subjective considerations could have achieved the specialization of modern science. A materialist scholar, Emil Dubois-Reymond (1882), drew a sharp dividing line between the objectives of science, as they served the purpose of accumulating a body of known facts, and man's ambition to control these facts. He rejected the results of Goethe's labors; but the implications of Goethe's methodology transcended Dubois-Reymond's judgment: these implications do not lie in the scientific field. When a physicist of the stature of Wilhelm von Helmholtz (1892) evaluated Goethe's contributions, he likewise rejected Goethe's findings; but he considered Goethe a "Vorahner kommender naturwissenschaftlicher Ideen" who had rendered a valuable service to theoretical science in his discovery of the ideal "type," the ideal pattern of the "Urphänomen." Yet he felt that Goethe had failed in his investigations where only consistently applied inductive method could have shown the way.

FAUST *and 19th-century history of literature.* Thus the real content of FAUST was left to a specialized science, literary history or, even more specifically, to "Goethe philology," which, in self-defense against the natural sciences, imitated the scientific method of empirical and detailed analysis and subjected Goethe's FAUST to a most minute scrutiny.

Now began the unearthing of the poem's historical, biographical, and literary "sources." The numerous splinters of the legendary Faust tradition were collected and compared. A search was undertaken through mystical and alchemistic literature, through philosophical works and theological tracts, through ancient and medieval poets — not merely to trace the origin of particular themes, images or words, but in the hope of determining the precise intellectual pattern in which this information was present in Goethe's mind when he wrote his poem.

Still, literary scholars could not ignore the factor of poetic imagination, which has its own laws outside the realm of cause and effect and analogy. Now different "schools" of interpretation developed which, by and large, could be grouped into two distinct camps: there were the "unitarians" who believed that the FAUST poem, in spite of many inconsistent details, has a fundamental "unity" of composition and idea — and there were the "anti-unitarians," the "fragmentists," who denied that there was any evidence of a fundamental "unity" in the poem, and contended that Goethe had used his FAUST as a receptacle of many profound and poetic ideas which, nevertheless, appear irrelevant to the Faust theme. There is no doubt that the historical and critical method cultivated by Wilhelm Scherer (1841–1886) showed the way again to the work of poetry itself, to that which Goethe himself had said and written. It was Scherer who first suspected that Goethe's first FAUST version must have been written in prose. Not until after Scherer's death was this hypothesis at least partially confirmed by Erich Schmidt's discovery of the URFAUST.

The numerous FAUST commentaries by Düntzer (1850), von Loeper (1870), Schröer (1881), Thomas (1892–1895), Minor (1901), Erich Schmidt (1903–1906), Witkowski (1906–1949), Traumann (1913), Trendelenburg (1919), Petsch (1926), and many others have made their indisputable contribution toward illuminating the mysteries of the poem for thousands of intelligent students who became influential citizens. Together with a host of Goethe biographies and countless critical studies, they have made available an immense fund of detailed information concerning the growth of the poem, its structure, and the imaginative resources of its author.

And still there are wide lacunae of obscurity left, where only the scholarship and the experience of coming generations of thoughtful readers may provide elucidation.

FAUST *and the 19th-century public.* Meanwhile, the general public had by no means overlooked the author of FAUST. Streets and schools in many German cities were named for the great "classic poet," whose works were alleged to be profound in wisdom, even if sometimes of doubtful morality. It was more significant that FAUST was presented at least every few years on any stage that cared for its reputation. The greatest public contribution, perhaps, was made by the many German publishers, scholars, and editors, who saw to it that not only every public library but almost every middle-class family could have its set of Goethe's works. The foundation of a Goethe Society in Weimar, the conversion into museums and archives of "Goethe" houses in Frankfurt and Weimar showed a public awareness of Goethe's share in shaping German thinking and civilization.

In the days before the first World War, the memory of Bismarck, founder of the German Reich (1871), was celebrated in students' torchlight parades and in speeches on the eve of the summer solstice. The memory of Goethe did not wholly fit into such surroundings; yet, when Goethe's name was sometimes mentioned, as one of those who were considered the "greatest" of the nation, it reflected a faint protest of *Geist* against *Macht.* The closing chorus of Richard Wagner's MEISTERSINGER VON NÜRNBERG (1862) — "Ehrt eure deutschen Meister!" — reminded the German "Bürger" that even if the "heil'ge Römische Reich" might dissolve, the "heil'ge deutsche Kunst" would survive. A similar sentiment was expressed by Richard Wagner when, in 1876, he was invited to compose a festival march commemorating the centennial of the American Declaration of Independence. Mingling national pride and cosmopolitan spirit, he inscribed on the title page of his PHILADELPHIA MARCH the words from FAUST:

> Nur der verdient sich Freiheit wie das Leben,
> der täglich sie erobern muß. (11 576)

Probably no hero-worshipping patriotic Goethe cult was possible on the basis of Goethe's works. In none of them — above all, not in FAUST — can there be found testimony for that harmonious personality that has often been attributed to Goethe. Quite the contrary: taken as a whole, Goethe's poetry reveals a constant struggle within himself — a struggle for objectivity and intellectual independence, a lifelong dissatisfaction with himself and with his achievements. It was the insight into these aspects of Goethe's personality which led to a renewed occupation with and rediscovery of FAUST.

5. FAUST RENAISSANCE

FAUST *revival.* The Romantic Movement, which swept the twenty-three year old Goethe into a frame of mind in which he became interested in the problems of Doctor Faustus, was still very much alive some 130 years later when a generation of young German writers discovered that the problems contained in Goethe's FAUST were not of merely historical or academic interest, but of vital importance. To them, FAUST was neither the property of philological specialists, nor the heritage of a stodgy bourgeoisie. A peculiar "vitalism" ran through German literature around the turn of the 19th and 20th centuries and for some decades thereafter. This vitalism, which was characteristic of the Youth Movement, found an outlet in the holiday exodus from crowded cities — and it expressed itself also in a new literary trend, first labelled "Neo-Romanticism," then "Expressionism."

It must be borne in mind that the neo-romantic vitalism did not arise merely in opposition to the advance of scientific knowledge or the growing mechanization of daily life. Often the agnostic, pantheistic creed, expressed by materialistic scientists themselves, was carried over into literature in the form of a confused "reverence for life" as such. The atheist teachings of the "Deutscher Monistenbund," called into existence by the Jena biologist Ernst Haeckel, were as thought-provoking as the spiritual consolation derived from Goethe's poem, "Prometheus." FAUST, too, was experienced by this generation in a manner comparable to Goethe's experience of Storm and Stress pantheism. Once again, youth looked for "Erlebnis," not "Wissen," and — like Faust — wanted to be "von allem Wissensqualm entladen"; once again it protested against the optimistic philosophy of material progress, as Goethe had protested against it when he satirized it in Famulus Wagner's words of contented pride: — "Und wie wir's dann zuletzt so herrlich weit gebracht."

In the literature of the early 20th century the observer finds the same terminology which once had been in vogue in Goethe's youth — "originality," "enjoyment of life," "totality," "creativeness." This was the language and the sentiment of FAUST, particularly that of Part I and of URFAUST. In the wake of such a revival of interest in FAUST, a new spirit of "activated" humanism began to spread against what was considered the over-mechanization of living. And just as Goethe had "discovered" the philosophy of Spinoza and interpreted it to suit his own purposes, the generation of the early 20th century "discovered" the philosophies of Schopenhauer (1788–1860) and of Nietzsche (1844–1900) and found that their interpretation of tragic heroism furnished a key to a new understanding of Goethe's FAUST.

Schopenhauer. In its systematic aspects, Schopenhauer's pessimism (as presented in his main work, DIE WELT ALS WILLE UND VORSTELLUNG, 1819), has little in common with Goethe's sanction and worship of life in any form. Sharing with Kant the assumption that *reality* is inaccessible to man, Schopenhauer maintained that the essence of the world is primeval *will*, unreasoning *impulse*. This "Will" manifests itself in nature and in man in various emotions and drives, which have only one aim: to exist, to be — even to the extent of annihilating any finite forces or forms which stand in the way of the self-realization of infinite "Will."

In the human world, the "Will" desires to exist forever — in the species; and yet, in order to realize this aim, it has to make — and break — the individual. Individuals come and go, teetering between desire and gratification; behind them, "Will" exerts its formidable power. Life would be unendurable if man were not endowed with the protective illusion of the "Idea" — in the form of reasoning, morals, science, religion, the arts — all of which afford him at least the illusion of security in a seemingly well-ordered universe. In this framework, life is a continuous, wholly irrational, process of suffering, relieved only occasionally by moments when pain is absent, when man has sought refuge behind the "veil" of the "idea."

Nietzsche. Schopenhauer's pessimism contains a peculiarly heroic justification of the individual who, although aware that he must die and be obliterated by absolute "Will," still wills his own existence in defiance of inescapable destruction. In this belief Schopenhauer found a successor in Nietzsche who, in his GEBURT DER TRAGÖDIE AUS DEM GEIST DER MUSIK (1871), interpreted the rise of the Greek tragedy as the heroic conquest of Art over Nature, of Idea over Will, or — to use Nietzsche's own terminology — of the "Apollinian" over the "Dionysian" element in man. At the moment in which man saw himself, as a tragic hero, succumbing to his fate, he acknowledged the nature of existence; and yet, in that aesthetic experience, he raised himself above existence, as an individual.

In Nietzsche's eyes, the "Dionysian" was the instinctive element in man, that unconscious will and unreasoning desire which are present in every human animal. The "Apollinian" on the other hand, was the element of reason and clarity, deliberation and consciousness, through which man distinguishes himself from other animals. Human civilizations are formed by the control which the Apollinian asserts over the forces of instinct and will, suppressing them, as if in a dreamlike spell. But there are moments when the "Dionysian" "remembers" its origin, when it breaks through the bondage and, forgetting *itself*, rejoins the "All," the Universal Will.

In his later writings, particularly in ALSO SPRACH ZARATHUSTRA (1883), Nietzsche revised his early pessimistic views into an unreserved affirmation of life. But then the figure of Zarathustra, the prophet of the Superman, became wholly ambiguous — at least insofar as the Faust problem is concerned. Zarathustra completely disavowed the existence of a transcendental world (which even Schopenhauer had admitted, as the realm of the Will) and became the daemon of "Will" which recognized no present but only a future, and considered man as "something that must be overcome."

The Superman whom Zarathustra envisages no longer feels "two souls in his breast," as Faust did. Dionysian *and* Apollinian, he lives in a world which does not "exist" but always "becomes" — a world of paradox in which reason is will, and instinct is the only power of contemplation. For the Superman is the being who is driven by the Will to exist, the Will to Power, and, at the same time, is driven by that Will to observe himself acting and experiencing.

There can be no doubt that Nietzsche's vitalism derived its inspiration from the fundamental problem of FAUST, as far as the concept of "Werden" and "Steigerung" is concerned. "Steigerung" is the underlying essence of Faust's experience. As a work of literature (or, as the Middle Ages would have called it, a "vision"), ZARATHUSTRA is the product of nihilism and despair. It reflects the experience of a completely dualistic world and the desire to overcome the dualism. Behind Zarathustra lies Nietzsche's experience of both the materialism of science and of the idealism of Christianity. Between these, Nietzsche finds himself in a desperate dilemma: he is attracted by both, but he cannot accept the one without refusing the other.

While Nietzsche decries science for its ignorance of an ultimate goal, he denounces Christianity as "fake ideology." Faust, in his unconditional and never satisfied search for truth, at least knew his limitations, his nature. Zarathustra knows no such limitations; and his "passion for knowledge" (*Leidenschaft der Erkenntnis*) is his Will to Power. That is why, for Zarathustra, his striving to be the Superman *must* be "right," dogmatic and uncompromising, whereas in FAUST we are told that man must strive, even though, striving, he errs. FAUST does not represent a philosophy of pure "daemonic" will, or a tragedy of man's ultimate defiance and desperation. Zarathustra is not a latter-day Faust, except as he has absorbed within himself both Faust and Mephistopheles — two principles which Goethe, wisely, kept separate. Indeed, if one had to trace the spiritual ancestry of his Zarathustra to any one of Goethe's characters, he would have to point to Prometheus, the lonely demigod who created men in his image because he had been forsaken by his gods.

As for Goethe's FAUST, Nietzsche rejected, violently and with an almost Mephistophelian rage, the final reception of Faust into Divine Grace. Perhaps Nietzsche was convinced that he had received a more profound inspiration from Mephistopheles, the Son of Chaos and Spirit of Negation, than from Faust, who is, after all, only one of the "langbeinige Zikaden." Ultimately, Nietzsche's longing for the future, his passion for "life," are outgrowths of his despair about the present. This is the background of his ironical nihilism, of his gift of clairvoyance. Why the modern age no longer has any ultimate values, why it cannot have them — these were the fundamental questions of Nietzsche's inquiry; and these questions made him one of the keenest, psychologically most alert, most *suspecting* observers of modern times.

Nietzsche's psychological analysis has left a lasting imprint on modern German literature. Scarcely a modern writer has been able to ignore him; three German Nobel Prize winners — Gerhart Hauptmann, Thomas Mann, Hermann Hesse — clearly bear the mark of Nietzsche's influence. Applying Nietzsche's pattern of analysis to FAUST was only reasonable: Was Faust not a "Dionysian" individual in his pangs of existence and his search for self-realization and "power"? And did he not also come under the spell of the "Apollinian" element in the contemplative scene "Wald und Höhle," in the timeless Arcadian idyll, and in the decisive dialogue with Dame Care? In many respects Nietzschean views have aided in discovering in Goethe's characters "human" sides which had been concealed by the worship of Goethe, the Olympian.

Spengler. In World War I, it has been reported, FAUST was among the most popular books German soldiers took with them to the trenches. It may be suspected that many of these soldiers read Goethe through Nietzsche's eyes.

Much the same may be said of a spectacular book which appeared at the end of that war and was discussed the world over — Oswald Spengler's philosophy of history, DER UNTERGANG DES ABENDLANDES (1918). Spengler conceived a *history of civilizations*, which, he said, was not blurred by the arbitrary, subjective (though traditional) division of history into "Ancient, Medieval, Modern." Instead, Spengler surveyed individual *cultures* as living things which run their life courses like plants: they come up, they mature, flourish, decline and die — and are replaced by other cultures.

In a *morphological* manner — derived from Goethe's nature studies — Spengler presented a thoroughly deterministic view of historical development, with some support from the pessimism of Schopenhauer: in spite of infinite individual variations, all cultures run a similar course; and when they have reached their greatest degree of self-realization, they can but prepare for their fall, and no precautions — frantic or deliberate — will avert it. While the anticipation of a decline of the western world indicated Spengler's indebtedness to Nietzsche's concept of decadence, it was Goethe's FAUST which induced Spengler to speak of western (occidental) civilization as governed by a dynamic will, a "Faustian soul" which, discovering limitless space, set out to "realize itself" in its arts, its sciences, its faiths — thus revealing its unconditional longing for life.

The reception of FAUST is as fascinating a chapter of intellectual history as the poem itself. Infinite are the variations in which the idea of striving and the experience of failure are interwoven. In 1919, when the constitution of the German Republic was being written in Weimar, the memory of Goethe and his FAUST was alive in every German mind. In the celebrations of 1949, commemorating the bicentennial of Goethe's birth, the question whether Faust was meant by Goethe as an exemplar or as a warning to his nation was often asked again, and the answers were as manifold as the philosophies of the interpreters.

In the history of the interpretation of FAUST, the demand for clarity has alternated with the surrender to allegory, as in Thomas Mann's DOKTOR FAUSTUS (1949), which subtly reasserted what Heinrich Heine had said a century earlier: "The German nation itself is that learned Doctor Faustus." Mann's keen psychological analysis of sickness, his probing into the mysteries of biological and intellectual heritages, suggest the spiritual heritage of Nietzsche. But in regard to its literary ancestry, Mann's novel represents a return to the medieval Doctor Faustus of the folk legend, who succumbed to his diabolical tempter, rather than a return to Goethe's Faust, for whom Mephistopheles is the Devil who spurs him on, in spite of himself, to "immer höhere und reinere Tätigkeit bis ans Ende."

FAUST is a human, not merely a German, problem. Writers of many nations have participated in the attempt to solve it, stressing the need and desire for ultimate faith in man. Active humanitarians, like Albert Schweitzer, and contemplative humanists, like Arnold J. Toynbee, have been inspired and challenged by Goethe's poem.

In his advanced age, when he had read Carlyle's attempt at popularizing Goethe's works, the poet remarked with gentle resignation:

Meine Sachen können nicht populär werden; wer daran denkt und dafür strebt, ist in einem Irrtum. Sie sind nicht für die Masse geschrieben, sondern nur für einzelne Menschen, die etwas Ähnliches wollen und suchen und die in ähnlichen Richtungen begriffen sind.

(*Conversation with Eckermann, October 11, 1828*)

Compared with this, the words which the Swiss historian Jacob Burckhardt (1818–1897) wrote to a young friend are more encouraging:

Irren Sie im FAUST herum! Die edelsten Geister haben alle diesen Weg gehen müssen, weil sie feste Wahrheiten suchten; das Gedicht neckte sie, zog sie dann tief in seine unter- und überirdischen Gänge hinein und hinterließ ihnen zuletzt gar keine *Wahrheiten,* aber einen geläuterten Trieb zur *Wahrheit,* — wie die Beschäftigung mit hohen geistigen Dingen ihn überhaupt hervorrufen soll.

VII. Rhythm and Rime

To deal exhaustively with the rhythmic patterns employed in FAUST would demand much more time and space than can profitably be given to such an undertaking in this book. Any interested student can begin a more comprehensive study by referring to the article "Rhythmus und Persönlichkeit in Goethes Faust" by Eduard Prokosch in the STUDIES IN HONOR OF ALEXANDER RUDOLPH HOHLFELD [= *Wisconsin Studies in Language and Literature*, Number 22, 1925].

RHYTHMIC UNITS

The essence of rhythm in German verse is the alternation of strongly stressed syllables with less strongly, or weakly, stressed (or, as we sometimes say, "unstressed") syllables. The rhythmic unit is the MEASURE, which consists of one heavily stressed syllable and the less heavily stressed syllable or syllables which "belong with" it. We may recognize the following simple units or measures:

iambic × −́ gezeigt
trochaic −́ × fühlet
anapestic × × −́ zu entstehn
dactylic −́ × × fürchtete
spondaic −́ −̀ Nachbar

CADENCE AND ANACRUSIS

Lines in the iambic or anapestic pattern may have what is called a *masculine* cadence, or they may have a *feminine* cadence. In a masculine cadence the line ends with the last stressed syllable; in a feminine cadence there is an "extra" unstressed syllable after the last stressed syllable. Thus:

33 Ihr beiden, die ihr mir so oft masculine cadence
× −́/× −́/× −́/ ×−́

34 in Not und Trübsal beigestanden, feminine cadence
× −́/ × −́/ × −́/ ×−́ ⁝ ×

Lines in the trochaic, dactylic, or choriambic pattern may have anacrusis. *Anacrusis* is the setting of an unstressed syllable (or sometimes two unstressed syllables) at the beginning of a line before a measure which begins with a stressed syllable. Thus:

12 070 Du Ohnegleiche, monosyllabic anacrusis
×⁝ −́ ×/−́ ×

1269 Denn er tat uns allen dissyllabic anacrusis
× ×⁝ −́ × /−́ ×

THE FAUST VERSE

While there is a great variety of rhythmic pattern and stanzaic structure in Goethe's FAUST, there is still a dominant verse type, which we may call, with Prokosch, the FAUST Verse. This is basically a four-beat iambic line with rime, in part regular and in part irregular (1) as to the number of unaccented syllables, or (2) as to the "inversion" of the first measure, or (3) as to *schwebende Betonung*, or (4) as to the introduction of anapests into the iambic pattern. Examples are:

355 Juristerei und Medizin normal line
× ´/ × ´/ × ´/ × ´

357 durchaus studiert, mit heißem Bemühn. irregular fourth measure
× ´ / × ´/ × ´/ × × ´

354 Habe nun, ach, Philosophie, inverted first measure
´ ×/ × ´ / × ´/ × ´

2028 Dann habt Ihr sie all' unterm Hut schwebende Betonung
` ´ /× ´/ × ´ /× ´

366 Zwar bin ich gescheiter als alle die Laffen, anapests for iambs and feminine cadence
× ´/ × × ´ / × × ´/× × ´ ⁝ ×

Variation of the line pattern in passages of this FAUST verse is accomplished most often by interspersing five-beat or six-beat iambic lines among the regular four-beat verses, while retaining the rime scheme. For example:

447 Wie alles sich zum Ganzen webt, normal FAUST verse
× ´/ × ´/ × ´/ × ´

448 eins in dem andern wirkt und lebt! inverted first measure
´ ×/ × ´ / × ´/ × ´

449 Wie Himmelskräfte auf und nieder steigen five-beat line with feminine cadence
× ´/ × ´/ × ´ / × ´/ × ´ ⁝ ×

450 und sich die goldnen Eimer reichen! normal FAUST verse with feminine cadence
× ´ / × ´ / × ´/ × ´ ⁝ ×

FIVE-BEAT IAMBIC LINES

There are at least two types of five-beat iambic lines in FAUST. The first is the rimed five-beat line, similar to the English "heroic verse" (commonly found in English in the heroic couplet). The second is the unrimed five-beat iambic line, commonly called "blank verse."

The rimed five-beat iambic line occurs either as a variation of the FAUST verse, as illustrated above (449), or in longer groups of lines. For example:

634 Dem Herrlichsten, was auch der Geist empfangen,
× ´ /× ´/ × ´ / × ´ /× ´ ⁝ ×

635 drängt immer fremd und fremder Stoff sich an;
× ´ /× ´ / × ´/ × ´/ × ´

636 wenn wir zum Guten dieser Welt gelangen,
× ´/ × ´/ × ´/× ´ / × ´ ⁝ ×

637 dann heißt das Bess're Trug und Wahn.
× ´/ × ´/ × ´ / × ´

The unrimed five-beat iambic line (*blank verse*) is not much used in FAUST, but it does occur prominently in the monologue of the scene *Wald und Höhle.* For example:

3217 Erhabner Geist, du gabst mir, gabst mir alles,
× ´/ × ´/ × ´/ × ´ / × ´⁝×

3218 warum ich bat. Du hast mir nicht umsonst
×´ /× ´ / × ´ / × ´ /× ´

3219 dein Angesicht im Feuer zugewendet.
× ´/ ×´/ × ´/× ´/× ´⁝×

SIX-BEAT IAMBIC LINES

The six-beat iambic lines of FAUST are of at least three types: the Alexandrine, the expanded FAUST verse, and the iambic trimeter.

The *Alexandrine* as used in FAUST differs from the expanded FAUST verse chiefly in the location of the *caesura* (pause) after the third beat. For example:

129 Ich sag' Euch: gebt nur mehr und immer, immer mehr
× ´/ × ´/ × ´ ‖ × ´ /× ´ / × ´

225 Was heute nicht geschieht, ist morgen nicht getan,
× ´/×´ / × ´ ‖ × ´/× ´ / ×´

The *expanded* FAUST *verse* may have a caesura after any but the third beat, or it may have no caesura. For example:

685 nur was der Augenblick erschafft, das kann er nützen.
` ´/ × ´/× ´ / × ´ ‖ ` ´ / × ´⁝×

769 und doch, an diesen Klang von Jugend auf gewöhnt,
× ´ ‖ × ´/× ´ / × ´/ × ´ /×´

773 da klang so ahnungsvoll des Glockentones Fülle,
× ´ / ×´ / × ´ / × ´/ × ´/ × ´⁝×

The *iambic trimeter* is a six-beat unrimed line with the caesura either after the fifth or after the seventh syllable. For example:

7017 des Nachbars Willen, eignem stolzen Sinn gemäß.
× ´/ ` ´/× ‖ ´/ × ´/× ´ / × ´

7020 der Freiheit holder, tausendblumiger Kranz zerreißt,
× ´/ ` ´ / × ‖ ´ /× ´ / ×× ´ / ×´

or

7012 Wie oft schon wiederholt' sich's! Wird sich immerfort
×´ / × ´/ × ´ /× ‖ ´ / × ´/ ×´

7013 ins Ewige wiederholen . . . Keiner gönnt das Reich
× ´/× ×´/ ×´ / × ‖ ´ /× ´ / × ´

Occasionally, as in 7013 and 8495, an iamb is replaced by an anapest.

8495 der Rückkehr samt den tapfersten seiner Krieger sich.
× ´ /× ´ / × ´/× × ´/× ´/×´

Rarely, a seven-beat iambic line is found among the trimeters. An example is line 10 039.

TROCHAIC LINES

Apart from occasional trochaic lines in the lyric and choral portions of FAUST, the use of the trochaic measure is largely confined to the second part of the poem. There are two major types of trochaic lines which require illustration, the four-beat trochaic dimeter (which is commonly rimed), and the eight-beat trochaic tetrameter.

Trochaic dimeter

7249 Rege dich, du Schilfgeflüster!
´ × / ´ × / ´ × / ´ ×

7250 Hauche leise, Rohrgeschwister,
´ × / ´ × / ´ × / ´ ×

7251 säuselt, leichte Weidensträuche,
´ × / ´ × / ´ × / ´ ×

7252 lispelt, Pappelzitterzweige,
´ × / ´ × / ´ × / ´ ×

Trochaic tetrameter

The *trochaic tetrameter* is an eight-beat trochaic line with the caesura usually after the fourth measure. Occasionally one of these lines is *catalectic* — that is, it lacks the final syllable of the last trochee, as in 9597 below.

9596 Allerdings, ihr Unerfahrnen! Das sind unerforschte Tiefen:
´ × / ´ × / ´ × / ´ × ‖ ´ × / ´ × / ´ × / ´ ×

9597 Saal an Sälen, Hof an Höfen, diese spürt' ich sinnend aus.
´ × / ´ × / ´ × / ´ × ‖ ´ × / ´ × / ´ × / ´ ∧

9598 Doch auf einmal ein Gelächter echot in den Höhlenräumen;
´ × / ´ × / ´ × / ´ × ‖ ´ × / ´ × / ´ × / ´ ×

LYRIC AND CHORAL VERSES

There are many lyric passages in FAUST and a considerable number of choral passages. We shall not attempt to present a systematic analysis of all of the verse and stanzaic patterns which can be found in these lines. It will suffice if the general principles are made clear. On the whole, these lyric lines are short lines. They may be iambic, or trochaic, or dactylic, or they may combine two of these forms. In addition, however, there are other forms which should not be resolved into iambs and trochees, because they represent imitations of classic measures, such as the choriambus.

Iambic measures

1609 die schöne Welt,
× ´ / × ´

2567 Die hohe Kraft
× ´ / × ´

Trochaic measures

12 069 Neige, neige,
´ ×/ ´ ×

12 070 du Ohnegleiche,
× ⁝ ´ × / ´ ×

Dactylic measures

738 Freude dem Sterblichen,
´ × × / ´ × ×

739 den die verderblichen,
´ × × / ´ × ×

740 schleichenden, erblichen
´ × × / ´ × ×

741 Mängel umwanden.
´ × × / ´ × ∧

Anapestic measures

9153 wie so sittig herab mit verweilendem Tritt
× × ´ / × × ´ / × × ´ / × × ´

9163 denn in ähnlichem Fall, da erfüllte der Mund
× × ´ / × × ´ / × × ´ / × × ´

With slight variation of the first measure:

9159 etwa des Haupts Lockhaar um die blendende Stirn,
× × × ´ / ` ´ / × × ´ / × × ´

Choriambic measures

9168 Stufen zum Thron,
´ × × ´

9169 Teppich und Sitz,
´ × × ´

With anacrusis:

9166 sie kommen daher;
× ⁝ ´ × × ´

9167 was tragen sie nur?
× ⁝ ´ × × ´

Verses with contiguous stresses

8883 Mißblickende, Mißredende du!
´ ` × × / ´ ` × × / ´

8887 Denn der Bösartige, wohltätig erscheinend,
× × ⁝ ´ ` × × / ´ ` × × / ´ ×

9083 unzugängliche Mauer.
´ ` ´ × × / ´ ×

FREE RHYTHMS

Passages written in free rhythms (*freie Rhythmen*) are characterized by the lack of uniformity of rhythmical pattern from line to line and by the variation in the length of the rhythmical periods used. Obviously, no set pattern of this irregularity can be cited in illustration of free rhythms, and opinion often varies as to how they should be analyzed metrically. However, good examples may be studied in lines 3438–3450, 3776–3834.

RIME

The peculiar function of *rime*, apart from its purely musical values, is that of binding lines together into larger units. This is accomplished by the repetition of identical (or strongly similar) sounds. Acoustically, the vowels are more prominent in rime than the consonants, but the consonants are important. If either the vowels or the consonants are not completely identical in a patterned repetition, we speak of *assonance* or *impure rime*. For example: *Gestalten : behalten* is an exact or pure rime; *spaße : Nase* is a case of assonance; *blöde : Rede* is an inexact or impure rime.

Rime is the feature on which the structure of larger units of several lines may be built. Such larger units are *strophes* or *stanzas* and there are many different kinds of them in FAUST. A convenient illustration is the *Zueignung*. This is composed of four stanzas, each of which is an *ottava rima* (the Italian term). In German this is called *die Stanze*. This is a group of eight rimed five-beat iambic lines, held together by the rime sequence which we describe as *abababcc* (see lines 1–8).

Another stanzaic form is the Italian *terza rima* (*die Terzine*). Here the rimes are arranged in sets of three and so made that the middle rime of one set becomes the initial rime of the next. This results in a continuous flow of verses, with a rime sequence *aba bcb cdc ded* . . . and so on indefinitely. An example is found in lines 4679–4727.

A native stanzaic form is the tripartite strophe of the German *Meistergesang*. This is composed of three groups of lines, the first two being usually very much alike, while the third is different in structure. The first two members are called the *Stollen* and *Gegenstollen* respectively and together make up the *Aufgesang*. The third group is called the *Abgesang*. An example is found in lines 4897–4916. Here there are two six-line groups (*Stollen* and *Gegenstollen*), followed by an eight-line *Abgesang*.

There are a number of peculiar features in Goethe's rime practice to which attention should be called. It is quite clear, for instance, that in his usage rounded front vowels are freely rimed with the corresponding unrounded ones: **ü** with **i**, **ö** with **e**, and the diphthong **eu** (**äu**) with **ei**. The lists we give are not intended to be exhaustive, but simply to illustrate what you may expect to find.

Rimes of **ü** with **ie**:

440–441	Zügen:liegen
620–621	genießen:büßen
669–671	Bügel:Riegel
842–844	geniert:führt
2869–2870	betrüben:lieben

Rimes of **ü** with **i**:

435–436	stillen:füllen
904–905	Blick:-glück
1267–1268	nützen:sitzen
3036–3038	müssen:wissen

Rimes of **ö** with **e** or **ä** (long):

811–812	gehn:schön
1587–1589	Seele:-höhle
1764–1765	blöde:Rede
1814–1815	höher:näher
2795–2796	gehören:wären
3052–3053	Ehren:betören
3946–3947	Dröhnen:Gähnen

Rimes of **ö** with **e** (short):

1395–1397	Schwelle:Hölle
2805–2806	Elemente:könnte
3422–3423	könnte:Sakramente

Rimes of **eu** or **äu** with **ei**:

1238–1239	teilen:Heulen
1595–1597	heuchelt:schmeichelt
1772–1773	greifen:häufen
2670–2671	Freuden:weiden
3900–3901	Mäuse:-weise
4026–4028	-gleichen:Sträuchen

For Goethe these were "pure" rimes; for modern readers they are "impure" because of the disparity between the vowel qualities of the two words thus linked together. It is best in reading Faust to use the modern German standard pronunciation, rather than to try to read the lines as they may have sounded to Goethe. This means that we treat such pairs as those cited above as "inexact" or "impure" rimes.

There are also some peculiarities as to the consonants in the rimes of Faust. These result mainly from Goethe's having rimed together consonants which (for modern readers) are *voiced* with consonants which are *voiceless*. In the case of **g** there is a further disparity for us in that a *stop* (**g**) is rimed with an *open* consonant (**ch**). For example:

Intervocalic **g** rimed with intervocalic **ch:**

449–450	steigen:reichen
730–731	reichen:zeigen
3463–3464	Tage:Sprache
3587–3588	neige:-reiche

Intervocalic **s** rimed with intervocalic **ß:**

699–700	hinausgewiesen:Füßen
710–712	aufzureißen:beweisen
2321–2322	spaße:Nase
4356–4358	diesen:schließen

Occasionally an intervocalic or a postconsonantal **d** is rimed with a **t.** In these cases, also, one does well to use the standard modern German pronunciation and to regard them as cases of assonance. For example:

1934–1935	-orten:geworden
3515–3516	schaden:raten
3902–3905	Heide:Geleite

VIII. The Three Stages of FAUST I

URFAUST (early 1770s) — FAUST: EIN FRAGMENT (1790) — FAUST: DER TRAGÖDIE ERSTER TEIL (1808)

URFAUST (EARLY 1770S)

1. Nacht. In einem hochgewölbten engen gothischen Zimmer (354–605) *

Faust, in a long soliloquy, reviews his career and his dissatisfaction with his present condition: his knowledge is incomplete, he has no confidence that his efforts as a teacher and scholar are helping mankind, he lacks both wealth and fame. Hence he has resorted to magic, as a possible road to real insight into the nature of the world — an insight which conventional scholarship has not given him. As he watches the moon rise, he feels the impulse to escape from his study. His books and scientific apparatus, arrayed row on row on dusty shelves, seem to imprison him in the bonds of professorial traditions; so he turns to a book of magical symbols and charms, which gives him a sense of intuitive understanding of the structure of the universe. When he turns from the symbol of the Macrocosm to that of the Spirit of the Earth, he is even more deeply affected; he pronounces the incantation of the Spirit of the Earth, and a terrifying apparition proclaims itself the ever-changing, everlasting weaver of God's gar-

* The line numbers refer to the corresponding material in the final version.

ment. Faust claims companionship with the Spirit, but is repulsed as too weak, too limited. The Spirit vanishes. A knock on the door announces Faust's famulus, Wagner. Wagner starts a conversation about oratory and rhetoric: Faust shows his contempt for mere technical tricks of oratory or the routine study of books as a substitute for sincerity, and at the same time warns against the danger of revealing one's true opinions to the prejudiced, narrow-minded, reactionary masses.

[606–1769 added in the final version; 1770–1867 added in FRAGMENT. See table, pages 162–163.]

2. Mephistoph. im Schlafrock, eine grose Perrücke auf. (1868–1881; 1896–1963; 2001–2050, and some lines not in the final version) [1882–1895; 1964–2000; 2051–2072 added in FRAGMENT]

Mephistopheles, disguised as Faust, advises an entering student. The lad is troubled by the bareness of the university buildings and the poverty he sees on all sides. For the time being, he has comfortable quarters at an inn, but Mephistopheles advises him to live in a student rooming house and eat what is set before him, forgetting his mother's good cooking. Next, the program of study is discussed. The student plans to study medicine. Mephistopheles satirizes the curriculum — the logic which does not teach one to think, the teachers who repeat the textbook slavishly and demand an echo of their lectures from the student. The medical course is not too difficult, he suggests, especially if one has a way with women patients. The student is dismissed with a motto: "You shall be as God, knowing good and evil."

[2051–2072 added in FRAGMENT]

3. Auerbachs Keller in Leipzig. (Chiefly prose; roughly equivalent to 2073–2336 of the final version)

A group of students are drinking, making jokes, playing pranks, and singing. Mephistopheles shows Faust how the students have fun, and promises Faust this kind of diversion every evening, if Faust enjoys it. They join the students, joke and drink with them. Mephistopheles sings "The Song of the Flea"; Faust performs a magic trick: — he bores holes in the table, from which wine flows into the students' glasses. The party becomes boisterous. A fight is about to break out when the students suspect Faust of being an agent of the Devil. Faust casts a spell upon them. He and Mephistopheles escape; when the students come to, one of them remembers seeing the strangers ride up the steps on a barrel. The students are nervous about returning home, and decide to get police protection.

4. Land Strase (four lines of verse, not used in later versions)

Faust and Mephistopheles pass a wayside cross. Mephistopheles hurries past, lowering his eyes. Faust asks him why; Mephistopheles admits it is only a prejudice, but says that a cross is obnoxious to him.

[2337–2604 added in FRAGMENT]

5. Strase (2605–2673; four additional lines not used in later versions)

Faust sees Gretchen on her way home from church, where she has confessed and been absolved from her sins. He tries to strike up an acquaintance, but she rebuffs him. Faust, much taken with her looks and liveliness, orders Mephistopheles to obtain Gretchen for him. Mephistopheles objects that the winning of a girl like Gretchen is difficult, even impossible. Faust insists, and threatens to break with Mephistopheles unless the girl is in his arms that very night. Mephistopheles agrees to take Faust to Gretchen's home during her absence, so that Faust can enjoy the sense of being, in a way, near her. Faust commands Mephistopheles to get a present for her; Mephistopheles, grumbling, leaves.

[2674–2677 added in FRAGMENT]

6. Abend. Ein kleines reinliches Zimmer (2678–2804)

Gretchen is braiding her hair. She wonders who the striking gentleman who spoke to her could have been. — After she leaves, Mephistopheles and Faust enter. Faust dismisses Mephistopheles and looks about him. The quiet neatness of the room fills him with an awareness of Gretchen's simple but admirable nature. The old furniture speaks to him of generations of devoted family love, of Gretchen's infancy and childhood. Suddenly Faust is ashamed of the heedless selfishness of his passion. To Mephistopheles, returning, Faust declares that he will never come back to this room. But Mephistopheles insists that Faust leave a jewel casket for Gretchen. Faust is reluctant; but Mephistopheles puts the casket in a wardrobe and leads Faust away, just before Gretchen enters. — She notices an oppressive, heavy atmosphere in the room; but she controls her fears and sings the song about "The King in Thule" — a song of love faithful unto death. As she opens the wardrobe, she sees the unfamiliar jewel casket. Curious, she opens it, and is amazed at the jewelry. She arrays herself in it, before the mirror, with mingled pleasure in the finery and regret that it is not hers — beauty without wealth is not enough!

7. Allee (2805–2864 — called "*Spaziergang*" in later versions)

Mephistopheles is cursing furiously. He tells Faust what has happened to the jewels they left in Gretchen's room: Gretchen's mother had insisted on asking the priest's advice about keeping the jewels. The priest commended her caution and appropriated the jewels for the church, promising the women a reward in heaven. Mephistopheles reports that Gretchen is more than a little disappointed at losing the jewels, and filled with curiosity about the giver. — Faust orders Mephistopheles to get some more, and finer, jewels; Mephistopheles grumbles but must obey.

8. Nachbaarinn Haus (2865–3024)

Mrs. Marthe Schwerdlein is wondering where her wandering husband is, whether he is perhaps dead — and she without a death certificate for him! — Gretchen enters, with a jewel box, even finer than the first, she says. Marthe warns her not to say anything about it to her mother. Gretchen puts on this new jewelry; she and Marthe are admiring it when there is a knock at the door. Mephistopheles enters, asks for Frau Marthe Schwerdlein, offers to withdraw in the pretended belief that Gretchen is an aristocratic young lady whose conversation with Marthe must not be interrupted. Gretchen modestly explains that the jewels are not hers. Mephistopheles, after complimenting Gretchen, proceeds with his business with Marthe: he has to tell her that her husband is dead and buried in Padua. Marthe is overcome, and angry at the fact that not even a penny had been sent to her. As Marthe weeps, Mephistopheles flatters Gretchen as deserving to be a bride, or the sweetheart of some dashing young fellow. To Marthe, Mephistopheles then gives a plausible account of the last days of Schwerdlein, delicately revealing a career of piracy and sin and misfortune. Marthe is both angry and sad; but when Mephistopheles suggests that she should look to the future and plan to remarry, her reaction is so swift and positive as to alarm him. He prepares to leave. Marthe asks Mephistopheles to testify to her husband's death, so that she may have a death certificate in proper legal form. Mephistopheles points out that two witnesses are required, and offers to bring a friend as second witness, suggesting that Gretchen be present at the interview. The appointment is made for that evening, in Marthe's garden, back of the house.

9. ——— (3025–3072 — called "*Straße*" in later versions)

Faust is impatiently waiting to hear Mephistopheles' report on his exploratory visit. Mephistopheles is optimistic; Marthe, he says, is the perfect go-between. He tells Faust of the little service that must be performed: swearing to Schwerdlein's death. Faust refuses to commit perjury. Mephistopheles ridicules this scruple. As a professor, he says, Faust had dogmatized about things he didn't really know; and as a lover Faust will deceitfully swear eternal fidelity to Gretchen. Faust insists that his protestations to Gretchen will be sincere, will be true expressions of overpowering emotion. Mephistopheles is not impressed; and Faust, somewhat deflated, agrees to lie about Schwerdlein's death, as a necessary step to obtaining Gretchen.

10. Garten (3073–3204)

The two couples, Faust and Gretchen, Mephistopheles and Marthe, are walking in Marthe's garden. They cross the stage alternately, one speaking while the other is unheard, deeper in the garden. Gretchen and Faust cross the stage first. Gretchen is apologetic about her lack of education; Faust flatters her. — As Gretchen and Faust withdraw, Mephistopheles and Marthe come forward. Marthe warns Mephistopheles of the disadvantages of a bachelor's life; Mephistopheles seems to be impressed. They withdraw. — Faust and Gretchen come forward. Faust is explaining the superiority of unaffected naturalness over mere external sophistication, and he asks Gretchen about her home life. Gretchen describes her simple domestic duties: she lives alone with her widowed mother; they have no maid; her brother is a soldier and away from home; her little sister is dead. Gretchen tells in some detail how she had to care for the child when the mother had been near death. Faust almost envies her the happiness she had with the child; she points out that there were hours of discouragement and weariness to be remembered, too. — As they withdraw, Marthe and Mephistopheles come forward. Marthe is encouraging Mephistopheles to display an interest in matrimony; Mephistopheles deftly avoids giving any direct answer. — They withdraw, and Faust and Gretchen come forward again. Faust asks Gretchen whether she recognized him as the man who had spoken to her as she left the church. She admits that she had, and tells him of her confusion at that time — concern that she might have behaved indecorously so as to provoke such attention, and yet an almost instinctive liking for Faust at first sight. She takes a flower and plucks its petals: "He loves me — loves me not — loves me — loves me not — — He loves me!" Faust seizes her hands and declares that love such as his must be eternal; Gretchen returns the pressure of his hands, then flees to a little gardenhouse. Faust hesitates a moment, then follows her. — Marthe and Mephistopheles return. It is getting dark, and Mephistopheles plans to depart. Marthe agrees that it is time, since her neighbors are likely to gossip.

11. Ein Gartenhäusgen (3205–3216)

Faust finds Gretchen in the gardenhouse and kisses her. As Gretchen exclaims: "Schon lange lieb' ich dich," there is a knock at the door. Mephistopheles and Marthe point out that it is time for the gentlemen to leave. Gretchen refuses Faust's offer to escort her home, since her mother would disapprove. After Faust and Mephistopheles leave, Gretchen muses wonderingly at Faust's interest in her, an ignorant small-town girl. [3217–3373 added in FRAGMENT, incorporating URFAUST scene 18]

12. Gretgens Stube (3374–3413)

Gretchen, alone, spinning, sings of her lost peace of mind, of her misery when she is not with Faust, her longing to see him, to hear his voice, to kiss him.

13. Marthens Garten (3414–3543)

Gretchen is worried about Faust's religious belief. He protests that he is kindly and tolerant, and respects the sacraments. He says that his reverence for God is immediate and emotional, not formal: he worships the Creator and Sustainer of the Universe, the God of Love; the emotion, not the name, is important. Gretchen does not quite understand what Faust is telling her, and she is still uneasy about his soul's salvation. Also, she feels intuitively that Faust's companion is an evil influence. Faust evades her implied questions about his relationship with Mephistopheles, and asks Gretchen to arrange an opportunity for him to visit her. She points out that her mother is a light sleeper, and would certainly discover them. Faust gives her a soporific to give to her mother; Gretchen, after some hesitation, accepts it. — As Gretchen leaves, Mephistopheles appears and taunts Faust for submitting docilely to Gretchen's catechizing. Mephistopheles observes that women are interested in their men's orthodoxy, believing that conformity in religion indicates a willingness to submit to a wife's control. Faust protests, and denounces Mephistopheles as incapable of understanding Gretchen's sincere concern for the soul of her beloved. Mephistopheles sneers at Gretchen's insight into his own peculiar nature and asks Faust: "And tonight?" adding that he has his own pleasure too in Faust's deception of Gretchen.

14. Am Brunnen (3544–3586)

At the well, Gretchen and Lieschen (a neighbor girl) are filling their pitchers. Lieschen is delightedly gossiping about another girl, Barbara, who has become pregnant, and whose lover has left town. Lieschen anticipates with malicious satisfaction the public penance Barbara will have to perform; and if the lover should return and marry her, the other young people will make a mockery of the wedding. As Gretchen goes home, she reflects sadly that she, too, was once ready to censure — and now she is herself vulnerable to just such blame. But the impulses which led her to her present condition were in themselves so good, so dear to her!

15. Zwinger (3587–3619)

Gretchen fills some vases at a nearby well, puts fresh flowers into them, and presents them to a statue of the Sorrowing Virgin in a wall niche. Gretchen prays for rescue from the shame and death, which, in her lonely despair, she sees looming before her.

[3620–3645, in the final version, were moved forward from scene 17 of URFAUST; 3646–3649 were added in the final version; 3650–3659 were moved forward from scene 18 of URFAUST; 3660–3775 were added in the final version.]

16. Dom. Exequien der Mutter Gretgens (3776–3834)

Gretchen is surrounded by her relatives — and, behind her, the Evil Spirit of her despairing conscience. The Evil Spirit reproaches Gretchen with the difference between *Then* and *Now* — once she had grasped the prayerbook with childlike faith; today she is praying for the soul of her mother, sent in her drugged sleep to long torment; today there is a terrifying something beneath her heart, growing and tormenting her with thoughts of a birth marked for disgrace. As the Chorus sings the grim hymn, "The Day of Wrath," the Evil Spirit interprets and applies the portentous menace of the hymn to Gretchen's own state of sin. Gretchen, distracted and terrified, faints.

17. Nacht. Vor Gretgens Haus (3620–3645; in the final version, this monologue was moved forward, to begin the scene "*Nacht. Straße vor Gretchens Türe,*" which, in FAUST I, precedes the scene "*Dom*")

Valentin, Gretchen's brother, a soldier, is bitterly contrasting the *Then* and *Now*. Once Gretchen had been the undisputed epitome of a girl's excellence, recognized as such even by Valentin's rough comrades. Today, no one need conceal pity for Valentin and contempt for his fallen sister. And the worst of it is that Valentin can smash their heads together, but he can't honestly call them liars.

18. ——— (3650–3659, omitted in FRAGMENT, but incorporated in the final version as part of the scene "*Nacht. Straße vor Gretchens Türe*"; 3342–3369, incorporated in FRAGMENT as part of the scene "*Wald und Höhle*")

(3650–3659) Faust and Mephistopheles appear. Faust is depressed; the gleam of light from a nearby church window, faintly shining and lost in the shadows, is a picture of his mood. Mephistopheles, on the other hand, feels wonderful, like a lustful tomcat. — (3342–3369) Faust, on his way to Gretchen, is still unable to feel the appropriate sentiments. He knows that the delights of Gretchen's embrace cannot blunt his awareness of being a destructive force in her life, like an Alpine torrent that undermines a peaceful cottage. Mephistopheles is impatiently reproachful of these scruples. "Go and make her happy, you fool," he tells Faust.

[3660–3775 and 3835–4398 were added in the final version; 3776–3834 = scene "*Dom*"]

19. ——— (prose; *Trüber Tag* 1–66)

Some time has passed. Faust has just discovered what has happened to Gretchen: she has borne a child, and in her despair and shame she has drowned it. She has been captured, sentenced to death, and is now in prison awaiting her execution. Faust is hysterical in his denunciations of Mephistopheles for concealing these tragic events. Mephistopheles is coldly realistic: Gretchen is not the first girl in world history to find herself in trouble; and who is responsible, Mephistopheles or Faust? Faust demands that Mephistopheles liberate Gretchen; but Mephistopheles says he has no power to interfere with verdicts of murder. What he can do, he will do — take Faust to the prison, and let Faust free her with human hands after the jailer has been put to sleep by Mephistopheles.

20. Nacht. Offen Feld (4399–4404)

As Faust and Mephistopheles rush along on black horses past an execution place, they see dim figures moving weirdly about the platform.

21. Kercker (prose; 4405–4612, except that here there is nothing corresponding to 4611 b)

Faust is unlocking the prison gate when he hears Gretchen within, singing a mad song. When he enters, Gretchen mistakes him for the executioner; she begs for a little more time; she begs to be allowed to nurse her child once more. Faust in anguish calls her name; she recognizes the voice. Faust entreats her to escape with him; but she insists on holding and kissing him. Then she thinks of the horror of the past year: she is responsible for her mother's death, she has killed her child. And Faust's hand seems to her to be wet with blood! As Faust repeats his pleas, she again refuses to leave the prison. — *They* are waiting outside for her, she says; but Faust must go and save their child; perhaps it is still alive in the pool where she had thrown it. Gretchen imagines that she and Faust are going up the path together, and that the way is barred by her mother, dazedly shaking her head slowly. — Dawn is growing gray in the east. Faust makes a last plea. But Gretchen's confused mind is focused on her execution: she imagines it step by step, up to the moment of sudden silence when the axe falls. Mephistopheles bursts in. Gretchen feels new horror at the sight of him. She calls on the angels to protect her, for now she feels horror at Faust, too. Mephistopheles drags Faust away, dismissing Gretchen with "She has been judged." As Faust vanishes, a reverberating cry "Heinrich! Heinrich!" is heard from the cell.

Faust: Ein Fragment (1790)

1. Nacht: 354–605

(= Urfaust 1. Faust's soliloquy — The Spirit of the Earth — The conversation with Wagner.)

[606–1769 added in final version of 1808]

2. ———: 1770–2072

(= The student scene from Urfaust 2, with about a hundred lines of introductory conversation between Faust and Mephistopheles, and with considerable modification of the interview between Mephistopheles and the student.)

(1770–1867) Faust and Mephistopheles are talking. Faust explains that he desires to encompass all the extremes of all human experiences. Mephistopheles objects that the limitations of a human being forbid such universality, and that human activities are so contradictory that it is a logical, as well as a practical, impossibility to participate in all human experiences. Instead, Mephistopheles urges Faust to make the most of the resources within the reach of an individual, and give up fruitless speculations and desires. The first step, says Mephistopheles, is to get out of the professorial study and find something better to do than teach half-truths to uninterested students. At that moment, a student is heard approaching Professor Faust's study. Faust does not want to see the lad; Mephistopheles puts on Faust's academic robe and prepares to play the role of a professor. As Faust leaves, Mephistopheles soliloquizes: Let Faust turn his back upon knowledge, and he must fall into the Devil's clutches; Faust's innate drive for ever more experience gives Mephistopheles (he thinks) the opportunity to take him through excitement and boredom until unsatisfied, insatiable longings drive him to disaster. — (1868–2050) The student enters, and Mephistopheles gives him advice. (The discussion of rooming and boarding facilities, in the Urfaust, is omitted.) Mephistopheles satirizes the required courses in logic and metaphysics. Then they discuss the choice of a field of concentration. The student has no desire to study law; and Mephistopheles agrees that law and justice are not synonymous. Theology is depicted as a hazardous undertaking, full of the peril of subtle heresy. But medicine is recommended, especially if one has a way with the women. The student is dismissed with the motto: "You shall be as God, knowing good and evil." — (2051–2072) Faust returns after the student leaves. Mephistopheles outlines their program: first the little, then the great world. Faust distrusts his ability to adjust to ordinary human society, but Mephistopheles reassures him. Mephistopheles' magic cloak is ready to take them into a new career for Faust.

3. Auerbachs Keller in Leipzig: 2073–2336

(Roughly = Urfaust 3; but now in verse throughout, and it is Mephistopheles, not Faust, who performs the showy tricks. — The drunken students — The magic tricks.)

4. Hexenküche: 2337–2604

The scene is a grotesque, quasi-alchemistic laboratory. The witch's household pets are a family of apes. Faust is revolted at the tasteless hocus-pocus. But Mephistopheles and the apes enjoy an idiotic conversation, with overtones of satire of human follies. Meanwhile, Faust is looking at a magic mirror, in which he sees the image of a supremely beautiful woman; Mephistopheles promises to find him a sweetheart equal to that image. The witch descends through the chimney. Mephistopheles quickly establishes his identity, and his authority; and he and the witch converse, somewhat at length and somewhat improperly, before he explains his mission: Faust is to be given a rejuvenating drink. The witch obeys; she prepares the drink, she recites a ritual of wild illogic. Faust drinks. Mephistopheles insists on Faust's leaving at once, despite Faust's desire to look once more into the mirror. Mephistopheles predicts that with the drink of youth in him, Faust will be able to see Helen of Troy in every woman.

5. Straße: 2605–2677

(= Urfaust 5. Faust accosts Gretchen; Faust orders Mephistopheles to obtain her. As a first step, Faust asks Mephistopheles to get a present for Gretchen. Mephistopheles approves this approach.)

6. Abend: 2678–2804

(= Urfaust 6. Faust in Gretchen's room — The jewel casket — "The King in Thule" — Gretchen finds the casket.)

7. Spatziergang: 2805–2864

(= Urfaust 7, Allee. Mephistopheles reports that the priest has Gretchen's jewels.)

8. Der Nachbarinn Haus: 2865–3024

(= Urfaust 8. Mephistopheles calls on Marthe, reports the death of her husband, and arranges to bring Faust to testify to Schwerdlein's death.)

9. Straße: 3025–3072

(= Urfaust 9. Mephistopheles reports to Faust, who is reluctant to commit perjury, but finally agrees.)

10. Garten: 3073–3204

(= Urfaust 10. The Faust-Gretchen and Mephistopheles-Marthe conversations.)

11. Ein Gartenhäuschen: 3205–3216

(= URFAUST 11, except that Gretchen now says "Von Herzen lieb' ich dich!" — Gretchen confesses her love. Faust and Mephistopheles leave.)

12. Grethchens Stube: 3374–3413

(= URFAUST 12. Gretchen at the spinning wheel, singing.)

13. Marthens Garten: 3414–3543

(= URFAUST 13. The discussion of religion — The soporific, and the appointment for that night — Mephistopheles' cynicism.)

14. Am Brunnen: 3544–3586

(= URFAUST 14. Lieschen tells Gretchen about Barbara's disgrace.)

15. Wald und Höhle: 3217–3373 (3342–3369 from URFAUST 18)

[In FRAGMENT, scene "*Wald und Höhle*" comes between "*Am Brunnen*" and "*Zwinger.*" In the final version, it was moved forward to a position between "*Ein Gartenhäuschen*" and "*Gretchens Stube.*"]

Faust has withdrawn to a forest wilderness, where he reviews his relationships with Mephistopheles and with Gretchen. He has gained a new insight into Nature and humanity; but he has been chained to a devil who debases his aspirations and drives him from one indulgence to another. Mephistopheles appears and fears that Faust has reverted to professorial theorizing. Such flights of fancy, he tells Faust, had once brought the professor close to suicide, and only Mephistopheles' services had prevented Faust's killing himself in despair. He scoffs at Faust's philosophical speculations, and incites him to return to Gretchen, telling Faust of Gretchen's misery because of his absence, conjuring up the picture of Gretchen's appealing beauty, scolding Faust as a heartless fool for refusing the girl the love she yearns for. Faust is bitterly self-reproachful about the destruction of Gretchen's peace that he has caused. Mephistopheles is coldly cynical: Gretchen wants comfort, and Faust can comfort her.

16. Zwinger: 3587–3619

(= URFAUST 15. Gretchen prays to the Sorrowing Virgin, and puts flowers before the wall-niche statue.)

[URFAUST scenes 17 and 18 — Valentin's soliloquy and the conversation between Faust and Mephistopheles — are omitted in FRAGMENT.]

17. Dom. Amt, Orgel und Gesang: 3776–3834

(= URFAUST 16. Gretchen and the Evil Spirit — "The Day of Wrath" — Gretchen faints.)

[The following parts of URFAUST are omitted in FRAGMENT: 17. *Nacht. Vor Gretgens Haus;* 19. *Trüber Tag;* 20. *Nacht. Offen Feld;* 21. *Kercker.* Lines 3835–4398 were added in the final version.]

Faust: Der Tragödie erster Teil
(final version, 1808)

Zueignung 1–32

The poet returns to the Faust theme somewhat reluctantly. The friends of his early twenties are far away; some of them are dead. The attraction of the subject is stronger as it has been so long put aside; the figures of the story and the words of his poem come to him dimly and like the sound of an Aeolian harp. Deeply moved, the poet's stern heart is softened, the present recedes from his view, and he is once more amid the images of the vanished past.

1. Vorspiel auf dem Theater 33–242

Three interested persons — the business manager, the author, the comedian — meet on the afternoon of the day when a new play, Faust, is to be presented to an audience which is already clamoring for tickets. (The play is not yet written!) The manager emphasizes the necessity of presenting something interesting, but still not trivial. The author insists on perfection of form and genuineness of emotion. The comedian insists on an admixture of fun in the final product, where reason, common sense, sentiment, and emotion also play their parts. The author is reluctant to debase his ethereal visions to fit the comprehension of the crowd. But the director and the comedian placate and bully him into producing a play which can make some of the poet's inspiration understandable to the ordinary spectator, using the devices of sensationalism, variety, human interest, and all the resources of the stage.

2. Prolog im Himmel 243–353

The Archangels Raphael, Gabriel, and Michael exalt the splendors of the Lord's Creation. Mephistopheles deplores the plight of mankind. Faust, described by the Lord as His servant, is taken as an example of humanity: Mephistopheles is confident that he can lead Faust away from the Lord's service; and the Lord defies Mephistopheles to divert Faust or any honest human soul from its striving, which is God's will for man. — The Lord instructs the loyal angels to rejoice in the beauty of the Cosmos, which is visible despite, and because of, continual change.

3. Nacht 354–807

(354–605 = Fragment 1, Urfaust 1: Faust's soliloquy — The Spirit of the Earth — The conversation with Wagner.)

(606–807) Faust relapses into despair, now intensified by the realization that the Spirit of the Earth is beyond his powers to understand. Neither a comprehension of nature nor the attainment of happiness seems possible; he resolves on suicide. As he lifts the poison to his lips, the sound of

Easter morning bells and choruses restrains him. Although he has lost faith in the message proclaimed by the bells and songs, the memory of a religious childhood overcomes the impulse of suicide.

4. Vor dem Tor 808–1177

It is Easter afternoon; outside the city walls, various groups of citizens are enjoying the spring sunshine. Apprentices, housemaids, students, taxpayers, a beggar, a fortuneteller, girls of middle-class families, soldiers — each group passes across the stage. Faust and Wagner stroll along; Faust comments gravely on the universal awakening of nature and mankind. They pass by a group of peasants, dancing and singing. An old peasant offers Faust a drink, recalling the services of Faust and his father in a time of pestilence. Faust thanks him; he and Wagner move on. Faust tells Wagner bitterly of the self-reproach he felt at the peasant's praise and gratitude; Faust now knows that the alchemistic medicine he and his father had given the sufferers was worse than the disease itself. Wagner tries to comfort him with the reflection that every generation makes its contribution to progress. Faust turns momentarily from his gloomy thoughts to contemplate the sunset. The thought of the sun's receding from his sight to bring another day elsewhere stirs in him the desire to soar high above the earth, westward, following the sun. One part of Faust's nature binds him to the comforts and rewards of common-sense accomplishment; the other yearns for transcendent adventure. Faust wishes that whatever superhuman spirits there may be should descend and carry him off to a new and exciting life in another realm. Wagner warns Faust against invoking the wily powers of the spirit world. As they return home, they notice a black poodle running in ever-narrowing circles around them. Faust thinks he sees a phosphorescence in the dog's wake; but when the poodle comes close, Faust agrees with Wagner that it is a quite ordinary dog. The poodle accompanies them back through the city gate.

5. Studierzimmer (I) 1178–1529

Faust enters his study, accompanied by the poodle. As Faust prepares to spend an evening of reading and study, the dog becomes restless. When Faust starts to translate the Gospel, the dog howls. Faust orders it to leave his study. But the dog assumes one queer shape after another; at last, after Faust has recited a series of increasingly potent charms, the room fills with a cloud of mist, and a spirit in the form of a medieval itinerant student steps forth. It is Mephistopheles. He identifies himself variously as a part of the spirit who always works for evil and always accomplishes good, the spirit of negation, at home in sin and destruction, the enemy of light and organic order of any sort. He is a son of Chaos and hopes to see the world reduced once more to chaos. When Faust tries to continue the discussion on an intellectual level, Mephistopheles asks to be excused, promising to return later. Faust is puzzled: if Mephistopheles wishes to leave, why doesn't he go? Mephistopheles explains that a magic symbol on Faust's threshold is holding him captive: a five-pointed star, imperfectly drawn, has a small opening that let him get in, but none to allow him to escape. Faust draws the inference that even the devils must obey some laws and live up to some contracts. Mephistopheles accepts the suggestion of an agreement between himself and Faust, but begs to be allowed to depart now, promising to return soon. Faust does not consent to let him go; so Mephistopheles summons his minions to beguile Faust with a song. They lull Faust in kaleidoscopic visions of beauty. Faust falls asleep; Mephistopheles summons a rat to gnaw through the restraining point of the star, and escapes. Faust, awakening, realizes that he has been disappointed once again.

6. Studierzimmer (II) 1530–2072

Faust is in his study; Mephistopheles knocks and enters; they converse. Mephistopheles is dressed as a cavalier and urges Faust to dress similarly and begin to live. Faust rejects any easy remedy for his sadness: he is too old for games, too young for resignation. Life seems to have only one answer to his strivings: "You must do without!" By day he has to face disappointments; at night he is plagued by bad dreams. Within him there is a force which rules him and moves him to mighty desires; but this force lacks power to affect the outside world so as to gratify those desires. Life, therefore, is a burden; death would be a boon. After Mephistopheles has teased him with a reference to Faust's once having rejected suicide, Faust passionately curses the impulses which held him back from self-destruction, which delude mankind into senselessly continuing a pointless existence: he curses intellectual ambition, aesthetic enjoyment, fame and wealth, wine, love, hope, faith, and — above all — patience. A chorus of spirits sings a dirge for this world of values which Faust is destroying; they urge Faust to rebuild a finer world for himself. Mephistopheles urges Faust to abandon his fruitless melancholy and associate with people. Mephistopheles offers to serve Faust in this world; Faust can repay him with service in the next world. Faust is not interested: he is not concerned about what may happen in any future life, but he simply doesn't believe that Mephistopheles has power to satisfy Faust's desires on this earth. Instead, Faust offers a wager: If Mephistopheles can do what he claims — satisfy Faust's human longings — then Faust will acknowledge himself beaten, will be willing to die, and accept as unimportant whatever consequences there may be in a future life. The test case shall be this: If Mephistopheles can so completely satisfy Faust that Faust wishes the moment of satisfaction to last forever, then Faust loses. Mephistopheles accepts this wager; Faust attests it by signing a document with his own blood. He assures Mephistopheles of good faith, for his greatest desire is to achieve just the complete satisfaction which will cause Mephistopheles to win the wager. To this end, he dedicates himself to a life of impulse, pleasure and pain, success and frustration, hate and love. — (1770–2072 = FRAGMENT 2: Mephistopheles urges Faust to be realistic and enjoy life as it comes. — The student is interviewed by Mephistopheles. — Faust and Mephistopheles depart on the magic cloak.)

7. Auerbachs Keller in Leipzig 2073–2336

(= FRAGMENT 3, URFAUST 3: The drunken students — Mephistopheles' tricks.)

8. Hexenküche 2337–2604

(= FRAGMENT 4: Faust is disgusted by the hocus-pocus, but entranced by the figure in the mirror. He is rejuvenated by the witch's potion.)

9. Straße 2605–2677

(= FRAGMENT 5, URFAUST 5: Faust sees Gretchen and orders Mephistopheles to obtain her.)

10. Abend 2678–2804

(= FRAGMENT 6, URFAUST 6: Faust in Gretchen's room — The jewel casket — "The King in Thule" — Gretchen finds the casket.)

11. Spaziergang 2805–2864

(= FRAGMENT 7, URFAUST 7: Mephistopheles reports that the priest has Gretchen's jewels.)

12. Der Nachbarin Haus 2865–3024

(= FRAGMENT 8, URFAUST 8: Mephistopheles calls on Marthe, reports the death of her husband, and arranges to bring Faust to testify to Schwerdtlein's death.)

13. Straße 3025–3072

(= FRAGMENT 9, URFAUST 9: Mephistopheles reports to Faust, who is reluctant to commit perjury, but finally agrees.)

14. Garten 3073–3204

(= FRAGMENT 10, URFAUST 10: The Faust-Gretchen and the Mephistopheles-Marthe conversations.)

15. Ein Gartenhäuschen 3205–3216

(= FRAGMENT 11, URFAUST 11: Gretchen confesses her love. Faust and Mephistopheles leave.)

16. Wald und Höhle 3217–3373

(= Fragment 15; 3342–3369 = Urfaust 18, in part: Faust in the wilderness reviews his relationships with Mephistopheles and Gretchen. Mephistopheles incites Faust to return to Gretchen. Faust yields, although he realizes that he may bring disaster to her.)

17. Gretchens Stube 3374–3413

(= Fragment 12, Urfaust 12: Gretchen at the spinning wheel, singing.)

18. Marthens Garten 3414–3543

(= Fragment 13, Urfaust 13: The discussion of religion — The soporific, and the appointment for that night — Mephistopheles' cynicism.)

19. Am Brunnen 3544–3586

(= Fragment 14, Urfaust 14: Lieschen tells Gretchen about Barbara's disgrace.)

20. Zwinger 3587–3619

(= Fragment 16, Urfaust 15: Gretchen prays to the Sorrowing Virgin, and puts flowers before the wall-niche statue.)

21. Nacht. Straße vor Gretchens Türe 3620–3775

(3620–3645 = Urfaust 17: Valentin contrasts his former pride in Gretchen with his present shame at her disgrace.) Valentin catches sight of two men approaching his sister's home. (3650–3659 = Urfaust 18, in part: Faust and Mephistopheles enter, Faust melancholy, Mephistopheles full of lustful high spirits.) Mephistopheles is looking forward to Walpurgis-Night. Faust finds some jewelry for Gretchen, a pearl necklace in a buried pot which also contains some coins. Mephistopheles sings a satirical serenade to Gretchen. Valentin steps out of the shadows and challenges his sister's betrayer to a duel. Mephistopheles parries Valentin's blows, Faust inflicts a mortal wound on Valentin. Faust and Mephistopheles flee. Marthe and Gretchen hear the tumult: they and other neighbors come out and find a dying man in the street. Valentin recognizes them and bitterly denounces Gretchen; he prophesies a life of disgrace for her, and curses her. He dies.

22. Dom 3776–3834

(= Fragment 17, Urfaust 16: Gretchen and the Evil Spirit — "The Day of Wrath.")

23. Walpurgisnacht 3835–4222

Mephistopheles takes Faust to the witches' annual gathering on the Brocken in the Harz Mountains — a scene of wild revelry. They go up the mountain side amid unearthly sights and sounds. Mephistopheles takes Faust to various parts of the mountain — past Mammon's palace, near the thoroughfare along which the wizards and witches are arriving, to a dying campfire where some neglected old men are outliving their reputations, by the booth of a huckster-witch, to a lewd dance, past a grumbling critic. During the dance, Faust is startled by two uncanny happenings: a red mouse jumps out of the mouth of the pretty young witch he is dancing with; and off to one side he sees a disturbing figure — Gretchen, with a thin red cord around her neck. Mephistopheles explains that Faust must have seen Medusa, the spectre that appears to every man in the form of his beloved. To distract Faust, Mephistopheles takes him to a hillside where some amateur players are presenting *A Walpurgis-Night's Dream.*

24. Walpurgisnachtstraum 4223–4398

The play (a pageant) is produced, ostensibly on the occasion of a reconciliation between Oberon and Titania, King and Queen of the fairies. [In the context of FAUST, Part I, it is the utmost of escapist irrelevance: amiable satire of literary and philosophical vagaries of the last decades of the eighteenth century — the ethereal end of the spectrum of humanity, contrasted with the animal, gross aspects of mankind depicted in the preceding scene.]

25. Trüber Tag TT 1–66

(= URFAUST 19: Faust has learned of Gretchen's plight. In a frenzy, he berates Mephistopheles, and demands that Gretchen be liberated. Mephistopheles is coldly realistic as to Faust's responsibility for Gretchen's tragedy, but offers to help Faust free her from prison.)

26. Nacht. Offen Feld 4399–4404

(= URFAUST 20: As Faust and Mephistopheles rush along past the execution place, on black horses, they see dim figures moving about the platform.)

27. Kerker 4405–4612

(= URFAUST 21, but now in verse throughout: Faust finds Gretchen, insane, in prison. Slowly she recognizes him, but only dully. She refuses to leave the prison with him, since she feels she must atone for her sins. She thinks of the happy past, of her and Faust's dying child, of her mother, of the coming execution. Mephistopheles appears, terrifying Gretchen and dragging Faust away. But in this final version, there is a reply to Mephistopheles' cold "She has been judged." — A Voice from Above answers: "She has been saved!")

Lines	URFAUST Scene	FRAGMENT Scene	FAUST I Scene
1–32			Zueignung
33–242			1. Vorspiel auf dem Theater
243–353			2. Prolog im Himmel
354–605	1	1	3. Nacht
606–807			3. Nacht
808–1177			4. Vor dem Tor
1178–1529			5. Studierzimmer (I)
1530–1769			6. Studierzimmer (II)
1770–1867		2	6. Studierzimmer (II)
1868–1881	2	2	6. Studierzimmer (II)
1882–1895		2	6. Studierzimmer (II)
1896–1963	2	2	6. Studierzimmer (II)
1964–2000		2	6. Studierzimmer (II)
2001–2050	2	2	6. Studierzimmer (II)
2051–2072		2	6. Studierzimmer (II)
2073–2336	3*	3	7. Auerbachs Keller
	4	omitted	omitted
2337–2604		4	8. Hexenküche
2605–2673	5	5	9. Straße
2674–2677		5	9. Straße
2678–2804	6	6	10. Abend
2805–2864	7	7	11. Spaziergang
2865–3024	8	8	12. Der Nachbarin Haus
3025–3072	9	9	13. Straße
3073–3204	10	10	14. Garten
3205–3216	11	11	15. Ein Gartenhäuschen
3217–3341		15	16. Wald und Höhle
3342–3369	18	15	16. Wald und Höhle
3370–3373		15	16. Wald und Höhle
3374–3413	12	12	17. Gretchens Stube
3414–3543	13	13	18. Marthens Garten
3544–3586	14	14	19. Am Brunnen
3587–3619	15	16	20. Zwinger
3620–3645	17		21. Nacht. Straße vor Gretchens Türe.
3646–3649			21. Nacht. Straße vor Gretchens Türe.
3650–3659	18		21. Nacht. Straße vor Gretchens Türe.
3660–3775			21. Nacht. Straße vor Gretchens Türe.

* In prose.

Lines	URFAUST Scene	FRAGMENT Scene	FAUST I Scene
3776–3834	16	17	22. Dom
3835–4222			23. Walpurgisnacht
4223–4398			24. Walpurgisnachtstraum
TT 1–66	19*		25. Trüber Tag*
4399–4404	20		26. Nacht. Offen Feld.
4405–4612	21*		27. Kerker

* In prose.

FAUST

Eine Tragödie

24 years had therefore elapsed since the first scenes of the work written. The poet - 48 yrs old and the shadowy forms of the drama which he again attempts to seize and hold, bring with them the phantoms of the friends to whom his earliest songs were sung: Cornelia, Lenz, Merck, Basedow, Gotter etc.

Zueignung

Ihr naht euch wieder, schwankende Gestalten,
die früh sich einst dem trüben Blick gezeigt.
Versuch' ich wohl, euch diesmal festzuhalten?
Fühl' ich mein Herz noch jenem Wahn geneigt?
Ihr drängt euch zu! Nun gut, so mögt ihr walten,
wie ihr aus Dunst und Nebel um mich steigt;
mein Busen fühlt sich jugendlich erschüttert
vom Zauberhauch, der euren Zug umwittert.

Ihr bringt mit euch die Bilder froher Tage,
und manche liebe Schatten steigen auf;
gleich einer alten, halbverklungnen Sage
kommt erste Lieb' und Freundschaft mit herauf;
der Schmerz wird neu, es wiederholt die Klage
des Lebens labyrinthisch irren Lauf
und nennt die Guten, die, um schöne Stunden
vom Glück getäuscht, vor mir hinweggeschwunden.

Sie hören nicht die folgenden Gesänge,
die Seelen, denen ich die ersten sang;
zerstoben ist das freundliche Gedränge,
verklungen, ach, der erste Widerklang!
Mein Leid ertönt der unbekannten Menge,
ihr Beifall selbst macht meinem Herzen bang;
und was sich sonst an meinem Lied erfreuet,
wenn es noch lebt, irrt in der Welt zerstreuet.

Und mich ergreift ein längst entwöhntes Sehnen
nach jenem stillen, ernsten Geisterreich;
es schwebet nun in unbestimmten Tönen
mein lispelnd Lied, der Äolsharfe gleich.
Ein Schauer faßt mich, Träne folgt den Tränen;
das strenge Herz, es fühlt sich mild und weich.
Was ich besitze, seh' ich wie im Weiten,
und was verschwand, wird mir zu Wirklichkeiten.

Goethe uses this scene to exhibit 3 attitudes toward dramatic poetry

1- Director - who wishes action with variety to bring crowds (Mannigfaltigkeit)

2- Comedian - a romantic piece with shifting emotions and a direct bond with contempory life

3. Poet - who wishes not to be constrained to write for the use of the vulgar crowd but rather in composure to form his work for posterity. (Nachkommenschaft)

1 Vorspiel auf dem Theater

Direktor. Theaterdichter. Lustige Person.

DIREKTOR

Ihr beiden, die ihr mir so oft
in Not und Trübsal beigestanden,
sagt, was ihr wohl in deutschen Landen
von unsrer Unternehmung hofft!
Ich wünschte sehr, der Menge zu behagen,
besonders weil sie lebt und leben läßt.
Die Pfosten sind, die Bretter aufgeschlagen,
und jedermann erwartet sich ein Fest.
Sie sitzen schon mit hohen Augenbraunen
gelassen da und möchten gern erstaunen.
Ich weiß, wie man den Geist des Volks versöhnt;
doch so verlegen bin ich nie gewesen:
zwar sind sie an das Beste nicht gewöhnt,
allein sie haben schrecklich viel gelesen.
Wie machen wir's, daß alles frisch und neu
und mit Bedeutung auch gefällig sei?
Denn freilich mag ich gern die Menge sehen,
wenn sich der Strom nach unsrer Bude drängt
und mit gewaltig wiederholten Wehen
sich durch die enge Gnadenpforte zwängt,
bei hellem Tage, schon vor Vieren,
mit Stößen sich bis an die Kasse ficht
und, wie in Hungersnot um Brot an Bäckertüren,
um ein Billett sich fast die Hälse bricht.
Dies Wunder wirkt auf so verschiedne Leute
der Dichter nur. Mein Freund, o tu es heute!

DICHTER

O sprich mir nicht von jener bunten Menge,
bei deren Anblick uns der Geist entflieht.
Verhülle mir das wogende Gedränge,
das wider Willen uns zum Strudel zieht.
Nein, führe mich zur stillen Himmelsenge,
wo nur dem Dichter reine Freude blüht,
wo Lieb' und Freundschaft unsres Herzens Segen
mit Götterhand erschaffen und erpflegen!

Ach, was in tiefer Brust uns da entsprungen,
was sich die Lippe schüchtern vorgelallt,
mißraten jetzt und jetzt vielleicht gelungen,
verschlingt des wilden Augenblicks Gewalt.
Oft, wenn es erst durch Jahre durchgedrungen,
erscheint es in vollendeter Gestalt.
Was glänzt, ist für den Augenblick geboren;
das Echte bleibt der Nachwelt unverloren.

LUSTIGE PERSON

Wenn ich nur nichts von Nachwelt hören sollte!
Gesetzt, daß ich von Nachwelt reden wollte,
wer machte denn der Mitwelt Spaß?
Den will sie doch und soll ihn haben!
Die Gegenwart von einem braven Knaben
ist, dächt' ich, immer auch schon was.
Wer sich behaglich mitzuteilen weiß,
den wird des Volkes Laune nicht erbittern;
er wünscht sich einen großen Kreis,
um ihn gewisser zu erschüttern.
Drum seid nur brav und zeigt Euch musterhaft:
laßt Phantasie mit allen ihren Chören,
Vernunft, Verstand, Empfindung, Leidenschaft,
doch, merkt Euch wohl, nicht ohne Narrheit hören!

DIREKTOR

Besonders aber laßt genug geschehn!
Man kommt zu schaun, man will am liebsten sehn.
Wird vieles vor den Augen abgesponnen,
so daß die Menge staunend gaffen kann,
da habt Ihr in der Breite gleich gewonnen:
Ihr seid ein vielgeliebter Mann.
Die Masse könnt Ihr nur durch Masse zwingen,
ein jeder sucht sich endlich selbst was aus.
Wer vieles bringt, wird manchem etwas bringen;
und jeder geht zufrieden aus dem Haus.
Gebt Ihr ein Stück, so gebt es gleich in Stücken!
Solch ein Ragout, es muß Euch glücken;
leicht ist es vorgelegt, so leicht als ausgedacht.
Was hilft's, wenn Ihr ein Ganzes dargebracht?
Das Publikum wird es Euch doch zerpflücken.

DICHTER

Ihr fühlet nicht, wie schlecht ein solches Handwerk sei,
wie wenig das dem echten Künstler zieme!
Der saubern Herren Pfuscherei
ist, merk' ich, schon bei Euch Maxime.

DIREKTOR

Ein solcher Vorwurf läßt mich ungekränkt:
ein Mann, der recht zu wirken denkt,
muß auf das beste Werkzeug halten.
Bedenkt, Ihr habet weiches Holz zu spalten,
und seht nur hin, für wen Ihr schreibt!
Wenn diesen Langeweile treibt,
kommt jener satt vom übertischten Mahle,
und, was das allerschlimmste bleibt,
gar mancher kommt vom Lesen der Journale.
Man eilt zerstreut zu uns, wie zu den Maskenfesten,
und Neugier nur beflügelt jeden Schritt;
die Damen geben sich und ihren Putz zum besten
und spielen ohne Gage mit.
Was träumet Ihr auf Eurer Dichterhöhe?
Was macht ein volles Haus Euch froh?
Beseht die Gönner in der Nähe!
Halb sind sie kalt, halb sind sie roh.
Der, nach dem Schauspiel, hofft ein Kartenspiel,
der eine wilde Nacht an einer Dirne Busen.
Was plagt ihr armen Toren viel,
zu solchem Zweck, die holden Musen?
Ich sag' Euch: gebt nur mehr und immer, immer mehr,
so könnt Ihr Euch vom Ziele nie verirren.
Sucht nur die Menschen zu verwirren,
sie zu befriedigen, ist schwer — —
Was fällt Euch an? Entzückung oder Schmerzen?

DICHTER

Geh hin und such dir einen andern Knecht!
Der Dichter sollte wohl das höchste Recht,
das Menschenrecht, das ihm Natur vergönnt,
um deinetwillen freventlich verscherzen!
Wodurch bewegt er alle Herzen?
Wodurch besiegt er jedes Element?
Ist es der Einklang nicht, der aus dem Busen dringt

und in sein Herz die Welt zurückeschlingt?
Wenn die Natur des Fadens ew'ge Länge,
gleichgültig drehend, auf die Spindel zwingt,
wenn aller Wesen unharmon'sche Menge
verdrießlich durcheinander klingt,
wer teilt die fließend immer gleiche Reihe
belebend ab, daß sie sich rhythmisch regt?
Wer ruft das Einzelne zur allgemeinen Weihe,
wo es in herrlichen Akkorden schlägt?
Wer läßt den Sturm zu Leidenschaften wüten,
das Abendrot im ernsten Sinne glühn?
Wer schüttet alle schönen Frühlingsblüten
auf der Geliebten Pfade hin?
Wer flicht die unbedeutend grünen Blätter
zum Ehrenkranz Verdiensten jeder Art?
Wer sichert den Olymp, vereinet Götter? —
Des Menschen Kraft, im Dichter offenbart!

LUSTIGE PERSON

So braucht sie denn, die schönen Kräfte,
und treibt die dicht'rischen Geschäfte,
wie man ein Liebesabenteuer treibt!
Zufällig naht man sich, man fühlt, man bleibt,
und nach und nach wird man verflochten;
es wächst das Glück, dann wird es angefochten,
man ist entzückt, nun kommt der Schmerz heran,
und eh' man sich's versieht, ist's eben ein Roman.
Laßt uns auch so ein Schauspiel geben!
Greift nur hinein ins volle Menschenleben!
Ein jeder lebt's, nicht vielen ist's bekannt,
und wo Ihr's packt, da ist's interessant.
In bunten Bildern wenig Klarheit,
viel Irrtum und ein Fünkchen Wahrheit:
so wird der beste Trank gebraut,
der alle Welt erquickt und auferbaut.
Dann sammelt sich der Jugend schönste Blüte
vor Eurem Spiel und lauscht der Offenbarung,
dann sauget jedes zärtliche Gemüte
aus Eurem Werk sich melanchol'sche Nahrung,
dann wird bald dies, bald jenes aufgeregt;
ein jeder sieht, was er im Herzen trägt.
Noch sind sie gleich bereit, zu weinen und zu lachen,

sie ehren noch den Schwung, erfreuen sich am Schein;
wer fertig ist, dem ist nichts recht zu machen;
ein Werdender wird immer dankbar sein.

DICHTER

So gib mir auch die Zeiten wieder,
da ich noch selbst im Werden war,
da sich ein Quell gedrängter Lieder
ununterbrochen neu gebar,
da Nebel mir die Welt verhüllten,
die Knospe Wunder noch versprach,
da ich die tausend Blumen brach,
die alle Täler reichlich füllten.
Ich hatte nichts und doch genug:
den Drang nach Wahrheit und die Lust am Trug.
Gib ungebändigt jene Triebe,
das tiefe, schmerzenvolle Glück,
des Hasses Kraft, die Macht der Liebe, —
gib meine Jugend mir zurück!

LUSTIGE PERSON

Der Jugend, guter Freund, bedarfst du allenfalls,
wenn dich in Schlachten Feinde drängen,
wenn mit Gewalt an deinen Hals
sich allerliebste Mädchen hängen,
wenn fern des schnellen Laufes Kranz
vom schwer erreichten Ziele winket,
wenn nach dem heft'gen Wirbeltanz
die Nächte schmausend man vertrinket.
Doch ins bekannte Saitenspiel
mit Mut und Anmut einzugreifen,
nach einem selbstgesteckten Ziel
mit holdem Irren hinzuschweifen, —
das, alte Herrn, ist eure Pflicht,
und wir verehren euch darum nicht minder.
Das Alter macht nicht kindisch, wie man spricht,
es findet uns nur noch als wahre Kinder.

DIREKTOR

Der Worte sind genug gewechselt,
laßt mich auch endlich Taten sehn!
Indes ihr Komplimente drechselt,
kann etwas Nützliches geschehn.
Was hilft es, viel von Stimmung reden?

Dem Zaudernden erscheint sie nie.
Gebt ihr euch einmal für Poeten,
so kommandiert die Poesie!
Euch ist bekannt, was wir bedürfen.
Wir wollen stark Getränke schlürfen:
nun braut mir unverzüglich dran!
Was heute nicht geschieht, ist morgen nicht getan,
und keinen Tag soll man verpassen.
Das Mögliche soll der Entschluß
beherzt sogleich beim Schopfe fassen:
er will es dann nicht fahren lassen
und wirket weiter, weil er muß.

Ihr wißt, auf unsern deutschen Bühnen
probiert ein jeder, was er mag.
Drum schonet mir an diesem Tag
Prospekte nicht und nicht Maschinen!
Gebraucht das groß' und kleine Himmelslicht,
die Sterne dürfet Ihr verschwenden;
an Wasser, Feuer, Felsenwänden,
an Tier' und Vögeln fehlt es nicht.
So schreitet in dem engen Bretterhaus
den ganzen Kreis der Schöpfung aus
und wandelt, mit bedächt'ger Schnelle,
vom Himmel durch die Welt zur Hölle!

2 Prolog im Himmel

Der Herr. Die himmlischen Heerscharen. Nachher Mephistopheles.

Die drei Erzengel treten vor.

Dramatic Purpose: To state the problem of Faust and M. The Lord permits M to attempt to lead Faust astray.

RAPHAEL

Die Sonne tönt nach alter Weise
in Brudersphären Wettgesang,
und ihre vorgeschriebne Reise
vollendet sie mit Donnergang.
Ihr Anblick gibt den Engeln Stärke,
wenn keiner sie ergründen mag;
die unbegreiflich hohen Werke
sind herrlich wie am ersten Tag.

GABRIEL

Und schnell und unbegreiflich schnelle
dreht sich umher der Erde Pracht;
es wechselt Paradieseshelle
mit tiefer, schauervoller Nacht.
Es schäumt das Meer in breiten Flüssen
am tiefen Grund der Felsen auf,
und Fels und Meer wird fortgerissen
in ewig schnellem Sphärenlauf.

MICHAEL

Und Stürme brausen um die Wette
vom Meer aufs Land, vom Land aufs Meer,
und bilden wütend eine Kette
der tiefsten Wirkung ringsumher.
Da flammt ein blitzendes Verheeren
dem Pfade vor des Donnerschlags;
doch deine Boten, Herr, verehren
das sanfte Wandeln deines Tags.

DIE ERZENGEL: *zu drei.*

Der Anblick gibt den Engeln Stärke,
da keiner dich ergründen mag,
und alle deine hohen Werke
sind herrlich wie am ersten Tag.

MEPHISTOPHELES

Da du, o Herr, dich einmal wieder nahst
und fragst, wie alles sich bei uns befinde,
und du mich sonst gewöhnlich gerne sahst,
so siehst du mich auch unter dem Gesinde.
Verzeih! Ich kann nicht hohe Worte machen,
und wenn mich auch der ganze Kreis verhöhnt;
mein Pathos brächte dich gewiß zum Lachen,
hättst du dir nicht das Lachen abgewöhnt.
Von Sonn' und Welten weiß ich nichts zu sagen;
ich sehe nur, wie sich die Menschen plagen.
Der kleine Gott der Welt bleibt stets von gleichem Schlag
und ist so wunderlich als wie am ersten Tag.
Ein wenig besser würd' er leben,
hättst du ihm nicht den Schein des Himmelslichts gegeben;
er nennt's Vernunft und braucht's allein,
nur tierischer als jedes Tier zu sein.
Er scheint mir, mit Verlaub von Euer Gnaden,
wie eine der langbeinigen Zikaden,
die immer fliegt und fliegend springt
und gleich im Gras ihr altes Liedchen singt;
und läg' er nur noch immer in dem Grase! —
In jeden Quark begräbt er seine Nase.

DER HERR

Hast du mir weiter nichts zu sagen?
Kommst du nur immer anzuklagen?
Ist auf der Erde ewig dir nichts recht?

MEPHISTOPHELES

Nein, Herr! Ich find' es dort, wie immer, herzlich schlecht.
Die Menschen dauern mich in ihren Jammertagen;
ich mag sogar die armen selbst nicht plagen.

DER HERR

Kennst du den Faust?

MEPHISTOPHELES

Den Doktor?

DER HERR

Meinen Knecht!

MEPHISTOPHELES

Fürwahr, er dient Euch auf besondre Weise!
Nicht irdisch ist des Toren Trank noch Speise.
Ihn treibt die Gärung in die Ferne.
Er ist sich seiner Tollheit halb bewußt:
vom Himmel fordert er die schönsten Sterne
und von der Erde jede höchste Lust,
und alle Näh' und alle Ferne
befriedigt nicht die tiefbewegte Brust.

DER HERR

Wenn er mir jetzt auch nur verworren dient,
so werd' ich ihn bald in die Klarheit führen.
Weiß doch der Gärtner, wenn das Bäumchen grünt,
daß Blüt' und Frucht die künft'gen Jahre zieren.

MEPHISTOPHELES

Was wettet Ihr? Den sollt Ihr noch verlieren,
wenn Ihr mir die Erlaubnis gebt,
ihn meine Straße sacht zu führen!

DER HERR

Solang er auf der Erde lebt,
so lange sei dir's nicht verboten.
Es irrt der Mensch, solang er strebt.

MEPHISTOPHELES

Da dank' ich Euch; denn mit den Toten
hab' ich mich niemals gern befangen.
Am meisten lieb' ich mir die vollen, frischen Wangen;
für einen Leichnam bin ich nicht zu Haus:
mir geht es wie der Katze mit der Maus.

DER HERR

Nun gut, es sei dir überlassen!
Zieh diesen Geist von seinem Urquell ab
und führ ihn, kannst du ihn erfassen,
auf deinem Wege mit herab, —
und steh beschämt, wenn du bekennen mußt:
ein guter Mensch, in seinem dunklen Drange,
ist sich des rechten Weges wohl bewußt.

MEPHISTOPHELES

Schon gut! Nur dauert es nicht lange.
Mir ist für meine Wette gar nicht bange.

Wenn ich zu meinem Zweck gelange,
erlaubt Ihr mir Triumph aus voller Brust.
Staub soll er fressen, und mit Lust,
wie meine Muhme, die berühmte Schlange.

Der Herr

Du darfst auch da nur frei erscheinen;
ich habe deinesgleichen nie gehaßt:
von allen Geistern, die verneinen,
ist mir der Schalk am wenigsten zur Last.
Des Menschen Tätigkeit kann allzuleicht erschlaffen,
er liebt sich bald die unbedingte Ruh;
drum geb' ich gern ihm den Gesellen zu,
der reizt und wirkt und muß als Teufel schaffen. —
Doch ihr, die echten Göttersöhne,
erfreut euch der lebendig reichen Schöne!
Das Werdende, das ewig wirkt und lebt,
umfass' euch mit der Liebe holden Schranken,
und was in schwankender Erscheinung schwebt,
befestiget mit dauernden Gedanken!

Der Himmel schließt, die Erzengel verteilen sich.

Mephistopheles, *allein.*

Von Zeit zu Zeit seh' ich den Alten gern
und hüte mich, mit ihm zu brechen.
Es ist gar hübsch von einem großen Herrn,
so menschlich mit dem Teufel selbst zu sprechen.

Der Tragödie erster Teil

3 Nacht

In einem hochgewölbten, engen gotischen Zimmer, ***Faust,*** *unruhig, auf seinem Sessel am Pulte.*

FAUST

Habe nun, ach, Philosophie,
Juristerei und Medizin
und leider auch Theologie
durchaus studiert, mit heißem Bemühn.
Da steh' ich nun, ich armer Tor,
und bin so klug als wie zuvor!
Heiße Magister, heiße Doktor gar,
und ziehe schon an die zehen Jahr
herauf, herab und quer und krumm
meine Schüler an der Nase herum —
und sehe, daß wir nichts wissen können!
Das will mir schier das Herz verbrennen.
Zwar bin ich gescheiter als alle die Laffen,
Doktoren, Magister, Schreiber und Pfaffen;
mich plagen keine Skrupel noch Zweifel,
fürchte mich weder vor Hölle noch Teufel. —
Dafür ist mir auch alle Freud' entrissen,
bilde mir nicht ein, was Recht's zu wissen,
bilde mir nicht ein, ich könnte was lehren,
die Menschen zu bessern und zu bekehren.
Auch hab' ich weder Gut noch Geld,
noch Ehr' und Herrlichkeit der Welt:
es möchte kein Hund so länger leben!
Drum hab' ich mich der Magie ergeben,
ob mir durch Geistes Kraft und Mund
nicht manch Geheimnis würde kund,
daß ich nicht mehr mit sauerm Schweiß
zu sagen brauche, was ich nicht weiß, —
daß ich erkenne, was die Welt
im Innersten zusammenhält,
schau' alle Wirkenskraft und Samen
und tu' nicht mehr in Worten kramen!

O, sähst du, voller Mondenschein,
zum letztenmal auf meine Pein,
den ich so manche Mitternacht
an diesem Pult herangewacht:
dann über Büchern und Papier,
trübsel'ger Freund, erschienst du mir! —
Ach, könnt' ich doch auf Bergeshöh'n
in deinem lieben Lichte gehn,
um Bergeshöhle mit Geistern schweben,
auf Wiesen in deinem Dämmer weben,
von allem Wissensqualm entladen
in deinem Tau gesund mich baden!

Weh! Steck' ich in dem Kerker noch?
Verfluchtes, dumpfes Mauerloch,
wo selbst das liebe Himmelslicht
trüb durch gemalte Scheiben bricht!
Beschränkt von diesem Bücherhauf,
den Würme nagen, Staub bedeckt,
den, bis ans hohe Gewölb' hinauf,
ein angeraucht Papier umsteckt!
Mit Gläsern, Büchsen rings umstellt,
mit Instrumenten vollgepfropft,
Urväter-Hausrat drein gestopft! —
Das ist deine Welt! Das heißt eine Welt!

Und fragst du noch, warum dein Herz
sich bang in deinem Busen klemmt,
warum ein unerklärter Schmerz
dir alle Lebensregung hemmt?
Statt der lebendigen Natur,
da Gott die Menschen schuf hinein,
umgibt in Rauch und Moder nur
dich Tiergeripp' und Totenbein.

Flieh! Auf! Hinaus ins weite Land!
Und dies geheimnisvolle Buch,
von Nostradamus' eigner Hand,
ist dir es nicht Geleit genug?
Erkennest dann der Sterne Lauf,
und wenn Natur dich unterweist,
dann geht die Seelenkraft dir auf,
wie spricht ein Geist zum andern Geist.

Umsonst, daß trocknes Sinnen hier
die heil'gen Zeichen dir erklärt.
Ihr schwebt, ihr Geister, neben mir:
antwortet mir, wenn ihr mich hört!

Er schlägt das Buch auf und erblickt das Zeichen des Makrokosmus.

Ha! Welche Wonne fließt in diesem Blick
auf einmal mir durch alle meine Sinnen!
Ich fühle junges, heil'ges Lebensglück
neuglühend mir durch Nerv' und Adern rinnen.
War es ein Gott, der diese Zeichen schrieb,
die mir das innre Toben stillen,
das arme Herz mit Freude füllen,
und mit geheimnisvollem Trieb
die Kräfte der Natur rings um mich her enthüllen?
Bin ich ein Gott? Mir wird so licht!
Ich schau' in diesen reinen Zügen
die wirkende Natur vor meiner Seele liegen.
Jetzt erst erkenn' ich, was der Weise spricht:
„Die Geisterwelt ist nicht verschlossen;
dein Sinn ist zu, dein Herz ist tot!
Auf! Bade, Schüler, unverdrossen
die ird'sche Brust im Morgenrot!"

Er beschaut das Zeichen.

Wie alles sich zum Ganzen webt,
eins in dem andern wirkt und lebt!
Wie Himmelskräfte auf und nieder steigen
und sich die goldnen Eimer reichen!
Mit segenduftenden Schwingen
vom Himmel durch die Erde dringen,
harmonisch all das All durchklingen!

Welch Schauspiel! Aber ach, ein Schauspiel nur!
Wo fass' ich dich, unendliche Natur —
euch Brüste, wo? Ihr Quellen alles Lebens,
an denen Himmel und Erde hängt,
dahin die welke Brust sich drängt —
ihr quellt, ihr tränkt, und schmacht' ich so vergebens?

Er schlägt unwillig das Buch um und erblickt das Zeichen des Erdgeistes.

Wie anders wirkt dies Zeichen auf mich ein!
Du, Geist der Erde, bist mir näher:

schon fühl' ich meine Kräfte höher,
schon glüh' ich wie von neuem Wein;
ich fühle Mut, mich in die Welt zu wagen,
der Erde Weh, der Erde Glück zu tragen,
mit Stürmen mich herumzuschlagen
und in des Schiffbruchs Knirschen nicht zu zagen. —
Es wölkt sich über mir!
Der Mond verbirgt sein Licht!
Die Lampe schwindet!
Es dampft! Es zucken rote Strahlen
mir um das Haupt! — Es weht
ein Schauer vom Gewölb' herab
und faßt mich an! —
Ich fühl's, du schwebst um mich, erflehter Geist.
Enthülle dich!
Ha! Wie's in meinem Herzen reißt!
Zu neuen Gefühlen
all' meine Sinnen sich erwühlen!
Ich fühle ganz mein Herz dir hingegeben!
Du mußt! Du mußt! Und kostet' es mein Leben!

Er faßt das Buch und spricht das Zeichen des Geistes geheimnisvoll aus. Es zuckt eine rötliche Flamme, der Geist erscheint in der Flamme.

GEIST

Wer ruft mir?

FAUST, *abgewendet.*

Schreckliches Gesicht!

GEIST

Du hast mich mächtig angezogen,
an meiner Sphäre lang gesogen,
und nun —

FAUST

Weh! Ich ertrag' dich nicht!

GEIST

Du flehst eratmend, mich zu schauen,
meine Stimme zu hören, mein Antlitz zu sehn;
mich neigt dein mächtig Seelenflehn:
da bin ich! . . . Welch erbärmlich Grauen
faßt Übermenschen dich! Wo ist der Seele Ruf?
Wo ist die Brust, die eine Welt in sich erschuf

und trug und hegte, die mit Freudebeben
erschwoll, sich uns, den Geistern, gleich zu heben?
Wo bist du, Faust, des Stimme mir erklang,
der sich an mich mit allen Kräften drang?
Bist du es, der, von meinem Hauch umwittert,
in allen Lebenstiefen zittert,
ein furchtsam weggekrümmter Wurm?

FAUST

Soll ich dir, Flammenbildung, weichen?
Ich bin's, bin Faust, bin deinesgleichen!

GEIST

In Lebensfluten, im Tatensturm
wall' ich auf und ab,
webe hin und her!
Geburt und Grab,
ein ewiges Meer,
ein wechselnd Weben,
ein glühend Leben:
so schaff' ich am sausenden Webstuhl der Zeit
und wirke der Gottheit lebendiges Kleid.

FAUST

Der du die weite Welt umschweifst,
geschäftiger Geist, wie nah fühl' ich mich dir!

GEIST

Du gleichst dem Geist, den du begreifst,
nicht mir!

Verschwindet.

FAUST, *zusammenstürzend.*

Nicht dir?
Wem denn?
Ich Ebenbild der Gottheit!
Und nicht einmal dir!

Es klopft.

O Tod! Ich kenn's! Das ist mein Famulus!
Es wird mein schönstes Glück zunichte!
Daß diese Fülle der Gesichte
der trockne Schleicher stören muß!

Wagner, im Schlafrocke und der Nachtmütze, eine Lampe in der Hand. Faust wendet sich unwillig.

Wagner

Verzeiht! Ich hör' Euch deklamieren;
Ihr last gewiß ein griechisch Trauerspiel?
In dieser Kunst möcht' ich was profitieren,
denn heutzutage wirkt das viel.
Ich hab' es öfters rühmen hören:
ein Komödiant könnt' einen Pfarrer lehren.

Faust

Ja, wenn der Pfarrer ein Komödiant ist, —
wie das denn wohl zuzeiten kommen mag.

Wagner

Ach, wenn man so in sein Museum gebannt ist
und sieht die Welt kaum einen Feiertag,
kaum durch ein Fernglas, nur von weiten,
wie soll man sie durch Überredung leiten?

Faust

Wenn ihr's nicht fühlt, ihr werdet's nicht erjagen,
wenn es nicht aus der Seele dringt
und mit urkräftigem Behagen
die Herzen aller Hörer zwingt.
Sitzt ihr nur immer! Leimt zusammen,
braut ein Ragout von andrer Schmaus
und blast die kümmerlichen Flammen
aus eurem Aschenhäufchen 'raus!
Bewundrung von Kindern und Affen,
wenn euch darnach der Gaumen steht —
doch werdet ihr nie Herz zu Herzen schaffen,
wenn es euch nicht von Herzen geht.

Wagner

Allein der Vortrag macht des Redners Glück;
ich fühl' es wohl, noch bin ich weit zurück.

Faust

Such' Er den redlichen Gewinn!
Sei Er kein schellenlauter Tor!
Es trägt Verstand und rechter Sinn
mit wenig Kunst sich selber vor;
und wenn's euch Ernst ist, was zu sagen,
ist's nötig, Worten nachzujagen?
Ja, eure Reden, die so blinkend sind,
in denen ihr der Menschheit Schnitzel kräuselt,

sind unerquicklich wie der Nebelwind,
der herbstlich durch die dürren Blätter säuselt!

WAGNER

Ach Gott! Die Kunst ist lang,
und kurz ist unser Leben.
Mir wird, bei meinem kritischen Bestreben,
doch oft um Kopf und Busen bang.
Wie schwer sind nicht die Mittel zu erwerben,
durch die man zu den Quellen steigt!
Und eh' man nur den halben Weg erreicht,
muß wohl ein armer Teufel sterben.

FAUST

Das Pergament, ist das der heil'ge Bronnen,
woraus ein Trunk den Durst auf ewig stillt?
Erquickung hast du nicht gewonnen,
wenn sie dir nicht aus eigner Seele quillt.

WAGNER

Verzeiht! Es ist ein groß Ergötzen,
sich in den Geist der Zeiten zu versetzen,
zu schauen, wie vor uns ein weiser Mann gedacht,
und wie wir's dann zuletzt so herrlich weit gebracht.

FAUST

O ja, bis an die Sterne weit!
Mein Freund, die Zeiten der Vergangenheit
sind uns ein Buch mit sieben Siegeln.
Was ihr den Geist der Zeiten heißt,
das ist im Grund der Herren eigner Geist,
in dem die Zeiten sich bespiegeln.
Da ist's denn wahrlich oft ein Jammer!
Man läuft euch bei dem ersten Blick davon:
ein Kehrichtfaß und eine Rumpelkammer
und höchstens eine Haupt- und Staatsaktion
mit trefflichen pragmatischen Maximen,
wie sie den Puppen wohl im Munde ziemen!

WAGNER

Allein die Welt! Des Menschen Herz und Geist!
Möcht' jeglicher doch was davon erkennen.

FAUST

Ja, was man so „erkennen" heißt!
Wer darf das Kind beim rechten Namen nennen?

Die wenigen, die was davon erkannt,
die, töricht g'nug, ihr volles Herz nicht wahrten,
dem Pöbel ihr Gefühl, ihr Schauen offenbarten,
hat man von je gekreuzigt und verbrannt. —
Ich bitt' Euch, Freund, es ist tief in der Nacht,
wir müssen's diesmal unterbrechen.

WAGNER

Ich hätte gern nur immer fortgewacht,
um so gelehrt mit Euch mich zu besprechen.
Doch morgen, als am ersten Ostertage,
erlaubt mir ein' und andre Frage.
Mit Eifer hab' ich mich der Studien beflissen;
zwar weiß ich viel, doch möcht' ich alles wissen.

Ab.

FAUST, *allein.*

Wie nur dem Kopf nicht alle Hoffnung schwindet,
der immerfort an schalem Zeuge klebt,
mit gier'ger Hand nach Schätzen gräbt,
und froh ist, wenn er Regenwürmer findet!

Darf eine solche Menschenstimme hier,
wo Geisterfülle mich umgab, ertönen?
Doch ach, für diesmal dank' ich dir,
dem ärmlichsten von allen Erdensöhnen.
Du rissest mich von der Verzweiflung los,
die mir die Sinne schon zerstören wollte.
Ach, die Erscheinung war so riesengroß,
daß ich mich recht als Zwerg empfinden sollte.

Ich, Ebenbild der Gottheit, das sich schon
ganz nah gedünkt dem Spiegel ew'ger Wahrheit,
sein selbst genoß in Himmelsglanz und Klarheit,
und abgestreift den Erdensohn, —
ich, mehr als Cherub, dessen freie Kraft
schon durch die Adern der Natur zu fließen
und, schaffend, Götterleben zu genießen
sich ahnungsvoll vermaß, wie muß ich's büßen!
Ein Donnerwort hat mich hinweggerafft.

Nicht darf ich dir zu gleichen mich vermessen!
Hab' ich die Kraft dich anzuziehn besessen,
so hatt' ich dich zu halten keine Kraft.
In jenem sel'gen Augenblicke

ich fühlte mich so klein, so groß;
du stießest grausam mich zurücke,
ins ungewisse Menschenlos.
  Wer lehret mich? Was soll ich meiden?
Soll ich gehorchen jenem Drang?
Ach, unsre Taten selbst, so gut als unsre Leiden,
sie hemmen unsres Lebens Gang.

Dem Herrlichsten, was auch der Geist empfangen,
drängt immer fremd und fremder Stoff sich an;
wenn wir zum Guten dieser Welt gelangen,
dann heißt das Bess're Trug und Wahn.
Die uns das Leben gaben, herrliche Gefühle,
erstarren in dem irdischen Gewühle.

Wenn Phantasie sich sonst mit kühnem Flug
und hoffnungsvoll zum Ewigen erweitert,
so ist ein kleiner Raum ihr nun genug,
wenn Glück auf Glück im Zeitenstrudel scheitert.
Die Sorge nistet gleich im tiefen Herzen,
dort wirket sie geheime Schmerzen,
unruhig wiegt sie sich und störet Lust und Ruh;
sie deckt sich stets mit neuen Masken zu:
sie mag als Haus und Hof, als Weib und Kind erscheinen,
als Feuer, Wasser, Dolch und Gift;
du bebst vor allem, was nicht trifft,
und was du nie verlierst, das mußt du stets beweinen.

Den Göttern gleich' ich nicht! Zu tief ist es gefühlt!
Dem Wurme gleich' ich, der den Staub durchwühlt,
den, wie er sich im Staube nährend lebt,
des Wandrers Tritt vernichtet und begräbt.

Ist es nicht Staub, was diese hohe Wand
aus hundert Fächern mir verenget:
der Trödel, der mit tausendfachem Tand
in dieser Mottenwelt mich dränget?
Hier soll ich finden, was mir fehlt?
Soll ich vielleicht in tausend Büchern lesen,
daß überall die Menschen sich gequält,
daß hie und da ein Glücklicher gewesen?
  Was grinsest du mir, hohler Schädel, her,
als daß dein Hirn, wie meines, einst verwirret
den leichten Tag gesucht und in der Dämmrung schwer,

Faust relapses into despair now intensified by the realization that the Spirit of the Earth is beyond his powers to understand. Neither a comprehension of nature nor the attainment of happiness seems possible; he resolves on suicide

mit Lust nach Wahrheit, jämmerlich geirret?
Ihr Instrumente freilich spottet mein
mit Rad und Kämmen, Walz' und Bügel:
ich stand am Tor, ihr solltet Schlüssel sein;
zwar euer Bart ist kraus, doch hebt ihr nicht die Riegel.
Geheimnisvoll am lichten Tag,
läßt sich Natur des Schleiers nicht berauben;
und was sie deinem Geist nicht offenbaren mag,
das zwingst du ihr nicht ab mit Hebeln und mit Schrauben.
Du alt Geräte, das ich nicht gebraucht,
du stehst nur hier, weil dich mein Vater brauchte.
Du alte Rolle, du wirst angeraucht,
solang an diesem Pult die trübe Lampe schmauchte.
Weit besser hätt' ich doch mein Weniges verpraßt,
als mit dem Wenigen belastet hier zu schwitzen!
Was du ererbt von deinen Vätern hast,
erwirb es, um es zu besitzen!
Was man nicht nützt, ist eine schwere Last;
nur was der Augenblick erschafft, das kann er nützen.

Doch warum heftet sich mein Blick auf jene Stelle?
Ist jenes Fläschchen dort den Augen ein Magnet?
Warum wird mir auf einmal lieblich helle,
als wenn im nächt'gen Wald uns Mondenglanz umweht?

Ich grüße dich, du einzige Phiole,
die ich mit Andacht nun herunterhole!
In dir verehr' ich Menschenwitz und Kunst.
Du Inbegriff der holden Schlummersäfte,
du Auszug aller tödlich-feinen Kräfte,
erweise deinem Meister deine Gunst!
Ich sehe dich, es wird der Schmerz gelindert,
ich fasse dich, das Streben wird gemindert,
des Geistes Flutstrom ebbet nach und nach.
Ins hohe Meer werd' ich hinausgewiesen,
die Spiegelflut erglänzt zu meinen Füßen,
zu neuen Ufern lockt ein neuer Tag.

Ein Feuerwagen schwebt auf leichten Schwingen
an mich heran! Ich fühle mich bereit,
auf neuer Bahn den Äther zu durchdringen,
zu neuen Sphären reiner Tätigkeit.—
Dies hohe Leben, diese Götterwonne!

Du, erst noch Wurm, und die verdienest du?
Ja, kehre nur der holden Erdensonne
entschlossen deinen Rücken zu!
Vermesse dich, die Pforten aufzureißen,
vor denen jeder gern vorüberschleicht!
Hier ist es Zeit, durch Taten zu beweisen,
daß Manneswürde nicht der Götterhöhe weicht, —
vor jener dunkeln Höhle nicht zu beben,
in der sich Phantasie zu eigner Qual verdammt, —
nach jenem Durchgang hinzustreben,
um dessen engen Mund die ganze Hölle flammt, —
zu diesem Schritt sich heiter zu entschließen,
und wär' es mit Gefahr, ins Nichts dahinzufließen.
Nun komm herab, kristallne reine Schale,
hervor aus deinem alten Futterale,
an die ich viele Jahre nicht gedacht!
Du glänztest bei der Väter Freudenfeste,
erheitertest die ernsten Gäste,
wenn einer dich dem andern zugebracht.
Der vielen Bilder künstlich reiche Pracht
— des Trinkers Pflicht, sie reimweis zu erklären,
auf einen Zug die Höhlung auszuleeren, —
erinnert mich an manche Jugendnacht.
Ich werde jetzt dich keinem Nachbar reichen;
ich werde meinen Witz an deiner Kunst nicht zeigen. —
Hier ist ein Saft, der eilig trunken macht;
mit brauner Flut erfüllt er deine Höhle. —
Den ich bereitet, den ich wähle,
der letzte Trunk sei nun, mit ganzer Seele,
als festlich hoher Gruß, dem Morgen zugebracht!

Er setzt die Schale an den Mund.
Glockenklang und Chorgesang.

CHOR DER ENGEL

Christ ist erstanden!
Freude dem Sterblichen,
den die verderblichen,
schleichenden, erblichen
Mängel umwanden!

FAUST

Welch tiefes Summen, welch ein heller Ton
zieht mit Gewalt das Glas von meinem Munde?

Verkündiget ihr dumpfen Glocken schon
des Osterfestes erste Feierstunde?
Ihr Chöre, singt ihr schon den tröstlichen Gesang,
der einst um Grabes Nacht von Engelslippen klang,
Gewißheit einem neuen Bunde?

CHOR DER WEIBER

Mit Spezereien
hatten wir ihn gepflegt;
wir, seine Treuen,
hatten ihn hingelegt;
Tücher und Binden
reinlich umwanden wir, —
ach, und wir finden
Christ nicht mehr hier!

CHOR DER ENGEL

Christ ist erstanden!
Selig der Liebende,
der die betrübende,
heilsam' und übende
Prüfung bestanden!

FAUST

Was sucht ihr, mächtig und gelind,
ihr Himmelstöne, mich am Staube?
Klingt dort umher, wo weiche Menschen sind!
Die Botschaft hör' ich wohl, allein mir fehlt der Glaube;
das Wunder ist des Glaubens liebstes Kind.
Zu jenen Sphären wag' ich nicht zu streben,
woher die holde Nachricht tönt;
und doch, an diesen Klang von Jugend auf gewöhnt,
ruft er auch jetzt zurück mich in das Leben.
Sonst stürzte sich der Himmelsliebe Kuß
auf mich herab in ernster Sabbatstille;
da klang so ahnungsvoll des Glockentones Fülle,
und ein Gebet war brünstiger Genuß;
ein unbegreiflich holdes Sehnen
trieb mich, durch Wald und Wiesen hinzugehn,
und unter tausend heißen Tränen
fühlt' ich mir eine Welt entstehn.
Dies Lied verkündete der Jugend muntre Spiele,
der Frühlingsfeier freies Glück;
Erinnrung hält mich nun mit kindlichem Gefühle

vom letzten, ernsten Schritt zurück.
O tönet fort, ihr süßen Himmelslieder!
Die Träne quillt, die Erde hat mich wieder!

CHOR DER JÜNGER

Hat der Begrabene
schon sich nach oben,
lebend Erhabene,
herrlich erhoben, —
ist er in Werdelust
schaffender Freude nah, —
ach, an der Erde Brust
sind wir zum Leide da! —
Ließ er die Seinen,
schmachtend uns hier zurück, —
ach, wir beweinen,
Meister, dein Glück!

CHOR DER ENGEL

Christ ist erstanden
aus der Verwesung Schoß!
Reißet von Banden
freudig euch los!
Tätig ihn preisenden,
Liebe beweisenden,
brüderlich speisenden,
predigend reisenden,
Wonne verheißenden,
euch ist der Meister nah,
euch ist er da!

4 Vor dem Tor

Spaziergänger aller Art ziehen hinaus.

EINIGE HANDWERKSBURSCHE

Warum denn dort hinaus?

ANDRE

Wir gehn hinaus aufs Jägerhaus.

Die ersten
Wir aber wollen nach der Mühle wandern.

Ein Handwerksbursch
Ich rat' euch, nach dem Wasserhof zu gehn.

Zweiter
Der Weg dahin ist gar nicht schön.

Die zweiten
Was tust denn du?

Ein dritter
Ich gehe mit den andern.

Vierter
Nach Burgdorf kommt herauf! Gewiß dort findet ihr
die schönsten Mädchen und das beste Bier
und Händel von der ersten Sorte!

Fünfter
Du überlustiger Gesell,
juckt dich zum drittenmal das Fell?
Ich mag nicht hin, mir graut es vor dem Orte.

Dienstmädchen
Nein, nein! Ich gehe nach der Stadt zurück.

Andre
Wir finden ihn gewiß bei jenen Pappeln stehen.

Erste
Das ist für mich kein großes Glück;
er wird an deiner Seite gehen,
mit dir nur tanzt er auf dem Plan.
Was gehn mich deine Freuden an?

Andre
Heut ist er sicher nicht allein:
der Krauskopf, sagt er, würde bei ihm sein.

Schüler
Blitz, wie die wackern Dirnen schreiten!
Herr Bruder, komm! Wir müssen sie begleiten.
Ein starkes Bier, ein beizender Toback
und eine Magd im Putz, das ist nun mein Geschmack.

Bürgermädchen
Da sieh mir nur die schönen Knaben!
Es ist wahrhaftig eine Schmach:

Gesellschaft könnten sie die allerbeste haben, —
und laufen diesen Mägden nach!

ZWEITER SCHÜLER, *zum ersten.*

Nicht so geschwind! Dort hinten kommen zwei.
Sie sind gar niedlich angezogen.
's ist meine Nachbarin dabei;
ich bin dem Mädchen sehr gewogen.
Sie gehen ihren stillen Schritt
und nehmen uns doch auch am Ende mit.

ERSTER

Herr Bruder, nein! Ich bin nicht gern geniert.
Geschwind, daß wir das Wildbret nicht verlieren!
Die Hand, die samstags ihren Besen führt,
wird sonntags dich am besten karessieren.

BÜRGER

Nein, er gefällt mir nicht, der neue Burgemeister!
Nun, da er's ist, wird er nur täglich dreister,
und für die Stadt was tut denn er?
Wird es nicht alle Tage schlimmer?
Gehorchen soll man mehr als immer
und zahlen mehr als je vorher.

BETTLER, *singt.*

Ihr guten Herrn, ihr schönen Frauen,
so wohlgeputzt und backenrot,
belieb' es euch, mich anzuschauen,
und seht und mildert meine Not!
Laßt hier mich nicht vergebens leiern!
Nur der ist froh, der geben mag.
Ein Tag, den alle Menschen feiern,
er sei für mich ein Erntetag!

ANDRER BÜRGER

Nichts Besser's weiß ich mir an Sonn- und Feiertagen
als ein Gespräch von Krieg und Kriegsgeschrei,
wenn hinten, weit, in der Türkei,
die Völker aufeinander schlagen.
Man steht am Fenster, trinkt sein Gläschen aus
und sieht den Fluß hinab die bunten Schiffe gleiten;
dann kehrt man abends froh nach Haus
und segnet Fried' und Friedenszeiten.

DRITTER BÜRGER

Herr Nachbar, ja! So lass' ich's auch geschehn:
sie mögen sich die Köpfe spalten,
mag alles durcheinander gehn;
doch nur zu Hause bleib's beim alten!

ALTE, *zu den Bürgermädchen.*

Ei! Wie geputzt! Das schöne junge Blut!
Wer soll sich nicht in euch vergaffen? —
Nur nicht so stolz! Es ist schon gut!
Und was ihr wünscht, das wüßt' ich wohl zu schaffen.

BÜRGERMÄDCHEN

Agathe, fort! Ich nehme mich in acht,
mit solchen Hexen öffentlich zu gehen;
sie ließ mich zwar in Sankt Andreas' Nacht
den künft'gen Liebsten leiblich sehen.

DIE ANDRE

Mir zeigte sie ihn im Kristall,
soldatenhaft, mit mehreren Verwegnen;
ich seh' mich um, ich such' ihn überall,
allein mir will er nicht begegnen.

SOLDATEN

Burgen mit hohen
Mauern und Zinnen,
Mädchen mit stolzen,
höhnenden Sinnen
möcht' ich gewinnen!
Kühn ist das Mühen,
herrlich der Lohn!

Und die Trompete
lassen wir werben,
wie zu der Freude
so zum Verderben.
Das ist ein Stürmen!
Das ist ein Leben!
Mädchen und Burgen
müssen sich geben.
Kühn ist das Mühen,
herrlich der Lohn!
Und die Soldaten
ziehen davon.

Faust und Wagner.

FAUST

Vom Eise befreit sind Strom und Bäche
durch des Frühlings holden, belebenden Blick;
im Tale grünet Hoffnungsglück.
Der alte Winter, in seiner Schwäche,
zog sich in rauhe Berge zurück.
Von dorther sendet er, fliehend, nur
ohnmächtige Schauer körnigen Eises
in Streifen über die grünende Flur.
Aber die Sonne duldet kein Weißes, —
überall regt sich Bildung und Streben, —
alles will sie mit Farben beleben;
doch an Blumen fehlt's im Revier,
sie nimmt geputzte Menschen dafür.
Kehre dich um, von diesen Höhen
nach der Stadt zurückzusehen!
Aus dem hohlen, finstern Tor
dringt ein buntes Gewimmel hervor.
Jeder sonnt sich heute so gern.
Sie feiern die Auferstehung des Herrn,
denn sie sind selber auferstanden:
aus niedriger Häuser dumpfen Gemächern,
aus Handwerks- und Gewerbesbanden,
aus dem Druck von Giebeln und Dächern,
aus der Straßen quetschender Enge,
aus der Kirchen ehrwürdiger Nacht
sind sie alle ans Licht gebracht.
Sieh nur! Sieh, wie behend sich die Menge
durch die Gärten und Felder zerschlägt,
wie der Fluß, in Breit' und Länge,
so manchen lustigen Nachen bewegt,
und, bis zum Sinken überladen,
entfernt sich dieser letzte Kahn.
Selbst von des Berges fernen Pfaden
blinken uns farbige Kleider an.
Ich höre schon des Dorfs Getümmel,
hier ist des Volkes wahrer Himmel,
zufrieden jauchzet groß und klein:
hier bin ich Mensch, hier darf ich's sein!

WAGNER

Mit Euch, Herr Doktor, zu spazieren
ist ehrenvoll und ist Gewinn;
doch würd' ich nicht allein mich her verlieren,
weil ich ein Feind von allem Rohen bin.
Das Fiedeln, Schreien, Kegelschieben
ist mir ein gar verhaßter Klang;
sie toben, wie vom bösen Geist getrieben,
und nennen's Freude, nennen's Gesang.

BAUERN UNTER DER LINDE.

Tanz und Gesang.

Der Schäfer putzte sich zum Tanz
mit bunter Jacke, Band und Kranz, —
schmuck war er angezogen.
Schon um die Linde war es voll,
und alles tanzte schon wie toll.
Juchhe! Juchhe!
Juchheisa! Heisa! He!
So ging der Fiedelbogen.

Er drückte hastig sich heran,
da stieß er an ein Mädchen an
mit seinem Ellenbogen;
die frische Dirne kehrt' sich um
und sagte: „Nun, das find' ich dumm!"
Juchhe! Juchhe!
Juchheisa! Heisa! He!
„Seid nicht so ungezogen!"

Doch hurtig in dem Kreise ging's,
sie tanzten rechts, sie tanzten links,
und alle Röcke flogen.
Sie wurden rot, sie wurden warm
und ruhten atmend Arm in Arm
— Juchhe! Juchhe!
Juchheisa! Heisa! He! —
und Hüft' an Ellenbogen.

„Und tu mir doch nicht so vertraut!
Wie mancher hat nicht seine Braut
belogen und betrogen!"
Er schmeichelte sie doch beiseit,
und von der Linde scholl es weit:

Juchhe! Juchhe!
Juchheisa! Heisa! He!
Geschrei und Fiedelbogen.

ALTER BAUER

Herr Doktor, das ist schön von Euch,
daß Ihr uns heute nicht verschmäht
und unter dieses Volksgedräng',
als ein so Hochgelahrter, geht.
So nehmet auch den schönsten Krug,
den wir mit frischem Trunk gefüllt!
Ich bring' ihn zu und wünsche laut,
daß er nicht nur den Durst Euch stillt:
die Zahl der Tropfen, die er hegt,
sei Euren Tagen zugelegt!

FAUST

Ich nehme den Erquickungstrank,
erwidr' euch allen Heil und Dank.

Das Volk sammelt sich im Kreis umher.

ALTER BAUER

Fürwahr, es ist sehr wohl getan,
daß Ihr am frohen Tag erscheint;
habt Ihr es vormals doch mit uns
an bösen Tagen gut gemeint!
Gar mancher steht lebendig hier,
den Euer Vater noch zuletzt
der heißen Fieberwut entriß,
als er der Seuche Ziel gesetzt.
Auch damals Ihr, ein junger Mann,
Ihr gingt in jedes Krankenhaus;
gar manche Leiche trug man fort,
Ihr aber kamt gesund heraus,
bestandet manche harte Proben:
dem Helfer half der Helfer droben.

ALLE

Gesundheit dem bewährten Mann,
daß er noch lange helfen kann!

FAUST

Vor jenem droben steht gebückt,
der helfen lehrt und Hülfe schickt!

Er geht mit Wagnern weiter.

WAGNER

Welch ein Gefühl mußt du, o großer Mann,
bei der Verehrung dieser Menge haben!
O glücklich, wer von seinen Gaben
solch einen Vorteil ziehen kann!
Der Vater zeigt dich seinem Knaben,
ein jeder fragt und drängt und eilt,
die Fiedel stockt, der Tänzer weilt.
Du gehst, in Reihen stehen sie,
die Mützen fliegen in die Höh';
und wenig fehlt, so beugten sich die Knie,
als käm' das Venerabile. – Blessed Sacrament in Procession

FAUST

Nur wenig Schritte noch hinauf zu jenem Stein. —
Hier wollen wir von unsrer Wandrung rasten.
Hier saß ich oft gedankenvoll allein
und quälte mich mit Beten und mit Fasten.
An Hoffnung reich, im Glauben fest,
mit Tränen, Seufzen, Händeringen
dacht' ich das Ende jener Pest
vom Herrn des Himmels zu erzwingen.
Der Menge Beifall tönt mir nun wie Hohn.
O, könntest du in meinem Innern lesen,
wie wenig Vater und Sohn
solch eines Ruhmes wert gewesen!
  Mein Vater war ein dunkler Ehrenmann,
der über die Natur und ihre heil'gen Kreise,
in Redlichkeit, jedoch auf seine Weise,
mit grillenhafter Mühe sann, —
der, in Gesellschaft von Adepten,
sich in die schwarze Küche schloß
und nach unendlichen Rezepten
das Widrige zusammengoß.
Da ward ein roter Leu, ein kühner Freier,
im lauen Bad der Lilie vermählt,
und beide dann mit offnem Flammenfeuer
aus einem Brautgemach ins andere gequält.
Erschien darauf mit bunten Farben
die junge Königin im Glas,
hier war die Arzenei; die Patienten starben,
und niemand fragte, wer genas.

So haben wir mit höllischen Latwergen
in diesen Tälern, diesen Bergen
weit schlimmer als die Pest getobt.
Ich habe selbst den Gift an Tausende gegeben;
sie welkten hin, ich muß erleben,
daß man die frechen Mörder lobt!

WAGNER

Wie könnt Ihr Euch darum betrüben!
Tut nicht ein braver Mann genug,
die Kunst, die man ihm übertrug,
gewissenhaft und pünktlich auszuüben?
Wenn du als Jüngling deinen Vater ehrst,
so wirst du gern von ihm empfangen;
wenn du als Mann die Wissenschaft vermehrst,
so kann dein Sohn zu höhrem Ziel gelangen.

FAUST

O glücklich, wer noch hoffen kann,
aus diesem Meer des Irrtums aufzutauchen!
Was man nicht weiß, das eben brauchte man,
und was man weiß, kann man nicht brauchen. —
Doch laß uns dieser Stunde schönes Gut
durch solchen Trübsinn nicht verkümmern!
Betrachte, wie in Abendsonneglut
die grünumgebnen Hütten schimmern!
Sie rückt und weicht, der Tag ist überlebt,
dort eilt sie hin und fördert neues Leben.
O, daß kein Flügel mich vom Boden hebt,
ihr nach und immer nach zu streben!
Ich säh' im ewigen Abendstrahl
die stille Welt zu meinen Füßen,
entzündet alle Höh'n, beruhigt jedes Tal,
den Silberbach in goldne Ströme fließen.
Nicht hemmte dann den göttergleichen Lauf
der wilde Berg mit allen seinen Schluchten.
Schon tut das Meer sich mit erwärmten Buchten
vor den erstaunten Augen auf.
Doch scheint die Göttin endlich wegzusinken.
Allein der neue Trieb erwacht,
ich eile fort, ihr ew'ges Licht zu trinken,
vor mir den Tag und hinter mir die Nacht,
den Himmel über mir und unter mir die Wellen . . .

Ein schöner Traum, indessen sie entweicht.
Ach! Zu des Geistes Flügeln wird so leicht
kein körperlicher Flügel sich gesellen.
Doch ist es jedem eingeboren,
daß sein Gefühl hinauf und vorwärts dringt,
wenn über uns, im blauen Raum verloren,
ihr schmetternd Lied die Lerche singt,
wenn über schroffen Fichtenhöhen
der Adler ausgebreitet schwebt,
und über Flächen, über Seen
der Kranich nach der Heimat strebt.

WAGNER

Ich hatte selbst oft grillenhafte Stunden,
doch solchen Trieb hab' ich noch nie empfunden.
Man sieht sich leicht an Wald und Feldern satt;
des Vogels Fittich werd' ich nie beneiden.
Wie anders tragen uns die Geistesfreuden
von Buch zu Buch, von Blatt zu Blatt!
Da werden Winternächte hold und schön,
ein selig Leben wärmet alle Glieder,
und ach, entrollst du gar ein würdig Pergamen,
so steigt der ganze Himmel zu dir nieder!

FAUST

Du bist dir nur des einen Triebs bewußt;
o lerne nie den andern kennen!
Zwei Seelen wohnen, ach, in meiner Brust,
die eine will sich von der andern trennen:
die eine hält in derber Liebeslust
sich an die Welt mit klammernden Organen;
die andre hebt gewaltsam sich vom Dust
zu den Gefilden hoher Ahnen.

O, gibt es Geister in der Luft,
die zwischen Erd' und Himmel herrschend weben,
so steiget nieder aus dem goldnen Duft
und führt mich weg zu neuem, buntem Leben!
Ja, wäre nur ein Zaubermantel mein!
Und trüg' er mich in fremde Länder,
mir sollt' er um die köstlichsten Gewänder,
nicht feil um einen Königsmantel sein!

WAGNER

Berufe nicht die wohlbekannte Schar,
die strömend sich im Dunstkreis überbreitet,
dem Menschen tausendfältige Gefahr
von allen Enden her bereitet.
Von Norden dringt der scharfe Geisterzahn
auf dich herbei mit pfeilgespitzten Zungen;
von Morgen ziehn vertrocknend sie heran
und nähren sich von deinen Lungen.
Wenn sie der Mittag aus der Wüste schickt,
die Glut auf Glut um deinen Scheitel häufen,
so bringt der West den Schwarm, der erst erquickt,
um dich und Feld und Aue zu ersäufen.
Sie hören gern, zum Schaden froh gewandt,
gehorchen gern, weil sie uns gern betrügen;
sie stellen wie vom Himmel sich gesandt
und lispeln englisch, wenn sie lügen.
Doch gehen wir! Ergraut ist schon die Welt,
die Luft gekühlt, der Nebel fällt.
Am Abend schätzt man erst das Haus. —
Was stehst du so und blickst erstaunt hinaus?
Was kann dich in der Dämmrung so ergreifen?

FAUST

Siehst du den schwarzen Hund durch Saat und Stoppel streifen?

WAGNER

Ich sah ihn lange schon. Nicht wichtig schien er mir.

FAUST

Betracht ihn recht! Für was hältst du das Tier?

WAGNER

Für einen Pudel, der auf seine Weise
sich auf der Spur des Herren plagt.

FAUST

Bemerkst du, wie in weitem Schneckenkreise
er um uns her und immer näher jagt?
Und irr' ich nicht, so zieht ein Feuerstrudel
auf seinen Pfaden hinterdrein.

WAGNER

Ich sehe nichts als einen schwarzen Pudel;
es mag bei Euch wohl Augentäuschung sein.

FAUST

Mir scheint es, daß er magisch leise Schlingen
zu künft'gem Band um unsre Füße zieht.

WAGNER

Ich seh' ihn ungewiß und furchtsam uns umspringen,
weil er statt seines Herrn zwei Unbekannte sieht.

FAUST

Der Kreis wird eng! Schon ist er nah!

WAGNER

Du siehst: ein Hund, und kein Gespenst ist da.
Er knurrt und zweifelt, legt sich auf den Bauch;
er wedelt. — Alles Hundebrauch.

FAUST

Geselle dich zu uns! Komm hier!

WAGNER

Es ist ein pudelnärrisch Tier.
Du stehest still, er wartet auf;
du sprichst ihn an, er strebt an dir hinauf;
verliere was, er wird es bringen,
nach deinem Stock ins Wasser springen.

FAUST

Du hast wohl recht: ich finde nicht die Spur
von einem Geist, und alles ist Dressur.

WAGNER

Dem Hunde, wenn er gut gezogen,
wird selbst ein weiser Mann gewogen.
Ja, deine Gunst verdient er ganz und gar,
er, der Studenten trefflicher Skolar.

Sie gehen in das Stadttor.

5 Studierzimmer

Faust, mit dem Pudel hereintretend.

FAUST

Verlassen hab' ich Feld und Auen,
die eine tiefe Nacht bedeckt,
mit ahnungsvollem, heil'gem Grauen
in uns die bess're Seele weckt.
Entschlafen sind nun wilde Triebe
mit jedem ungestümen Tun;
es reget sich die Menschenliebe,
die Liebe Gottes regt sich nun.

Sei ruhig, Pudel! Renne nicht hin und wider!
An der Schwelle was schnoperst du hier?
Lege dich hinter den Ofen nieder!
Mein bestes Kissen geb' ich dir.
Wie du draußen auf dem bergigen Wege
durch Rennen und Springen ergötzt uns hast,
so nimm nun auch von mir die Pflege
als ein willkommner, stiller Gast.

Ach, wenn in unsrer engen Zelle
die Lampe freundlich wieder brennt,
dann wird's in unserm Busen helle,
im Herzen, das sich selber kennt.
Vernunft fängt wieder an zu sprechen,
und Hoffnung wieder an zu blühn;
man sehnt sich nach des Lebens Bächen,
ach, nach des Lebens Quelle hin.

Knurre nicht, Pudel! Zu den heiligen Tönen,
die jetzt meine ganze Seel' umfassen,
will der tierische Laut nicht passen.
Wir sind gewohnt, daß die Menschen verhöhnen,
was sie nicht verstehn,
daß sie vor dem Guten und Schönen,
das ihnen oft beschwerlich ist, murren;
will es der Hund, wie sie, beknurren?

Aber ach! Schon fühl' ich, bei dem besten Willen,
Befriedigung nicht mehr aus dem Busen quillen.
Aber warum muß der Strom so bald versiegen,
und wir wieder im Durste liegen?
Davon hab' ich so viel Erfahrung. —
Doch dieser Mangel läßt sich ersetzen:
wir lernen das Überirdische schätzen,
wir sehnen uns nach Offenbarung,
die nirgends würd'ger und schöner brennt
als in dem Neuen Testament.
Mich drängt's, den Grundtext aufzuschlagen,
mit redlichem Gefühl einmal
das heilige Original
in mein geliebtes Deutsch zu übertragen.

Er schlägt ein Volum auf und schickt sich an.

Geschrieben steht: „Im Anfang war das Wort!"
Hier stock' ich schon! Wer hilft mir weiter fort?
Ich kann das Wort so hoch unmöglich schätzen,
ich muß es anders übersetzen,
wenn ich vom Geiste recht erleuchtet bin.
Geschrieben steht: Im Anfang war der Sinn.
Bedenke wohl die erste Zeile,
daß deine Feder sich nicht übereile!
Ist es der Sinn, der alles wirkt und schafft?
Es sollte stehn: Im Anfang war die Kraft!
Doch, auch indem ich dieses niederschreibe,
schon warnt mich was, daß ich dabei nicht bleibe.
Mir hilft der Geist! Auf einmal seh' ich Rat
und schreibe getrost: Im Anfang war die Tat!

Soll ich mit dir das Zimmer teilen,
Pudel, so laß das Heulen,
so laß das Bellen!
Solch einen störenden Gesellen
mag ich nicht in der Nähe leiden.
Einer von uns beiden
muß die Zelle meiden.
Ungern heb' ich das Gastrecht auf;
die Tür ist offen, hast freien Lauf.

Aber was muß ich sehen!
Kann das natürlich geschehen?
Ist es Schatten? Ist's Wirklichkeit?

Wie wird mein Pudel lang und breit!
Er hebt sich mit Gewalt, —
das ist nicht eines Hundes Gestalt!
Welch ein Gespenst bracht' ich ins Haus!
Schon sieht er wie ein Nilpferd aus,
mit feurigen Augen, schrecklichem Gebiß.
O! Du bist mir gewiß!
Für solche halbe Höllenbrut
ist Salomonis Schlüssel gut.

GEISTER, *auf dem Gange.*

Drinnen gefangen ist einer!
Bleibet haußen! Folg' ihm keiner!
Wie im Eisen der Fuchs,
zagt ein alter Höllenluchs.
Aber gebt acht!
Schwebet hin, schwebet wider,
auf und nieder,
und er hat sich losgemacht.
Könnt ihr ihm nützen,
laßt ihn nicht sitzen!
Denn er tat uns allen
schon viel zu Gefallen.

FAUST

Erst, zu begegnen dem Tiere,
brauch' ich den Spruch der Viere:

Salamander soll glühen,
Undene sich winden,
Sylphe verschwinden,
Kobold sich mühen.

Wer sie nicht kennte,
die Elemente,
ihre Kraft
und Eigenschaft,
wäre kein Meister
über die Geister.

Verschwind in Flammen,
Salamander!
Rauschend fließe zusammen,
Undene!
Leucht in Meteoren-Schöne,
Sylphe!

Bring häusliche Hülfe,
Incubus! Incubus!
Tritt hervor und mache den Schluß!

Keines der Viere
steckt in dem Tiere.
Es liegt ganz ruhig und grinst mich an;
ich hab' ihm noch nicht weh getan.
Du sollst mich hören
stärker beschwören.

Bist du, Geselle,
ein Flüchtling der Hölle?
So sieh dies Zeichen,
dem sie sich beugen,
die schwarzen Scharen!

Schon schwillt es auf mit borstigen Haaren.

Verworfnes Wesen!
Kannst du ihn lesen,
den nie Entsproßnen,
Unausgesprochnen,
durch alle Himmel Gegoßnen,
freventlich Durchstochnen?

Hinter den Ofen gebannt,
schwillt es wie ein Elefant,
den ganzen Raum füllt es an,
es will zum Nebel zerfließen.
Steige nicht zur Decke hinan!
Lege dich zu des Meisters Füßen!
Du siehst, daß ich nicht vergebens drohe.
Ich versenge dich mit heiliger Lohe!
Erwarte nicht
das dreimal glühende Licht!
Erwarte nicht
die stärkste von meinen Künsten!

Mephistopheles tritt, indem der Nebel fällt, gekleidet wie ein fahrender Scholastikus, hinter dem Ofen hervor.

MEPHISTOPHELES

Wozu der Lärm? Was steht dem Herrn zu Diensten?

FAUST

Das also war des Pudels Kern!
Ein fahrender Skolast? Der Kasus macht mich lachen.

MEPHISTOPHELES

Ich salutiere den gelehrten Herrn!
Ihr habt mich weidlich schwitzen machen.

FAUST

Wie nennst du dich?

MEPHISTOPHELES

Die Frage scheint mir klein
für einen, der das Wort so sehr verachtet,
der, weit entfernt von allem Schein,
nur in der Wesen Tiefe trachtet.

FAUST

Bei euch, ihr Herrn, kann man das Wesen
gewöhnlich aus dem Namen lesen,
wo es sich allzudeutlich weist,
wenn man euch Fliegengott, Verderber, Lügner heißt.
Nun gut, wer bist du denn?

MEPHISTOPHELES

Ein Teil von jener Kraft,
die stets das Böse will und stets das Gute schafft.

FAUST

Was ist mit diesem Rätselwort gemeint?

MEPHISTOPHELES

Ich bin der Geist, der stets verneint!
Und das mit Recht; denn alles, was entsteht,
ist wert, daß es zugrunde geht;
drum besser wär's, daß nichts entstünde.
So ist denn alles, was ihr Sünde,
Zerstörung, kurz das Böse nennt,
mein eigentliches Element.

FAUST

Du nennst dich einen Teil, und stehst doch ganz vor mir?

MEPHISTOPHELES

Bescheidne Wahrheit sprech' ich dir.
Wenn sich der Mensch, die kleine Narrenwelt,
gewöhnlich für ein Ganzes hält:
ich bin ein Teil des Teils, der anfangs alles war,
ein Teil der Finsternis, die sich das Licht gebar,
das stolze Licht, das nun der Mutter Nacht
den alten Rang, den Raum ihr streitig macht.
Und doch gelingt's ihm nicht, da es, soviel es strebt,

verhaftet an den Körpern klebt:
von Körpern strömt's, die Körper macht es schön,
ein Körper hemmt's auf seinem Gange;
so, hoff' ich, dauert es nicht lange,
und mit den Körpern wird's zugrunde gehn.

FAUST

Nun kenn' ich deine würd'gen Pflichten!
Du kannst im Großen nichts vernichten
und fängst es nun im Kleinen an.

MEPHISTOPHELES

Und freilich ist nicht viel damit getan.
Was sich dem Nichts entgegenstellt,
das Etwas, diese plumpe Welt,
soviel als ich schon unternommen,
ich wußte nicht ihr beizukommen,
mit Wellen, Stürmen, Schütteln, Brand —
geruhig bleibt am Ende Meer und Land!
Und dem verdammten Zeug, der Tier- und Menschenbrut,
dem ist nun gar nichts anzuhaben!
Wie viele hab' ich schon begraben,
und immer zirkuliert ein neues, frisches Blut!
So geht es fort, man möchte rasend werden!
Der Luft, dem Wasser, wie der Erden
entwinden tausend Keime sich,
im Trocknen, Feuchten, Warmen, Kalten!
Hätt' ich mir nicht die Flamme vorbehalten,
ich hätte nichts Apart's für mich.

FAUST

So setzest du der ewig regen,
der heilsam schaffenden Gewalt
die kalte Teufelsfaust entgegen,
die sich vergebens tückisch ballt!
Was anders suche zu beginnen
des Chaos wunderlicher Sohn!

MEPHISTOPHELES

Wir wollen wirklich uns besinnen.
Die nächsten Male mehr davon!
Dürft' ich wohl diesmal mich entfernen?

FAUST

Ich sehe nicht, warum du fragst.

Ich habe jetzt dich kennen lernen,
besuche nun mich, wie du magst.
Hier ist das Fenster, hier die Türe,
ein Rauchfang ist dir auch gewiß.

MEPHISTOPHELES

Gesteh' ich's nur! Daß ich hinausspaziere,
verbietet mir ein kleines Hindernis:
der Drudenfuß auf Eurer Schwelle —

FAUST

Das Pentagramma macht dir Pein?
Ei, sage mir, du Sohn der Hölle:
wenn das dich bannt, wie kamst du denn herein?
Wie ward ein solcher Geist betrogen?

MEPHISTOPHELES

Beschaut es recht! Es ist nicht gut gezogen;
der eine Winkel, der nach außen zu,
ist, wie du siehst, ein wenig offen.

FAUST

Das hat der Zufall gut getroffen!
Und mein Gefangner wärst denn du?
Das ist von ungefähr gelungen!

MEPHISTOPHELES

Der Pudel merkte nichts, als er hereingesprungen.
Die Sache sieht jetzt anders aus:
der Teufel kann nicht aus dem Haus.

FAUST

Doch warum gehst du nicht durchs Fenster?

MEPHISTOPHELES

's ist ein Gesetz der Teufel und Gespenster:
wo sie hereingeschlüpft, da müssen sie hinaus.
Das erste steht uns frei, beim zweiten sind wir Knechte.

FAUST

Die Hölle selbst hat ihre Rechte?
Das find' ich gut! Da ließe sich ein Pakt,
und sicher wohl, mit euch, ihr Herren, schließen?

MEPHISTOPHELES

Was man verspricht, das sollst du rein genießen,
dir wird davon nichts abgezwackt.
Doch das ist nicht so kurz zu fassen,

und wir besprechen das zunächst;
doch jetzo bitt' ich hoch und höchst,
für dieses Mal mich zu entlassen.

Faust

So bleibe doch noch einen Augenblick,
um mir erst gute Mär zu sagen.

Mephistopheles

Jetzt laß mich los! Ich komme bald zurück;
dann magst du nach Belieben fragen.

Faust

Ich habe dir nicht nachgestellt,
bist du doch selbst ins Garn gegangen.
Den Teufel halte, wer ihn hält!
Er wird ihn nicht so bald zum zweiten Male fangen.

Mephistopheles

Wenn dir's beliebt, so bin ich auch bereit,
dir zur Gesellschaft hier zu bleiben;
doch mit Bedingnis, dir die Zeit
durch meine Künste würdig zu vertreiben.

Faust

Ich seh' es gern, das steht dir frei;
nur daß die Kunst gefällig sei!

Mephistopheles

Du wirst, mein Freund, für deine Sinnen
in dieser Stunde mehr gewinnen
als in des Jahres Einerlei.
Was dir die zarten Geister singen,
die schönen Bilder, die sie bringen,
sind nicht ein leeres Zauberspiel.
Auch dein Geruch wird sich ergötzen,
dann wirst du deinen Gaumen letzen,
und dann entzückt sich dein Gefühl.
Bereitung braucht es nicht voran;
beisammen sind wir, fanget an!

Geister

Schwindet, ihr dunkeln
Wölbungen droben!
Reizender schaue
freundlich der blaue
Äther herein!
Wären die dunkeln

Wolken zerronnen!
Sternelein funkeln,
mildere Sonnen
scheinen darein.
Himmlischer Söhne
geistige Schöne,
schwankende Beugung
schwebet vorüber.
Sehnende Neigung
folget hinüber;
und der Gewänder
flatternde Bänder
decken die Länder,
decken die Laube,
wo sich fürs Leben,
tief in Gedanken,
Liebende geben.
Laube bei Laube!
Sprossende Ranken!
Lastende Traube
stürzt ins Behälter
drängender Kelter;
stürzen in Bächen
schäumende Weine,
rieseln durch reine,
edle Gesteine,
lassen die Höhen
hinter sich liegen,
breiten zu Seen
sich ums Genügen
grünender Hügel.
Und das Geflügel
schlürfet sich Wonne,
flieget der Sonne,
flieget den hellen
Inseln entgegen,
die sich auf Wellen
gauklend bewegen,
wo wir in Chören
Jauchzende hören,
über den Auen
Tanzende schauen,
die sich im Freien

alle zerstreuen.
Einige klimmen
über die Höhen,
andere schwimmen
über die Seen,
andere schweben:
alle zum Leben,
alle zur Ferne
liebender Sterne,
seliger Huld.

MEPHISTOPHELES

Er schläft! So recht, ihr luft'gen, zarten Jungen!
Ihr habt ihn treulich eingesungen!
Für dies Konzert bin ich in eurer Schuld.

Du bist noch nicht der Mann, den Teufel festzuhalten.

Umgaukelt ihn mit süßen Traumgestalten,
versenkt ihn in ein Meer des Wahns!
Doch dieser Schwelle Zauber zu zerspalten,
bedarf ich eines Rattenzahns.
Nicht lange brauch' ich zu beschwören,
schon raschelt eine hier und wird sogleich mich hören.

Der Herr der Ratten und der Mäuse,
der Fliegen, Frösche, Wanzen, Läuse
befiehlt dir, dich hervorzuwagen
und diese Schwelle zu benagen,
so wie er sie mit Öl betupft. —
Da kommst du schon hervorgehupft!
Nur frisch ans Werk! Die Spitze, die mich bannte,
sie sitzt ganz vornen an der Kante.
Noch einen Biß, so ist's geschehn!

Nun, Fauste, träume fort, bis wir uns wiedersehn!

Ab.

FAUST, *erwachend.*

Bin ich denn abermals betrogen?
Verschwindet so der geisterreiche Drang,
daß mir ein Traum den Teufel vorgelogen,
und daß ein Pudel mir entsprang?

6 Studierzimmer

Faust. Nachher Mephistopheles.

FAUST
Es klopft? Herein! Wer will mich wieder plagen?

MEPHISTOPHELES
Ich bin's.

FAUST
Herein!

MEPHISTOPHELES
Du mußt es dreimal sagen.

FAUST
Herein denn!

MEPHISTOPHELES
So gefällst du mir!
Wir werden, hoff' ich, uns vertragen.
Denn dir die Grillen zu verjagen,
bin ich als edler Junker hier —
in rotem, goldverbrämtem Kleide,
das Mäntelchen von starrer Seide,
die Hahnenfeder auf dem Hut,
mit einem langen, spitzen Degen —
und rate nun dir, kurz und gut,
dergleichen gleichfalls anzulegen,
damit du, losgebunden, frei,
erfahrest, was das Leben sei.

FAUST
In jedem Kleide werd' ich wohl die Pein
des engen Erdelebens fühlen.
Ich bin zu alt, um nur zu spielen,
zu jung, um ohne Wunsch zu sein.
Was kann die Welt mir wohl gewähren?
„Entbehren sollst du! Sollst entbehren!"
Das ist der ewige Gesang,
der jedem an die Ohren klingt,
den, unser ganzes Leben lang,
uns heiser jede Stunde singt.
Nur mit Entsetzen wach' ich morgens auf;
ich möchte bittre Tränen weinen,

den Tag zu sehn, der mir in seinem Lauf
nicht einen Wunsch erfüllen wird, nicht einen,
der selbst die Ahnung jeder Lust
mit eigensinnigem Krittel mindert,
die Schöpfung meiner regen Brust
mit tausend Lebensfratzen hindert.
Auch muß ich, wenn die Nacht sich niedersenkt,
mich ängstlich auf das Lager strecken;
auch da wird keine Rast geschenkt,
mich werden wilde Träume schrecken.
Der Gott, der mir im Busen wohnt,
kann tief mein Innerstes erregen;
der über allen meinen Kräften thront,
er kann nach außen nichts bewegen:
und so ist mir das Dasein eine Last,
der Tod erwünscht, das Leben mir verhaßt.

MEPHISTOPHELES

Und doch ist nie der Tod ein ganz willkommner Gast.

FAUST

O selig der, dem er im Siegesglanze
die blut'gen Lorbeern um die Schläfe windet,
den er, nach rasch durchrastem Tanze,
in eines Mädchens Armen findet!
O, wär' ich vor des hohen Geistes Kraft
entzückt, entseelt dahingesunken!

MEPHISTOPHELES

Und doch hat jemand einen braunen Saft
in jener Nacht nicht ausgetrunken.

FAUST

Das Spionieren, scheint's, ist deine Lust.

MEPHISTOPHELES

Allwissend bin ich nicht; doch viel ist mir bewußt.

FAUST

Wenn aus dem schrecklichen Gewühle
ein süß bekannter Ton mich zog,
den Rest von kindlichem Gefühle
mit Anklang froher Zeit betrog,
so fluch' ich allem, was die Seele
mit Lock- und Gaukelwerk umspannt
und sie in diese Trauerhöhle

mit Blend- und Schmeichelkräften bannt!
Verflucht voraus die hohe Meinung,
womit der Geist sich selbst umfängt!
Verflucht das Blenden der Erscheinung,
die sich an unsre Sinne drängt!
Verflucht, was uns in Träumen heuchelt,
des Ruhms, der Namensdauer Trug!
Verflucht, was als Besitz uns schmeichelt,
als Weib und Kind, als Knecht und Pflug!
Verflucht sei Mammon, wenn mit Schätzen
er uns zu kühnen Taten regt,
wenn er zu müßigem Ergötzen
die Polster uns zurechtelegt!
Fluch sei dem Balsamsaft der Trauben!
Fluch jener höchsten Liebeshuld!
Fluch sei der Hoffnung! Fluch dem Glauben!
Und Fluch vor allen der Geduld!

GEISTERCHOR, *unsichtbar.*

Weh! weh!
Du hast sie zerstört,
die schöne Welt,
mit mächtiger Faust;
sie stürzt, sie zerfällt!
Ein Halbgott hat sie zerschlagen!
Wir tragen
die Trümmern ins Nichts hinüber
und klagen
über die verlorne Schöne.
Mächtiger
der Erdensöhne,
prächtiger
baue sie wieder!
In deinem Busen baue sie auf!
Neuen Lebenslauf
beginne
mit hellem Sinne!
Und neue Lieder
tönen darauf!

MEPHISTOPHELES

Dies sind die Kleinen
von den Meinen.

Höre, wie zu Lust und Taten
altklug sie raten!
In die Welt weit,
aus der Einsamkeit,
wo Sinnen und Säfte stocken,
wollen sie dich locken.

Hör auf, mit deinem Gram zu spielen,
der wie ein Geier dir am Leben frißt!
Die schlechteste Gesellschaft läßt dich fühlen,
daß du ein Mensch mit Menschen bist.
Doch so ist's nicht gemeint,
dich unter das Pack zu stoßen.
Ich bin keiner von den Großen;
doch willst du mit mir vereint
deine Schritte durchs Leben nehmen,
so will ich mich gern bequemen,
dein zu sein, auf der Stelle.
Ich bin dein Geselle
und mach' ich dir's recht,
bin ich dein Diener, bin dein Knecht!

Faust

Und was soll ich dagegen dir erfüllen?

Mephistopheles

Dazu hast du noch eine lange Frist.

Faust

Nein, nein! Der Teufel ist ein Egoist
und tut nicht leicht um Gottes willen,
was einem andern nützlich ist.
Sprich die Bedingung deutlich aus!
Ein solcher Diener bringt Gefahr ins Haus.

Mephistopheles

Ich will mich hier zu deinem Dienst verbinden,
auf deinen Wink nicht rasten und nicht ruhn;
wenn wir uns drüben wiederfinden,
so sollst du mir das Gleiche tun.

Faust

Das Drüben kann mich wenig kümmern.
Schlägst du erst diese Welt zu Trümmern,
die andre mag darnach entstehn.
Aus dieser Erde quillen meine Freuden,

und diese Sonne scheinet meinen Leiden;
kann ich mich erst von ihnen scheiden,
dann mag, was will und kann, geschehn.
Davon will ich nichts weiter hören,
ob man auch künftig haßt und liebt,
und ob es auch in jenen Sphären
ein Oben oder Unten gibt.

MEPHISTOPHELES

In diesem Sinne kannst du's wagen.
Verbinde dich! Du sollst in diesen Tagen
mit Freuden meine Künste sehn;
ich gebe dir, was noch kein Mensch gesehn.

FAUST

Was willst du armer Teufel geben?
Ward eines Menschen Geist, in seinem hohen Streben,
von deinesgleichen je gefaßt?
Doch hast du Speise, die nicht sättigt, hast
du rotes Gold, das ohne Rast,
Quecksilber gleich, dir in der Hand zerrinnt,
ein Spiel, bei dem man nie gewinnt,
ein Mädchen, das an meiner Brust
mit Äugeln schon dem Nachbar sich verbindet,
der Ehre schöne Götterlust,
die wie ein Meteor verschwindet.
Zeig mir die Frucht, die fault, eh' man sie bricht,
und Bäume, die sich täglich neu begrünen!

MEPHISTOPHELES

Ein solcher Auftrag schreckt mich nicht,
mit solchen Schätzen kann ich dienen.
Doch, guter Freund, die Zeit kommt auch heran,
wo wir was Gut's in Ruhe schmausen mögen.

FAUST

Werd' ich beruhigt je mich auf ein Faulbett legen,
so sei es gleich um mich getan!
Kannst du mich schmeichelnd je belügen,
daß ich mir selbst gefallen mag,
kannst du mich mit Genuß betrügen,
das sei für mich der letzte Tag!
Die Wette biet' ich!

MEPHISTOPHELES

Topp!

FAUST

Und Schlag auf Schlag!
Werd' ich zum Augenblicke sagen:
„Verweile doch, du bist so schön!"
dann magst du mich in Fesseln schlagen,
dann will ich gern zugrunde gehn!
Dann mag die Totenglocke schallen,
dann bist du deines Dienstes frei,
die Uhr mag stehn, der Zeiger fallen,
es sei die Zeit für mich vorbei!

MEPHISTOPHELES

Bedenk es wohl! Wir werden's nicht vergessen.

FAUST

Dazu hast du ein volles Recht!
Ich habe mich nicht freventlich vermessen:
wie ich beharre, bin ich Knecht,
ob dein, was frag' ich, oder wessen!

MEPHISTOPHELES

Ich werde heute gleich, beim Doktorschmaus,
als Diener meine Pflicht erfüllen.
Nur eins! — Um Lebens oder Sterbens willen
bitt' ich mir ein paar Zeilen aus.

FAUST

Auch was Geschriebnes forderst du Pedant?
Hast du noch keinen Mann, nicht Manneswort gekannt?
Ist's nicht genug, daß mein gesprochnes Wort
auf ewig soll mit meinen Tagen schalten?
Rast nicht die Welt in allen Strömen fort,
und mich soll ein Versprechen halten?
Doch dieser Wahn ist uns ins Herz gelegt, —
wer mag sich gern davon befreien?
Beglückt, wer Treue rein im Busen trägt,
kein Opfer wird ihn je gereuen!
Allein ein Pergament, beschrieben und beprägt,
ist ein Gespenst, vor dem sich alle scheuen.
Das Wort erstirbt schon in der Feder,
die Herrschaft führen Wachs und Leder.
Was willst du, böser Geist, von mir?
Erz? Marmor? Pergament? Papier?
Soll ich mit Griffel, Meißel, Feder schreiben?
Ich gebe jede Wahl dir frei.

MEPHISTOPHELES

Wie magst du deine Rednerei
nur gleich so hitzig übertreiben!
Ist doch ein jedes Blättchen gut.
Du unterzeichnest dich mit einem Tröpfchen Blut.

FAUST

Wenn dies dir völlig G'nüge tut,
so mag es bei der Fratze bleiben.

MEPHISTOPHELES

Blut ist ein ganz besondrer Saft.

FAUST

Nur keine Furcht, daß ich dies Bündnis breche!
Das Streben meiner ganzen Kraft
ist grade das, was ich verspreche.
Ich habe mich zu hoch gebläht;
in deinen Rang gehör' ich nur.
Der große Geist hat mich verschmäht,
vor mir verschließt sich die Natur.
Des Denkens Faden ist zerrissen,
mir ekelt lange vor allem Wissen.
Laß in den Tiefen der Sinnlichkeit
uns glühende Leidenschaften stillen!
In undurchdrungnen Zauberhüllen
sei jedes Wunder gleich bereit!
Stürzen wir uns in das Rauschen der Zeit,
ins Rollen der Begebenheit!
Da mag denn Schmerz und Genuß,
Gelingen und Verdruß
miteinander wechseln, wie es kann;
nur rastlos betätigt sich der Mann.

MEPHISTOPHELES

Euch ist kein Maß und Ziel gesetzt.
Beliebt's Euch, überall zu naschen,
im Fliehen etwas zu erhaschen,
bekomm' Euch wohl, was Euch ergötzt!
Nur greift mir zu und seid nicht blöde!

FAUST

Du hörest ja, von Freud' ist nicht die Rede.
Dem Taumel weih' ich mich, dem schmerzlichsten Genuß,
verliebtem Haß, erquickendem Verdruß.

Mein Busen, der vom Wissensdrang geheilt ist,
soll keinen Schmerzen künftig sich verschließen,
und was der ganzen Menschheit zugeteilt ist,
will ich in meinem innern Selbst genießen,
mit meinem Geist das Höchst' und Tiefste greifen,
ihr Wohl und Weh auf meinen Busen häufen
und so mein eigen Selbst zu ihrem Selbst erweitern —
und, wie sie selbst, am End' auch ich zerscheitern.

MEPHISTOPHELES

O glaube mir, der manche tausend Jahre
an dieser harten Speise kaut,
daß von der Wiege bis zur Bahre
kein Mensch den alten Sauerteig verdaut!
Glaub unsereinem: dieses Ganze
ist nur für einen Gott gemacht!
Er findet sich in einem ew'gen Glanze,
uns hat er in die Finsternis gebracht,
und euch taugt einzig Tag und Nacht.

FAUST

Allein ich will!

MEPHISTOPHELES

Das läßt sich hören!
Doch nur vor einem ist mir bang:
die Zeit ist kurz, die Kunst ist lang.
Ich dächt', Ihr ließet Euch belehren.
Assoziiert Euch mit einem Poeten,
laßt den Herrn in Gedanken schweifen
und alle edlen Qualitäten
auf Euren Ehrenscheitel häufen:
des Löwen Mut,
des Hirsches Schnelligkeit,
des Italieners feurig Blut,
des Nordens Dau'rbarkeit.
Laßt ihn Euch das Geheimnis finden,
Großmut und Arglist zu verbinden
und Euch, mit warmen Jugendtrieben,
nach einem Plane, zu verlieben.
Möchte selbst solch einen Herren kennen,
würd' ihn Herrn Mikrokosmus nennen.

FAUST

Was bin ich denn, wenn es nicht möglich ist,
der Menschheit Krone zu erringen,
nach der sich alle Sinne dringen?

MEPHISTOPHELES

Du bist am Ende — was du bist.
Setz dir Perücken auf von Millionen Locken,
setz deinen Fuß auf ellenhohe Socken, —
du bleibst doch immer, was du bist.

FAUST

Ich fühl's, vergebens hab' ich alle Schätze
des Menschengeists auf mich herbeigerafft,
und wenn ich mich am Ende niedersetze,
quillt innerlich doch keine neue Kraft;
ich bin nicht um ein Haarbreit höher,
bin dem Unendlichen nicht näher.

MEPHISTOPHELES

Mein guter Herr, Ihr seht die Sachen,
wie man die Sachen eben sieht;
wir müssen das gescheiter machen,
eh' uns des Lebens Freude flieht.
Was Henker! Freilich, Händ' und Füße
und Kopf und H — —, die sind dein;
doch alles, was ich frisch genieße,
ist das drum weniger mein?
Wenn ich sechs Hengste zahlen kann,
sind ihre Kräfte nicht die meine?
Ich renne zu und bin ein rechter Mann,
als hätt' ich vierundzwanzig Beine.
Drum frisch! Laß alles Sinnen sein,
und grad mit in die Welt hinein!
Ich sag' es dir: ein Kerl, der spekuliert,
ist wie ein Tier, auf dürrer Heide
von einem bösen Geist im Kreis herumgeführt,
und ringsumher liegt schöne grüne Weide.

FAUST

Wie fangen wir das an?

MEPHISTOPHELES

Wir gehen eben fort.
Was ist das für ein Marterort?
Was heißt das für ein Leben führen,

sich und die Jungens ennuyieren?
Laß du das dem Herrn Nachbar Wanst!
Was willst du dich das Stroh zu dreschen plagen?
Das Beste, was du wissen kannst,
darfst du den Buben doch nicht sagen. —
Gleich hör' ich einen auf dem Gange!

FAUST

Mir ist's nicht möglich, ihn zu sehn.

MEPHISTOPHELES

Der arme Knabe wartet lange,
der darf nicht ungetröstet gehn.
Komm, gib mir deinen Rock und Mütze!
Die Maske muß mir köstlich stehn.

Er kleidet sich um.

Nun überlaß es meinem Witze!
Ich brauche nur ein Viertelstündchen Zeit;
indessen mache dich zur schönen Fahrt bereit!

Faust ab.

MEPHISTOPHELES, *in Fausts langem Kleide.*

Verachte nur Vernunft und Wissenschaft,
des Menschen allerhöchste Kraft,
laß nur in Blend- und Zauberwerken
dich von dem Lügengeist bestärken,
so hab' ich dich schon unbedingt. —
Ihm hat das Schicksal einen Geist gegeben,
der ungebändigt immer vorwärts dringt,
und dessen übereiltes Streben
der Erde Freuden überspringt.
Den schlepp' ich durch das wilde Leben,
durch flache Unbedeutenheit;
er soll mir zappeln, starren, kleben,
und seiner Unersättlichkeit
soll Speis' und Trank vor gier'gen Lippen schweben;
er wird Erquickung sich umsonst erflehn;
und hätt' er sich auch nicht dem Teufel übergeben,
er müßte doch zugrunde gehn.

Ein Schüler tritt auf.

SCHÜLER

Ich bin allhier erst kurze Zeit
und komme voll Ergebenheit,

einen Mann zu sprechen und zu kennen,
den alle mir mit Ehrfurcht nennen.

MEPHISTOPHELES

Eure Höflichkeit erfreut mich sehr!
Ihr seht einen Mann wie andre mehr.
Habt Ihr Euch sonst schon umgetan?

SCHÜLER

Ich bitt' Euch, nehmt Euch meiner an!
Ich komme mit allem guten Mut,
leidlichem Geld und frischem Blut;
meine Mutter wollte mich kaum entfernen;
möchte gern was Recht's hieraußen lernen.

MEPHISTOPHELES

Da seid Ihr eben recht am Ort.

SCHÜLER

Aufrichtig, möchte schon wieder fort!
In diesen Mauern, diesen Hallen
will es mir keineswegs gefallen.
Es ist ein gar beschränkter Raum,
man sieht nichts Grünes, keinen Baum,
und in den Sälen, auf den Bänken
vergeht mir Hören, Sehn und Denken.

MEPHISTOPHELES

Das kommt nur auf Gewohnheit an.
So nimmt ein Kind der Mutter Brust
nicht gleich im Anfang willig an,
doch bald ernährt es sich mit Lust.
So wird's Euch an der Weisheit Brüsten
mit jedem Tage mehr gelüsten.

SCHÜLER

An ihrem Hals will ich mit Freuden hangen!
Doch sagt mir nur: wie kann ich hingelangen?

MEPHISTOPHELES

Erklärt Euch, eh' Ihr weiter geht:
was wählt Ihr für eine Fakultät?

SCHÜLER

Ich wünschte, recht gelehrt zu werden,
und möchte gern, was auf der Erden
und in dem Himmel ist, erfassen,
die Wissenschaft und die Natur.

M. satirizes the required courses in logic and metaphysics. Then they discuss the choice of a field of concentration. The student has no desire to study law. M. agrees that law + justice are not synonymous. Theology is depicted as a hazardous undertaking, full of the peril of subtle heresy. But medicine is recommended especially if one has a way with women. He is dismissed with motto. "You shall be as God, knowing good and evil."

MEPHISTOPHELES

Da seid Ihr auf der rechten Spur;
doch müßt Ihr Euch nicht zerstreuen lassen.

SCHÜLER

Ich bin dabei mit Seel' und Leib;
doch freilich würde mir behagen
ein wenig Freiheit und Zeitvertreib
an schönen Sommerfeiertagen.

MEPHISTOPHELES

Gebraucht der Zeit, sie geht so schnell von hinnen.
Doch Ordnung lehrt Euch Zeit gewinnen.
Mein teurer Freund, ich rat' Euch drum
zuerst *Collegium Logicum*.
Da wird der Geist Euch wohl dressiert,
in spanische Stiefeln eingeschnürt,
daß er bedächtiger so fortan
hinschleiche die Gedankenbahn
und nicht etwa, die Kreuz und Quer,
irrlichteliere hin und her.
Dann lehret man Euch manchen Tag,
daß, was Ihr sonst auf einen Schlag
getrieben, wie Essen und Trinken frei,
Eins! Zwei! Drei! dazu nötig sei.
Zwar ist's mit der Gedankenfabrik
wie mit einem Weber-Meisterstück,
wo *ein* Tritt tausend Fäden regt,
die Schifflein herüber hinüber schießen,
die Fäden ungesehen fließen,
ein Schlag tausend Verbindungen schlägt.
Der Philosoph, der tritt herein
und beweist Euch, es müßt' so sein:
das Erst' wär' so, das Zweite so
und drum das Dritt' und Vierte so;
und wenn das Erst' und Zweit' nicht wär',
das Dritt' und Viert' wär' nimmermehr.
Das preisen die Schüler allerorten,
sind aber keine Weber geworden.
Wer will was Lebendig's erkennen und beschreiben,
sucht erst den Geist herauszutreiben;
dann hat er die Teile in seiner Hand,
fehlt leider nur das geistige Band.

Philosopher can analyze but can't create a masterpiece

Encheiresin naturae nennt's die Chemie,
spottet ihrer selbst und weiß nicht wie.

SCHÜLER

Kann Euch nicht eben ganz verstehen.

MEPHISTOPHELES

Das wird nächstens schon besser gehen,
wenn Ihr lernt alles reduzieren - reduction of propositions to basic terms
und gehörig klassifizieren. 'according to characteristic features

SCHÜLER

Mir wird von alle dem so dumm,
als ging' mir ein Mühlrad im Kopf herum.

MEPHISTOPHELES

Nachher, vor allen andern Sachen,
müßt Ihr Euch an die Metaphysik machen!
Da seht, daß Ihr tiefsinnig faßt,
was in des Menschen Hirn nicht paßt;
für was drein geht und nicht drein geht,
ein prächtig Wort zu Diensten steht.
Doch vorerst dieses halbe Jahr
nehmt ja der besten Ordnung wahr!
Fünf Stunden habt Ihr jeden Tag;
seid drinnen mit dem Glockenschlag!
Habt Euch vorher wohl präpariert,
Paragraphos wohl einstudiert,
damit Ihr nachher besser seht,
daß er nichts sagt, als was im Buche steht.
Doch Euch des Schreibens ja befleißt,
als diktiert' Euch der Heilig' Geist!

SCHÜLER

Das sollt Ihr mir nicht zweimal sagen!
Ich denke mir, wie viel es nützt;
denn was man schwarz auf weiß besitzt,
kann man getrost nach Hause tragen.

MEPHISTOPHELES

Doch wählt mir eine Fakultät! Choice of field of concentration

SCHÜLER Jurisprudence

Zur Rechtsgelehrsamkeit kann ich mich nicht bequemen.

MEPHISTOPHELES

Ich kann es Euch so sehr nicht übelnehmen,
ich weiß, wie es um diese Lehre steht.

Es erben sich Gesetz' und Rechte
wie eine ew'ge Krankheit fort;
sie schleppen von Geschlecht sich zum Geschlechte
und rücken sacht von Ort zu Ort.
Vernunft wird Unsinn, Wohltat Plage;
weh dir, daß du ein Enkel bist!
Vom Rechte, das mit uns geboren ist,
von dem ist leider nie die Frage.

SCHÜLER

Mein Abscheu wird durch Euch vermehrt.
O glücklich der, den Ihr belehrt!
Fast möcht' ich nun Theologie studieren.

MEPHISTOPHELES

Ich wünschte nicht, Euch irrezuführen.
Was diese Wissenschaft betrifft,
es ist so schwer, den falschen Weg zu meiden;
es liegt in ihr so viel verborgnes Gift,
und von der Arzenei ist's kaum zu unterscheiden.
Am besten ist's auch hier, wenn Ihr nur *einen* hört
und auf des Meisters Worte schwört.
Im ganzen — haltet Euch an Worte!
Dann geht Ihr durch die sichre Pforte
zum Tempel der Gewißheit ein.

SCHÜLER

Doch ein Begriff muß bei dem Worte sein!

MEPHISTOPHELES

Schon gut! Nur muß man sich nicht allzu ängstlich quälen;
denn eben wo Begriffe fehlen,
da stellt ein Wort zur rechten Zeit sich ein.
Mit Worten läßt sich trefflich streiten,
mit Worten ein System bereiten,
an Worte läßt sich trefflich glauben,
von einem Wort läßt sich kein Jota rauben.

SCHÜLER

Verzeiht! Ich halt' Euch auf mit vielen Fragen,
allein ich muß Euch noch bemühn.
Wollt Ihr mir von der Medizin
nicht auch ein kräftig Wörtchen sagen?
Drei Jahr ist eine kurze Zeit,
und, Gott, das Feld ist gar zu weit!

Wenn man einen Fingerzeig nur hat,
läßt sich's schon eher weiter fühlen.

MEPHISTOPHELES, *für sich.*

Ich bin des trocknen Tons nun satt,
muß wieder recht den Teufel spielen.

Laut.

Der Geist der Medizin ist leicht zu fassen!
Ihr durchstudiert die groß' und kleine Welt,
um es am Ende gehn zu lassen,
wie's Gott gefällt.
Vergebens, daß Ihr ringsum wissenschaftlich schweift,
ein jeder lernt nur, was er lernen kann;
doch der den Augenblick ergreift,
das ist der rechte Mann.
Ihr seid noch ziemlich wohlgebaut,
an Kühnheit wird's Euch auch nicht fehlen,
und wenn Ihr Euch nur selbst vertraut,
vertrauen Euch die andern Seelen.
Besonders lernt die Weiber führen!
Es ist ihr ewig Weh und Ach
so tausendfach
aus *einem* Punkte zu kurieren;
und wenn Ihr halbweg ehrbar tut,
dann habt Ihr sie all' unterm Hut.
Ein Titel muß sie erst vertraulich machen,
daß Eure Kunst viel Künste übersteigt;
zum Willkomm tappt Ihr dann nach allen Siebensachen,
um die ein andrer viele Jahre streicht,
versteht das Pülslein wohl zu drücken
und fasset sie, mit feurig schlauen Blicken,
wohl um die schlanke Hüfte frei,
zu sehn, wie fest geschnürt sie sei.

SCHÜLER

Das sieht schon besser aus! Man sieht doch, wo und wie!

MEPHISTOPHELES

Grau, teurer Freund, ist alle Theorie,
und grün des Lebens goldner Baum.

SCHÜLER

Ich schwör' Euch zu, mir ist's als wie ein Traum.
Dürft' ich Euch wohl ein andermal beschweren,
von Eurer Weisheit auf den Grund zu hören?

MEPHISTOPHELES

Was ich vermag, soll gern geschehn.

SCHÜLER

Ich kann unmöglich wieder gehn,
ich muß Euch noch mein Stammbuch überreichen.
Gönn' Eure Gunst mir dieses Zeichen!

MEPHISTOPHELES

Sehr wohl.

Er schreibt und gibt's.

SCHÜLER, *liest.*

„*Eritis sicut Deus, scientes bonum et malum.*"

Macht's ehrerbietig zu und empfiehlt sich.

MEPHISTOPHELES

Folg nur dem alten Spruch und meiner Muhme, der Schlange,
dir wird gewiß einmal bei deiner Gottähnlichkeit bange!

Faust tritt auf.

FAUST

Wohin soll es nun gehn?

MEPHISTOPHELES

Wohin es dir gefällt.
Wir sehn die kleine, dann die große Welt.
Mit welcher Freude, welchem Nutzen,
wirst du den *Cursum* durchschmarutzen!

FAUST

Allein bei meinem langen Bart
fehlt mir die leichte Lebensart.
Es wird mir der Versuch nicht glücken;
ich wußte nie, mich in die Welt zu schicken.
Vor andern fühl' ich mich so klein;
ich werde stets verlegen sein.

MEPHISTOPHELES

Mein guter Freund, das wird sich alles geben;
sobald du dir vertraust, sobald weißt du zu leben.

FAUST

Wie kommen wir denn aus dem Haus?
Wo hast du Pferde, Knecht und Wagen?

MEPHISTOPHELES

Wir breiten nur den Mantel aus,
der soll uns durch die Lüfte tragen.

Du nimmst bei diesem kühnen Schritt
nur keinen großen Bündel mit.
Ein bißchen Feuerluft, die ich bereiten werde,
hebt uns behend von dieser Erde,
und sind wir leicht, so geht es schnell hinauf. —
Ich gratuliere dir zum neuen Lebenslauf.

p 316

7 Auerbachs Keller in Leipzig

Zeche lustiger Gesellen.

FROSCH

Will keiner trinken, keiner lachen?
Ich will euch lehren Gesichter machen!
Ihr seid ja heut wie nasses Stroh
und brennt sonst immer lichterloh.

BRANDER

Das liegt an dir: du bringst ja nichts herbei,
nicht eine Dummheit, keine Sauerei.

Frosch gießt ihm ein Glas Wein über den Kopf.

FROSCH

Da hast du beides!

BRANDER

Doppelt Schwein!

FROSCH

Ihr wollt es ja, man soll es sein!

SIEBEL

Zur Tür hinaus, wer sich entzweit!
Mit offner Brust singt Runda, sauft und schreit!
Auf! Holla! Ho!

ALTMAYER

Weh mir! Ich bin verloren!
Baumwolle her! Der Kerl sprengt mir die Ohren.

SIEBEL

Wenn das Gewölbe widerschallt,
fühlt man erst recht des Basses Grundgewalt.

M not Faust performs the showy tricks
a group of students are drinking, making jokes, playing pranks and singing.
M. promises F this kind of diversion every eve. if F. enjoys it

FROSCH

So recht! Hinaus mit dem, der etwas übelnimmt!
A! tara lara da!

ALTMAYER

A! tara lara da!

FROSCH

Die Kehlen sind gestimmt.

Singt.

Das liebe Heil'ge Röm'sche Reich,
wie hält's nur noch zusammen?

BRANDER

Ein garstig Lied! Pfui! Ein politisch Lied!
Ein leidig Lied! Dankt Gott mit jedem Morgen,
daß ihr nicht braucht fürs Röm'sche Reich zu sorgen!
Ich halt' es wenigstens für reichlichen Gewinn,
daß ich nicht Kaiser oder Kanzler bin.
Doch muß auch uns ein Oberhaupt nicht fehlen;
wir wollen einen Papst erwählen.
Ihr wißt, welch eine Qualität
den Ausschlag gibt, den Mann erhöht.

FROSCH, *singt.*

Schwing dich auf, Frau Nachtigall,
grüß mir mein Liebchen zehentausendmal!

SIEBEL

Dem Liebchen keinen Gruß! Ich will davon nichts hören!

FROSCH

Dem Liebchen Gruß und Kuß! Du wirst mir's nicht verwehren!

Singt.

Riegel auf! in stiller Nacht.
Riegel auf! der Liebste wacht.
Riegel zu! des Morgens früh.

SIEBEL

Ja, singe, singe nur, und lob und rühme sie!
Ich will zu meiner Zeit schon lachen.
Sie hat mich angeführt, dir wird sie's auch so machen.
Zum Liebsten sei ein Kobold ihr beschert!
Der mag mit ihr auf einem Kreuzweg schäkern;
ein alter Bock, wenn er vom Blocksberg kehrt,
mag im Galopp noch „Gute Nacht!" ihr meckern!
Ein braver Kerl von echtem Fleisch und Blut
ist für die Dirne viel zu gut.

Ich will von keinem Gruße wissen,
als ihr die Fenster eingeschmissen!

BRANDER, *auf den Tisch schlagend.*

Paßt auf! Paßt auf! Gehorchet mir!
Ihr Herrn, gesteht: ich weiß zu leben!
Verliebte Leute sitzen hier,
und diesen muß, nach Standsgebühr,
zur guten Nacht ich was zum besten geben.
Gebt acht! Ein Lied vom neusten Schnitt!
Und singt den Rundreim kräftig mit!

Er singt.

Es war eine Ratt' im Kellernest,
lebte nur von Fett und Butter,
hatte sich ein Ränzlein angemäst't,
als wie der Doktor Luther.
Die Köchin hatt' ihr Gift gestellt;
da ward's so eng ihr in der Welt,
als hätte sie Lieb' im Leibe.

CHORUS, *jauchzend.*

Als hätte sie Lieb' im Leibe.

BRANDER

Sie fuhr herum, sie fuhr heraus
und soff aus allen Pfützen,
zernagt', zerkratzt' das ganze Haus;
wollte nichts ihr Wüten nützen!
Sie tät gar manchen Ängstesprung,
bald hatte das arme Tier genung,
als hätt' es Lieb' im Leibe.

CHORUS

Als hätt' es Lieb' im Leibe.

BRANDER

Sie kam vor Angst am hellen Tag
der Küche zugelaufen,
fiel an den Herd und zuckt' und lag
und tät erbärmlich schnaufen.
Da lachte die Vergifterin noch:
„Ha! Sie pfeift auf dem letzten Loch,
als hätte sie Lieb' im Leibe."

CHORUS

Als hätte sie Lieb' im Leibe.

SIEBEL

Wie sich die platten Bursche freuen!
Es ist mir eine rechte Kunst,
den armen Ratten Gift zu streuen!

BRANDER

Sie stehn wohl sehr in deiner Gunst?

ALTMAYER

Der Schmerbauch mit der kahlen Platte!
Das Unglück macht ihn zahm und mild;
er sieht in der geschwollnen Ratte
sein ganz natürlich Ebenbild.

Faust und Mephistopheles treten auf.

MEPHISTOPHELES

Ich muß dich nun vor allen Dingen
in lustige Gesellschaft bringen,
damit du siehst, wie leicht sich's leben läßt.
Dem Volke hier wird jeder Tag ein Fest.
Mit wenig Witz und viel Behagen
dreht jeder sich im engen Zirkeltanz,
wie junge Katzen mit dem Schwanz.
Wenn sie nicht über Kopfweh klagen,
solang der Wirt nur weiter borgt,
sind sie vergnügt und unbesorgt.

BRANDER

Die kommen eben von der Reise,
man sieht's an ihrer wunderlichen Weise;
sie sind nicht eine Stunde hier.

FROSCH

Wahrhaftig, du hast recht! Mein Leipzig lob' ich mir!
Es ist ein klein Paris und bildet seine Leute.

SIEBEL

Für was siehst du die Fremden an?

FROSCH

Laßt mich nur gehn! Bei einem vollen Glase
zieh' ich, wie einen Kinderzahn,
den Burschen leicht die Würmer aus der Nase.
Sie scheinen mir aus einem edlen Haus:
sie sehen stolz und unzufrieden aus.

BRANDER
Marktschreier sind's gewiß, ich wette!
ALTMAYER
Vielleicht.
FROSCH
Gib acht, ich schraube sie!
MEPHISTOPHELES, *zu Faust.*
Den Teufel spürt das Völkchen nie,
und wenn er sie beim Kragen hätte!
FAUST
Seid uns gegrüßt, ihr Herrn!
SIEBEL
Viel Dank zum Gegengruß!
Leise, Mephistopheles von der Seite ansehend.
Was hinkt der Kerl auf einem Fuß?
MEPHISTOPHELES
Ist es erlaubt, uns auch zu euch zu setzen?
Statt eines guten Trunks, den man nicht haben kann,
soll die Gesellschaft uns ergötzen.
ALTMAYER
Ihr scheint ein sehr verwöhnter Mann.
FROSCH
Ihr seid wohl spät von Rippach aufgebrochen?
Habt ihr mit Herren Hans noch erst zu Nacht gespeist?
MEPHISTOPHELES
Heut sind wir ihn vorbeigereist!
Wir haben ihn das letztemal gesprochen.
Von seinen Vettern wußt' er viel zu sagen,
viel Grüße hat er uns an jeden aufgetragen.
Er neigt sich gegen Frosch.
ALTMAYER, *leise.*
Da hast du's! Der versteht's!
SIEBEL
Ein pfiffiger Patron!
FROSCH
Nun, warte nur, ich krieg' ihn schon!
MEPHISTOPHELES
Wenn ich nicht irrte, hörten wir
geübte Stimmen Chorus singen?

Gewiß, Gesang muß trefflich hier
von dieser Wölbung widerklingen!

FROSCH

Seid Ihr wohl gar ein Virtuos?

MEPHISTOPHELES

O nein! Die Kraft ist schwach, allein die Lust ist groß.

ALTMAYER

Gebt uns ein Lied!

MEPHISTOPHELES

Wenn ihr begehrt, die Menge!

SIEBEL

Nur auch ein nagelneues Stück!

MEPHISTOPHELES

Wir kommen erst aus Spanien zurück,
dem schönen Land des Weins und der Gesänge.

Singt.

Es war einmal ein König,
der hatt' einen großen Floh,—

FROSCH

Horcht! Einen Floh! Habt ihr das wohl gefaßt?
Ein Floh ist mir ein saubrer Gast.

MEPHISTOPHELES, *singt.*

Es war einmal ein König,
der hatt' einen großen Floh,
den liebt' er gar nicht wenig,
als wie seinen eignen Sohn.
Da rief er seinen Schneider,
der Schneider kam heran:
„Da, miß dem Junker Kleider
und miß ihm Hosen an!“

BRANDER

Vergeßt nur nicht, dem Schneider einzuschärfen,
daß er mir aufs genauste mißt,
und daß, so lieb sein Kopf ihm ist,
die Hosen keine Falten werfen!

MEPHISTOPHELES

In Sammet und in Seide
war er nun angetan,
hatte Bänder auf dem Kleide,

hatt' auch ein Kreuz daran,
und war sogleich Minister
und hatt' einen großen Stern.
Da wurden seine Geschwister
bei Hof auch große Herrn.

all his relations became great lords at court

Und Herrn und Fraun am Hofe,
die waren sehr geplagt,
die Königin und die Zofe
gestochen und genagt,
und durften sie nicht knicken
und weg sie jucken nicht.
Wir knicken und ersticken
doch gleich, wenn einer sticht.

did not dare to brush them

CHORUS, *jauchzend.*

Wir knicken und ersticken
doch gleich, wenn einer sticht.

FROSCH

Bravo! Bravo! Das war schön!

SIEBEL

So soll es jedem Floh ergehn!

BRANDER

Spitzt die Finger und packt sie fein!

ALTMAYER

Es lebe die Freiheit! Es lebe der Wein!

MEPHISTOPHELES

Ich tränke gern ein Glas, die Freiheit hoch zu ehren,
wenn eure Weine nur ein bißchen besser wären.

SIEBEL

Wir mögen das nicht wieder hören!

MEPHISTOPHELES

Ich fürchte nur, der Wirt beschweret sich;
sonst gäb' ich diesen werten Gästen
aus unserm Keller was zum besten.

SIEBEL

Nur immer her! Ich nehm's auf mich.

FROSCH

Schafft Ihr ein gutes Glas, so wollen wir Euch loben.
Nur gebt nicht gar zu kleine Proben!

Denn wenn ich judizieren soll,
verlang' ich auch das Maul recht voll.

ALTMAYER, *leise.*

Sie sind vom Rheine, wie ich spüre.

MEPHISTOPHELES

Schafft einen Bohrer an!

BRANDER

Was soll mit dem geschehn?
Ihr habt doch nicht die Fässer vor der Türe?

ALTMAYER

Dahinten hat der Wirt ein Körbchen Werkzeug stehn.

Mephistopheles nimmt den Bohrer.

MEPHISTOPHELES, *zu Frosch.*

Nun sagt: was wünschet Ihr zu schmecken?

FROSCH

Wie meint Ihr das? Habt Ihr so mancherlei?

MEPHISTOPHELES

Ich stell' es einem jeden frei.

ALTMAYER, *zu Frosch.*

Aha! Du fängst schon an, die Lippen abzulecken.

FROSCH

Gut! Wenn ich wählen soll, so will ich Rheinwein haben.
Das Vaterland verleiht die allerbesten Gaben.

MEPHISTOPHELES, *indem er an dem Platz, wo Frosch sitzt, ein Loch in den Tischrand bohrt.*

Verschafft ein wenig Wachs, die Pfropfen gleich zu machen!

ALTMAYER

Ach, das sind Taschenspielersachen!

MEPHISTOPHELES, *zu Brander.*

Und Ihr?

BRANDER

Ich will Champagner Wein,
und recht moussierend soll er sein!

Mephistopheles bohrt; einer hat indessen die Wachspfropfen gemacht und verstopft.

BRANDER

Man kann nicht stets das Fremde meiden,
das Gute liegt uns oft so fern.

Ein echter deutscher Mann mag keinen Franzen leiden,
doch ihre Weine trinkt er gern.

Siebel, *indem sich Mephistopheles seinem Platze nähert.*

Ich muß gestehn: den sauern mag ich nicht.
Gebt mir ein Glas vom echten süßen!

Mephistopheles, *bohrt.*

Euch soll sogleich Tokayer fließen.

Altmayer

Nein, Herren, seht mir ins Gesicht!
Ich seh' es ein, ihr habt uns nur zum besten.

Mephistopheles

Ei! Ei! Mit solchen edlen Gästen
wär' es ein bißchen viel gewagt.
Geschwind! Nur grad heraus gesagt!
Mit welchem Weine kann ich dienen?

Altmayer

Mit jedem. Nur nicht lang gefragt!

Nachdem die Löcher alle gebohrt und verstopft sind,
Mephistopheles, *mit seltsamen Gebärden.*

Trauben trägt der Weinstock,
Hörner der Ziegenbock!
Der Wein ist saftig, Holz die Reben:
der hölzerne Tisch kann Wein auch geben.
Ein tiefer Blick in die Natur!
Hier ist ein Wunder: glaubet nur!

Nun zieht die Pfropfen und genießt!

Alle, *indem sie die Pfropfen ziehen, und jedem der verlangte Wein ins Glas läuft.*

O schöner Brunnen, der uns fließt!

Mephistopheles

Nur hütet euch, daß ihr mir nichts vergießt!

Sie trinken wiederholt.

Alle, *singen.*

Uns ist ganz kannibalisch wohl,
als wie fünfhundert Säuen!

Mephistopheles

Das Volk ist frei! Seht an, wie wohl's ihm geht!

Faust — Wants to leave

Ich hätte Lust, nun abzufahren.

MEPHISTOPHELES

Gib nur erst acht! Die Bestialität
wird sich gar herrlich offenbaren.

Siebel trinkt unvorsichtig, der Wein fließt auf die Erde und wird zur Flamme.

SIEBEL

Helft! Feuer! Helft! Die Hölle brennt!

MEPHISTOPHELES, *die Flamme besprechend.*

Sei ruhig, freundlich Element!

Zu dem Gesellen.

Für diesmal war es nur ein Tropfen Fegefeuer.

SIEBEL

Was soll das sein? Wart't! Ihr bezahlt es teuer!
Es scheinet, daß Ihr uns nicht kennt.

FROSCH

Lass' Er uns das zum zweiten Male bleiben!

ALTMAYER

Ich dächt', wir hießen ihn ganz sachte seitwärts gehn.

SIEBEL

Was, Herr? Er will sich unterstehn,
und hier Sein Hokuspokus treiben?

MEPHISTOPHELES

Still, altes Weinfaß!

SIEBEL

Besenstiel!

Du willst uns gar noch grob begegnen?

BRANDER

Wart nur! Es sollen Schläge regnen!

Altmayer zieht einen Pfropf aus dem Tisch. Es springt ihm Feuer entgegen.

ALTMAYER

Ich brenne! Ich brenne!

SIEBEL

Zauberei!

Stoßt zu! Der Kerl ist vogelfrei!

Sie ziehen die Messer und gehn auf Mephistopheles los.

MEPHISTOPHELES, *mit ernsthafter Gebärde.*

Falsch Gebild und Wort
verändern Sinn und Ort!

Seid hier und dort!

Sie stehn erstaunt und sehn einander an.

ALTMAYER

Wo bin ich? Welches schöne Land!

FROSCH

Weinberge! Seh' ich recht?

SIEBEL

Und Trauben gleich zur Hand!

BRANDER

Hier unter diesem grünen Laube,
seht, welch ein Stock! Seht, welche Traube!

Er faßt Siebeln bei der Nase. Die andern tun es wechselseitig und heben die Messer.

MEPHISTOPHELES, *wie oben.*

Irrtum, laß los der Augen Band! —
Und merkt euch, wie der Teufel spaße!

Er verschwindet mit Faust, die Gesellen fahren auseinander.

SIEBEL

Was gibt's?

ALTMAYER

Wie?

FROSCH

War das deine Nase?

BRANDER, *zu Siebel.*

Und deine hab' ich in der Hand!

ALTMAYER

Es war ein Schlag, der ging durch alle Glieder!
Schafft einen Stuhl, ich sinke nieder!

When the students come to one of them remembers seeing the strangers ride up the steps on a barrel.

FROSCH

Nein, sagt mir nur! Was ist geschehn?

SIEBEL

Wo ist der Kerl? Wenn ich ihn spüre,
er soll mir nicht lebendig gehn!

ALTMAYER

Ich hab' ihn selbst hinaus zur Kellertüre —
auf einem Fasse reiten sehn. — —
Es liegt mir bleischwer in den Füßen.

Sich nach dem Tische wendend.

Mein! Sollte wohl der Wein noch fließen?

SIEBEL
Betrug war alles, Lug und Schein!
FROSCH
Mir deuchte doch, als tränk' ich Wein.
BRANDER
Aber wie war es mit den Trauben?
ALTMAYER
Nun sag' mir eins, man soll kein Wunder glauben!

Faust is disgusted by the hocus-pocus but entranced by a figure in the mirror. He is rejuvenated by the witches potion & predicts he'll see Helen of Troy in every woman.

8 Hexenküche

Auf einem niedrigen Herde steht ein großer Kessel über dem Feuer. In dem Dampfe, der davon in die Höhe steigt, zeigen sich verschiedene Gestalten. Eine Meerkatze sitzt bei dem Kessel und schäumt ihn und sorgt, daß er nicht überläuft. Der Meerkater mit den Jungen sitzt darneben und wärmt sich. Wände und Decke sind mit dem seltsamsten Hexenhausrat ausgeschmückt.

Faust. Mephistopheles.

FAUST
Mir widersteht das tolle Zauberwesen!
Versprichst du mir, ich soll genesen
in diesem Wust von Raserei? frantic mess
Verlang' ich Rat von einem alten Weibe?
Und schafft die Sudelköcherei filthy slops
wohl dreißig Jahre mir vom Leibe?
Weh mir, wenn du nichts Besser's weißt!
Schon ist die Hoffnung mir verschwunden.
Hat die Natur und hat ein edler Geist
nicht irgendeinen Balsam ausgefunden?

MEPHISTOPHELES
Mein Freund, nun sprichst du wieder klug!
Dich zu verjüngen, gibt's auch ein natürlich Mittel;
allein es steht in einem andern Buch
und ist ein wunderlich Kapitel.

FAUST

Ich will es wissen!

MEPHISTOPHELES

Gut! Ein Mittel, ohne Geld
und Arzt und Zauberei zu haben:
begib dich gleich hinaus aufs Feld,
fang an zu hacken und zu graben,
erhalte dich und deinen Sinn
in einem ganz beschränkten Kreise,
ernähre dich mit ungemischter Speise,
leb mit dem Vieh als Vieh, und acht es nicht für Raub,
den Acker, den du erntest, selbst zu düngen!
Das ist das beste Mittel, glaub,
auf achtzig Jahr dich zu verjüngen!

FAUST

Das bin ich nicht gewöhnt, ich kann mich nicht bequemen,
den Spaten in die Hand zu nehmen.
Das enge Leben steht mir gar nicht an.

MEPHISTOPHELES

So muß denn doch die Hexe dran.

FAUST

Warum denn just das alte Weib!
Kannst du den Trank nicht selber brauen?

MEPHISTOPHELES

Das wär' ein schöner Zeitvertreib!
Ich wollt' indes wohl tausend Brücken bauen.
Nicht Kunst und Wissenschaft allein,
Geduld will bei dem Werke sein.
Ein stiller Geist ist Jahre lang geschäftig;
die Zeit nur macht die feine Gärung kräftig.
Und alles, was dazu gehört,
es sind gar wunderbare Sachen!
Der Teufel hat sie's zwar gelehrt;
allein der Teufel kann's nicht machen.

Die Tiere erblickend.

Sieh, welch ein zierliches Geschlecht!
Das ist die Magd! Das ist der Knecht!

Zu den Tieren.

Es scheint, die Frau ist nicht zu Hause?

Die Tiere

Beim Schmause,
aus dem Haus
zum Schornstein hinaus!

Mephistopheles

Wie lange pflegt sie wohl zu schwärmen?

Die Tiere

Solange wir uns die Pfoten wärmen.

Mephistopheles, *zu Faust.*

Wie findest du die zarten Tiere?

Faust

So abgeschmackt, als ich nur jemand sah!

Mephistopheles

Nein, ein Diskurs wie dieser da
ist grade der, den ich am liebsten führe!

Zu den Tieren.

So sagt mir doch, verfluchte Puppen:
was quirlt ihr in dem Brei herum?

Die Tiere

Wir kochen breite Bettelsuppen.

Mephistopheles

Da habt ihr ein groß Publikum.

Der Kater macht sich herbei und schmeichelt dem Mephistopheles.

Der Kater

O würfle nur gleich
und mache mich reich
und laß mich gewinnen!
Gar schlecht ist's bestellt,
und wär' ich bei Geld,
so wär' ich bei Sinnen.

Mephistopheles

Wie glücklich würde sich der Affe schätzen,
könnt' er nur auch ins Lotto setzen!

Indessen haben die jungen Meerkätzchen mit einer großen Kugel gespielt und rollen sie hervor.

Der Kater

Das ist die Welt:
sie steigt und fällt
und rollt beständig;

sie klingt wie Glas,
— wie bald bricht das! —
ist hohl inwendig.
Hier glänzt sie sehr
und hier noch mehr.
— Ich bin lebendig! —
Mein lieber Sohn,
halt dich davon!
Du mußt sterben!
Sie ist von Ton:
es gibt Scherben!

MEPHISTOPHELES

Was soll das Sieb?

Der Kater holt es herunter.

DER KATER

Wärst du ein Dieb,
wollt' ich dich gleich erkennen.

Er läuft zur Kätzin und läßt sie durchsehen.

Sieh durch das Sieb!
Erkennst du den Dieb
und darfst ihn nicht nennen?

MEPHISTOPHELES, *sich dem Feuer nähernd.*

Und dieser Topf?

KATER und KÄTZIN

Der alberne Tropf!
Er kennt nicht den Topf,
er kennt nicht den Kessel!

MEPHISTOPHELES

Unhöfliches Tier!

DER KATER

Den Wedel nimm hier
und setz dich in Sessel!

Er nötigt den Mephistopheles zu sitzen.

FAUST, *welcher diese Zeit über vor einem Spiegel gestanden, sich ihm bald genähert, bald sich von ihm entfernt hat.*

Was seh' ich? Welch ein himmlisch Bild
zeigt sich in diesem Zauberspiegel!
O Liebe, leihe mir den schnellsten deiner Flügel
und führe mich in ihr Gefild!
Ach, wenn ich nicht auf dieser Stelle bleibe,
wenn ich es wage, nah zu gehn,

kann ich sie nur als wie im Nebel sehn!
Das schönste Bild von einem Weibe!
Ist's möglich, ist das Weib so schön?
Muß ich an diesem hingestreckten Leibe
den Inbegriff von allen Himmeln sehn?
So etwas findet sich auf Erden?

MEPHISTOPHELES

Natürlich, wenn ein Gott sich erst sechs Tage plagt
und selbst am Ende „Bravo!" sagt,
da muß es was Gescheites werden!
Für diesmal sieh dich immer satt!
Ich weiß dir so ein Schätzchen auszuspüren,
und selig, wer das gute Schicksal hat,
als Bräutigam sie heimzuführen!

Faust sieht immerfort in den Spiegel. MEPHISTOPHELES, *sich in dem Sessel dehnend und mit dem Wedel spielend, fährt fort zu sprechen:*

Hier sitz' ich wie der König auf dem Throne,
den Zepter halt' ich hier, es fehlt nur noch die Krone.

DIE TIERE, *welche bisher allerlei wunderliche Bewegungen durcheinander gemacht haben, bringen dem Mephistopheles eine Krone mit großem Geschrei.*

O sei doch so gut,
mit Schweiß und mit Blut
die Krone zu leimen!

Sie gehn ungeschickt mit der Krone um und zerbrechen sie in zwei Stücke, mit welchen sie herumspringen.

Nun ist es geschehn!
Wir reden und sehn,
wir hören und reimen, —

FAUST, *gegen den Spiegel.*

Weh mir! Ich werde schier verrückt.

MEPHISTOPHELES, *auf die Tiere deutend.*

Nun fängt mir an fast selbst der Kopf zu schwanken.

DIE TIERE

— und wenn es uns glückt,
und wenn es sich schickt,
so sind es Gedanken!

FAUST, *wie oben.*

Mein Busen fängt mir an zu brennen!
Entfernen wir uns nur geschwind!

MEPHISTOPHELES, *in obiger Stellung.*

Nun, wenigstens muß man bekennen,
daß es aufrichtige Poeten sind.

Der Kessel, welchen die Kätzin bisher außer acht gelassen, fängt an überzulaufen; es entsteht eine große Flamme, welche zum Schornstein hinausschlägt. Die Hexe kommt durch die Flamme mit entsetzlichem Geschrei heruntergefahren.

DIE HEXE

Au! Au! Au! Au!
Verdammtes Tier! Verfluchte Sau!
Versäumst den Kessel, versengst die Frau!
Verfluchtes Tier!

Faust und Mephistopheles erblickend.

Was ist das hier?
Wer seid ihr hier?
Was wollt ihr da?
Wer schlich sich ein? —
Die Feuerpein
euch ins Gebein!

Sie fährt mit dem Schaumlöffel in den Kessel und spritzt Flammen nach Faust, Mephistopheles und den Tieren. Die Tiere winseln.

MEPHISTOPHELES, *welcher den Wedel, den er in der Hand hält, umkehrt und unter die Gläser und Töpfe schlägt.*

Entzwei! Entzwei!
Da liegt der Brei!
Da liegt das Glas!
Es ist nur Spaß,
der Takt, du Aas,
zu deiner Melodei!

Indem die Hexe voll Grimm und Entsetzen zurücktritt.

Erkennst du mich? Gerippe! Scheusal du!
Erkennst du deinen Herrn und Meister?
Was hält mich ab, so schlag' ich zu,
zerschmettre dich und deine Katzengeister!
Hast du vorm roten Wams nicht mehr Respekt?
Kannst du die Hahnenfeder nicht erkennen?

Hab' ich dies Angesicht versteckt?
Soll ich mich etwa selber nennen?

DIE HEXE

O Herr, verzeiht den rohen Gruß!
Seh' ich doch keinen Pferdefuß.
Wo sind denn Eure beiden Raben?

MEPHISTOPHELES

Für diesmal kommst du so davon;
denn freilich ist es eine Weile schon,
daß wir uns nicht gesehen haben.
Auch die Kultur, die alle Welt beleckt,
hat auf den Teufel sich erstreckt;
das nordische Phantom ist nun nicht mehr zu schauen:
wo siehst du Hörner, Schweif und Klauen?
Und was den Fuß betrifft, den ich nicht missen kann,
der würde mir bei Leuten schaden;
darum bedien' ich mich, wie mancher junge Mann,
seit vielen Jahren falscher Waden.

DIE HEXE, *tanzend.*

Sinn und Verstand verlier' ich schier,
seh' ich den Junker Satan wieder hier!

MEPHISTOPHELES

Den Namen, Weib, verbitt' ich mir!

DIE HEXE

Warum? Was hat er Euch getan?

MEPHISTOPHELES

Er ist schon lang ins Fabelbuch geschrieben;
allein die Menschen sind nichts besser dran:
den Bösen sind sie los, die Bösen sind geblieben.
Du nennst mich Herr Baron, so ist die Sache gut;
ich bin ein Kavalier wie andre Kavaliere.
Du zweifelst nicht an meinem edlen Blut;
sieh her: das ist das Wappen, das ich führe!

Er macht eine unanständige Gebärde. Die Hexe lacht unmäßig.

DIE HEXE

Ha! Ha! Das ist in Eurer Art!
Ihr seid ein Schelm, wie Ihr nur immer wart!

Mephistopheles, *zu Faust.*
Mein Freund, das lerne wohl verstehn!
Dies ist die Art, mit Hexen umzugehn.

Die Hexe
Nun sagt, ihr Herren, was ihr schafft.

Mephistopheles
Ein gutes Glas von dem bekannten Saft!
Doch muß ich Euch ums ält'ste bitten:
die Jahre doppeln seine Kraft.

Die Hexe
Gar gern! Hier hab' ich eine Flasche,
aus der ich selbst zuweilen nasche,
die auch nicht mehr im mind'sten stinkt;
ich will Euch gern ein Gläschen geben.
Leise.
Doch wenn es dieser Mann unvorbereitet trinkt,
so kann er, wißt Ihr wohl, nicht eine Stunde leben.

Mephistopheles
Es ist ein guter Freund, dem es gedeihen soll;
ich gönn' ihm gern das Beste deiner Küche.
Zieh deinen Kreis, sprich deine Sprüche,
und gib ihm eine Tasse voll!

Die Hexe, mit seltsamen Gebärden, zieht einen Kreis und stellt wunderbare Sachen hinein; indessen fangen die Gläser an zu klingen, der Kessel zu tönen, und machen Musik. Zuletzt bringt sie ein großes Buch, stellt die Meerkatzen in den Kreis, die ihr zum Pult dienen und die Fackel halten müssen. Sie winkt Fausten, zu ihr zu treten.

Faust, *zu Mephistopheles.*
Nein, sage mir: was soll das werden?
Das tolle Zeug, die rasenden Gebärden,
der abgeschmackteste Betrug,
sind mir bekannt, verhaßt genug.

Mephistopheles
Ei, Possen! Das ist nur zum Lachen;
sei nur nicht ein so strenger Mann!
Sie muß als Arzt ein Hokuspokus machen,
damit der Saft dir wohl gedeihen kann.

Er nötigt Fausten, in den Kreis zu treten. Die Hexe, mit großer Emphase, fängt an, aus dem Buche zu deklamieren.

Die Hexe

Du mußt verstehn!
Aus Eins mach Zehn
und Zwei laß gehn
und Drei mach gleich,
so bist du reich.
Verlier die Vier!
Aus Fünf und Sechs
— so sagt die Hex' —
mach Sieben und Acht,
so ist's vollbracht:
und Neun ist Eins,
und Zehn ist keins.
Das ist das Hexen-Einmaleins.

Faust

Mich dünkt, die Alte spricht im Fieber.

Mephistopheles

Das ist noch lange nicht vorüber,
ich kenn' es wohl, so klingt das ganze Buch.
Ich habe manche Zeit damit verloren,
denn ein vollkommner Widerspruch
bleibt gleich geheimnisvoll für Kluge wie für Toren.
Mein Freund, die Kunst ist alt und neu.
Es war die Art zu allen Zeiten,
durch Drei und Eins, und Eins und Drei
Irrtum statt Wahrheit zu verbreiten.
So schwätzt und lehrt man ungestört;
wer will sich mit den Narrn befassen?
Gewöhnlich glaubt der Mensch, wenn er nur Worte hört,
es müsse sich dabei doch auch was denken lassen.

Die Hexe, *fährt fort:*

Die hohe Kraft
der Wissenschaft,
der ganzen Welt verborgen!
Und wer nicht denkt,
dem wird sie geschenkt:
er hat sie ohne Sorgen.

Faust

Was sagt sie uns für Unsinn vor?
Es wird mir gleich der Kopf zerbrechen.

Mich dünkt, ich hör' ein ganzes Chor
von hunderttausend Narren sprechen.

MEPHISTOPHELES

Genug, genug, o treffliche Sibylle!
Gib deinen Trank herbei und fülle
die Schale rasch bis an den Rand hinan!
Denn meinem Freund wird dieser Trunk nicht schaden:
er ist ein Mann von vielen Graden,
der manchen guten Schluck getan.

Die Hexe, mit vielen Zeremonien, schenkt den Trank in eine Schale; wie sie Faust an den Mund bringt, entsteht eine leichte Flamme.

MEPHISTOPHELES

Nur frisch hinunter! Immer zu!
Es wird dir gleich das Herz erfreuen.
Bist mit dem Teufel du und du,
und willst dich vor der Flamme scheuen?

Die Hexe löst den Kreis. Faust tritt heraus.

MEPHISTOPHELES

Nun frisch hinaus! Du darfst nicht ruhn.

DIE HEXE

Mög' Euch das Schlückchen wohl behagen!

MEPHISTOPHELES, *zur Hexe.*

Und kann ich dir was zu Gefallen tun,
so darfst du mir's nur auf Walpurgis sagen.

DIE HEXE

Hier ist ein Lied! Wenn Ihr's zuweilen singt,
so werdet Ihr besondre Wirkung spüren.

MEPHISTOPHELES, *zu Faust.*

Komm nur geschwind und laß dich führen;
du mußt notwendig transpirieren,
damit die Kraft durch Inn- und Äußres dringt.
Den edlen Müßiggang lehr' ich hernach dich schätzen,
und bald empfindest du mit innigem Ergötzen,
wie sich Cupido regt und hin und wider springt.

FAUST

Laß mich nur schnell noch in den Spiegel schauen!
Das Frauenbild war gar zu schön!

MEPHISTOPHELES

Nein! Nein! Du sollst das Muster aller Frauen
nun bald leibhaftig vor dir sehn.

Leise.

Du siehst, mit diesem Trank im Leibe,
bald Helenen in jedem Weibe.

9 Straße

Faust. Margarete, vorübergehend.

FAUST

Mein schönes Fräulein! Darf ich wagen,
meinen Arm und Geleit Ihr anzutragen?

MARGARETE

Bin weder Fräulein, weder schön.
Kann ungeleitet nach Hause gehn.

Sie macht sich los und ab.

FAUST

Beim Himmel, dieses Kind ist schön!
So etwas hab' ich nie gesehn.
Sie ist so sitt- und tugendreich,
und etwas schnippisch doch zugleich.
Der Lippe Rot, der Wange Licht, —
die Tage der Welt vergess' ich's nicht!
Wie sie die Augen niederschlägt,
hat tief sich in mein Herz geprägt;
wie sie kurz angebunden war,
das ist nun zum Entzücken gar!

Mephistopheles tritt auf.

FAUST

Hör, du mußt mir die Dirne schaffen!

MEPHISTOPHELES

Nun, welche?

FAUST

Sie ging just vorbei.

MEPHISTOPHELES

Da die? Sie kam von ihrem Pfaffen,
der sprach sie aller Sünden frei.
— Ich schlich mich hart am Stuhl vorbei. —
Es ist ein gar unschuldig Ding,
das eben für nichts zur Beichte ging:
über die hab' ich keine Gewalt!

FAUST

Ist über vierzehn Jahr doch alt.

MEPHISTOPHELES

Du sprichst ja wie Hans Liederlich:
der begehrt jede liebe Blum' für sich,
und dünkelt ihm, es wär' kein' Ehr'
und Gunst, die nicht zu pflücken wär';
geht aber doch nicht immer an.

FAUST

Mein Herr Magister Lobesan,
lass' Er mich mit dem Gesetz in Frieden!
Und das sag' ich Ihm kurz und gut:
wenn nicht das süße junge Blut
heut nacht in meinen Armen ruht,
so sind wir um Mitternacht geschieden.

MEPHISTOPHELES

Bedenkt, was gehn und stehen mag!
Ich brauche wenigstens vierzehn Tag',
nur die Gelegenheit auszuspüren.

FAUST

Hätt' ich nur sieben Stunden Ruh,
brauchte den Teufel nicht dazu,
so ein Geschöpfchen zu verführen.

MEPHISTOPHELES

Ihr sprecht schon fast wie ein Franzos!
Doch bitt' ich, laßt's Euch nicht verdrießen:
was hilft's, nur grade zu genießen?
Die Freud' ist lange nicht so groß,
als wenn Ihr erst herauf, herum,
durch allerlei Brimborium,
das Püppchen geknetet und zugericht't,
wie's lehret manche welsche Geschicht'.

FAUST

Hab' Appetit auch ohne das.

MEPHISTOPHELES

Jetzt ohne Schimpf und ohne Spaß!
Ich sag' Euch: mit dem schönen Kind
geht's ein für allemal nicht geschwind.
Mit Sturm ist da nichts einzunehmen;
wir müssen uns zur List bequemen.

FAUST

Schaff mir etwas vom Engelsschatz!
Führ mich an ihren Ruheplatz!
Schaff mir ein Halstuch von ihrer Brust,
ein Strumpfband meiner Liebeslust!

MEPHISTOPHELES

Damit Ihr seht, daß ich Eurer Pein
will förderlich und dienstlich sein,
wollen wir keinen Augenblick verlieren;
will Euch noch heut in ihr Zimmer führen.

FAUST

Und soll sie sehn, — sie haben?

MEPHISTOPHELES

Nein!
Sie wird bei einer Nachbarin sein.
Indessen könnt Ihr ganz allein
an aller Hoffnung künft'ger Freuden
in ihrem Dunstkreis satt Euch weiden.

FAUST

Können wir hin?

MEPHISTOPHELES

Es ist noch zu früh.

FAUST

Sorg du mir für ein Geschenk für sie!

Ab.

MEPHISTOPHELES

Gleich schenken? Das ist brav! Da wird er reüssieren!
Ich kenne manchen schönen Platz
und manchen altvergrabnen Schatz;
ich muß ein bißchen revidieren.

Ab.

10 Abend

Ein kleines, reinliches Zimmer.

Margarete, ihre Zöpfe flechtend und aufbindend.

MARGARETE

Ich gäb' was drum, wenn ich nur wüßt',
wer heut der Herr gewesen ist!
Er sah gewiß recht wacker aus
und ist aus einem edlen Haus;
das konnt' ich ihm an der Stirne lesen —
er wär' auch sonst nicht so keck gewesen.

Ab.

Mephistopheles und Faust treten auf.

MEPHISTOPHELES

Herein, ganz leise, nur herein!

FAUST, *nach einigem Stillschweigen.*

Ich bitte dich, laß mich allein!

MEPHISTOPHELES, *herumspürend.*

Nicht jedes Mädchen hält so rein.

Ab.

FAUST, *rings aufschauend.*

Willkommen, süßer Dämmerschein,
der du dies Heiligtum durchwebst!
Ergreif mein Herz, du süße Liebespein,
die du vom Tau der Hoffnung schmachtend lebst!
Wie atmet rings Gefühl der Stille,
der Ordnung, der Zufriedenheit!
In dieser Armut welche Fülle!
In diesem Kerker welche Seligkeit!

Er wirft sich auf den ledernen Sessel am Bette.

O nimm mich auf, der du die Vorwelt schon
bei Freud' und Schmerz im offnen Arm empfangen!
Wie oft, ach, hat an diesem Väterthron
schon eine Schar von Kindern rings gehangen!
Vielleicht hat, dankbar für den heil'gen Christ,
mein Liebchen hier, mit vollen Kinderwangen,
dem Ahnherrn fromm die welke Hand geküßt.

The function of this scene is to make vivid the basic antagonism between G's simple purity of heart + the baseness of the threat to her peace. Neither Faust's heedless passion nor M's lewd sensuality is compatible with the cleanliness of the room + its occupant. The atmosphere of the room has its effect on Faust. His passion is, for the moment, sublimated in a romantic analysis of the objects around him until he finally realizes the incongruity of his present undertaking with his former standards of conduct (2720) M. intervenes before this turn of thought can become effective in a decision which might disrupt his plans.

Ich fühl', o Mädchen, deinen Geist
der Füll' und Ordnung um mich säuseln,
der mütterlich dich täglich unterweist,
den Teppich auf den Tisch dich reinlich breiten heißt,
sogar den Sand zu deinen Füßen kräuseln.
O liebe Hand, so göttergleich!
Die Hütte wird durch dich ein Himmelreich.
Und hier! . . .

Er hebt einen Bettvorhang auf.

Was faßt mich für ein Wonnegraus!
Hier möcht' ich volle Stunden säumen.
Natur, hier bildetest in leichten Träumen
den eingebornen Engel aus!
Hier lag das Kind, mit warmem Leben
den zarten Busen angefüllt;
und hier mit heilig reinem Weben
entwirkte sich das Götterbild!
Und du! Was hat dich hergeführt?
Wie innig fühl' ich mich gerührt!
Was willst du hier? Was wird das Herz dir schwer?
Armsel'ger Faust! Ich kenne dich nicht mehr.
Umgibt mich hier ein Zauberduft?
Mich drang's, so grade zu genießen,
und fühle mich in Liebestraum zerfließen!
Sind wir ein Spiel von jedem Druck der Luft?
Und träte sie den Augenblick herein,
wie würdest du für deinen Frevel büßen!
Der große Hans, ach, wie so klein,
läg', hingeschmolzen, ihr zu Füßen.

Mephistopheles kommt.

MEPHISTOPHELES

Geschwind! Ich seh' sie unten kommen.

FAUST

Fort! Fort! Ich kehre nimmermehr!

MEPHISTOPHELES

Hier ist ein Kästchen leidlich schwer.
Ich hab's woanders hergenommen.
Stellt's hier nur immer in den Schrein!
Ich schwör' Euch, ihr vergehn die Sinnen;
ich tat Euch Sächelchen hinein,
um eine andre zu gewinnen, —
zwar Kind ist Kind, und Spiel ist Spiel.

FAUST

Ich weiß nicht, — soll ich?

MEPHISTOPHELES

Fragt Ihr viel?
Meint Ihr vielleicht den Schatz zu wahren?
Dann rat' ich Eurer Lüsternheit,
die liebe schöne Tageszeit
und mir die weitre Müh' zu sparen.
Ich hoff' nicht, daß Ihr geizig seid!
Ich kratz' den Kopf, reib' an den Händen,

Er stellt das Kästchen in den Schrein und drückt das Schloß wieder zu.

— Nur fort! Geschwind! —
um Euch das süße junge Kind
nach Herzens Wunsch und Will' zu wenden;
und Ihr seht drein,
als solltet Ihr in den Hörsaal hinein,
als stünden grau leibhaftig vor Euch da
Physik und Metaphysika!
Nur fort!

Ab.

Margarete, mit einer Lampe.

MARGARETE

Es ist so schwül, so dumpfig hie . . .

Sie macht das Fenster auf.

und ist doch eben so warm nicht drauß.
Es wird mir so, ich weiß nicht wie —
Ich wollt', die Mutter käm' nach Haus!
Mir läuft ein Schauer übern ganzen Leib —
Bin doch ein töricht-furchtsam Weib!

Sie fängt an zu singen, indem sie sich auszieht.

Es war ein König in Thule,
gar treu bis an das Grab,
dem sterbend seine Buhle
einen goldnen Becher gab.

Es ging ihm nichts darüber,
er leert' ihn jeden Schmaus;
die Augen gingen ihm über,
so oft er trank daraus.

Und als er kam zu sterben,
zählt' er seine Städt' im Reich,
gönnt' alles seinem Erben,
den Becher nicht zugleich.

Er saß beim Königsmahle,
die Ritter um ihn her,
auf hohem Vätersaale,
dort, auf dem Schloß am Meer.

Dort stand der alte Zecher,
trank letzte Lebensglut
und warf den heiligen Becher
hinunter in die Flut.

Er sah ihn stürzen, trinken
und sinken tief ins Meer.
Die Augen täten ihm sinken,
trank nie einen Tropfen mehr.

Sie eröffnet den Schrein, ihre Kleider einzuräumen, und erblickt das Schmuckkästchen.

Wie kommt das schöne Kästchen hier herein?
Ich schloß doch ganz gewiß den Schrein.
Es ist doch wunderbar! Was mag wohl drinne sein?
Vielleicht bracht's jemand als ein Pfand,
und meine Mutter lieh darauf.
Da hängt ein Schlüsselchen am Band,
ich denke wohl, ich mach' es auf! —
Was ist das? Gott im Himmel! Schau!
So was hab' ich mein' Tage nicht gesehn!
Ein Schmuck! Mit dem könnt' eine Edelfrau
am höchsten Feiertage gehn. —
Wie sollte mir die Kette stehn?
Wem mag die Herrlichkeit gehören?

Sie putzt sich damit auf und tritt vor den Spiegel.

Wenn nur die Ohrring' meine wären!
Man sieht doch gleich ganz anders drein.
Was hilft Euch Schönheit, junges Blut?
Das ist wohl alles schön und gut,
allein man läßt's auch alles sein;
man lobt Euch halb mit Erbarmen. —
Nach Golde drängt,
am Golde hängt
doch alles. Ach, wir Armen!

The function of this scene is threefold: 1. It retards the progress of the main action of the G. adventure. 2. It introduces G's mother as an opposing force in the conflict. 3. It removes the last uncertainty as to Faust's scruples or his determination to have the girl.

11 Spaziergang

Faust, in Gedanken auf und ab gehend. **Zu ihm Mephi-***stopheles.*

Mephistopheles

Bei aller verschmähten Liebe! Beim höllischen Elemente! —
Ich wollt', ich wüßte was Ärger's, daß ich's fluchen könnte!

Faust

Was hast? Was kneipt dich denn so sehr?
So kein Gesicht sah ich in meinem Leben!

Mephistopheles

Ich möcht' mich gleich dem Teufel übergeben,
wenn ich nur selbst kein Teufel wär'!

Faust

Hat sich dir was im Kopf verschoben?
Dich kleidet's, wie ein Rasender zu toben!

Mephistopheles

Denkt nur! Den Schmuck, für Gretchen angeschafft,
den hat ein Pfaff hinweggerafft! —
Die Mutter kriegt das Ding zu schauen,
gleich fängt's ihr heimlich an zu grauen.
Die Frau hat gar einen feinen Geruch,
schnuffelt immer im Gebetbuch
und riecht's einem jeden Möbel an,
ob das Ding heilig ist oder profan.
Und an dem Schmuck, da spürt sie's klar,
daß dabei nicht viel Segen war.
„Mein Kind," rief sie, „ungerechtes Gut
befängt die Seele, zehrt auf das Blut.
Wollen's der Mutter Gottes weihen!
Wird uns mit Himmelsmanna erfreuen."
Margretlein zog ein schiefes Maul.
„Ist halt," dacht' sie, „ein geschenkter Gaul,
und wahrlich, gottlos ist nicht der,

scent of evil about the whole matter

What about the gift horse?

der ihn so fein gebracht hierher.“
Die Mutter ließ einen Pfaffen kommen.
Der hatte kaum den Spaß vernommen,
ließ sich den Anblick wohl behagen.
Er sprach: „So ist man recht gesinnt!
Wer überwindet, der gewinnt.
Die Kirche hat einen guten Magen,
hat ganze Länder aufgefressen
und doch noch nie sich übergessen.
Die Kirch' allein, meine lieben Frauen,
kann ungerechtes Gut verdauen.“

FAUST

Das ist ein allgemeiner Brauch,
ein Jud' und König kann es auch.

MEPHISTOPHELES

Strich drauf ein Spange, Kett' und Ring',
als wären's eben Pfifferling';
dankt' nicht weniger und nicht mehr,
als ob's ein Korb voll Nüsse wär';
versprach ihnen allen himmlischen Lohn. —
Und sie waren sehr erbaut davon.

FAUST

Und Gretchen?

MEPHISTOPHELES

Sitzt nun unruhvoll,
weiß weder, was sie will noch soll;
denkt ans Geschmeide Tag und Nacht,
noch mehr an den, der's ihr gebracht.

FAUST

Des Liebchens Kummer tut mir leid.
Schaff du ihr gleich ein neu Geschmeid'!
Am ersten war ja so nicht viel.

MEPHISTOPHELES

O ja, dem Herrn ist alles Kinderspiel!

FAUST

Und mach, und richt's nach meinem Sinn!
Häng dich an ihre Nachbarin!
Sei Teufel doch nur nicht wie Brei,
und schaff einen neuen Schmuck herbei!

MEPHISTOPHELES

Ja, gnäd'ger Herr, von Herzen gerne! —

Faust ab.

MEPHISTOPHELES

So ein verliebter Tor verpufft
Euch Sonne, Mond und alle Sterne
zum Zeitvertreib dem Liebchen in die Luft.

Ab.

12 Der Nachbarin Haus

Marthe allein.

MARTHE

Gott verzeih's meinem lieben Mann,
er hat an mir nicht wohl getan!
Geht da stracks in die Welt hinein
und läßt mich auf dem Stroh allein.
Tät ihn doch wahrlich nicht betrüben,
tät ihn, weiß Gott, recht herzlich lieben.

Sie weint.

Vielleicht ist er gar tot! — O Pein! —
Hätt' ich nur einen Totenschein!

Margarete kommt.

MARGARETE

Frau Marthe!

MARTHE

Gretelchen, was soll's?

MARGARETE

Fast sinken mir die Kniee nieder!
Da find' ich so ein Kästchen wieder
in meinem Schrein! Von Ebenholz!
Und Sachen herrlich ganz und gar!
Weit reicher, als das erste war!

MARTHE

Das muß Sie nicht der Mutter sagen;
tät's wieder gleich zur Beichte tragen.

MARGARETE

Ach seh' Sie nur! Ach schau' Sie nur!

Marthe putzt sie auf.

MARTHE

O du glücksel'ge Kreatur!

MARGARETE

Darf mich leider nicht auf der Gassen
noch in der Kirche mit sehen lassen.

MARTHE

Komm du nur oft zu mir herüber
und leg den Schmuck hier heimlich an!
Spazier ein Stündchen lang dem Spiegelglas vorüber;
wir haben unsre Freude dran.
Und dann gibt's einen Anlaß, gibt's ein Fest,
wo man's so nach und nach den Leuten sehen läßt:
ein Kettchen erst, die Perle dann ins Ohr;
die Mutter sieht's wohl nicht, man macht ihr auch was vor.

MARGARETE

Wer konnte nur die beiden Kästchen bringen?
Es geht nicht zu mit rechten Dingen!

Es klopft.

MARGARETE

Ach Gott! Mag das meine Mutter sein?

MARTHE, *durchs Vorhängel guckend.*

Es ist ein fremder Herr. —Herein!

Mephistopheles tritt auf.

MEPHISTOPHELES

Bin so frei, grad hereinzutreten,
muß bei den Frauen Verzeihn erbeten.

Tritt ehrerbietig vor Margareten zurück.

Wollte nach Frau Marthe Schwerdtlein fragen.

MARTHE

Ich bin's! Was hat der Herr zu sagen?

MEPHISTOPHELES, *leise zu ihr.*

Ich kenne Sie jetzt, mir ist das genug;
Sie hat da gar vornehmen Besuch.
Verzeiht die Freiheit, die ich genommen!
Will nach Mittage wieder kommen.

MARTHE, *laut.*

Denk, Kind! Um alles in der Welt!
Der Herr dich für ein Fräulein hält!

MARGARETE

Ich bin ein armes junges Blut —
Ach Gott! Der Herr ist gar zu gut:
Schmuck und Geschmeide sind nicht mein.

MEPHISTOPHELES

Ach, es ist nicht der Schmuck allein;
Sie hat ein Wesen, einen Blick so scharf!
Wie freut mich's, daß ich bleiben darf.

MARTHE

Was bringt Er denn? Verlange sehr —

MEPHISTOPHELES

Ich wollt', ich hätt' eine frohere Mär!
Ich hoffe, Sie läßt mich's drum nicht büßen:
Ihr Mann ist tot und läßt Sie grüßen.

MARTHE

Ist tot? Das treue Herz! O weh!
Mein Mann ist tot! — Ach, ich vergeh'!

MARGARETE

Ach, liebe Frau, verzweifelt nicht!

MEPHISTOPHELES

So hört die traurige Geschicht'!

MARGARETE

Ich möchte drum mein' Tag' nicht lieben;
würde mich Verlust zu Tode betrüben.

MEPHISTOPHELES

Freud' muß Leid, Leid muß Freude haben.

MARTHE

Erzählt mir seines Lebens Schluß!

MEPHISTOPHELES

Er liegt in Padua begraben
beim heiligen Antonius,
an einer wohlgeweihten Stätte
zum ewig kühlen Ruhebette.

MARTHE

Habt Ihr sonst nichts an mich zu bringen?

MEPHISTOPHELES

Ja, eine Bitte, groß und schwer:
lass' Sie doch ja für ihn dreihundert Messen singen!
Im übrigen sind meine Taschen leer.

MARTHE

Was! Nicht ein Schaustück? Kein Geschmeid'?
Was jeder Handwerksbursch im Grund des Säckels spart,
zum Angedenken aufbewahrt,
und lieber hungert, lieber bettelt —

MEPHISTOPHELES

Madam, es tut mir herzlich leid!
Allein er hat sein Geld wahrhaftig nicht verzettelt.
Auch er bereute seine Fehler sehr,
ja, und bejammerte sein Unglück noch viel mehr.

MARGARETE

Ach, daß die Menschen so unglücklich sind!
Gewiß, ich will für ihn manch Requiem noch beten.

MEPHISTOPHELES

Ihr wäret wert, gleich in die Eh' zu treten:
Ihr seid ein liebenswürdig Kind.

MARGARETE

Ach nein, das geht jetzt noch nicht an.

MEPHISTOPHELES

Ist's nicht ein Mann, sei's derweil ein Galan!
's ist eine der größten Himmelsgaben,
so ein lieb Ding im Arm zu haben.

MARGARETE

Das ist des Landes nicht der Brauch.

MEPHISTOPHELES

Brauch oder nicht! — Es gibt sich auch!

MARTHE

Erzählt mir doch!

MEPHISTOPHELES

Ich stand an seinem Sterbebette
— es war was besser als von Mist —
von halbgefaultem Stroh. Allein er starb als Christ
und fand, daß er weit mehr noch auf der Zeche hätte.
„Wie," rief er, „muß ich mich von Grund aus hassen,
so mein Gewerb, mein Weib so zu verlassen!

Ach, die Erinnrung tötet mich!
Vergäb' sie mir nur noch in diesem Leben!"

MARTHE, *weinend.*

Der gute Mann! Ich hab' ihm längst vergeben.

MEPHISTOPHELES

„Allein, weiß Gott, sie war mehr schuld als ich."

MARTHE

Das lügt er! Was! Am Rand des Grabs zu lügen!

MEPHISTOPHELES

Er fabelte gewiß in letzten Zügen,
wenn ich nur halb ein Kenner bin.
„Ich hatte," sprach er, „nicht zum Zeitvertreib zu gaffen,
erst Kinder und dann Brot für sie zu schaffen
— und Brot im allerweit'sten Sinn! —
und konnte nicht einmal mein Teil in Frieden essen."

MARTHE

Hat er so aller Treu', so aller Lieb' vergessen,
der Plackerei bei Tag und Nacht?

MEPHISTOPHELES

Nicht doch. Er hat Euch herzlich dran gedacht.
Er sprach: „Als ich nun weg von Malta ging,
da betet' ich für Frau und Kinder brünstig.
Uns war denn auch der Himmel günstig,
daß unser Schiff ein türkisch Fahrzeug fing,
das einen Schatz des großen Sultans führte.
Da ward der Tapferkeit ihr Lohn,
und ich empfing denn auch, wie sich's gebührte,
mein wohlgemeßnes Teil davon."

MARTHE

Ei wie! Ei wo! Hat er's vielleicht vergraben?

MEPHISTOPHELES

Wer weiß, wo nun es die vier Winde haben!
Ein schönes Fräulein nahm sich seiner an,
als er in Napel fremd umherspazierte;
sie hat an ihm viel Lieb's und Treu's getan,
daß er's bis an sein selig Ende spürte.

MARTHE

Der Schelm! Der Dieb an seinen Kindern!
Auch alles Elend, alle Not
konnt' nicht sein schändlich Leben hindern!

MEPHISTOPHELES

Ja seht! Dafür ist er nun tot!
Wär' ich nun jetzt an Eurem Platze,
betraurt' ich ihn ein züchtig Jahr,
visierte dann unterweil nach einem neuen Schatze.

MARTHE

Ach Gott! Wie doch mein erster war,
find' ich nicht leicht auf dieser Welt den andern!
Es konnte kaum ein herziger Närrchen sein.
Er liebte nur das allzuviele Wandern,
und fremde Weiber, und fremden Wein,
und das verfluchte Würfelspiel!

MEPHISTOPHELES

Nun, nun, so konnt' es gehn und stehen,
wenn er Euch ungefähr so viel
von seiner Seite nachgesehen.
Ich schwör' Euch zu: mit dem Beding
wechselt' ich selbst mit Euch den Ring!

MARTHE

O, es beliebt dem Herrn zu scherzen!

MEPHISTOPHELES, *für sich.*

Nun mach' ich mich beizeiten fort!
Die hielte wohl den Teufel selbst beim Wort.

Zu Gretchen.

Wie steht es denn mit Ihrem Herzen?

MARGARETE

Was meint der Herr damit?

MEPHISTOPHELES, *für sich.*

Du gut's, unschuldig's Kind!

Laut.

Lebt wohl, ihr Fraun!

MARGARETE

Lebt wohl!

MARTHE

O sagt mir doch geschwind!
Ich möchte gern ein Zeugnis haben,
wo, wie und wann mein Schatz gestorben und begraben.
Ich bin von je der Ordnung Freund gewesen,
möcht' ihn auch tot im Wochenblättchen lesen.

MEPHISTOPHELES

Ja, gute Frau, durch zweier Zeugen Mund
wird allerwegs die Wahrheit kund.
Habe noch gar einen feinen Gesellen,
den will ich Euch vor den Richter stellen.
Ich bring' ihn her.

MARTHE

O tut das ja!

MEPHISTOPHELES

Und hier die Jungfrau ist auch da?
Ein braver Knab'! Ist viel gereist,
Fräuleins alle Höflichkeit erweist.

MARGARETE

Müßte vor dem Herren schamrot werden.

MEPHISTOPHELES

Vor keinem Könige der Erden!

MARTHE

Da hinterm Haus in meinem Garten
wollen wir der Herrn heut abend warten.

13 Straße

This scene exhibits the state of Faust's emotions & furnishes motivation for the scene which follows.

Faust. Mephistopheles.

FAUST

Wie ist's? Will's fördern? Will's bald gehn?

MEPHISTOPHELES

Ah bravo! Find' ich Euch in Feuer?
In kurzer Zeit ist Gretchen Euer!
Heut abend sollt Ihr sie bei Nachbar' Marthen sehn:
das ist ein Weib wie auserlesen
zum Kuppler- und Zigeunerwesen!

FAUST

So recht!

MEPHISTOPHELES

Doch wird auch was von uns begehrt.

FAUST

Ein Dienst ist wohl des andern wert.

M. reports to Faust who is reluctant to commit perjury but finally agrees.

MEPHISTOPHELES

Wir legen nur ein gültig Zeugnis nieder,
daß ihres Ehherrn ausgereckte Glieder
in Padua an heil'ger Stätte ruhn.

FAUST

Sehr klug! Wir werden erst die Reise machen müssen!

MEPHISTOPHELES

Sancta Simplicitas! Darum ist's nicht zu tun;
bezeugt nur, ohne viel zu wissen!

FAUST

Wenn Er nichts Besser's hat, so ist der Plan zerrissen.

MEPHISTOPHELES

O heil'ger Mann! Da wärt Ihr's nun!
Ist es das erstemal in Eurem Leben,
daß Ihr falsch Zeugnis abgelegt?
Habt Ihr von Gott, der Welt und was sich drin bewegt,
vom Menschen, was sich ihm in Kopf und Herzen regt,
Definitionen nicht mit großer Kraft gegeben,
mit frecher Stirne, kühner Brust?
Und wollt Ihr recht ins Innre gehen,
habt Ihr davon, — Ihr müßt es grad gestehen —
so viel als von Herrn Schwerdtleins Tod gewußt!

FAUST

Du bist und bleibst ein Lügner, ein Sophiste.

MEPHISTOPHELES

Ja, wenn man's nicht ein bißchen tiefer wüßte!
Denn morgen wirst, in allen Ehren,
das arme Gretchen nicht betören
und alle Seelenlieb' ihr schwören?

FAUST

Und zwar von Herzen!

MEPHISTOPHELES

Gut und schön!
Dann wird von ewiger Treu' und Liebe,
von einzig überallmächt'gem Triebe —
Wird das auch so von Herzen gehn?

FAUST

Laß das! Es wird! — Wenn ich empfinde,
für das Gefühl, für das Gewühl
nach Namen suche, keinen finde,

dann durch die Welt mit allen Sinnen schweife,
nach allen höchsten Worten greife
und diese Glut, von der ich brenne,
unendlich, ewig, ewig nenne, —
ist das ein teuflisch Lügenspiel?

MEPHISTOPHELES

Ich hab' doch recht!

FAUST

Hör! Merk dir dies
— ich bitte dich! — und schone meine Lunge:
wer recht behalten will und hat nur eine Zunge,
behält's gewiß.
Und komm, ich hab' des Schwätzens Überdruß,
denn du hast recht, vorzüglich weil ich muß.

p391

above all

Faust concedes that he means to deceive and betray Gretchen. He says he's being forced to this action by his inability to resist the compelling of his impulses?

14 Garten

Margarete an Faustens Arm, Marthe mit Mephistopheles, auf und ab spazierend.

MARGARETE

Ich fühl' es wohl, daß mich der Herr nur schont,
herab sich läßt, mich zu beschämen.
Ein Reisender ist so gewohnt,
aus Gütigkeit fürliebzunehmen;
ich weiß zu gut, daß solch erfahrnen Mann
mein arm Gespräch nicht unterhalten kann.

FAUST

Ein Blick von dir, ein Wort mehr unterhält
als alle Weisheit dieser Welt.

Er küßt ihre Hand.

MARGARETE

Inkommodiert Euch nicht! Wie könnt Ihr sie nur küssen?
Sie ist so garstig, ist so rauh!
Was hab' ich nicht schon alles schaffen müssen!
Die Mutter ist gar zu genau.

Gehn vorüber.

The chief function of this scene is to demonstrate the purity of the girl and the genuineness of her attraction to Faust.

The contrasts of the two conversations emphasizes the diff. between nature at work and the Devil at play.

MARTHE

Und Ihr, mein Herr, Ihr reist so immer fort?

MEPHISTOPHELES

Ach, daß Gewerb und Pflicht uns dazu treiben!
Mit wie viel Schmerz verläßt man manchen Ort
und darf doch nun einmal nicht bleiben!

MARTHE

In raschen Jahren geht's wohl an,
so um und um frei durch die Welt zu streifen;
doch kömmt die böse Zeit heran,
und sich als Hagestolz allein zum Grab zu schleifen, —
das hat noch keinem wohlgetan.

MEPHISTOPHELES

Mit Grausen seh' ich das von weiten.

MARTHE

Drum, werter Herr, beratet Euch in Zeiten!

Gehn vorüber.

MARGARETE

Ja, aus den Augen, aus dem Sinn!
Die Höflichkeit ist Euch geläufig;
allein Ihr habt der Freunde häufig,
sie sind verständiger, als ich bin.

FAUST

O Beste! Glaube, was man so „verständig" nennt,
ist oft mehr Eitelkeit und Kurzsinn.

MARGARETE

Wie?

FAUST

Ach, daß die Einfalt, daß die Unschuld nie
sich selbst und ihren heil'gen Wert erkennt!
Daß Demut, Niedrigkeit, die höchsten Gaben
der liebevoll austeilenden Natur —

MARGARETE

Denkt Ihr an mich ein Augenblickchen nur,
ich werde Zeit genug an Euch zu denken haben.

FAUST

Ihr seid wohl viel allein?

MARGARETE

Ja, unsre Wirtschaft ist nur klein,
und doch will sie versehen sein.
Wir haben keine Magd; muß kochen, fegen, stricken
und nähn und laufen früh und spat;
und meine Mutter ist in allen Stücken
so akkurat!
Nicht, daß sie just so sehr sich einzuschränken hat;
wir könnten uns weit eh'r als andre regen:
mein Vater hinterließ ein hübsch Vermögen,
ein Häuschen und ein Gärtchen vor der Stadt.
Doch hab' ich jetzt so ziemlich stille Tage:
mein Bruder ist Soldat,
mein Schwesterchen ist tot.
Ich hatte mit dem Kind wohl meine liebe Not;
doch übernähm' ich gern noch einmal alle Plage,
so lieb war mir das Kind.

FAUST

Ein Engel, wenn dir's glich!

MARGARETE

Ich zog es auf, und herzlich liebt' es mich.
Es war nach meines Vaters Tod geboren.
Die Mutter gaben wir verloren,
so elend wie sie damals lag,
und sie erholte sich sehr langsam, nach und nach.
Da konnte sie nun nicht dran denken,
das arme Würmchen selbst zu tränken;
und so erzog ich's ganz allein,
mit Milch und Wasser; so ward's mein.
Auf meinem Arm, in meinem Schoß
war's freundlich, zappelte, ward groß.

FAUST

Du hast gewiß das reinste Glück empfunden.

MARGARETE

Doch auch gewiß gar manche schwere Stunden.
Des Kleinen Wiege stand zu Nacht
an meinem Bett: es durfte kaum sich regen,
war ich erwacht.
Bald mußt' ich's tränken, bald es zu mir legen,
bald, wenn's nicht schwieg, vom Bett aufstehn
und tänzelnd in der Kammer auf und nieder gehn,

und früh am Tage schon am Waschtrog stehn,
dann auf dem Markt und an dem Herde sorgen,
und immer fort wie heut so morgen.
Da geht's, mein Herr, nicht immer mutig zu;
doch schmeckt dafür das Essen, schmeckt die Ruh.

Gehn vorüber.

MARTHE

Die armen Weiber sind doch übel dran:
ein Hagestolz ist schwerlich zu bekehren.

MEPHISTOPHELES

Es käme nur auf Euresgleichen an,
mich eines Bessern zu belehren.

MARTHE

Sagt grad, mein Herr: habt Ihr noch nichts gefunden?
Hat sich das Herz nicht irgendwo gebunden?

MEPHISTOPHELES

Das Sprichwort sagt: „Ein eigner Herd,
ein braves Weib sind Gold und Perlen wert.“

MARTHE

Ich meine: ob Ihr niemals Lust bekommen?

MEPHISTOPHELES

Man hat mich überall recht höflich aufgenommen.

MARTHE

Ich wollte sagen: ward's nie Ernst in Eurem Herzen?

MEPHISTOPHELES

Mit Frauen soll man sich nie unterstehn zu scherzen.

MARTHE

Ach, Ihr versteht mich nicht!

MEPHISTOPHELES

Das tut mir herzlich leid!
Doch ich versteh', — daß Ihr sehr gütig seid.

Gehn vorüber.

FAUST

Du kanntest mich, o kleiner Engel, wieder,
gleich als ich in den Garten kam?

MARGARETE

Saht Ihr es nicht? Ich schlug die Augen nieder.

FAUST

Und du verzeihst die Freiheit, die ich nahm,
was sich die Frechheit unterfangen,
als du jüngst aus dem Dom gegangen?

MARGARETE

Ich war bestürzt! Mir war das nie geschehn;
es konnte niemand von mir Übel's sagen.
Ach, dacht' ich, hat er in deinem Betragen
was Freches, Unanständiges gesehn?
Es schien ihn gleich nur anzuwandeln,
mit dieser Dirne gradehin zu handeln.
Gesteh' ich's doch! Ich wußte nicht, was sich
zu Eurem Vorteil hier zu regen gleich begonnte;
allein gewiß, ich war recht bös auf mich,
daß ich auf Euch nicht böser werden konnte.

FAUST

Süß Liebchen!

MARGARETE

Laßt einmal!

Sie pflückt eine Sternblume und zupft die Blätter ab, eins nach dem andern.

FAUST

Was soll das? Einen Strauß?

MARGARETE

Nein, es soll nur ein Spiel.

FAUST

Wie?

MARGARETE

Geht! Ihr lacht mich aus.

Sie rupft und murmelt.

FAUST

Was murmelst du?

MARGARETE, *halblaut.*

Er liebt mich — liebt mich nicht —

FAUST

Du holdes Himmelsangesicht!

MARGARETE, *fährt fort:*

liebt mich — nicht — liebt mich — nicht — —

Das letzte Blatt ausrupfend, mit holder Freude.

Er liebt mich!

FAUST

Ja, mein Kind! Laß dieses Blumenwort
dir Götterausspruch sein: er liebt dich!
Verstehst du, was das heißt? Er liebt dich!

Er faßt ihre beiden Hände.

MARGARETE

Mich überläuft's!

FAUST

O schaudre nicht! Laß diesen Blick,
laß diesen Händedruck dir sagen,
was unaussprechlich ist:
sich hinzugeben ganz und eine Wonne
zu fühlen, die ewig sein muß!
Ewig! — Ihr Ende würde Verzweiflung sein . . .
Nein, kein Ende! Kein Ende!

Margarete drückt ihm die Hände, macht sich los und läuft weg. Er steht einen Augenblick in Gedanken, dann folgt er ihr.

MARTHE, *kommend.*

Die Nacht bricht an.

MEPHISTOPHELES

Ja, und wir wollen fort.

MARTHE

Ich bät' Euch, länger hier zu bleiben,
allein es ist ein gar zu böser Ort:
es ist, als hätte niemand nichts zu treiben
und nichts zu schaffen,
als auf des Nachbarn Schritt und Tritt zu gaffen;
und man kommt ins Gered', wie man sich immer stellt. —
Und unser Pärchen?

MEPHISTOPHELES

Ist den Gang dort aufgeflogen. —
Mutwill'ge Sommervögel!

MARTHE

Er scheint ihr gewogen.

MEPHISTOPHELES

Und sie ihm auch. Das ist der Lauf der Welt.

15 Ein Gartenhäuschen

Margarete springt herein, steckt sich hinter die Tür, hält die Fingerspitze an die Lippen und guckt durch die Ritze.

MARGARETE
Er kommt!
Faust kommt.
FAUST
Ach, Schelm, so neckst du mich . . .
Treff' ich dich!
Er küßt sie.
MARGARETE, *ihn fassend und den Kuß zurückgebend.*
Bester Mann! Von Herzen lieb' ich dich!
Mephistopheles klopft an.
FAUST, *stampfend.*
Wer da?
MEPHISTOPHELES
Gut Freund!
FAUST
Ein Tier!
MEPHISTOPHELES
Es ist wohl Zeit zu scheiden.
Marthe kommt.
MARTHE
Ja, es ist spät, mein Herr.
FAUST
Darf ich Euch nicht geleiten?
MARGARETE
Die Mutter würde mich — Lebt wohl!
FAUST
Muß ich denn gehn?
Lebt wohl!
MARTHE
Ade!
MARGARETE
Auf baldig Wiedersehn!
Faust und Mephistopheles ab.

MARGARETE

Du lieber Gott! Was so ein Mann
nicht alles, alles denken kann!
Beschämt nur steh' ich vor ihm da
und sag' zu allen Sachen „Ja".
Bin doch ein arm, unwissend Kind.
Begreife nicht, was er an mir find't.

Ab.

16 Wald und Höhle

Faust allein.

FAUST

Erhabner Geist, du gabst mir, gabst mir alles,
warum ich bat. Du hast mir nicht umsonst
dein Angesicht im Feuer zugewendet.
Gabst mir die herrliche Natur zum Königreich,
Kraft, sie zu fühlen, zu genießen. Nicht
kalt staunenden Besuch erlaubst du nur,
vergönnest mir, in ihre tiefe Brust
wie in den Busen eines Freunds zu schauen.
Du führst die Reihe der Lebendigen
vor mir vorbei und lehrst mich meine Brüder
im stillen Busch, in Luft und Wasser kennen.
Und wenn der Sturm im Walde braust und knarrt,
die Riesenfichte stürzend Nachbaräste
und Nachbarstämme quetschend niederstreift,
und ihrem Fall dumpf-hohl der Hügel donnert, —
dann führst du mich zur sichern Höhle, zeigst
mich dann mir selbst, und meiner eignen Brust
geheime tiefe Wunder öffnen sich.
Und steigt vor meinem Blick der reine Mond
besänftigend herüber, schweben mir
von Felsenwänden, aus dem feuchten Busch,
der Vorwelt silberne Gestalten auf
und lindern der Betrachtung strenge Lust.

O, daß dem Menschen nichts Vollkommnes wird,
empfind' ich nun. Du gabst zu dieser Wonne,

die mich den Göttern nah und näher bringt,
mir den Gefährten, den ich schon nicht mehr
entbehren kann, wenn er gleich, kalt und frech,
mich vor mir selbst erniedrigt, und zu Nichts,
mit einem Worthauch, deine Gaben wandelt.
Er facht in meiner Brust ein wildes Feuer
nach jenem schönen Bild geschäftig an.
So tauml' ich von Begierde zu Genuß,
und im Genuß verschmacht' ich nach Begierde.—

Mephistopheles tritt auf.

MEPHISTOPHELES

Habt Ihr nun bald das Leben g'nug geführt?
Wie kann's Euch in die Länge freuen?
Es ist wohl gut, daß man's einmal probiert;
dann aber wieder zu was Neuen!

FAUST

Ich wollt', du hättest mehr zu tun,
als mich am guten Tag zu plagen.

MEPHISTOPHELES

Nun, nun! Ich lass' dich gerne ruhn;
du darfst mir's nicht im Ernste sagen.
An dir Gesellen, unhold, barsch und toll,
ist wahrlich wenig zu verlieren.
Den ganzen Tag hat man die Hände voll!
Was ihm gefällt und was man lassen soll,
kann man dem Herrn nie an der Nase spüren.

FAUST

Das ist so just der rechte Ton!
Er will noch Dank, daß Er mich ennuyiert.

MEPHISTOPHELES

Wie hätt'st du, armer Erdensohn,
dein Leben ohne mich geführt?
Vom Kribskrabs der Imagination
hab' ich dich doch auf Zeiten lang kuriert.
Und wär' ich nicht, so wärst du schon
von diesem Erdball abspaziert.
Was hast du da in Höhlen, Felsenritzen
dich wie ein Schuhu zu versitzen?
Was schlurfst aus dumpfem Moos und triefendem Gestein,
wie eine Kröte, Nahrung ein?

Ein schöner, süßer Zeitvertreib!
Dir steckt der Doktor noch im Leib!

FAUST

Verstehst du, was für neue Lebenskraft
mir dieser Wandel in der Öde schafft?
Ja, würdest du es ahnen können,
du wärest Teufel g'nug, mein Glück mir nicht zu gönnen.

MEPHISTOPHELES

Ein überirdisches Vergnügen!
In Nacht und Tau auf den Gebirgen liegen,
und Erd' und Himmel wonniglich umfassen,
zu einer Gottheit sich aufschwellen lassen,
der Erde Mark mit Ahnungsdrang durchwühlen,
alle sechs Tagewerk' im Busen fühlen,
in stolzer Kraft ich weiß nicht was genießen,
bald liebewonniglich in alles überfließen,
verschwunden ganz der Erdensohn,
und dann die hohe Intuition —

Mit einer Gebärde.

ich darf nicht sagen, wie — zu schließen!

FAUST

Pfui über dich!

MEPHISTOPHELES

Das will Euch nicht behagen;
Ihr habt das Recht, gesittet „Pfui" zu sagen.
Man darf das nicht vor keuschen Ohren nennen,
was keusche Herzen nicht entbehren können.
Und kurz und gut, ich gönn' Ihm das Vergnügen,
gelegentlich sich etwas vorzulügen;
doch lange hält Er das nicht aus.
Du bist schon wieder abgetrieben
und, währt es länger, aufgerieben
in Tollheit — oder Angst und Graus.
Genug damit! Dein Liebchen sitzt dadrinne,
und alles wird ihr eng und trüb.
Du kommst ihr gar nicht aus dem Sinne,
sie hat dich übermächtig lieb.
Erst kam deine Liebeswut übergeflossen,
wie vom geschmolznen Schnee ein Bächlein übersteigt;
du hast sie ihr ins Herz gegossen,

nun ist dein Bächlein wieder seicht.
Mich dünkt, anstatt in Wäldern zu thronen,
ließ' es dem großen Herren gut,
das arme, affenjunge Blut
für seine Liebe zu belohnen.
Die Zeit wird ihr erbärmlich lang;
sie steht am Fenster, sieht die Wolken ziehn
über die alte Stadtmauer hin.
„Wenn ich ein Vöglein wär'!" — so geht ihr Gesang
Tage lang, halbe Nächte lang.
Einmal ist sie munter, meist betrübt,
einmal recht ausgeweint,
dann wieder ruhig, wie's scheint, —
und immer verliebt.

FAUST

Schlange! Schlange!

MEPHISTOPHELES, *für sich.*

Gelt, daß ich dich fange!

FAUST

Verruchter! Hebe dich von hinnen
und nenne nicht das schöne Weib!
Bring die Begier zu ihrem süßen Leib
nicht wieder vor die halbverrückten Sinnen!

MEPHISTOPHELES

Was soll es denn? Sie meint, du seist entflohn,
und halb und halb bist du es schon.

FAUST

Ich bin ihr nah, und wär' ich noch so fern;
ich kann sie nie vergessen, nie verlieren!
Ja, ich beneide schon den Leib des Herrn,
wenn ihre Lippen ihn indes berühren.

MEPHISTOPHELES

Gar wohl, mein Freund! Ich hab' Euch oft beneidet
ums Zwillingspaar, das unter Rosen weidet.

FAUST

Entfliehe, Kuppler!

MEPHISTOPHELES

Schön! Ihr schimpft, und ich muß lachen.
Der Gott, der Bub' und Mädchen schuf,

erkannte gleich den edelsten Beruf,
auch selbst Gelegenheit zu machen.
Nur fort, es ist ein großer Jammer!
Ihr sollt in Eures Liebchens Kammer,
nicht etwa in den Tod!

FAUST

Was ist die Himmelsfreud' in ihren Armen!
Laß mich an ihrer Brust erwarmen!
Fühl' ich nicht immer ihre Not?
Bin ich der Flüchtling nicht, der Unbehauste,
der Unmensch ohne Zweck und Ruh,
der wie ein Wassersturz von Fels' zu Felsen brauste,
begierig wütend, nach dem Abgrund zu?
Und seitwärts sie, mit kindlich dumpfen Sinnen,
im Hüttchen auf dem kleinen Alpenfeld,
und all ihr häusliches Beginnen
umfangen in der kleinen Welt.
Und ich, der Gottverhaßte,
hatte nicht genug,
daß ich die Felsen faßte
und sie zu Trümmern schlug!
Sie, ihren Frieden mußt' ich untergraben!
Du, Hölle, mußtest dieses Opfer haben!
Hilf, Teufel, mir die Zeit der Angst verkürzen!
Was muß geschehn, mag's gleich geschehn!
Mag ihr Geschick auf mich zusammenstürzen
und sie mit mir zugrunde gehn!

MEPHISTOPHELES

Wie's wieder siedet, wieder glüht!
Geh ein und tröste sie, du Tor!
Wo so ein Köpfchen keinen Ausgang sieht,
stellt er sich gleich das Ende vor.
Es lebe, wer sich tapfer hält!
Du bist doch sonst so ziemlich eingeteufelt:
nichts Abgeschmackter's find' ich auf der Welt
als einen Teufel, der verzweifelt.

17 Gretchens Stube

Gretchen, am Spinnrade, allein.

GRETCHEN

Meine Ruh ist hin,
mein Herz ist schwer;
ich finde sie nimmer
und nimmermehr.

Wo ich ihn nicht hab',
ist mir das Grab;
die ganze Welt
ist mir vergällt.

Mein armer Kopf
ist mir verrückt,
mein armer Sinn
ist mir zerstückt.

Meine Ruh ist hin,
mein Herz ist schwer;
ich finde sie nimmer
und nimmermehr.

Nach ihm nur schau' ich
zum Fenster hinaus,
nach ihm nur geh' ich
aus dem Haus.

Sein hoher Gang,
sein' edle Gestalt,
seines Mundes Lächeln,
seiner Augen Gewalt,

und seiner Rede
Zauberfluß,
sein Händedruck —
und ach, sein Kuß!

Meine Ruh ist hin,
mein Herz ist schwer;
ich finde sie nimmer
und nimmermehr.

Gretchen is in love and is robbed of her peace. This scene is a necessary antecedant and motivation to the discussion of religion in Martha's garden. Also without this scene we could not understand G's acceptance of the sleeping potion for her mother.

Mein Busen drängt
sich nach ihm hin.
Ach, dürft' ich fassen
und halten ihn
und küssen ihn,
so wie ich wollt',
an seinen Küssen
vergehen sollt'!

18 Marthens Garten

Margarete. Faust.

MARGARETE

Versprich mir, Heinrich!

FAUST

Was ich kann!

MARGARETE

Nun sag: wie hast du's mit der Religion?
Du bist ein herzlich guter Mann,
allein ich glaub', du hältst nicht viel davon.

FAUST

Laß das, mein Kind! Du fühlst, ich bin dir gut;
für meine Lieben ließ' ich Leib und Blut,
will niemand sein Gefühl und seine Kirche rauben.

MARGARETE

Das ist nicht recht, man muß dran glauben!

FAUST

Muß man?

MARGARETE

Ach, wenn ich etwas auf dich könnte!
Du ehrst auch nicht die heil'gen Sakramente!

FAUST

Ich ehre sie.

MARGARETE

Doch ohne Verlangen!
Zur Messe, zur Beichte bist du lange nicht gegangen.
Glaubst du an Gott?

FAUST

Mein Liebchen, wer darf sagen:
„Ich glaub' an Gott"?
Magst Priester oder Weise fragen,
und ihre Antwort scheint nur Spott
über den Frager zu sein.

MARGARETE

So glaubst du nicht?

FAUST

Mißhör mich nicht, du holdes Angesicht!
Wer darf ihn nennen
und wer bekennen:
„Ich glaub' ihn" —
wer empfinden
und sich unterwinden
zu sagen: „Ich glaub' ihn nicht"?
Der Allumfasser,
der Allerhalter,
faßt und erhält er nicht
dich, mich, sich selbst?
Wölbt sich der Himmel nicht da droben?
Liegt die Erde nicht hier unten fest?
Und steigen freundlich blickend
ewige Sterne nicht herauf?
Schau' ich nicht Aug' in Auge dir?
Und drängt nicht alles
nach Haupt und Herzen dir
und webt in ewigem Geheimnis
unsichtbar sichtbar neben dir?
Erfüll davon dein Herz, so groß es ist!
Und wenn du ganz in dem Gefühle selig bist,
nenn es dann, wie du willst!
Nenn's Glück! Herz! Liebe! Gott!
Ich habe keinen Namen
dafür! Gefühl ist alles, —
Name ist Schall und Rauch,
umnebelnd Himmelsglut.

MARGARETE

Das ist alles recht schön und gut.
Ungefähr sagt das der Pfarrer auch,
nur mit ein bißchen andern Worten.

FAUST

Es sagen's allerorten
alle Herzen unter dem himmlischen Tage,
jedes in seiner Sprache;
warum nicht ich in der meinen?

MARGARETE

Wenn man's so hört, möcht's leidlich scheinen,
steht aber doch immer schief darum;
denn du hast kein Christentum.

FAUST

Lieb's Kind!

MARGARETE

Es tut mir lang schon weh,
daß ich dich in d e r Gesellschaft seh'.

FAUST

Wieso?

MARGARETE

Der Mensch, den du da bei dir hast,
ist mir in tiefer, innrer Seele verhaßt!
Es hat mir in meinem Leben
so nichts einen Stich ins Herz gegeben,
als des Menschen widrig Gesicht.

FAUST

Liebe Puppe, fürcht ihn nicht!

MARGARETE

Seine Gegenwart bewegt mir das Blut.
Ich bin sonst allen Menschen gut;
aber wie ich mich sehne, dich zu schauen,
hab' ich vor dem Menschen ein heimlich Grauen,
und halt' ihn für einen Schelm dazu!
Gott verzeih' mir's, wenn ich ihm Unrecht tu'!

FAUST

Es muß auch solche Käuze geben.

MARGARETE

Wollte nicht mit seinesgleichen leben!
Kommt er einmal zur Tür herein,
sieht er immer so spöttisch drein
und halb ergrimmt;
man sieht, daß er an nichts keinen Anteil nimmt.
Es steht ihm an der Stirn geschrieben,

daß er nicht mag eine Seele lieben.
Mir wird's so wohl in deinem Arm,
so frei, so hingegeben warm,
und seine Gegenwart schnürt mir das Innre zu.

FAUST

Du ahnungsvoller Engel du!

MARGARETE

Das übermannt mich so sehr,
daß, wo er nur mag zu uns treten,
mein' ich sogar, ich liebte dich nicht mehr!
Auch, wenn er da ist, könnt' ich nimmer beten,
und das frißt mir ins Herz hinein;
dir, Heinrich, muß es auch so sein.

FAUST

Du hast nun die Antipathie!

MARGARETE

Ich muß nun fort.

FAUST

Ach, kann ich nie
ein Stündchen ruhig dir am Busen hängen
und Brust an Brust und Seel' in Seele drängen?

MARGARETE

Ach, wenn ich nur alleine schlief'!
Ich ließ' dir gern heut nacht den Riegel offen.
Doch meine Mutter schläft nicht tief,
und würden wir von ihr betroffen,
ich wär' gleich auf der Stelle tot!

FAUST

Du Engel, das hat keine Not.
Hier ist ein Fläschchen. Drei Tropfen nur
in ihren Trank umhüllen
mit tiefem Schlaf gefällig die Natur.

MARGARETE

Was tu' ich nicht um deinetwillen!
Es wird ihr hoffentlich nicht schaden?

FAUST

Würd' ich sonst, Liebchen, dir es raten?

MARGARETE

Seh' ich dich, bester Mann, nur an,
weiß nicht, was mich nach deinem Willen treibt;

ich habe schon so viel für dich getan,
daß mir zu tun fast nichts mehr übrigbleibt.

Ab.

Mephistopheles tritt auf.

MEPHISTOPHELES

Der Grasaff'! Ist er weg?

FAUST

Hast wieder spioniert?

MEPHISTOPHELES

Ich hab's ausführlich wohl vernommen:
Herr Doktor wurden da katechisiert.
Hoff', es soll Ihnen wohl bekommen!
Die Mädels sind doch sehr interessiert,
ob einer fromm und schlicht nach altem Brauch.
Sie denken: „Duckt er da, folgt er uns eben auch."

FAUST

Du Ungeheuer siehst nicht ein,
wie diese treue, liebe Seele —
von ihrem Glauben voll,
der ganz allein
ihr seligmachend ist, — sich heilig quäle,
daß sie den liebsten Mann verloren halten soll.

MEPHISTOPHELES

Du übersinnlicher sinnlicher Freier,
ein Mägdelein nasführet dich! —

FAUST

Du Spottgeburt von Dreck und Feuer!

MEPHISTOPHELES

Und die Physiognomie versteht sie meisterlich:
in meiner Gegenwart wird's ihr, sie weiß nicht wie.
Mein Mäskchen da weissagt verborgnen Sinn:
sie fühlt, daß ich ganz sicher ein Genie,
vielleicht wohl gar der Teufel bin.
Nun, heute nacht —?

FAUST

Was geht dich's an?

MEPHISTOPHELES

Hab' ich doch meine Freude dran!

19 Am Brunnen

Gretchen und Lieschen, mit Krügen.

LIESCHEN
Hast nichts von Bärbelchen gehört?

GRETCHEN
Kein Wort. Ich komm' gar wenig unter Leute.

LIESCHEN
Gewiß, Sibylle sagt' mir's heute:
die hat sich endlich auch betört.
Das ist das Vornehmtun!

GRETCHEN
Wieso?

LIESCHEN
Es stinkt!
Sie füttert zwei, wenn sie nun ißt und trinkt.

GRETCHEN
Ach!

LIESCHEN
So ist's ihr endlich recht ergangen.
Wie lange hat sie an dem Kerl gehangen!
Das war ein Spazieren,
auf Dorf und Tanzplatz Führen!
Mußt' überall die Erste sein!
Kurtesiert' ihr immer mit Pastetchen und Wein.
Bild't' sich was auf ihre Schönheit ein;
war doch so ehrlos, sich nicht zu schämen,
Geschenke von ihm anzunehmen.
War ein Gekos' und ein Geschleck':
da ist denn auch das Blümchen weg!

GRETCHEN
Das arme Ding!

LIESCHEN
Bedauerst sie noch gar!
Wenn unsereins am Spinnen war,
uns nachts die Mutter nicht hinunterließ,
stand sie bei ihrem Buhlen süß;
auf der Türbank und im dunkeln Gang

ward ihnen keine Stunde zu lang.
Da mag sie denn sich ducken nun,
im Sünderhemdchen Kirchbuß' tun!

GRETCHEN

Er nimmt sie gewiß zu seiner Frau.

LIESCHEN

Er wär' ein Narr! Ein flinker Jung'
hat anderwärts noch Luft genung.
Er ist auch fort.

GRETCHEN

Das ist nicht schön!

LIESCHEN

Kriegt sie ihn, soll's ihr übel gehn:
das Kränzel reißen die Buben ihr,
und Häckerling streuen wir vor die Tür!

Ab.

GRETCHEN, *nach Hause gehend.*

Wie konnt' ich sonst so tapfer schmälen,
wenn tät ein armes Mägdlein fehlen!
Wie konnt' ich über andrer Sünden
nicht Worte g'nug der Zunge finden!
Wie schien mir's schwarz, und schwärzt's noch gar,
mir's immer doch nicht schwarz g'nug war,
und segnet' mich und tat so groß, —
und bin nun selbst der Sünde bloß!
Doch — alles, was dazu mich trieb,
Gott! war so gut — ach, war so lieb!

20 Zwinger

In der Mauerhöhle ein Andachtsbild der Mater dolorosa, *Blumenkrüge davor. Gretchen steckt frische Blumen in die Krüge.*

GRETCHEN

Ach, neige,
du Schmerzenreiche,
dein Antlitz gnädig meiner Not!
Das Schwert im Herzen,
mit tausend Schmerzen
blickst auf zu deines Sohnes Tod.
Zum Vater blickst du,
und Seufzer schickst du
hinauf um sein' und deine Not.

Wer fühlet,
wie wühlet
der Schmerz mir im Gebein?
Was mein armes Herz hier banget,
was es zittert, was verlanget,
weißt nur du, nur du allein!

Wohin ich immer gehe,
wie weh, wie weh, wie wehe
wird mir im Busen hier!
Ich bin, ach, kaum alleine,
ich wein', ich wein', ich weine,
das Herz zerbricht in mir.

Die Scherben vor meinem Fenster
betaut' ich mit Tränen, ach,
als ich am frühen Morgen
dir diese Blumen brach.
Schien hell in meine Kammer
die Sonne früh herauf,
saß ich in allem Jammer
in meinem Bett schon auf.

Hilf! Rette mich von Schmach und Tod!
Ach, neige,
du Schmerzenreiche,
dein Antlitz gnädig meiner Not!

G. prays for rescue from the shame and death, which in her lonely despair, she sees looming before her.

G's brother has learned of his sister's disgrace. He is lying in wait for her lover to avenge her betrayal. The dramatic function of this scene is to break off the G affair by forcing F to flee from town.

21 Nacht. Straße vor Gretchens Türe

Valentin: Soldat, Gretchens Bruder.

VALENTIN

Wenn ich so saß bei einem Gelag,
wo mancher sich berühmen mag,
und die Gesellen mir den Flor
der Mägdlein laut gepriesen vor,
mit vollem Glas das Lob verschwemmt, —
den Ellenbogen aufgestemmt,
saß ich in meiner sichern Ruh,
hört' all dem Schwadronieren zu
und streiche lächelnd meinen Bart
und kriege das volle Glas zur Hand
und sage: „Alles nach seiner Art!
Aber ist e i n e im ganzen Land,
die meiner trauten Gretel gleicht,
die meiner Schwester das Wasser reicht?"
Topp! Topp! Kling! Klang! Das ging herum;
die einen schrieen: „Er hat recht,
sie ist die Zier vom ganzen Geschlecht!"
Da saßen alle die Lober stumm.
  Und nun! — Um 's Haar sich auszuraufen
und an den Wänden hinaufzulaufen! —
Mit Stichelreden, Naserümpfen
soll jeder Schurke mich beschimpfen!
Soll wie ein böser Schuldner sitzen,
bei jedem Zufallswörtchen schwitzen!
Und möcht' ich sie zusammenschmeißen,
könnt' ich sie doch nicht Lügner heißen.

It also adds one more murder to the guilt of the lovers.

is a match to her

Was kommt heran? Was schleicht herbei?
Irr' ich nicht, es sind ihrer zwei.
Ist er's, gleich pack' ich ihn beim Felle!
Soll nicht lebendig von der Stelle!

Faust und Mephistopheles treten auf.

FAUST

Wie von dem Fenster dort der Sakristei
aufwärts der Schein des ew'gen Lämpchens flämmert
und schwach und schwächer seitwärts dämmert!

Und Finsternis drängt ringsum bei!
So sieht's in meinem Busen nächtig.

MEPHISTOPHELES

Und mir ist's wie dem Kätzlein schmächtig,
das an den Feuerleitern schleicht,
sich leis' dann um die Mauern streicht;
mir ist's ganz tugendlich dabei:
ein bißchen Diebsgelüst, ein bißchen Rammelei.
So spukt mir schon durch alle Glieder
die herrliche Walpurgisnacht.
Die kommt uns übermorgen wieder;
da weiß man doch, warum man wacht.

Faust is depressed. The light from the window reflects his mood. M, on the other hand, feels wonderful like a lustful tomcat.

FAUST

Rückt wohl der Schatz indessen in die Höh',
den ich dort hinten flimmern seh'?

MEPHISTOPHELES

Du kannst die Freude bald erleben,
das Kesselchen herauszuheben.
Ich schielte neulich so hinein,
sind herrliche Löwentaler drein.

FAUST

Nicht ein Geschmeide, nicht ein Ring,
meine liebe Buhle damit zu zieren?

MEPHISTOPHELES

Ich sah dabei wohl so ein Ding
als wie eine Art von Perlenschnüren.

FAUST

So ist es recht! Mir tut es weh,
wenn ich ohne Geschenke zu ihr geh'.

MEPHISTOPHELES

Es sollt' Euch eben nicht verdrießen,
umsonst auch etwas zu genießen. —
Jetzt, da der Himmel voller Sterne glüht,
sollt Ihr ein wahres Kunststück hören:
ich sing' ihr ein moralisch Lied,
um sie gewisser zu betören.

Singt zur Zither.

Was machst du mir
vor Liebchens Tür,
Kathrinchen, hier
bei frühem Tagesblicke?

Laß, laß es sein!
Er läßt dich ein,
als Mädchen ein,
als Mädchen nicht zurücke.
Nehmt euch in acht!
Ist es vollbracht,
dann gute Nacht,
ihr armen, armen Dinger!
Habt ihr euch lieb,
tut keinem Dieb
nur nichts zulieb',
als mit dem Ring am Finger!

VALENTIN, *tritt vor.*

Wen lockst du hier? Beim Element!
Vermaledeiter Rattenfänger!
Zum Teufel erst das Instrument!
Zum Teufel hinterdrein den Sänger!

MEPHISTOPHELES

Die Zither ist entzwei! An der ist nichts zu halten.

VALENTIN

Nun soll es an ein Schädelspalten!

MEPHISTOPHELES, *zu Faust.*

Herr Doktor, nicht gewichen! Frisch!
Hart an mich an, wie ich Euch führe!
Heraus mit Eurem Flederwisch!
Nur zugestoßen! Ich pariere.

VALENTIN

Pariere den!

MEPHISTOPHELES

Warum denn nicht?

VALENTIN

Auch den!

MEPHISTOPHELES

Gewiß!

VALENTIN

Ich glaub', der Teufel ficht!
Was ist denn das? Schon wird die Hand mir lahm!

MEPHISTOPHELES, *zu Faust.*

Stoß zu!

VALENTIN, *fällt.*

O weh!

MEPHISTOPHELES

Nun ist der Lümmel zahm!
Nun aber fort! Wir müssen gleich verschwinden,
denn schon entsteht ein mörderlich Geschrei.
Ich weiß mich trefflich mit der Polizei,
doch mit dem Blutbann schlecht mich abzufinden.

Faust und Mephistopheles ab.

MARTHE, *am Fenster.*

Heraus! Heraus!

GRETCHEN, *am Fenster.*

Herbei ein Licht!

MARTHE, *wie oben.*

Man schilt und rauft, man schreit und ficht!

VOLK

Da liegt schon einer tot!

MARTHE, *heraustretend.*

Die Mörder, sind sie denn entflohn?

GRETCHEN, *heraustretend.*

Wer liegt hier?

VOLK

Deiner Mutter Sohn!

GRETCHEN

Allmächtiger! Welche Not!

VALENTIN

Ich sterbe! — Das ist bald gesagt
und bälder noch getan. —
Was steht ihr Weiber, heult und klagt?
Kommt her und hört mich an!

Alle treten um ihn.

Mein Gretchen, sieh! Du bist noch jung,
bist gar noch nicht gescheit genung,
machst deine Sachen schlecht.
Ich sag' dir's im Vertrauen nur:
du bist doch nun einmal eine Hur';
so sei's auch eben recht!

GRETCHEN

Mein Bruder! Gott! Was soll mir das?

VALENTIN

Laß unsern Herrgott aus dem Spaß!
Geschehn ist leider nun geschehn,
und wie es gehn kann, so wird's gehn.
Du fingst mit einem heimlich an,
bald kommen ihrer mehre dran,
und wenn dich erst ein Dutzend hat,
so hat dich auch die ganze Stadt.
Wenn erst die Schande wird geboren,
wird sie heimlich zur Welt gebracht,
und man zieht den Schleier der Nacht
ihr über Kopf und Ohren;
ja, man möchte sie gern ermorden.
Wächst sie aber und macht sich groß,
dann geht sie auch bei Tage bloß
und ist doch nicht schöner geworden.
Je häßlicher wird ihr Gesicht,
je mehr sucht sie des Tages Licht.
Ich seh' wahrhaftig schon die Zeit,
daß alle brave Bürgersleut',
wie von einer angesteckten Leichen,
von dir, du Metze, seitab weichen.
Dir soll das Herz im Leib verzagen,
wenn sie dir in die Augen sehn!
Sollst keine goldne Kette mehr tragen!
In der Kirche nicht mehr am Altar stehn!
In einem schönen Spitzenkragen
dich nicht beim Tanze wohlbehagen!
In eine finstre Jammerecken
unter Bettler und Krüppel dich verstecken!
Und wenn dir denn auch Gott verzeiht,
auf Erden sein vermaledeit!

MARTHE

Befehlt Eure Seele Gott zu Gnaden!
Wollt Ihr noch Lästrung auf Euch laden?

VALENTIN

Könnt' ich dir nur an den dürren Leib,
du schändlich kupplerisches Weib,
da hofft' ich, aller meiner Sünden
Vergebung reiche Maß zu finden!

GRETCHEN

Mein Bruder! Welche Höllenpein!

VALENTIN

Ich sage, laß die Tränen sein!
Da du dich sprachst der Ehre los,
gabst mir den schwersten Herzensstoß.
Ich gehe durch den Todesschlaf
zu Gott ein als Soldat und brav.

Stirbt.

22 Dom

Amt, Orgel und Gesang.

Gretchen unter vielem Volke. *Böser Geist hinter Gretchen.*

BÖSER GEIST

Wie anders, Gretchen, war dir's,
als du noch voll Unschuld
hier zum Altar tratst,
aus dem vergriffnen Büchelchen
Gebete lalltest, —
halb Kinderspiele,
halb Gott im Herzen!
Gretchen!
Wo steht dein Kopf?
In deinem Herzen
welche Missetat?
Bet'st du für deiner Mutter Seele, die
durch dich zur langen, langen Pein hinüberschlief?
Auf deiner Schwelle wessen Blut?
Und unter deinem Herzen
regt sich's nicht quillend schon
und ängstet dich und sich
mit ahnungsvoller Gegenwart?

GRETCHEN

Weh! Weh!
Wär' ich der Gedanken los,
die mir herüber und hinüber gehen
wider mich!

CHOR

Dies irae, dies illa
solvet saeclum in favilla.

Orgelton.

Böser Geist

Grimm faßt dich!
Die Posaune tönt!
Die Gräber beben!
Und dein Herz,
aus Aschenruh
zu Flammenqualen
wieder aufgeschaffen,
bebt auf!

Gretchen

Wär' ich hier weg!
Mir ist, als ob die Orgel mir
den Atem versetzte,
Gesang mein Herz
im Tiefsten löste.

Chor

Judex ergo cum sedebit,
quidquid latet, adparebit;
nil inultum remanebit.

Gretchen

Mir wird so eng!
Die Mauernpfeiler
befangen mich!
Das Gewölbe
drängt mich! — Luft!

Böser Geist

Verbirg dich! Sünd' und Schande
bleibt nicht verborgen.
— Luft? Licht?
Weh dir!

Chor

Quid sum miser tunc dicturus,
quem patronum rogaturus,
cum vix justus sit securus?

Böser Geist

Ihr Antlitz wenden
Verklärte von dir ab.
Die Hände dir zu reichen,
schauert's den Reinen.
Weh!

Chor

Quid sum miser tunc dicturus?

Gretchen

Nachbarin! Euer Fläschchen! —

Sie fällt in Ohnmacht.

23 Walpurgisnacht

Harzgebirg. Gegend von Schierke und Elend.

Faust und Mephistopheles.

Mephistopheles

Verlangst du nicht nach einem Besenstiele?
Ich wünschte mir den allerderbsten Bock.
Auf diesem Weg sind wir noch weit vom Ziele.

Faust

Solang ich mich noch frisch auf meinen Beinen fühle,
genügt mir dieser Knotenstock.
Was hilft's, daß man den Weg verkürzt? —
Im Labyrinth der Täler hinzuschleichen,
dann diesen Felsen zu ersteigen,
von dem der Quell sich ewig sprudelnd stürzt, —
das ist die Lust, die solche Pfade würzt!
Der Frühling webt schon in den Birken,
und selbst die Fichte fühlt ihn schon;
sollt' er nicht auch auf unsre Glieder wirken?

Mephistopheles

Fürwahr, ich spüre nichts davon!
Mir ist es winterlich im Leibe,
ich wünschte Schnee und Frost auf meiner Bahn.
  Wie traurig steigt die unvollkommne Scheibe
des roten Monds mit später Glut heran
und leuchtet schlecht, daß man bei jedem Schritte
vor einen Baum, vor einen Felsen rennt!
Erlaub, daß ich ein Irrlicht bitte!
Dort seh' ich eins, das eben lustig brennt.
  Heda, mein Freund! Darf ich dich zu uns fodern?
Was willst du so vergebens lodern?
Sei doch so gut und leucht uns da hinauf!

IRRLICHT

Aus Ehrfurcht, hoff' ich, soll es mir gelingen,
mein leichtes Naturell zu zwingen;
nur zickzack geht gewöhnlich unser Lauf.

MEPHISTOPHELES

Ei! Ei! Er denkt's den Menschen nachzuahmen.
Geh' Er nur grad, in 's Teufels Namen!
Sonst blas' ich Ihm Sein Flackerleben aus.

IRRLICHT

Ich merke wohl, Ihr seid der Herr vom Haus,
und will mich gern nach Euch bequemen.
Allein bedenkt: der Berg ist heute zaubertoll,
und wenn ein Irrlicht Euch die Wege weisen soll,
so müßt Ihr's so genau nicht nehmen.

FAUST, MEPHISTOPHELES, IRRLICHT: *im Wechselgesang.*

In die Traum- und Zaubersphäre
sind wir, scheint es, eingegangen.
Führ uns gut und mach dir Ehre,
daß wir vorwärts bald gelangen
in den weiten, öden Räumen!

Seh' die Bäume hinter Bäumen,
wie sie schnell vorüberrücken,
und die Klippen, die sich bücken,
und die langen Felsennasen,
wie sie schnarchen, wie sie blasen!

Durch die Steine, durch den Rasen
eilet Bach und Bächlein nieder.
Hör' ich Rauschen? Hör' ich Lieder?
Hör' ich holde Liebesklage,
Stimmen jener Himmelstage?
Was wir hoffen, was wir lieben!
Und das Echo, wie die Sage
alter Zeiten, hallet wider.

„Uhu! Schuhu!" tönt es näher,
Kauz und Kiebitz und der Häher,
sind sie alle wachgeblieben?
Sind das Molche durchs Gesträuche?
Lange Beine, dicke Bäuche!

Und die Wurzeln, wie die Schlangen,
winden sich aus Fels und Sande,
strecken wunderliche Bande,
uns zu schrecken, uns zu fangen;
aus belebten, derben Masern
strecken sie Polypenfasern
nach dem Wandrer. Und die Mäuse,
tausendfärbig, scharenweise,
durch das Moos und durch die Heide!
Und die Funkenwürmer fliegen
mit gedrängten Schwärmezügen
zum verwirrenden Geleite.

Aber sag mir, ob wir stehen,
oder ob wir weitergehen?
Alles, alles scheint zu drehen:
Fels und Bäume, die Gesichter
schneiden, und die irren Lichter,
die sich mehren, die sich blähen.

MEPHISTOPHELES

Fasse wacker meinen Zipfel!
Hier ist so ein Mittelgipfel,
wo man mit Erstaunen sieht,
wie im Berg der Mammon glüht.

FAUST

Wie seltsam glimmert durch die Gründe
ein morgenrötlich trüber Schein!
Und selbst bis in die tiefen Schlünde
des Abgrunds wittert er hinein.
Da steigt ein Dampf, dort ziehen Schwaden,
hier leuchtet Glut aus Dunst und Flor,
dann schleicht sie wie ein zarter Faden,
dann bricht sie wie ein Quell hervor.
Hier schlingt sie eine ganze Strecke,
mit hundert Adern, sich durchs Tal,
und hier in der gedrängten Ecke
vereinzelt sie sich auf einmal.
Da sprühen Funken in der Nähe,
wie ausgestreuter goldner Sand.
Doch schau! In ihrer ganzen Höhe
entzündet sich die Felsenwand.

the demon of earthly riches
the 9th prince of hell puts on a show for his lord and master with special illumination of the deep abyss in which his treasure house of gold is hid.

MEPHISTOPHELES

Erleuchtet nicht zu diesem Feste
Herr Mammon prächtig den Palast?
Ein Glück, daß du's gesehen hast:
ich spüre schon die ungestümen Gäste.

FAUST

Wie rast die Windsbraut durch die Luft!
Mit welchen Schlägen trifft sie meinen Nacken!

MEPHISTOPHELES

Du mußt des Felsens alte Rippen packen,
sonst stürzt sie dich hinab in dieser Schlünde Gruft.
Ein Nebel verdichtet die Nacht.
Höre, wie's durch die Wälder kracht!
Aufgescheucht fliegen die Eulen.
Hör! Es splittern die Säulen
ewig grüner Paläste.
Girren und Brechen der Äste!
Der Stämme mächtiges Dröhnen!
Der Wurzeln Knarren und Gähnen!
Im fürchterlich verworrenen Falle
übereinander krachen sie alle,
und durch die übertrümmerten Klüfte
zischen und heulen die Lüfte.
Hörst du Stimmen in der Höhe?
In der Ferne? In der Nähe?
Ja, den ganzen Berg entlang
strömt ein wütender Zaubergesang!

HEXEN: *im Chor.*

Die Hexen zu dem Brocken ziehn,
die Stoppel ist gelb, die Saat ist grün.
Dort sammelt sich der große Hauf,
Herr Urian sitzt obenauf.
So geht es über Stein und Stock,
es f——t die Hexe, es st——t der Bock.

STIMME

Die alte Baubo kommt allein;
sie reitet auf einem Mutterschwein.

CHOR

So Ehre denn, wem Ehre gebührt!
Frau Baubo vor, und angeführt!

Ein tüchtig Schwein und Mutter drauf,
da folgt der ganze Hexenhauf.

STIMME

Welchen Weg kommst du her?

STIMME

Übern Ilsenstein!
Da guckt' ich der Eule ins Nest hinein.
Die macht' ein Paar Augen!

STIMME

O fahre zur Hölle!
Was reit'st du so schnelle?

STIMME

Mich hat sie geschunden.
Da sieh nur die Wunden!

HEXEN: *Chor.*

Der Weg ist breit, der Weg ist lang.
Was ist das für ein toller Drang!
Die Gabel sticht, der Besen kratzt,
das Kind erstickt, die Mutter platzt.

HEXENMEISTER: HALBES CHOR.

Wir schleichen wie die Schneck' im Haus,
die Weiber alle sind voraus.
Denn, geht es zu des Bösen Haus,
das Weib hat tausend Schritt voraus.

ANDRE HÄLFTE

Wir nehmen das nicht so genau.
Mit tausend Schritten macht's die Frau;
doch, wie sie auch sich eilen kann,
mit einem Sprunge macht's der Mann.

STIMME, *von oben.*

Kommt mit, kommt mit vom Felsensee!

STIMME, *von unten.*

Wir möchten gerne mit in die Höh'.
Wir waschen, und blank sind wir ganz und gar,
aber auch ewig unfruchtbar.

BEIDE CHÖRE

Es schweigt der Wind, es flieht der Stern,
der trübe Mond verbirgt sich gern.
Im Sausen sprüht das Zauberchor
viel tausend Feuerfunken hervor.

Stimme, *von unten.*

Halte! Halte!

Stimme, *von oben.*

Wer ruft da aus der Felsenspalte?

Stimme, *von unten.*

Nehmt mich mit! Nehmt mich mit!
Ich steige schon dreihundert Jahr
und kann den Gipfel nicht erreichen.
Ich wäre gern bei meinesgleichen.

Beide Chöre

Es trägt der Besen, trägt der Stock,
die Gabel trägt, es trägt der Bock;
wer heute sich nicht heben kann,
ist ewig ein verlorner Mann.

Halbhexe, *unten.*

Ich tripple nach, so lange Zeit;
wie sind die andern schon so weit!
Ich hab' zu Hause keine Ruh
und komme hier doch nicht dazu.

Chor der Hexen

Die Salbe gibt den Hexen Mut,
ein Lumpen ist zum Segel gut,
ein gutes Schiff ist jeder Trog;
der flieget nie, der heut nicht flog.

Beide Chöre

Und wenn wir um den Gipfel ziehn,
so streichet an dem Boden hin
und deckt die Heide weit und breit
mit eurem Schwarm der Hexenheit!

Sie lassen sich nieder.

Mephistopheles

Das drängt und stößt, das ruscht und klappert!
Das zischt und quirlt, das zieht und plappert!
Das leuchtet, sprüht und stinkt und brennt!
Ein wahres Hexenelement!
Nur fest an mir! Sonst sind wir gleich getrennt. —
Wo bist du?

Faust, *in der Ferne.*

Hier!

MEPHISTOPHELES

Was! Dort schon hingerissen?
Da werd' ich Hausrecht brauchen müssen.
Platz! Junker Voland kommt. Platz! Süßer Pöbel, Platz!
Hier, Doktor, fasse mich! Und nun, in einem Satz,
laß uns aus dem Gedräng' entweichen;
es ist zu toll, sogar für meinesgleichen.
Dort neben leuchtet was mit ganz besondrem Schein,
es zieht mich was nach jenen Sträuchen.
Komm, komm! Wir schlupfen da hinein.

FAUST

Du Geist des Widerspruchs! Nur zu! Du magst mich führen.
Ich denke doch, das war recht klug gemacht:
zum Brocken wandeln wir in der Walpurgisnacht,
um uns beliebig nun hieselbst zu isolieren!

They have come to the mt. for the very party from which they are now withdrawing.

MEPHISTOPHELES

Da sieh nur, welche bunten Flammen!
Es ist ein muntrer Klub beisammen.
Im Kleinen ist man nicht allein.

FAUST

Doch droben möcht' ich lieber sein!
Schon seh' ich Glut und Wirbelrauch.
Dort strömt die Menge zu dem Bösen;
da muß sich manches Rätsel lösen.

Faust wants to go to the summit where he may find answers about the nature of things

MEPHISTOPHELES

Doch manches Rätsel knüpft sich auch.
Laß du die große Welt nur sausen,
wir wollen hier im stillen hausen.
Es ist doch lange hergebracht,
daß in der großen Welt man kleine Welten macht.
Da seh' ich junge Hexchen, nackt und bloß,
und alte, die sich klug verhüllen.
Seid freundlich, nur um meinetwillen!
Die Müh' ist klein, der Spaß ist groß.
Ich höre was von Instrumenten tönen!
Verflucht Geschnarr! Man muß sich dran gewöhnen.
Komm mit! Komm mit! Es kann nicht anders sein:
ich tret' heran und führe dich herein,
und ich verbinde dich aufs neue.
Was sagst du, Freund? Das ist kein kleiner Raum:
da sieh nur hin! Du siehst das Ende kaum.

Ein Hundert Feuer brennen in der Reihe;
man tanzt, man schwatzt, man kocht, man trinkt, man liebt;
nun sage mir, wo es was Besser's gibt!

Faust

Willst du dich nun, um uns hier einzuführen,
als Zaubrer oder Teufel produzieren?

Mephistopheles

Zwar bin ich sehr gewohnt, inkognito zu gehn,
doch läßt am Galatag man seinen Orden sehn.
Ein Knieband zeichnet mich nicht aus,
doch ist der Pferdefuß hier ehrenvoll zu Haus.
Siehst du die Schnecke da? Sie kommt herangekrochen:
mit ihrem tastenden Gesicht
hat sie mir schon was abgerochen.
Wenn ich auch will, verleugn' ich hier mich nicht.
Komm nur! Von Feuer gehen wir zu Feuer;
ich bin der Werber, und du bist der Freier.

Zu einigen, die um verglimmende Kohlen sitzen.

Ihr alten Herrn, was macht ihr hier am Ende?
Ich lobt' euch, wenn ich euch hübsch in der Mitte fände,
von Saus umzirkt und Jugendbraus;
genug allein ist jeder ja zu Haus.

General

Wer mag auf Nationen trauen,
man habe noch so viel für sie getan!
Denn bei dem Volk, wie bei den Frauen,
steht immerfort die Jugend obenan.

a group of caricatures of the reactionaries of Goethe's day

Minister

Jetzt ist man von dem Rechten allzuweit,
ich lobe mir die guten Alten;
denn freilich, da wir alles galten,
da war die rechte goldne Zeit.

Parvenu

Wir waren wahrlich auch nicht dumm
und taten oft, was wir nicht sollten;
doch jetzo kehrt sich alles um und um,
und eben da wir's fest erhalten wollten.

Autor

Wer mag wohl überhaupt jetzt eine Schrift
von mäßig klugem Inhalt lesen!

Und was das liebe junge Volk betrifft,
das ist noch nie so naseweis gewesen.

MEPHISTOPHELES, *der auf einmal sehr alt erscheint.*

Zum Jüngsten Tag fühl' ich das Volk gereift,
da ich zum letztenmal den Hexenberg ersteige,
und weil mein Fäßchen trübe läuft,
so ist die Welt auch auf der Neige.

TRÖDELHEXE

Ihr Herren, geht nicht so vorbei!
Laßt die Gelegenheit nicht fahren!
Aufmerksam blickt nach meinen Waren!
Es steht dahier gar mancherlei.
Und doch ist nichts in meinem Laden,
— dem keiner auf der Erde gleicht, —
das nicht einmal zum tücht'gen Schaden
der Menschen und der Welt gereicht.
Kein Dolch ist hier, von dem nicht Blut geflossen,
kein Kelch, aus dem sich nicht, in ganz gesunden Leib,
verzehrend heißes Gift ergossen,
kein Schmuck, der nicht ein liebenswürdig Weib
verführt, kein Schwert, das nicht den Bund gebrochen,
nicht etwa hinterrücks den Gegenmann durchstochen.

Items offered suggest the Valentin-Gretchen outrages of the pair who pass by.

MEPHISTOPHELES

Frau Muhme! Sie versteht mir schlecht die Zeiten.
Getan, geschehn! Geschehn, getan!
Verleg' Sie sich auf Neuigkeiten!
Nur Neuigkeiten ziehn uns an.

M doesn't approve of the suggestions of the past

FAUST

Daß ich mich nur nicht selbst vergesse!
Heiß' ich mir das doch eine Messe!

MEPHISTOPHELES

Der ganze Strudel strebt nach oben;
du glaubst zu schieben und du wirst geschoben.

FAUST

Wer ist denn das?

MEPHISTOPHELES

Betrachte sie genau!
Lilith ist das.

FAUST

Wer?

MEPHISTOPHELES

Adams erste Frau.
Nimm dich in acht vor ihren schönen Haaren,
vor diesem Schmuck, mit dem sie einzig prangt!
Wenn sie damit den jungen Mann erlangt,
so läßt sie ihn so bald nicht wieder fahren.

FAUST

Da sitzen zwei, die Alte mit der Jungen;
die haben schon was Recht's gesprungen!

MEPHISTOPHELES

Das hat nun heute keine Ruh.
Es geht zum neuen Tanz. Nun komm, wir greifen zu!

FAUST, *mit der Jungen tanzend.*

Einst hatt' ich einen schönen Traum:
da sah ich einen Apfelbaum,
zwei schöne Äpfel glänzten dran;
sie reizten mich, ich stieg hinan.

DIE SCHÖNE

Der Äpfelchen begehrt ihr sehr,
und schon vom Paradiese her.
Von Freuden fühl' ich mich bewegt,
daß auch mein Garten solche trägt.

MEPHISTOPHELES, *mit der Alten.*

Einst hatt' ich einen wüsten Traum:
da sah ich einen gespaltnen Baum,
der hatt' ein —— —— ——;
so —— es war, gefiel mir's doch.

DIE ALTE

Ich biete meinen besten Gruß
dem Ritter mit dem Pferdefuß!
Halt' Er einen —— —— bereit,
wenn Er —— —— —— nicht scheut.

PROKTOPHANTASMIST

Verfluchtes Volk! Was untersteht ihr euch?
Hat man euch lange nicht bewiesen,
ein Geist steht nie auf ordentlichen Füßen?
Nun tanzt ihr gar, uns andern Menschen gleich!

DIE SCHÖNE, *tanzend.*

Was will denn der auf unserm Ball?

at this point Faust as sunk as low into sheer sensual lust as he can go

p 410

Faust, *tanzend.*

Ei! Der ist eben überall.
Was andre tanzen, muß er schätzen.
Kann er nicht jeden Schritt beschwätzen,
so ist der Schritt so gut als nicht geschehn.
Am meisten ärgert ihn, sobald wir vorwärts gehn.
Wenn ihr euch so im Kreise drehen wolltet,
wie er's in seiner alten Mühle tut,
das hieß' er allenfalls noch gut, —
besonders wenn ihr ihn darum begrüßen solltet.

Proktophantasmist

Ihr seid noch immer da! Nein, das ist unerhört.
Verschwindet doch! Wir haben ja aufgeklärt!
Das Teufelspack, es fragt nach keiner Regel.
Wir sind so klug, und dennoch spukt's in Tegel.
Wie lange hab' ich nicht am Wahn hinausgekehrt,
und nie wird's rein! Das ist doch unerhört!

Die Schöne

So hört doch auf, uns hier zu ennuyieren!

Proktophantasmist

Ich sag's euch Geistern ins Gesicht:
den Geistesdespotismus leid' ich nicht;
mein Geist kann ihn nicht exerzieren.

Es wird fortgetanzt.

Heut, seh' ich, will mir nichts gelingen;
doch eine Reise nehm' ich immer mit
und hoffe, noch vor meinem letzten Schritt
die Teufel und die Dichter zu bezwingen.

Mephistopheles

Er wird sich gleich in eine Pfütze setzen.
Das ist die Art, wie er sich soulagiert,
und wenn Blutegel sich an seinem Steiß ergötzen,
ist er von Geistern und von Geist kuriert.

Zu Faust, der aus dem Tanz getreten ist.

Was lässest du das schöne Mädchen fahren,
das dir zum Tanz so lieblich sang?

Faust

Ach, mitten im Gesange sprang
ein rotes Mäuschen ihr aus dem Munde!

Story of Nicolai
see p 410

p 411
During the dance F. is startled by 2 uncanny happenings.
1- a red mouse jumps out of the mouth of the pretty one witch he is dancing with

MEPHISTOPHELES

Das ist was Recht's! Das nimmt man nicht genau;
genug, die Maus war doch nicht grau!
Wer fragt darnach in einer Schäferstunde?

FAUST

Dann sah ich —

MEPHISTOPHELES

Was?

FAUST

Mephisto, siehst du dort
ein blasses, schönes Kind allein und ferne stehen?
Sie schiebt sich langsam nur vom Ort,
sie scheint mit geschloßnen Füßen zu gehen.
Ich muß bekennen, daß mir deucht,
daß sie dem guten Gretchen gleicht.

MEPHISTOPHELES

Laß das nur stehn! Dabei wird's niemand wohl.
Es ist ein Zauberbild, ist leblos, ein Idol.
Ihm zu begegnen ist nicht gut:
vom starren Blick erstarrt des Menschen Blut,
und er wird fast in Stein verkehrt . . .
Von der Meduse hast du ja gehört!

FAUST

Fürwahr, es sind die Augen eines Toten,
die eine liebende Hand nicht schloß!
Das ist die Brust, die Gretchen mir geboten,
das ist der süße Leib, den ich genoß!

MEPHISTOPHELES

Das ist die Zauberei, du leicht verführter Tor!
Denn jedem kommt sie wie sein Liebchen vor.

FAUST

Welch eine Wonne! Welch ein Leiden!
Ich kann von diesem Blick nicht scheiden.
Wie sonderbar muß diesen schönen Hals
ein einzig rotes Schnürchen schmücken,
nicht breiter als ein Messerrücken!

MEPHISTOPHELES

Ganz recht! Ich seh' es ebenfalls.
Sie kann das Haupt auch unterm Arme tragen;
denn Perseus hat's ihr abgeschlagen. —
Nur immer diese Lust zum Wahn! —

Komm doch das Hügelchen heran!
Hier ist's so lustig wie im Prater;
und hat man mir's nicht angetan,
so seh' ich wahrlich ein Theater.
Was gibt's denn da?

SERVIBILIS

Gleich fängt man wieder an:
ein neues Stück, das letzte Stück von sieben;
so viel zu geben, ist allhier der Brauch.
Ein Dilettant hat es geschrieben,
und Dilettanten spielen's auch.
Verzeiht, ihr Herrn, wenn ich verschwinde;
mich dilettiert's, den Vorhang aufzuziehn.

MEPHISTOPHELES

Wenn ich euch auf dem Blocksberg finde,
das find' ich gut; denn da gehört ihr hin.

24 Walpurgisnachtstraum

oder

Oberons und Titanias goldne Hochzeit

Intermezzo

THEATERMEISTER

Heute ruhen wir einmal,
Miedings wackre Söhne.
Alter Berg und feuchtes Tal,
das ist die ganze Szene!

HEROLD

Daß die Hochzeit golden sei,
soll'n funfzig Jahr sein vorüber;
aber ist der Streit vorbei,
das „golden" ist mir lieber.

OBERON

Seid ihr Geister, wo ich bin,
so zeigt's in diesen Stunden!
König und die Königin,
sie sind aufs neu verbunden.

Puck

Kommt der Puck und dreht sich quer
und schleift den Fuß im Reihen;
Hundert kommen hinterher,
sich auch mit ihm zu freuen.

Ariel

Ariel bewegt den Sang
in himmlisch reinen Tönen;
viele Fratzen lockt sein Klang,
doch lockt er auch die Schönen.

Oberon

Gatten, die sich vertragen wollen,
lernen's von uns beiden!
Wenn sich zweie lieben sollen,
braucht man sie nur zu scheiden.

Titania

Schmollt der Mann und grillt die Frau,
so faßt sie nur behende;
führt mir nach dem Mittag sie
und ihn an Nordens Ende!

Orchester Tutti, *fortissimo.*

Fliegenschnauz' und Mückennas'
mit ihren Anverwandten,
Frosch im Laub und Grill' im Gras,
das sind die Musikanten!

Solo

Seht, da kommt der Dudelsack!
Es ist die Seifenblase.
Hört den Schneckeschnickeschnack
durch seine stumpfe Nase!

Geist, der sich erst bildet

Spinnenfuß und Krötenbauch
und Flügelchen dem Wichtchen!
Zwar ein Tierchen gibt es nicht,
doch gibt es ein Gedichtchen.

Ein Pärchen

Kleiner Schritt und hoher Sprung
durch Honigtau und Düfte!
Zwar du trippelst mir genung,
doch geht's nicht in die Lüfte.

Neugieriger Reisender
Ist das nicht Maskeradenspott?
Soll ich den Augen trauen,
Oberon, den schönen Gott,
auch heute hier zu schauen?

Nikolai who disliked phantoms

Orthodox
Keine Klauen, keinen Schwanz!
Doch bleibt es außer Zweifel:
so wie die Götter Griechenlands,
so ist auch er ein Teufel.

aimed at Stolberg who found blasphemy in Schiller's poems

Nordischer Künstler
Was ich ergreife, das ist heut
fürwahr nur skizzenweise;
doch ich bereite mich beizeit
zur italien'schen Reise.

necessary for classic form

Purist
Ach, mein Unglück führt mich her:
wie wird nicht hier geludert!
Und von dem ganzen Hexenheer
sind zweie nur gepudert!

an academician of the narrow minded pedantic school

Junge Hexe
Der Puder ist so wie der Rock
für alt' und graue Weibchen;
drum sitz' ich nackt auf meinem Bock
und zeig' ein derbes Leibchen.

Matrone
Wir haben zu viel Lebensart,
um hier mit euch zu maulen;
doch hoff' ich, sollt ihr jung und zart,
so wie ihr seid, verfaulen.

Kapellmeister
Fliegenschnauz' und Mückennas',
umschwärmt mir nicht die Nackte!
Frosch im Laub und Grill' im Gras,
so bleibt doch auch im Takte!

Windfahne, *nach der einen Seite.*
Gesellschaft, wie man wünschen kann:
wahrhaftig lauter Bräute!
Und Junggesellen! Mann für Mann
die hoffnungsvollsten Leute!

WINDFAHNE, *nach der andern Seite.*

Und tut sich nicht der Boden auf,
sie alle zu verschlingen,
so will ich mit behendem Lauf
gleich in die Hölle springen.

XENIEN – Satirical Epigrams pub. by G. + Schiller. Dealt very severely with contemporary literary products in G.

Als Insekten sind wir da,
mit kleinen, scharfen Scheren,
Satan, unsern Herrn Papa,
nach Würden zu verehren.

HENNINGS – had attacked S's Horen + his Musealmanach

Seht, wie sie in gedrängter Schar
naiv zusammen scherzen!
Am Ende sagen sie noch gar,
sie hätten gute Herzen.

Leader of Muses – MUSAGET – collection of poems pub by Hennings.

Ich mag in diesem Hexenheer
mich gar zu gern verlieren;
denn freilich diese wüßt' ich eh'r
als Musen anzuführen.

CI-DEVANT GENIUS DER ZEIT

Mit rechten Leuten wird man was.
Komm, fasse meinen Zipfel!
Der Blocksberg, wie der deutsche Parnaß,
hat gar einen breiten Gipfel.

NEUGIERIGER REISENDER

Sagt: wie heißt der steife Mann?
Er geht mit stolzen Schritten.
Er schnopert, was er schnopern kann. —
„Er spürt nach Jesuiten."

KRANICH – Lavater - a pious religious poet

In dem Klaren mag ich gern
und auch im Trüben fischen;
darum seht ihr den frommen Herrn
sich auch mit Teufeln mischen.

WELTKIND – Goethe

Ja, für die Frommen, glaubet mir,
ist alles ein Vehikel;
sie bilden auf dem Blocksberg hier
gar manches Konventikel.

TÄNZER

Da kommt ja wohl ein neues Chor?
Ich höre ferne Trommeln.
Nur ungestört! Es sind im Rohr
die unisonen Dommeln.

TANZMEISTER

Wie jeder doch die Beine lupft!
Sich, wie er kann, herauszieht!
Der Krumme springt, der Plumpe hupft
und fragt nicht, wie es aussieht.

FIEDLER

Das haßt sich schwer, das Lumpenpack,
und gäb' sich gern das Restchen;
es eint sie hier der Dudelsack,
wie Orpheus' Leier die Bestjen.

DOGMATIKER

Ich lasse mich nicht irre schrein,
nicht durch Kritik noch Zweifel.
Der Teufel muß doch etwas sein;
wie gäb's denn sonst auch Teufel?

If he can by thinking arrive at "der Teufel" then "der Teufel" must correspond to reality

IDEALIST

Die Phantasie in meinem Sinn
ist diesmal gar zu herrisch.
Fürwahr, wenn ich das alles bin,
so bin ich heute närrisch.

All existence to him is the representation of his own mind the creator of everything he experiences

REALIST

Das Wesen ist mir recht zur Qual
und muß mich baß verdrießen;
ich stehe hier zum erstenmal
nicht fest auf meinen Füßen.

Accepts as real all objects of his perception

SUPERNATURALIST

Mit viel Vergnügen bin ich da
und freue mich mit diesen;
denn von den Teufeln kann ich ja
auf gute Geister schließen.

He believes in reality transcending our power to perceive

SKEPTIKER

Sie gehn den Flämmchen auf der Spur
und glaub'n sich nah dem Schatze.
Auf Teufel reimt der Zweifel nur;
da bin ich recht am Platze.

Regards all perception as delusive & denies the possibility of any truth.

KAPELLMEISTER

Frosch im Laub und Grill' im Gras,
verfluchte Dilettanten!
Fliegenschnauz' und Mückennas',
ihr seid doch Musikanten!

DIE GEWANDTEN

Sanssouci, so heißt das Heer
von lustigen Geschöpfen;
auf den Füßen geht's nicht mehr,
drum gehn wir auf den Köpfen.

DIE UNBEHÜLFLICHEN

Sonst haben wir manchen Bissen erschranzt,
nun aber Gott befohlen!
Unsere Schuhe sind durchgetanzt,
wir laufen auf nackten Sohlen.

IRRLICHTER

Von dem Sumpfe kommen wir,
woraus wir erst entstanden;
doch sind wir gleich im Reihen hier
die glänzenden Galanten.

STERNSCHNUPPE

Aus der Höhe schoß ich her
im Stern- und Feuerscheine,
liege nun im Grase quer:
wer hilft mir auf die Beine?

DIE MASSIVEN

Platz! Und Platz! Und ringsherum!
So gehn die Gräschen nieder.
Geister kommen, Geister auch,
sie haben plumpe Glieder!

PUCK

Tretet nicht so mastig auf
wie Elefantenkälber!
Und der Plumpst' an diesem Tag
sei Puck, der derbe, selber.

ARIEL

Gab die liebende Natur,
gab der Geist euch Flügel,
folget meiner leichten Spur!
Auf zum Rosenhügel!

ORCHESTER, *pianissimo.*

Wolkenzug und Nebelflor
erhellen sich von oben.
Luft im Laub und Wind im Rohr —
und alles ist zerstoben.

After his great emotional experience he seeks solitude in nature.

25 Trüber Tag

Feld.

Faust und Mephistopheles.

The dramatic function of this scene is to show F's return to his nobler self and his determination to risk everything to alleviate the suffering he has caused.

FAUST Im Elend! Verzweifelnd! Erbärmlich auf der Erde lange verirrt und nun gefangen! Als Missetäterin im Kerker zu entsetzlichen Qualen eingesperrt, das holde, unselige Geschöpf! Bis dahin! dahin! — Verräterischer, nichtswürdiger Geist, und das hast du mir verheimlicht! — Steh nur, steh! Wälze die teuflischen Augen ingrimmend im Kopf herum! Steh und trutze mir durch deine unerträgliche Gegenwart! — Gefangen! Im unwiederbringlichen Elend! Bösen Geistern übergeben und der richtenden, gefühllosen Menschheit! — [Und mich wiegst du indes in abgeschmackten Zerstreuungen, verbirgst mir ihren wachsenden Jammer und lässest sie hülflos verderben!]

lulled me with the most insipid dissipations

MEPHISTOPHELES [Sie ist die erste nicht.]

FAUST Hund! Abscheuliches Untier! — Wandle ihn, du unendlicher Geist! Wandle den Wurm wieder in seine Hundsgestalt, wie er sich oft nächtlicher Weile gefiel, vor mir herzutrotten, dem harmlosen Wandrer vor die Füße zu kollern und sich dem niederstürzenden auf die Schultern zu hängen. Wandl' ihn wieder in seine Lieblingsbildung, daß er vor mir im Sand auf dem Bauch krieche, ich ihn mit Füßen trete, den Verworfnen! — „Die erste nicht!" — Jammer! Jammer! Von keiner Menschenseele zu fassen, daß mehr als ein Geschöpf in die Tiefe dieses Elendes versank, daß nicht das erste genug tat für die Schuld aller übrigen in seiner windenden Todesnot vor den

Faust is hysterical in his denunciations of M. for concealing these tragic events. M. is coldly realistic. & not the first. Who was responsible? - F. or M.

Augen des ewig Verzeihenden! Mir wühlt es Mark und Leben durch, das Elend dieser Einzigen; du grinsest gelassen über das Schicksal von Tausenden hin!

MEPHISTOPHELES Nun sind wir schon wieder an der Grenze unsres Witzes, da, wo euch Menschen der Sinn überschnappt. Warum machst du Gemeinschaft mit uns, wenn du sie nicht durchführen kannst? Willst fliegen, und bist vorm Schwindel nicht sicher? Drangen wir uns dir auf, oder du dich uns?

FAUST Fletsche deine gefräßigen Zähne mir nicht so entgegen! Mir ekelt's! — Großer, herrlicher Geist, der du mir zu erscheinen würdigtest, der du mein Herz kennest und meine Seele, warum an den Schandgesellen mich schmieden, der sich am Schaden weidet und am Verderben sich letzt?

MEPHISTOPHELES Endigst du?

FAUST Rette sie! Oder weh dir! Den gräßlichsten Fluch über dich auf Jahrtausende!

MEPHISTOPHELES Ich kann die Bande des Rächers nicht lösen, seine Riegel nicht öffnen. — „Rette sie!" — Wer war's, der sie ins Verderben stürzte? Ich oder du?

Faust blickt wild umher.

MEPHISTOPHELES Greifst du nach dem Donner? Wohl, daß er euch elenden Sterblichen nicht gegeben ward! Den unschuldig Entgegnenden zu zerschmettern, das ist so Tyrannenart, sich in Verlegenheiten Luft zu machen.

FAUST Bringe mich hin! Sie soll frei sein!

MEPHISTOPHELES Und die Gefahr, der du dich aussetzest? Wisse! Noch liegt auf der Stadt Blutschuld von deiner Hand. Über des Erschlagenen Stätte schweben rächende Geister und lauern auf den wiederkehrenden Mörder.

FAUST Noch das von dir? Mord und Tod einer Welt über dich Ungeheuer! Führe mich hin, sag' ich, und befrei sie!

MEPHISTOPHELES Ich führe dich, und was ich tun kann, höre! Habe ich alle Macht im Himmel und auf

Erden? Des Türners Sinne will ich umnebeln; bemächtige dich der Schlüssel und führe sie heraus mit Menschenhand! Ich wache! Die Zauberpferde sind bereit, ich entführe euch. Das vermag ich.

FAUST Auf und davon!

26 Nacht. Offen Feld

Faust und Mephistopheles, auf schwarzen Pferden daherbrausend.

FAUST
Was weben die dort um den Rabenstein?
MEPHISTOPHELES
Weiß nicht, was sie kochen und schaffen.
FAUST
Schweben auf, schweben ab, neigen sich, beugen sich.
MEPHISTOPHELES
Eine Hexenzunft.
FAUST
Sie streuen und weihen.
MEPHISTOPHELES
Vorbei! Vorbei!

27 Kerker

Faust, mit einem Bund Schlüssel und einer Lampe, vor einem eisernen Türchen.

FAUST
Mich faßt ein längst entwohnter Schauer,
der Menschheit ganzer Jammer faßt mich an.
Hier wohnt sie, hinter dieser feuchten Mauer;
und ihr Verbrechen war ein guter Wahn! —
Du zauderst, zu ihr zu gehen?

Du fürchtest, sie wieder zu sehen?
Fort! Dein Zagen zögert den Tod heran.

Er ergreift das Schloß.

Es singt inwendig.

Meine Mutter, die Hur',
die mich umgebracht hat!
Mein Vater, der Schelm,
der mich gessen hat!
Mein Schwesterlein klein
hub auf die Bein'
an einem kühlen Ort.
Da ward ich ein schönes Waldvögelein,
fliege fort, fliege fort!

FAUST, *aufschließend.*

Sie ahnet nicht, daß der Geliebte lauscht,
die Ketten klirren hört, das Stroh, das rauscht.

Er tritt ein.

MARGARETE, *sich auf dem Lager verbergend.*

Weh! weh! Sie kommen. — Bittrer Tod!

FAUST, *leise.*

Still! Still! Ich komme, dich zu befreien.

MARGARETE, *sich vor ihn hinwälzend.*

Bist du ein Mensch, so fühle meine Not!

FAUST

Du wirst die Wächter aus dem Schlafe schreien!

Er faßt die Ketten, sie aufzuschließen.

MARGARETE, *auf den Knien.*

Wer hat dir, Henker, diese Macht
über mich gegeben?
Du holst mich schon um Mitternacht!
Erbarme dich und laß mich leben!
Ist's morgen früh nicht zeitig genung?

Sie steht auf.

Bin ich doch noch so jung, so jung —
und soll schon sterben!
Schön war ich auch, und das war mein Verderben.
Nah war der Freund, nun ist er weit;
zerrissen liegt der Kranz, die Blumen zerstreut —
Fasse mich nicht so gewaltsam an!

Schone mich! Was hab' ich dir getan?
Laß mich nicht vergebens flehen,
hab' ich dich doch mein' Tage nicht gesehen!

FAUST

Werd' ich den Jammer überstehen?

MARGARETE

Ich bin nun ganz in deiner Macht.
Laß mich nur erst das Kind noch tränken!
Ich herzt' es diese ganze Nacht;
sie nahmen mir's, um mich zu kränken,
und sagen nun, ich hätt' es umgebracht.
Und niemals werd' ich wieder froh . . .
Sie singen Lieder auf mich! Es ist bös von den Leuten!
Ein altes Märchen endigt so;
wer heißt sie's deuten?

a tale of a girl killing her own child.

FAUST, *wirft sich nieder.*

Ein Liebender liegt dir zu Füßen,
die Jammerknechtschaft aufzuschließen.

MARGARETE, *wirft sich zu ihm.*

O laß uns knien, die Heil'gen anzurufen!
Sieh! Unter diesen Stufen,
unter der Schwelle
siedet die Hölle!
Der Böse,
mit furchtbarem Grimme,
macht ein Getöse!

FAUST, *laut.*

Gretchen! Gretchen!

Sleepwalkers are awaken by calling out their name

MARGARETE, *aufmerksam.*

Das war des Freundes Stimme!

Sie springt auf. Die Ketten fallen ab.

Wo ist er? Ich hab' ihn rufen hören!
Ich bin frei! Mir soll niemand wehren!
An seinen Hals will ich fliegen,
an seinem Busen liegen!
Er rief „Gretchen!" Er stand auf der Schwelle.
Mitten durchs Heulen und Klappen der Hölle,
durch den grimmigen, teuflischen Hohn,
erkannt' ich den süßen, den liebenden Ton.

FAUST

Ich bin's!

MARGARETE

Du bist's! O sag es noch einmal!

Ihn fassend.

Er ist's! Er ist's! Wohin ist alle Qual?
Wohin die Angst des Kerkers, der Ketten?
Du bist's! Kommst, mich zu retten!
Ich bin gerettet!
Schon ist die Straße wieder da,
auf der ich dich zum ersten Male sah,
und der heitere Garten,
wo ich und Marthe deiner warten.

G. is overcome by the sweet memories of her past. This a demonstration of the insuperable power of her love impulse

FAUST, *fortstrebend.*

Komm mit! Komm mit!

MARGARETE

O weile!
Weil' ich doch so gern, wo du weilest!

Liebkosend.

FAUST

Eile!
Wenn du nicht eilest,
werden wir's teuer büßen müssen.

MARGARETE

Wie? Du kannst nicht mehr küssen?
Mein Freund, so kurz von mir entfernt,
und hast 's Küssen verlernt?
Warum wird mir an deinem Halse so bang,
wenn sonst von deinen Worten, deinen Blicken
ein ganzer Himmel mich überdrang,
und du mich küßtest, als wolltest du mich ersticken?
Küsse mich!
Sonst küss' ich dich!

Sie umfaßt ihn.

O weh! Deine Lippen sind kalt,
sind stumm.
Wo ist dein Lieben
geblieben?
Wer brachte mich drum?

Driven not by love but guilt

Sie wendet sich von ihm.

FAUST

Komm! Folge mir! Liebchen, fasse Mut!
Ich herze dich mit tausendfacher Glut,
nur folge mir! Ich bitte dich nur dies!

MARGARETE, *zu ihm gewendet.*

Und bist du's denn? Und bist du's auch gewiß?

FAUST

Ich bin's! Komm mit!

MARGARETE

Du machst die Fesseln los,
nimmst wieder mich in deinen Schoß.
Wie kommt es, daß du dich vor mir nicht scheust? —
Und weißt du denn, mein Freund, wen du befreist?

FAUST

Komm! Komm! Schon weicht die tiefe Nacht.

MARGARETE

Meine Mutter hab' ich umgebracht,
mein Kind hab' ich ertränkt.
War es nicht dir und mir geschenkt?
Dir auch. — Du bist's! Ich glaub' es kaum.
Gib deine Hand! Es ist kein Traum!
Deine liebe Hand! — Ach, aber sie ist feucht!
Wische sie ab! Wie mich deucht,
ist Blut dran.
Ach Gott! Was hast du getan!
Stecke den Degen ein,
ich bitte dich drum!

FAUST

Laß das Vergangne vergangen sein!
Du bringst mich um!

MARGARETE

Nein, du mußt übrigbleiben!
Ich will dir die Gräber beschreiben.
Für die mußt du sorgen
gleich morgen:
der Mutter den besten Platz geben,
meinen Bruder sogleich darneben,
mich ein wenig beiseit',
— nur nicht gar zu weit! —
und das Kleine mir an die rechte Brust.

Niemand wird sonst bei mir liegen! —
Mich an deine Seite zu schmiegen,
das war ein süßes, ein holdes Glück!
Aber es will mir nicht mehr gelingen;
mir ist's, als müßt' ich mich zu dir zwingen,
als stießest du mich von dir zurück;
und doch bist du's und blickst so gut, so fromm.

FAUST

Fühlst du, daß ich es bin, so komm!

MARGARETE

Dahinaus?

FAUST

Ins Freie!

MARGARETE

Ist das Grab drauß,
lauert der Tod, so komm!
Von hier ins ewige Ruhebett
und weiter keinen Schritt —
Du gehst nun fort? O Heinrich, könnt' ich mit!

She will only go with him to her death

FAUST

Du kannst! So wolle nur! Die Tür steht offen.

MARGARETE

Ich darf nicht fort, für mich ist nichts zu hoffen.
Was hilft es, fliehn? Sie lauern doch mir auf.
Es ist so elend, betteln zu müssen,
und noch dazu mit bösem Gewissen!
Es ist so elend, in der Fremde schweifen,
und sie werden mich doch ergreifen!

FAUST

Ich bleibe bei dir.

MARGARETE

Geschwind! Geschwind!
Rette dein armes Kind!
Fort! Immer den Weg
am Bach hinauf,
über den Steg,
in den Wald hinein,
links, wo die Planke steht,
im Teich!
Faß es nur gleich!

Es will sich heben,
es zappelt noch!
Rette! Rette!

FAUST

Besinne dich doch!
Nur einen Schritt, so bist du frei!

MARGARETE

Wären wir nur den Berg vorbei!
Da sitzt meine Mutter auf einem Stein,
— es faßt mich kalt beim Schopfe! —
da sitzt meine Mutter auf einem Stein
und wackelt mit dem Kopfe;
sie winkt nicht, sie nickt nicht, der Kopf ist ihr schwer,
sie schlief so lange, sie wacht nicht mehr.
Sie schlief, damit wir uns freuten . . .
Es waren glückliche Zeiten!

FAUST

Hilft hier kein Flehen, hilft kein Sagen,
so wag' ich's, dich hinwegzutragen.

MARGARETE

Laß mich! Nein, ich leide keine Gewalt!
Fasse mich nicht so mörderisch an!
Sonst hab' ich dir ja alles zulieb' getan.

FAUST

Der Tag graut! Liebchen! Liebchen!

MARGARETE

Tag! Ja, es wird Tag! Der letzte Tag dringt herein;
mein Hochzeittag sollt' es sein!
Sag niemand, daß du schon bei Gretchen warst.
Weh meinem Kranze!
Es ist eben geschehn!
Wir werden uns wiedersehn,
aber nicht beim Tanze. —
Die Menge drängt sich, man hört sie nicht.
Der Platz, die Gassen
können sie nicht fassen.
Die Glocke ruft, das Stäbchen bricht.
Wie sie mich binden und packen!
Zum Blutstuhl bin ich schon entrückt.
Schon zuckt nach jedem Nacken

die Schärfe, die nach meinem zückt . . .
Stumm liegt die Welt wie das Grab!

FAUST

O, wär' ich nie geboren!

MEPHISTOPHELES, *erscheint draußen.*

Auf! Oder ihr seid verloren!
Unnützes Zagen! Zaudern und Plaudern!
Meine Pferde schaudern,
der Morgen dämmert auf.

MARGARETE

Was steigt aus dem Boden herauf?
Der! Der! Schick ihn fort!
Was will der an dem heiligen Ort?
Er will mich!

FAUST

Du sollst leben!

MARGARETE

Gericht Gottes! Dir hab' ich mich übergeben! give

MEPHISTOPHELES, *zu Faust.*

Komm! Komm! Ich lasse dich mit ihr im Stich!

MARGARETE

Dein bin ich, Vater! Rette mich!—
Ihr Engel! Ihr heiligen Scharen!
Lagert euch umher, mich zu bewahren!
—Heinrich! Mir graut's vor dir!

MEPHISTOPHELES

Sie ist gerichtet!

STIMME, *von oben.*

Ist gerettet!

MEPHISTOPHELES, *zu Faust.*

Her zu mir!

Verschwindet mit Faust.

STIMME, *von innen, verhallend.*

Heinrich! Heinrich!—— Gott

(filled with terror)

Camp around me + from evils ward me. Psalm 34.7 The angel of Jehovah encampeth round them that fear him + delivereth them

The voice of love which will not pass away

G's terror for her lover results from the determination to follow God's judgement + her conviction that F. is not included therein
The conviction crystallizes when she sees M. with Faust.

Notes: *FAUST I*

FOREWORD

to the users of these notes

In these explanatory notes we have sought to give full information concerning each point of probable difficulty to an American college student. We have tried to give rather too much than too little, without allowing the notes to become too voluminous to be usable.

It has not been our purpose to discuss questions of textual criticism. We have instead made our choice of the various alternatives at each of the textual cruces and have then allowed our text to stand on its own merits without discussion. Only in the case of an unsatisfactory textual solution have we discussed the problem in our notes, in order to explain why the text as we print it is unsatisfactory.

We have not undertaken to present the many literary analogies, parallel passages, and "influences" which Goethe's text constantly suggests, unless it has seemed to us that a reference to these matters would help make the meaning of the text more apparent.

The complete vocabulary which we have prepared for FAUST has made it unnecessary for us to offer translations of individual words in our notes, but the student will find many paraphrases designed to make clear the over-all meaning of difficult lines, as well as an occasional direct rendition of the text into English.

Scholarly opinion is divided concerning the meaning of a number of passages in FAUST. We have not given the history of such divisions of opinion, but have tried to say what we believed the correct interpretation to be, and have then indicated the other opinions which seem to us tenable. In those few cases in which we could not ourselves agree, we have given all the interpretations which appear reasonable to any of us.

These notes do not attempt to deal with the many intricate problems of FAUST interpretation which are raised, particularly, by the second part of the poem. Our primary purpose is to make the text accessible to the student. We have endeavored to provide interpretation only when this appears to be needed for a first-level understanding of the text. Our efforts at higher-level interpretation are to be found in the introduction we provide, not in the notes.

Only one abbreviation which might be unfamiliar is used in these notes. This is **SD** which, when prefixed to a line number, indicates the stage direction at that place.

Bibliographical references are few and as a rule self-explanatory. The following list may, however, be useful:

URFAUST The earliest preserved form of Goethe's FAUST.

FRAGMENT The first form of FAUST published by Goethe, 1790.

Eckermann GESPRÄCHE MIT GOETHE IN DEN LETZTEN JAHREN SEINES LEBENS by Johann Peter Eckermann, Leipzig, 1836–1848. The pertinent passages for FAUST are also to be found in Gräf, H. G., GOETHE ÜBER SEINE DICHTUNGEN, 2. Teil, 2. Band, Frankfurt a. M., 1904.

Hederich, Benjamin: GRÜNDLICHES MYTHOLOGISCHES LEXIKON . . . , verbessert von J. J. Schwabe, Leipzig, 1770.

Zueignung

These four elegiac stanzas were first written in the summer of 1797, probably on June 24, seven years after the publication of Faust: Ein Fragment (see Introduction, p. 39), when Goethe had decided to resume work on this drama. The dedication is not an integral part of the Faust play, but belongs to it as a mood-setting preliminary chord belongs to a pianist's performance of a masterpiece. The title, 'Dedication,' can only be considered a reflection of the mood of the author, since the poem is not explicitly dedicated to any person or persons. Indeed, one may almost say that this dedication is the dedication of the poet to his theme.

1 **schwankende Gestalten** The 'figures' of the play — Faust, Gretchen, Mephistopheles, and the rest — not clearly seen in the poet's imagination, but uncertainly 'wavering,' as they return after years in which he has been otherwise occupied. The poet had once before seen them in his youthful (*früh*) and less lucid imagination. This reference to the *trüben Blick* (line 2) is the poet's criticism of his conception of these figures in his earlier work. Goethe's first interest in the Faust materials appears to have been aroused in 1769 (*cf.* the letter to Zelter, June 1, 1831).

4 **Wahn** 'fanciful idea': his youthful project of putting the figures of the Faust legend into a great drama, of catching these creatures of his imagination and giving them artistic form (*festzuhalten*).

5 **mögt ihr walten** The figures of this tale crowd upon the poet's mind, and he resolves to let them hold sway in his imagination rather than to try to put them away.

6 **Dunst und Nebel** Equivalent to *Nebeldunst*, 'misty haze.' The two nouns connected by the conjunction *und* are used instead of a compound or a modified noun in the figure of speech called hendiadys. This reference to *Dunst und Nebel* (also in a letter to Schiller, June 22, 1797), as the medium from which the figures of his play arise before his mind's eye, seems to imply not merely the dimness with which the persons of the tale are seen, but also the obscurity of the age to which they belong, when alchemy and sorcery flourished, as compared with the clarity and serenity of classic antiquity, as this is conventionally depicted.

8 **umwittert** A magic emanation seems to envelop the moving procession of these figures from the old story.

10 **Schatten** The shades of youthful friends, now dead or departed from the poet's life, the memories of youthful love and first friends, whose passing once caused him great pain.

13 **Klage** His present lament, as it recalls to his mind the names of these departed friends, causes him to retrace in memory the tortuous, labyrinth-like path of his early life.

15 **um schöne Stunden getäuscht** 'deprived of happy hours' (by a trick of fortune).

16 **hinweggeschwunden** Here, as very frequently, the auxiliary of

tense must be supplied from the context. In this case it would be *sind*, to make the present perfect tense '(they) have vanished away.'

17 **Gesänge** 'cantos.' The poet refers to his work as if to an epic poem in the traditional form of Milton's PARADISE LOST, or Dante's DIVINA COMMEDIA. This is a metaphor, since none of Goethe's FAUST has the form of epic poetry.

18 **die Seelen** Those friends and acquaintances in Frankfurt and in Weimar to whom Goethe had read his first FAUST scenes.

19 **Gedränge** The friendly crowd of enthusiastic young people, with whom Goethe associated in Frankfurt, Strassburg, and Wetzlar, and in whose response to his poetic creations his own feelings found an echo.

21 **Leid** The poem is thought of as the expression of the poet's deepest passion, his sufferings. In his youth he had read some FAUST scenes to friends who understood him; now, when his poem, with this dedication, is printed and published, it will be open for all to read and to hear. The use of *Leid* here is analogous to that in the distich, written but never published by Goethe, concerning his novel, DIE LEIDEN DES JUNGEN WERTHERS:

> Ach, wie hab' ich so oft die törichten Blätter verwünschet,
> die mein jugendlich Leid unter die Menschen gebracht.

[From the first version of the second "Römische Elegie," *Jubiläums-Ausgabe,* I, 351.]

22 **Beifall** The approval of the unknown multitude disturbs the poet. He fears that general public approval of his poem may indicate that it is less worthy than he had hoped, see lines 59–62. The phrase, *vielen gefallen ist schlimm,* reflects Goethe's aristocratically aloof attitude toward the literary taste of his time.

23 **was** Refers (like *es,* line 24) to anyone who may have enjoyed the early FAUST scenes, 'whoever . . . he.'

25 **längst entwöhntes Sehnen** The poet's youth lies far behind him (Goethe was now forty-eight years old). For years he has not allowed himself to indulge in reminiscent longing for those very happy early days, see lines 184–197. Now he longs again to be with the kindred souls, the *freundliche Gedränge* (19), who are but spirits in the silent realm of ghosts (26). As the dim figures of the past crowd upon his imagination, the poet's emotions are aroused and he feels himself transported far from present realities back into this remembered past.

28 **lispelnd** In poetry, the attributive adjective after an *ein*-word in the nominative or accusative neuter singular is quite frequently without the expected ending *-es.* — **Lied** This dedication, as the poet sings it, seems to him to fade away, to become faint like the whispering, uncertain sounds of the Aeolian harp, while the vanished past assumes for him increasing reality.

1. VORSPIEL AUF DEM THEATER

The underlying fiction of this scene is that these three persons, the theater director, the poet, and the clown, are about to undertake the production of a play, the FAUST, which is to follow. Goethe uses the scene to exhibit three attitudes toward dramatic poetry, that of (1) the director, who wishes action with variety, in order to bring crowds to his theater, (2) the comedian, who wants a romantic piece with shifting emotions and a direct bond with contemporary life, and (3) the poet, who wishes not to be constrained to write for the uses of the vulgar crowd, but rather in composure to form his work for posterity. The director prevails, and, so to speak, drives the poor poet to his task.

SD 33 **Direktor, Theaterdichter, Lustige Person.** The manager, the poet, and the comedian. The better theater companies employed a writer, whose job it was to prepare the scripts for the various plays presented, to compose occasional prologues and epilogues and, incidentally, a number of original plays each year. The comedian represents the performers of these plays, particularly the player of comic parts, such as the roles of the Fool in Shakespeare's plays.

35 **in deutschen Landen** The implication here is that this is one of those international traveling companies, notably groups of English, Dutch, or German players, who, toward the end of the sixteenth century, performed in the cities and at the courts of princes throughout Europe. This one appears to be uncertain about German conditions and the ensuing dialogue considers the problems posed by German audiences; yet the reference to *unsern deutschen Bühnen,* in line 231, appears to identify this company as a German troupe of the late eighteenth century.

39 Where no theater building existed, these troupes set up their own stages wherever they could — often in a barn, a warehouse, in the town hall, or in a temporary wooden structure (*Bude,* line 50), which they erected on the market place.

41 **Augenbraunen** Another form of *Augenbrauen,* used here for the rime.

46 This audience expects to be astonished (42), and this is the more difficult as its reading is extensive. It will not be easy to find something new for these people.

51 **Wehen** The throes of struggling in the crowd.

52 **Gnadenpforte** The entrance to the theater, which is compared by this allusion to the "gate . . . which leadeth unto life," Matthew 7.14.

53 **vor Vieren** Dative plural of *vier,* now no longer usual. The performances in Weimar usually began at half-past five or six o'clock. This crowd has gathered well in advance: indeed, the play for the evening has not yet been put together.

55 This line, like 104, 117, 119, 126 and a number of others is an Alexandrine: that is, it has six beats, with a caesura (a slight pause) after the third beat (*Hungersnot*). For further details see Introduction p. 140. — Goethe wrote two youthful plays in this French verse form. The effect of the line in the present context is something like that of the ornamentation of rococo architecture.

SD 59 This may be the same poet who spoke the dedication. At any rate he uses the same stanza form. He says that he cannot compose if he thinks of the motley crowd for whom his work will be performed.

62 **Strudel** 'whirlpool,' the symbol of distraction.

63 **Himmelsenge** A place of retreat, which will be like Heaven to the poet.

64 **wo nur** 'where alone.'

66 **Götterhand** The plural form *Götter*, 'of the gods,' is reminiscent of the usage of the Greek and Latin poets. It usually means simply 'divine,' with no direct reference to the Christian God.

67–69 The inspirations of the poet's heart, shyly and tentatively murmured, sometimes fail, sometimes succeed in achieving poetic form.

70 **verschlingt** The subject is *Gewalt*, the object is those thoughts (67–69) to which the poet has tried to give poetic form.

71 **durchgedrungen** Supply *ist*; see note to line 16.

71–74 The poetic product is valued in accordance with the conditions of the moment when it appears. Often a work which is not highly esteemed when first brought forth is found by later audiences to have high excellence. Here and now, brilliance may have a momentary effect; genuine artistry will be recognized even by a remote posterity, however blind the contemporary audience may be to its merits.

79 **Gegenwart** The future, or posterity, may have its values. But the present is worth something too, particularly the present of the fine young fellows whose patronage largely supports these actors.

82 The momentary whim of the public will not embitter the artist who knows how to say his say easily. The larger and less intimate his audience, the more certainly will such an artist find a ready response.

85 The comedian urges the poet to be a good fellow and give them an exemplary play for the evening.

86–88 It has been suggested that there is in these lines an allusion to allegorical figures such as appeared in the baroque plays of Daniel Caspar von Lohenstein, and in the plays of Andreas Gryphius. This does not appear to be altogether likely, since it is evident that no such allegorical figures do appear in our play. It seems rather that the poet is being urged to summon his own powers, his imagination, his reason, his common sense, his emotions, and his passions for this task, and admonished not to omit the comic element. One may compare here Goethe's *Maxime*: "Ein dramatisches Werk zu verfassen, dazu gehört Genie. Am Ende soll die Empfindung, in der Mitte die Vernunft, am Anfang der Verstand vorwalten und alles gleichmäßig durch eine lebhaft-klare Einbildungskraft vorgetragen werden."

93 **in der Breite** 'among the masses.'

99 **Stück:Stücken** A pun. When you give a 'play,' give it right off 'in pieces,' never mind about unity (*ein Ganzes*, 'an artistic whole'). — This is a satirical reference to the then prevalent custom of European theaters of giving performances in which only a series of

effective excerpts from a play, or even from several plays, was presented. Goethe quips at this frailty again at lines 4215–16. He deals with the matter more fully in WILHELM MEISTERS LEHRJAHRE, V, 4.

103 **zerpflücken** 'pick apart' into those portions which it (*das Publikum*) likes best. The director does not credit the general public with any sense for the unity of the play, even if there may be unity in it.

104 **sei** Like *zieme* (105), subjunctive in a subordinate clause of implied indirect discourse, introduced by *ihr fühlet nicht.* This use of the subjunctive after an introductory verb in the present tense has become comparatively unusual in present-day German, but it is very frequently found in Goethe's works. This subjunctive may be said often to have little distinctive meaning and the forms may be translated as if they were indicative forms.

106 **saubern** 'nice.' Used sarcastically to mean something quite different. There were a number of such play-smiths active in Germany in Goethe's day, and he was pretty vigorous in his contempt for them.

111 The poet's task, as described by the Director, is to present something fresh and new, something that will please the audience, while it also gives them something to think about (47–48). That task is here compared to the splitting of wood, and in this case, of soft wood. The people of his audience are without powers of concentration. Some come because of boredom; others come loaded down with overeating; still others come from the distraction of magazine reading. None of them are in any condition to appreciate a work of real artistic merit. They do not wish to be edified: they wish to be still further distracted. That, says the realistic Director, is easy, if only enough is made to happen on the stage.

117 **Maskenfesten** 'carnivals': the great masquerade parties, particularly at Shrovetide, just before Lent. These were especially gay in Cologne, Paris, and Rome. The spirit of such celebrations is well reflected in Berlioz' *Roman Carnival Overture.*

119 The ladies in their finery become an important part of the attraction which brings the audience to the theater, although they are not paid for thus contributing to the success of the evening.

121 **was** = *weshalb, warum,* as frequently; see 122, 127.

127 **ihr armen Toren** This poet and others like him, who think of their plays as works of high art, are thus classed by the realistic actor.

132 The dashes indicate interruption due to a gesture by the poet, perhaps a despairing glance toward Heaven.

135 **sollte** Expresses an intention or an expectation of someone else with respect to its subject: 'You expect the poet, I suppose, to . . .' or 'The poet is expected, I suppose, to . . .'

136 **Menschenrecht** 'Man's right' to perceive and describe the relationship between individual phenomena as these present themselves to his mind and the totality of the world as an entity: the right to philosophize, the right to think.

139 **Element** of nature.

140 **Einklang** That overpowering 'harmony' which springs from the poet's bosom and, encompassing the world's multiplicity of often unrelated events, sweeps these back into the poet's heart as a harmonious whole.

142 **Fadens** Nature is thought of as spinning a thread out of the events of life, eternally spinning, twisting this thread indifferently, and winding it on a spindle. All of these events involve beings which make sounds, and these sounds are unrelated and discordant, therefore vexing to the ear. The process seems endless and meaningless until the poet, perceiving the basic 'harmony' of life, organizes the form of these sounds, arranges the symbols of these events, so that a rhythm results. In this way the poet infuses life, interest, or reason into the dissonant jangle produced by nature.

148 **Weihe** The individual thing or happening has artistic importance only as it is a part of a whole. Only the universal element in the individual event consecrates it, relates it harmoniously to other events. Poetic art, if it is to be significant, must present an individual event in such a way that the universal truth which makes that event important can be perceived intuitively. This done, the individual event does indeed 'strike splendid chords' (149) in the hearts of discerning listeners.

150 **zu** 'as accompaniment to.'

154 **Blätter** The leaves of laurel are insignificant in themselves. But made into a wreath of honor and accompanied by a proper dedicatory or commemorative poem, they become a fit reward for any merit.

156 **Olymp** The seat of the Greek gods, a symbol for the highest aspirations of men, some kind of heaven. The force which creates this heaven, or which sustains and consolidates it, is the peculiarly human power of insight, revealed in the poet.

158–183 The comedian, urging the poet to action, to put together a piece for the evening, suggests that he start with anything that comes to mind (*zufällig* 161), and then let his emotions direct the further course of events. Take any subject from real life (167), he says, and your fine poetic insight will give you power to make your play a revelation to everyone, and then it will be interesting. Of course, you have to work through symbols (*Bildern* 170), and these need to be lively and somewhat perplexing, or at any rate not too clear: you need a lot of human error and a bit of truth to make a brew that will be at once refreshing and edifying. Go about it this way; then the young, the tender of heart, will find in your play the things they themselves have most in their own hearts. Don't try to write for the people who have ceased to grow; no one can please them.

181 **Schwung** The grand gesture, the soaring flight of the imagination, characteristic of the heroic drama of the seventeenth century. Examples abound in the plays of Gryphius and of Lohenstein.

182 **wer fertig ist** The antithesis of *ein Werdender*. People who have ceased to learn have ceased to grow, are 'finished.' They will not feel any attraction to such a play, but that can't be helped: they

don't approve of anything. Hence, write for the young, disregard the perfect, or those who think they are perfect.

184–197 These lines will find an echo in the heart of any man near or past fifty, as Goethe was when he wrote them. They belong intimately by mood to the dedication, and they say that to write for the young the poet needs to be young. This the comedian at once denies.

186 **gedrängter** 'crowding close, one upon the other.'

193 **Wahrheit . . . Trug** Neither of these words is easily defined, as Pilate discovered (John 18.38). Life is full of both things. Truth, however, is something apprehended by the mind, by the human intelligence; *Trug,* be it illusion or delusion, is something apprehended by the senses. The world of truth is a world of abstractions; the world of phenomena, from which these abstractions stem, is perhaps the world of delusion to which this poet refers. Because it appears in this context, this line also has a meaning more closely associated with the world of the theater. Hence *Wahrheit* can be taken to mean 'fidelity to nature,' and *Trug* to mean the 'sham of the stage.'

The two ideas of *Drang* and *Lust* are overtones of the contrast between *Wahrheit* and *Trug*, and suggest the conflict between the activating force of inner drive and the opiate of enjoyment which leads to passivity. This conflict is found in the lives of all and is especially exemplified in the story of Faust.

202 **Kranz** It was customary to hang the wreath intended for the winner of the race upon the goal, where approaching runners could see it.

204 **Wirbeltanz** The violent folk dances, which are physically exhausting, by contrast with the sedate minuet of the princely court.

206 The writing of poetry or of a play is compared to the playing of a lyre or harp, to the accompaniment of which ancient poetry was recited.

209 **mit holdem Irren** The comedian suggests that the poet may wend his way, unmethodically and leisurely, toward his self-set goal, and that the audience will find his meandering pleasant.

212 This *Vorspiel* was probably written in 1797, when Goethe was 48 years old. If there is any personal reference behind these lines, coupled with those of the poet at 184–197, it is to a Goethe who was mature and who needed a bit of urging to take up the task of completing his FAUST. He is an *alter Herr* (210) in the sense that he is a senior, not a junior, writer, but not in the sense that he is an old man.

218 **Stimmung** No one has mentioned 'mood' up to this point. But it is evidently expected that the poet will remonstrate and say that he has to find the right mood before he can compose his play. In his conversations with Eckermann (March 11, 1828) Goethe described two kinds of aesthetic productivity: one, the highest attainable, is beyond any poet's control. "Jede Produktivität höchster Art, jedes bedeutende Aperçu, jede Erfindung, jeder große Gedanke, der Früchte bringt und Folge hat, steht in niemandes Gewalt und ist über aller irdischen Macht erhaben. Dergleichen hat der Mensch

als unverhoffte Geschenke von oben . . ." The other kind of productivity is more subject to the will of the poet. "In diese Region zähle ich alles zur Ausführung eines Planes Gehörige, alle Mittelglieder einer Gedankenkette, deren Endpunkte bereits leuchtend dastehen; ich zähle dahin alles dasjenige, was den sichtbaren Leib und Körper eines Kunstwerkes ausmacht." This is the kind of productivity the director understands and urges his poet to undertake.

224 **braut . . . dran** 'set about brewing.'

228 **beim Schopfe fassen** Lysippos, a Greek sculptor (about 330 B.C.) made a statue of Kairos (Opportunity), in which this figure was depicted as having a lock of hair in front and being completely bald on the back of the head. Hence one seized Opportunity by the forelock or not at all, according to tradition based on this statue. Determination (*der Entschluß*), therefore, is to regard the possible as its opportunity. Having seized the possible by the forelock, determination will not let go, but will proceed from this beginning. In short, the director says: Take some subject at hand and begin; the rest will follow, because it has to do so.

232 The reference is to the unrestricted use of all sorts of apparatus and effects on the German stage, in contrast to the classic economy of the French plays of Corneille and Racine. There was no well established tradition in Germany to restrain the ebullient zeal of producers, and every device to surprise and overawe an audience was tried. Thus, *das groß' und kleine Himmelslicht* (235) are the stage properties which represent the sun and the moon, respectively.

238 **an Tier' und Vögeln,** for *an Tieren und Vögeln.* Rather frequently Goethe drops a suffix or an inflectional ending from a word joined by *und* to another which has the omitted morpheme, e.g., *das groß' und kleine Himmelslicht* 235, *von Sonn' und Welten* 279.

242 This need not be taken literally as an itinerary. It is a list of the stopping places in the *Kreis der Schöpfung* which the poet is to traverse. Faust does get into all of these places before he is finished, but not in this order. This whole scene is designed, perhaps principally, to prepare the audience for a most unusual variety in the sequence of scenes to follow.

2. Prolog im Himmel

The dramatic purpose of this scene is to state the problem of Mephistopheles and Faust. The issue is whether or not Mephistopheles can lead Faust away from the service of the Lord. The Lord appears to be in an indulgent mood, in that he permits, indeed encourages, Mephistopheles to attempt to lead Faust astray.

The analogy of this scene to the Biblical story of Job is evident. There the Lord points to his servant Job as an "upright man" and Satan proposes to destroy Job's character by destroying his possessions. The God of the Old Testament gives his approval to Satan's undertaking, and Job is subjected to grievous torments. In Faust

Mephistopheles proposes to win Faust away from God, not by persecution, but *sacht* (314) by easy allurements and by pleasures.

By locating this scene in Heaven and using God, Mephistopheles, and the Archangels as speaking characters Goethe achieves something of the atmosphere of the Mystery plays of the Middle Ages.

SD 243 **Der Herr** As this is usually produced on the stage, the Lord does not appear where the audience can see Him, but converses with the others through an opening into an inner court of Heaven. Conventionally this opening is overhead, and a great shaft of light falls from above while the Lord is present. It is cut off when the inner court is closed, line 349. — **Die himmlischen Heerscharen** are the Heavenly Hosts of Luke 2.13. — **Die drei Erzengel** We may assume that there are numerous archangels in Heaven, of whom these three step forward. The Bible mentions only Michael (Jude 9) as an archangel. The name of Raphael occurs in the apocryphal Book of Tobit (12.15). Gabriel is mentioned in the Book of Daniel (8.16) and in the Gospel of Luke (1.19, 26). Neither Gabriel nor Raphael is called an archangel in the Bible.

243 **die Sonne tönt** Aristotle says that some Pythagorean philosophers believed that the heavenly bodies produced musical notes as they moved along their courses. Those which moved slowly produced a low note, those which moved more rapidly produced a high note; so that there was a chance for harmony, if the relative speeds of the stars on their courses were integrally related. This idea has frequently been used by poets and musicians.

244 **Brudersphären Wettgesang** The mention of 'spheres' seems to indicate that Goethe was making poetic use of the ancient Ptolemaic cosmography as the basis for the relationships here presupposed. This doctrine envisaged the earth as a stationary sphere located at the center of the finite universe. This universe was viewed as a structure of hollow, concentric, transparent spheres around the earth: the closest easy analogy to this structure is that of a large onion. The sphere nearest the earth is that of the moon. Within each of the six spheres next outside the moon one of the planets moved on its own (epicyclic) course. Nearest the realm of the moon was the sphere of Mercury, then came the spheres of Venus, the sun, Mars, Jupiter, and Saturn, in that order. Beyond the sphere of Saturn was the sphere of the fixed stars. It is probably the spheres of the planets which are here thought of as 'brother spheres' to the sun. Each sphere as it revolves makes a sound and the whole is viewed as a friendly rivalry. In this Ptolemaic system, God resided outside the finite universe, beyond the *Primum Mobile*, in the Empyrean, the "tenth heaven" of Dante, "the abode of the blessed."

246 **vollendet** The sun cannot be said ever to complete its journey, in the sense that it arrives and ceases to travel. However, it does rotate on its axis and presumably travels around an orbit. It appears that at line 243 the sun was remote enough for its movement to sound a musical note (*tönt*), whereas at line 246 it has come close enough to the observer to produce a thunderous roar, rather than a musical tone.

248 **wenn** = *obwohl,* or perhaps *während.* — **sie** = *die Sonne.* — **mag** = *kann.*

249 **Werke** The works of Creation, described in the first chapter of Genesis, and referred to in Genesis 2.2: "Und also vollendete Gott am siebenten Tage seine Werke, die er machte . . ."

251 **schnell, schnelle** The adverbial form is *schnelle; schnell* is the adjectival form, used as an adverb, as almost any adjective may be used. — A point at the surface of the earth's equator is moving around the earth's axis at a speed of approximately 1000 miles per hour.

252 **dreht** The earth is seen to revolve, and rapidly. This means that the observer is not too remote, and that he is watching a point on the earth's surface move through space. It is apparent that the Ptolemaic cosmography, which viewed the earth as motionless, is not the basis of the conception here represented. It is not known how fully Goethe understood the true relationships of the sun to the other components of its galaxy, but it may be observed that what he here says can be understood to apply to the universe as we know it with less contradiction than it can be applied to the Ptolemaic system.

253 **Paradieseshelle** Daylight is apparently the norm in Paradise; see line 1782.

255 The sea is seen to strike violently in broad currents against a rocky coast, and then the whole — the sea and the coast — is whirled from the view of the archangels as the earth revolves.

261–262 **Kette der . . . Wirkung** The storms of the earth are seen as a series of events which are linked together by a causal connection, one event being in part at least the effect of those which have preceded it and the cause of those which follow.

263–264 **flammt . . . vor** The flashing devastation of lightning goes flaming before the path of the thunder.

265 **doch** Although the tremendous power of these natural forces is impressive, still the angels (*Boten*) are more deeply moved by the even, gentle movement of God's day. What is really impressive in the universe is its relative immutability, the regularity of the laws of nature amidst all movement and change.

267–270 These lines are to be compared with lines 247–250. There the angels derived strength from the sight of God's works, in particular the sun, *although* they were unable to understand them completely. Here the angels are strengthened by the sight of the gentle progress of God's day, *because* they know they cannot comprehend God directly.

SD 271 The name Mephistopheles, in one form or another (Mephostophilus, Mephistophilis, Mephistophiel), belongs to the Faust legend. Goethe's form is that of the FAUSTBUCH DES CHRISTLICH MEINENDEN (about 1725). A satisfactory explanation of the derivation of the name has not yet been found.

271 **wieder nahst** The assumption appears to be that God is making one of His periodic tours of inspection in Heaven, and that Mephistopheles, whose normal field of operations is not in Heaven, has come there expressly to see the Lord. However, he appears to identify

himself (*bei uns*) with the angels of this particular region of Heaven, and to have his place among them as one of the Lord's servants (*Gesinde*).

273 **sonst** Although Mephistopheles is engaged in the business of seducing souls from God's ways, he has in the past usually been well treated by God upon the occasion of such visits as this. He therefore makes bold to appear now. See lines 337–343.

277 **Pathos** Any attempt on the part of Mephistopheles to exhibit deep feelings (*hohe Worte*) of the sort shown by the archangels.

279 **Sonn' und Welten** See note to line 238.

281 **der kleine Gott** Man was created in God's image, but on a much smaller scale.

282 **wunderlich** In line 250 it was *herrlich*. One has to expect satire from the *Schalk* (339) Mephistopheles.

285 **Vernunft** This was the watchword, the new divinity, of the men of the French Revolution of 1789; and the two lines 285–286 may be taken as an allusion to this Revolution.

287 **Euer Gnaden** A fixed phrase used to address persons of high degree, 'Your Grace.'

288–292 Mephistopheles compares man's use of his intellectual powers in the effort to understand the workings of the universe with the vain leapings of the grasshopper, who, no matter how often or how high he leaps, lands once more in the grass from which he sprang. So man, despite his efforts, remains no better than before. But then, to be sure, man is so constituted that even if he stopped his leaping and lay always 'in the grass' — says Mephistopheles with disgust — he would still 'stick his nose' into everything, because of this peculiarly human inquisitive drive to understand.

294 **nur** There is a certain impatience with Mephistopheles in these lines. 'Do you always come here solely to complain, don't you ever find anything right on earth?' The earth is one of God's pet projects; He made it and, after making it, He peopled it with human beings.

297 **dauern** This is a bit of cynical, scornful irony.

298 **selbst** 'myself.'

299 The parallel here to the Book of Job is evident. There also when the "sons of God came to present themselves before Jehovah," Satan came along. Satan had been "down" on earth, "walking to and fro in it." Job 1.8: "And Jehovah said unto Satan, Hast thou considered my servant Job? for there is none like him in the earth, a perfect and upright man, one that feareth God and turneth away from evil." Satan replied that this fear of God was due to the special care God bestowed upon Job, and that if this were taken away, Job would renounce God openly. Jehovah then granted Satan permission to take away all Job's material wealth, saying (Job 1.12): "All that he hath is in thy power; only upon himself put not forth thy hand." The rest of the book tells of Satan's efforts and Job's sufferings, and his final victory, when God "blessed the latter end of Job more than his beginning," and permitted him long life (Job 42.16): "And after this Job lived a hundred and forty

years, and saw his sons, and his sons' sons, even four generations. So Job died, being old and full of days."

300 **Euch** The shift from *du* to *Ihr* (*Euch*) reflects a change in the attitude of Mephistopheles toward God. This is not a change from lesser to greater respect, but from sympathy to antipathy, — from the feeling that there was some bond between them to the awareness of the irreconcilable difference which sets Mephistopheles apart from the others.

301 **irdisch** 'of the earth, earthy,' — perhaps with some reminiscence of I Corinthians 15.47: "The first man is of the earth, earthy: the second man is of Heaven." This Faust is not the "natural" man, but is driven by a great ferment in his soul to seek the remote, the ultimate. Mephistopheles views this as a mad quest and reports that Faust is at least partially aware of the madness of his strivings. Goethe's problem here was to make Faust a very special case without thereby making him non-human, to make him exceptional but not atypical.

306 'And all things near and all things remote' which Faust is able to acquire or to achieve.

308 **Wenn . . . auch** = *obwohl*, 'even though.'

309 **bald** Just how 'soon' is not clear. Neither is it quite clear what *in die Klarheit führen* means, for it is reasonable to believe that this contrasts with *verworren*, and that both describe conditions under which Faust serves or is to serve the Lord. From lines 315–318 it would appear that clarity cannot be a state of human life on earth but must be a condition attainable only after death. Yet how Faust is to serve the Lord in Heaven is neither clear nor aesthetically important. The solution of the problem raised here might give important information concerning the state of Goethe's plans for Faust at the time he wrote these lines.

310 Supply the subject and read: *Es weiß doch der Gärtner.*

314 **meine Straße** Probably the "broad way that leadeth to destruction." (Matthew 7.13).

315 The Lord restricts the attempts of Mephistopheles to lead Faust astray. As long as Faust lives on earth, Mephistopheles may tempt him.

317 **strebt** Man's striving is the positive drive which leads him to seek his own highest development, the perfect realization of his potentialities. The guiding force in this striving is reason, the goal of which is truth. The negation of this drive, the acceptance of any state as satisfactory, is the most irrational of all errors; and the man who falls into it is in the gravest danger of losing his essential human attributes.

318 Mephistopheles evidently has to deal with numerous dead, presumably those whom he has succeeded in leading along his way (314); but he doesn't enjoy that, any more than a cat enjoys a dead mouse. He now has definite permission to attempt to win Faust over to his way, but no wager has been agreed to by the Lord.

320 **mir** The dative of the personal pronoun is frequently used to refer to its antecedent as the person particularly interested in the action, either in his mind or emotions (the "ethical dative," as

here), or in a practical way (the dative of interest or of advantage). The ethical dative is frequently best omitted from an English translation.

324 **Urquell** God.

326 **herab** 'down' (to perdition).

328 **ein guter Mensch** The attribute *guter* is positive, not negative. A good man is a man who strives toward truth and self-perfection. — **in seinem dunklen Drange** 'in the confusedly (308) directed drive' which carries such a man through the errors to which all are subject (317). Such a man may go astray, but he will discover that he has done so, and he will also know when he is on the right track. So long as he continues to fight the good fight he remains *ein guter Mensch*, and he may expect to come out all right in the end.

330 **nur** Mephistopheles concedes that this good man (Faust) knows the right way; only, he says, it won't take long to lead him away from it.

335 **Muhme** The serpent of Genesis 3, whom Mephistopheles claims as a relative. The degree of relationship intended by *Muhme* is not clear; it may mean 'aunt,' 'first cousin,' or some more remote (female) relative. Mephistopheles also calls the *Trödelhexe* (4110) "*Frau Muhme.*" — The punishment meted out to the serpent of Genesis 3 was that it should go upon its belly and eat dust all the days of its life.

336 **auch da** With respect to the celebration of this predicted victory. — The interpretation of this line depends on how one takes *nur*. Some take it to qualify *frei* and to mean 'not otherwise than free, quite freely.' Others take it to qualify *erscheinen* and to mean 'only appear to be free.' If one reads *nur* with *frei*, then *erscheinen* means 'to appear,' presumably before God as Mephistopheles is appearing at the moment. God gives permission to Mephistopheles to triumph or to appear to triumph freely in the event that Faust should succumb to his wiles. God knows Mephistopheles will fail (325–327), but Mephistopheles does not accept this as inevitable.

339 **Schalk** The crafty, ironical knave who irritates and confuses the good man by impugning the validity of his reason. There are other forces of evil which the Lord finds it more difficult to condone, but we are not told what these are.

343 **als Teufel schaffen** Probably the same idea, basically, as at 1336, where Mephistopheles himself admits that, although he always wishes to bring about evil, he always does bring about good. The present line justifies God's permitting this spirit of negation to try to entrap his servant Faust. Even with devilish intent, Mephistopheles will be obliged to produce good, because, in the sight of God, the only unforgivable sin of man is the lapsing into a state of unconditional repose (340–341).

344 **ihr** God turns from Mephistopheles to the archangels who surround His throne and calls them 'true, genuine' (*echt*), to distinguish them from Mephistopheles, who is one of the fallen angels and no longer deserves this approval.

345 **Schöne** An old form of the abstract noun, like *Länge*, *Breite*, *Tiefe*. *Schönheit* is now the usual form.

347 **umfass'** Optative, 'may the world of becoming (*das Werdende*) encompass you with the gentle bonds of love.'

349 **befestiget** Imperative; the archangels are instructed to give permanence to the unsteady world of phenomena by fixing it in lasting thoughts. They are to observe the things and events of the universe. From these, by means of their "pure" reason, they are to abstract the enduring part — the "ideas" (*noumena*), the principles, laws, relationships.

SD 349 **Der Himmel** The inner sanctum, where God has been. See note to SD 243.

353 **menschlich** 'humanely, like a human being, man to man.' — **mit dem Teufel.** The notion that Mephistopheles is *the* Devil is not consistently adhered to throughout the play. At times he is *a* devil, merely one of many evil spirits.

Der Tragödie erster Teil

3. Nacht

In the Prologue in Heaven Goethe has stated the problem of his Faust. Can Mephistopheles lead this man Faust from the paths of righteousness into eternal damnation, or will Faust, because of his inner qualities, remain invulnerable to the wiles of the Devil? There is a specific criterion of man's fall: his acquiescence in *die unbedingte Ruhe*, and the cessation of that striving which is the mark of man.

In the present scene we meet the chief protagonist, Faust. The method of the poet is primarily that of the soliloquy. There is very little dialogue in this scene, and no action in the usual sense. First we find the scholar Faust in his study, sunk in despair because of his inability to penetrate beyond the outward appearance of things to their reality, and sick of his cloistered life. By means of magic, of which he has become a practitioner, he attempts to find a way to transcend the limits which confine him. He feels himself momentarily exalted into the realm of spirits, evokes an apparition of one of them and, being rebuffed for his presumption, sinks back into his despair. He then conceives the idea that by committing suicide he may gain access to the realm of the spirits beyond this earth. He is about to drink poison when the sound of the Easter carols in the nearby church restrains him and he puts down the poison cup.

SD 354 **gotisch** Gothic architecture is the symbol of the medieval and romantic. The scene is characteristic of the age of the Reformation in sixteenth-century Germany. This is the period of Luther, Dürer, Erasmus, and Hans Sachs. The Gothic style of architecture, although it was developed during the fourteenth century, had not yet been superseded by later forms.

354 **Habe** Supply the subject *ich*. This kind of omission is not infrequent in Faust. — **Philosophie.** The German university was or-

ganized in four major units or colleges called faculties. These were Theology, Jurisprudence, Medicine, and Philosophy. The effect of this organization can still be seen in the kinds of doctoral degrees granted in our own universities. We still have doctors of theology, of law, of medicine, and of philosophy, the last including almost every type of scholarship not named in the other three classes.

355 **Juristerei** = *Jurisprudenz.* The word here has none of the derogatory connotation now associated with the suffix *–erei.*

356 **leider auch** Faust is particularly disappointed in his study of theology, because he had expected from it the greatest satisfaction of his hunger for truth. Instead he had got from it only unsatisfactory answers to his questions.

357 **Bemühn** Rimes with *Medizin.* In Goethe's rime practice there is no difference between rounded and unrounded vowels of the same type. The vowels *ü* and *i* belong to the type called "high front vowels" and may be rimed with each other, e.g. *Zügen:liegen* 440–441. The vowels *ö* and *e* are "mid front vowels" and may be rimed with each other, e.g. *Bergeshöh'n:gehn* 392–393, *näher:höher* 461–462. The diphthongs *ei* and *eu* may be rimed, e.g. *Zweifel:Teufel* 368–369; see Introduction, p. 144.

360 **Magister, Doktor** The two higher degrees in the sequence: *Baccalaureus, Magister, Doktor.*

361 **ziehe schon** A present tense where in English we should use a progressive present perfect 'I have now been leading.' — **an die zehen Jahr** 'almost ten years.' The accusative indicates approach toward a limit. *zehen Jahr* is archaic for *zehn Jahre.* Goethe used a plural form *Jahr* as well as the normal plural *Jahre.*

364 **wissen** Not merely 'to know,' but 'to know completely and with certainty.' This kind of use, in which more is implied than the words express, is called a "pregnant use" of words.

366 **Laffen** Faust holds his colleagues in contempt, regardless of their positions, enumerated in 367.

367 **Doktoren, Magister, Schreiber, Pfaffen** All are men of academic training. *Doktor* is the highest academic rank; *Magister* is next in order of eminence. *Schreiber* is a man learned in the law, a jurist perhaps; and *Pfaffe* is a member of the clergy. The word *Pfaffe* as used here does not of itself imply disrespect.

376 **möchte** = *könnte.* The verb *mögen* in older German usually meant 'to have the physical power to,' and in that sense 'to be able.'

377 **Magie** Not *magia diabolica,* the black art or necromancy, but *magia naturalis.* This was a craft of conjuration which did not involve an appeal to Satan or other evil spirits, but to the planetary and other good spirits, who were called upon to aid the sorcerer in his efforts to find out the secrets of nature. This dealing with spirits was not of necessity bad or sinful, but it involved some risk that the operator might be deceived by Satan and led to eternal damnation and hell-fire (369).

378 **ob** 'to see whether.'

379 **Geheimnis** Faust seeks answers to his questions about the mysterious nature of things. He wants to teach his students things

which will make them better and less sinful men (373), but the truth he seeks remains a mystery to him.

383 Faust wishes to know the nature of the inner cohesive force which holds the universe together. — There is a great gulf between the methods of alchemy and the methods of atomic fission, but the difference is rather in the tools than in the driving force of man's search for truth, which animates both quests.

384 Ostensibly technical terms of alchemy; *Wirkenskraft*, the energy of a living being; *Samen*, the primordial substances out of which things are formed. It seems likely that Goethe invented the term *Wirkenskraft*, while *Samen* is a well-known term in alchemy.

385 **tu'** An auxiliary verb here, and best not translated. — **kramen**, as a small shopkeeper retails small items from his stock to his customers, so Faust feels that he has been dealing out mere words to his students instead of real knowledge. Others take the verb *kramen* to mean 'rummage about in' and construe the line to refer to Faust's feeling of frustration when he finds himself manipulating mere words rather than fundamental facts in his studies.

386 **Mondenschein** Like *Sonnenschein*, a compound with the *-en* of the weak noun declension; now commonly *Mondschein*.

387 **zum letztenmal** Faust wishes that his vain search for truth might come to an end, and that he might join the spirits (394) who float about mountain caverns and meadows in the moonlight. In his imagination he does just that, only to be rudely awakened by the real things his eyes see about him (398).

389 **den ich . . . herangewacht** 'which, sleepless, I have watched approach.'

398–417 The target of this tirade is dead knowledge, the unorganized and meaningless heaping up of learning which generates no living, vital power. Faust's study has become his prison, into which the light of Nature's sun shines but dimly.

403 **Würme** An archaic plural form, now replaced by *Würmer*. Goethe uses both forms; see line 2176.

405 **ein angeraucht Papier** A collective singular: a mass of smoke-browned papers, bundles and rolls of manuscripts, lecture notes, and the like, piled and thrust into the shelves. The smoke came principally from the lamp in which much midnight oil has burned. Concerning the lack of adjective ending, see note to line 28, *lispelnd*.

408 This had been his father's study and laboratory. Faust's father had been an alchemist and a physician, and had possessed the equipment required for these arts (see 1034–1055). *Urväter* suggests that the contents of the room may have come in part from still earlier generations of Faust's family.

410 **du** Faust addresses himself.

415 The world of nature into which God put men, when He created them.

420 **Nostradamus** Latin form of the name of Michel de Nostredame (1503–1566), an astrologer and physician, a contemporary of the historical Dr. Faust (see Introduction, p. 18 f.). No such book as this from the hand of Nostradamus is known to us. Many of the features of the following conjurations have been traced to the ARCANA

COELESTIA (1749) of Emanuel von Swedenborg (1688–1772), the Swedish spiritualist, or *Geisterseher*.

424 The power to become a spiritualist, and thus to hold converse with the many spirits who people the regions around the earth, will be given him by revelation.

426 The intellectual explanation of the cabalistic symbols of his book does not bring him into communion with these spirits. According to Swedenborg's doctrine, such communication is accomplished through the senses, which are opened to the world of spirits by an act of divine or supernatural compassion.

SD 430 **Makrokosmus** The great world, the universe as a whole, contrasted with the microcosm, or man viewed as the epitome of the universe. The symbol of the macrocosm is to be thought of as a drawing which depicts the universe as a mechanism with intricately integrated parts, driven by a unitary force, moving harmoniously in a predestined course. Just which one of a number of such symbols Goethe may have had in mind is not known. None of the known symbols corresponds in detail to what follows here.

431 **Sinnen** Plural of *der Sinn.* Present-day German uses *Sinne*; see line 611.

433 **Nerv' und Adern** for *Nerven und Adern.* See note to line 238.

442 **der Weise** It is not likely that Goethe meant to refer to any single person here. In any event, no satisfactory identification of this sage or of the pretended quotation 443–446 has been made.

446 **Morgenrot** Not the 'dawn,' but "Aurora," in astrological literature a symbol for intuitive knowledge of the universe.

447–453 This vision is mystic and mysterious. Celestial powers ascend and descend on wings fragrant with blessing. They hand each other golden vessels and together they make harmonious sounds Just what is supposed to be in these golden vessels is not revealed.

454 This symbol of the *Makrokosmus* is, after all, only a spectacle, not reality; it is not nature itself.

455–456 Faust hungers after truth as an infant hungers for nourishment. The metaphor is often compared with that of Isaiah 66.11. In seventeenth and eighteenth century books on natural science, "Nature" is often pictured as a statue of a goddess (Isis) with many breasts. See also lines 1892–1893.

458 **dahin** Equivalent to the relative, *wohin.*

SD 460 **Erdgeist** The *Welt- und Tatengenius,* the tutelary spirit ('genius') of the acts of this world. The Earth Spirit may be taken here as an alchemistic, spiritualistic notion, a spirit which can be caused to appear by the utterance of an appropriate incantation. We do not know precisely what Goethe intended the function of this Earth Spirit in the economy of the Faust play to be (see Introduction p. 90).

464 The effect of Faust's contemplation of the symbol of the Earth Spirit differs from the effect of his contemplation of the symbol of the macrocosm. The latter excited Faust's soul to climb to transcendent heights of the world of spirit, the former moves him to plunge actively into the affairs of the earth. The two images sym-

bolize respectively man's drive toward understanding and his drive toward action.

478 These 'new feelings' are referred to in lines 614–621.

SD 481 A magic formula accompanies the symbol of the Earth Spirit in the book. When this is spoken by the right person under the proper circumstances, the spirit will appear. — In the theater, as Goethe planned it, a much enlarged "transparency" (a lantern slide) of a bust of Jupiter was to be thrown upon the wall of Faust's study. This image was to have flaming eyes and flaming hair.

483 The capacity of men to attract spirits and of spirits to attract men is assumed in the spiritualistic philosophy of Paracelsus and his followers. Swedenborg describes this attraction as "suction," *attractio seu suctio.* — Each spirit is supposed to have its own sphere (484).

488 **mächtig** for *mächtiges;* see note on *lispelnd* line 28. Similarly: *erbärmlich* 489, *wechselnd* 506, *glühend* 507, *griechisch* 523.

490 **Übermenschen** The Earth Spirit recognizes in Faust an unusual human being, a man of great and sincere longing to become like God in knowledge, to become an equal of the spirits of the earth and of the universe. But Faust's terror at the sight of the apparition moves the Earth Spirit to scorn. *Übermensch* is here used as a term of irony.

494 **des** Older form of the genitive case of the relative pronoun, for which *dessen* is now usual.

495 **sich . . . drang** Now usually *sich . . . drängte.*

501–509 Here the Earth Spirit indicates what he is: the guardian spirit, or "genius of deeds" in which the deity is made manifest. Just as clothes condition the outward appearance of their wearer, so life conditions the outward appearance of God.

510 In these words Faust may be said to betray his lack of comprehension of the Earth Spirit, who does not flit about, but is rather indwelling in all phenomena, and who is not restlessly busy *about* things, but universally active *within* living Nature.

519 **Glück** The joy of communing with spirits. The line is somewhat out of harmony with Faust's disappointment expressed in lines 514–517.

521 **Schleicher** The reference is to slow rather than to surreptitious movements of Wagner. He is honest enough, but not inspired, as Faust sees him.

524 **Kunst** The art of reading aloud effectively. The course of study in the liberal arts of the medieval university comprised two divisions with a total of seven fields: (a) the *trivium,* comprising grammar, dialectic, rhetoric, and (b) the *quadrivium,* comprising arithmetic, geometry, music, and astronomy. The *trivium* is concerned with the proper and effective use of language, and Faust, as a university teacher, may be supposed to have been interested in it. The reading of ancient Greek tragedy is to be thought of as an exercise in dialectic or rhetoric, in which Wagner believes Faust to be engaged as a part of his studies.

527 **Komödiant** Not 'comedian' in our modern sense, but rather any theatrical player, including even 'tragedians.' The essential factor of the comparison here is that the actor speaks lines written by someone else as though they were his own thoughts. When Wagner suggests that actors could well teach preachers how to declaim, Faust's immediate response (528–529) is that this is true enough, if the preacher has nothing of his own to say, but merely mouths the words of others. Of course, Wagner is interested in declamation as a part of the art of persuasion (533), necessary to any man in the public eye.

530 **Museum** The name once generally given to a scholar's study. The word, which was borrowed from Greek by way of Latin, originally meant 'dedicated to or belonging to the Muses.'

531 **einen Feiertag** The accusative, meaning about what English 'on,' in the phrase 'on a holiday,' would mean; the genitive case would be more natural in such a sentence and would mean 'of' (a holiday), but the rime with *mag* 529 prevented the use of *eines Feiertags* or *feiertags.*

532 **von weiten** Now usually *von weitem,* with the dative singular of the adjective *weit.* Goethe's form *weiten* is an archaic uninflected adverbial form. This phrase occurs again in lines 3094 and 8160.

533 **durch Überredung leiten** Wagner is thinking only of dialectic, of the art of persuasion. — Johann Christoph Gottsched (1700–1766) did much to improve German practice in this field through his book AUSFÜHRLICHE REDEKUNST. Although most of Goethe's references to Gottsched are uncomplimentary, there is little doubt that the arguments of Gottsched's book were in his mind as he composed this dialogue between Wagner and Faust.

534 The *es* of **ihr's** and **werdet's** represents the means of persuasion which Wagner seeks to understand. The only source of really persuasive arguments is one's feelings, one's heart or soul; purely external arts are not likely to be effective.

536 **mit urkräftigem Behagen** 'with the delight which comes from the vigor of spontaneous utterance.'

538 **leimt zusammen** 'Compile,' as Germans say, "*mit Kleister und Schere,*" by pasting together clippings from other people's (or indeed from one's own earlier) writings.

539 **andrer** Genitive plural of the pronoun: 'other people's.'

542 **Affen** Probably the same persons who were called *Laffen* 366. — The syntax of this clause and the dependent clause which follows it is incomplete. This phenomenon is called "anacoluthon," and there is a great deal of it in Goethe's FAUST. One can here supply the missing connection by inference from what follows. The meaning is: 'You can perhaps obtain the admiration of children and fools by the methods suggested, if your taste tends to such things.'

544 **Herz zu Herzen schaffen** 'work heart to heart' (with others).

546 **Allein** is ambiguous. It may mean either *nur* 'only,' or *doch* 'but.' We understand this line to mean: 'However, in spite of all you have just said, the success of the orator does depend upon his style of delivery.'

548 **Er** One of the three pronouns regularly used to address one person. Of these three the most intimate was *du*, next in degree of formality was *Er*, and most formal was *Ihr* with a plural verb. The shift from one form to another is often an effective device to indicate a change of mood. Faust has been speaking in general terms, as if to a group of Wagners, using the plural forms *ihr* 534, *euer* 541, and *euch* 543. *Er*, with the third person verb *Such'*, is correctly formal in address to Wagner but carries a hint of vexation, which seems to have disappeared at 568, where *du* is used. Only once (3524) in FAUST does Goethe use the modern "polite" form with *Sie* and a plural verb to a single person. — **redlichen Gewinn** This is contrasted with *Vortrag* 546. What is to be won by mere external qualities of style, as Wagner understands it, is contrasted with what is to be won by sheer honesty of utterance.

549 **schellenlaut** The cap and bells are the traditional insignia of the jester. Court fools in Shakespeare's times, and later, wore exotic costumes and weird caps, to which tiny jingling bells were attached.

550 **Verstand und rechter Sinn** are to be taken as the logical subject of *trägt*. The two are enough of a unit to justify the singular verb, though the singularity of the act of utterance rather than the nature of the subject probably determined the choice of the verb form.

552 **euch** Faust reverts to his general form of address, as if to a class or group of persons.

555 **Schnitzel kräuseln** A well-known pastime for the entertainment of children, the crimping and folding of odd and insignificant baubles out of pieces of paper. However, the ambiguous case-form of *der Menschheit* makes difficult a definitive interpretation of this line. Some take *der Menschheit* as genitive with *Schnitzel*, meaning 'Man's poorest shreds,' and thence understand the line to mean that such orators as Wagner admires serve up to their audiences mere baubles crimped from the remnants of humanity. We prefer to take *der Menschheit* as a dative, and to understand it to mean: 'curl paper baubles for humanity.' Such orators think their efforts should affect all men, but the curly gewgaws of their discourse are devoid of life and freshness. Paper flowers have no fragrance.

558 Wagner is a learned man. He quotes the first aphorism of the physician Hippokrates, which is universally known in its Latin form: *Ars longa, vita brevis*, or, as Longfellow put it: "Art is long, and time is fleeting."

It may be observed that Goethe here permits Wagner a good deal of *Schnitzel kräuseln* in the form of alliteration: *Kunst, kurz, kritisch, Kopf; Mittel, man, man, muß; lang, Leben; Bestreben, Busen, bang; erwerben, erreicht; steigt, sterben.* The rime scheme is artful: abbacddc.

560 **kritischen Bestreben** The labors of a philologist, the interpreter of ancient documents, whose first task is to establish by critical procedure the genuine or original text of the document and the history of its transmission. — Wagner here represents eighteenth century rationalism, the Age of Enlightenment, which was exceedingly proud of its own achievements (570–573). Judged by modern standards, the men of this day were very careless of historical ac-

curacy in their treatment of the past. Herder, and after him Goethe, were eloquent critics of this laxity, and sharply scornful of this pride.

561 **Kopf und Busen** The seats respectively of the intellect and the emotions. The preposition *um* is to be taken here in the local sense: 'around, in the neighborhood of.' The line thus means that Wagner feels both intellectual and emotional anxiety as he pursues his critical endeavors, not that he is worried about his head and his heart.

562 **Mittel** First, the knowledge of ancient languages (here Greek, Latin, and Hebrew), by means of which the sources become accessible to study; second, the books and manuscripts which contain these sources.

566 **Bronnen** A play on the meaning of *die Quelle,* 'source, fountain.' The word *Bronnen* belongs to a more elevated style of diction than the usual form *Brunnen.*

570 **Ergötzen** is all Wagner understands of *Erquickung* 568. *Ergötzen* is a receptive, passive experience, the effects of which soon pass away; *Erquickung* is a productive, activating experience, the effects of which are lasting.

576 The allusion is to the book with seven seals in the Revelation of John, Chapter 5.1 — Chapter 8.1.

577 Faust includes Wagner in his criticism of the historians of the *Aufklärung* (Age of Enlightenment), *die Herren* of 578.

583–585 **Haupt- und Staatsaktion** The "Tragedy of Blood," in which the rise and fall of princely tyrants was portrayed. This came to be a favorite theme for the puppet plays, many of which Goethe saw as a boy in Frankfurt. In these plays, as well as in many stage plays of that time, the actors were made to voice moralizing comments on human life, or "golden texts" conveying rules for the proper conduct of life.

587 **was** = *etwas.*

589 **das Kind** The truth as revealed by insight.

593 **gekreuzigt** Notably, Jesus Christ. — **verbrannt** The popular means of exterminating prophets or heretics in Faust's time. Some famous victims were: John Hus, burned at the stake in Constance 1415, Giordano Bruno, burned at the stake in Rome 1600. Girolamo Savonarola was strangled before his body was burned, in Rome 1498.

598 **als** 'since it is' Easter Sunday (*der erste Ostertag*). Easter Monday is *der zweite Ostertag.*

599 **ein' und andre** 'one or another.' An indefinite number, or 'this or that,' an indefinite kind of question.

605–606 This is one of the imperfect joints in the composition of the play. What follows was written many years, perhaps more than twenty years, after what precedes, and there are logical conflicts between the two conceptions of Faust's relationship to the Earth Spirit which cannot wholly be resolved. What is said after line 605 is in harmony with the *Prologue in Heaven.*

607 **Geisterfülle** A reference to the presence of the Earth Spirit and the other spirits (493) associated with it (520).

613 **sollte** Faust's feelings were determined by the will of another, the *Erdgeist:* 'I was made to . . .'

614–622 These lines describe in some detail the new feelings alluded to in lines 477–481.

615 **gedünkt** Supply *hatte.* — **Spiegel** This reference to truth reflected in a mirror suggests the *Monadology* of Leibnitz, who speaks of souls as living mirrors or images of the universe of creatures, while spirits are images of Divinity itself, capable of knowing the system of the universe. The pertinent passages of the *Monadology* are conveniently translated in Benjamin Rand's MODERN CLASSICAL PHILOSOPHERS, New York, 1908, p. 213.

616 **sein** Genitive of the reflexive, with *genoß*, instead of the now more usual accusative, *sich.*

617 **abgestreift** Supply *hatte;* 'and who had stripped off all earthly attributes' (*den Erdensohn*).

618 **Cherub** In the generally accepted hierarchy of spirits, the seraphim stand nearest to God. The cherubim are kept somewhat more remote from the deity, while mere angels are restricted to regions still farther from God. — The antecedent of **dessen** is *ich.*

619 A violent anthropomorphic metaphor, which sees Nature as a physiological organism through whose veins the free creative power of the deity flows: 'I, whose free strength presumptuously, with awed emotion, made bold to flow through nature's veins.'

622 **Donnerwort** See lines 512–513. The *du* of the following lines is the *Erdgeist.*

631 **jenem Drang** The impelling urge, exemplified in lines 455–459, to seek actively the source of all life.

632 **Taten : Leiden** The two terms are complementary, 'what we do, and what is done to us.'

634 **Geist** Antithesis to *Stoff.* Our most precious conceptions suffer the restrictions imposed by the fact that we belong to the world of matter. The more exalted the *Geist,* the more foreign and incompatible the *Stoff.*

635 **immer fremd und fremder** Involves two devices for emphasizing the increasing of the quality *fremd.* Either *immer fremder* or *fremder und fremder* would serve. The omission of the suffix *-er* from the first *fremder* is a trick often found in Goethe's poetry.

636–637 Our earth-bound, practical reason bids us accept and be content with that which is good. What appears to our imagination to be better, is likely, this practical reason tells us, to be a delusion. This doctrine is crystallized in sayings such as: "The grass is always greener in the other fellow's yard."

638 **Leben** Here in the pregnant sense: 'real life, life worth calling life,' which results only from exalted sentiments.

640 **sonst** 'formerly': prior to Faust's experience with the Earth Spirit.

643 **Glück auf Glück** 'one happiness after another.'

644 **die Sorge** This conception interested Goethe greatly and he has expressed himself about it in many places. Compare here Part II, lines 11 383 ff. — **gleich** = *sogleich.*

651 **nie : stets** The very fact that one might lose a thing which one greatly treasures, though one does not in fact lose it, causes one to worry about its possible loss and often even to imagine that one has lost it.

656 **Wand** Accusative. The *Fächer* are the shelves and compartments, or pigeonholes, into which are stuffed the *Urväter-Hausrat* of line 408 (the *Trödel* of line 658), which make the room seem oppressive to Faust.

666 **leicht : schwer** The day is contrasted with the dusk as light is contrasted with heavy. To a person who seeks the illumination of truth (the day), the obscurity of human understanding (dusk) is heavy, or difficult to bear. Goethe expressed the sentiments of lines 665–667 more directly in a *Gespräch* with the Jena Professor of History, Luden (1806), when he said of human life:

"... daß es zu allen Zeiten und in allen Ländern miserabel gewesen ist: die Menschen haben sich stets geängstigt und geplagt, sie haben sich und anderen das bißchen Leben sauer gemacht und die Schönheit der Welt und die Süßigkeit des Daseins weder zu achten noch zu genießen vermocht. Nur wenigen ist es bequem und erfreulich geworden."

It should be observed that at least two recent editors [Max Hecker, in the *Welt-Goethe-Ausgabe* (1932 and 1937) and Ernst Beutler (1939 and 1950)] have replaced *leichten* by *lichten*. They believe *leichten* to have been a printer's error for *lichten*, overlooked by everyone, including Goethe.

669 To think here of primitive electrostatic machines, as some do, is to charge the poet with a not too serious anachronism. The historical Faust was a personage of the sixteenth century. The electrostatic machine, with rotating disc and comblike collectors, was invented by Otto von Guericke (1602–1686) in the mid-seventeenth century. Goethe owned a large machine of this type. It is more probable, however, that the instruments here referred to were mechanical, rather than electric, for 'wheel, cogs, cylinder, bridle' are all terms of mechanics.

670 **Tor** The gateway to the mysteries of nature.

672–673 **Geheimnisvoll** An attribute of *Natur* 673. Faust says that the only avenue to the secret mysteries of Nature is that of revelation to the intellect or soul of an inspired man; that no mere plodding, methodical research will lead to the solution of these mysteries. The veil suggests the veiled statue of Isis, the Egyptian goddess, which stood in the temple at Sais, in Egypt. Schiller used this goddess as a symbol of truth in his ballad, *Das verschleierte Bild zu Sais* (1795).

678 **Rolle** Of paper; see 405. Because the lamp has burned dimly and with much smoke all these years, the roll of papers is becoming covered with soot.

682–683 **ererbt hast : besitzen** Many things which are inherited remain apart from one's own active interests. One may have such things, but unless one actively works with them, they are not one's very own. This *hast* may be taken independently of *ererbt*, and read:

'what you have, having inherited it from your forebears . . .' The sentiment is analogous to that of lines 11 574–11 576.

684–685 The reference here is not to antique furnishings, but to the things of the intellect. The mind can use at a given moment only the things which it creates at that moment. One can make use of the wisdom of the past only when one has won this wisdom for oneself. Then one's mind will produce it when confronted by the need of the moment, and thus it will be useful. — **nützt, nützen** instead of *benützen*, 'to make good use of.'

690 **einzige** = *einzigartige* 'unique,' hence 'very precious, highly treasured.'

692 **Kunst** Equivalent to *Menschenkunst.*

698 **Flutstrom** The intense emotional excitement under which Faust has been: the *Streben* of 697, the *Drang* of 631.

701 Faust, holding in his hands a phial of deadly poison, is contemplating suicide. Therefore the 'new day' is the life beyond death, where he hopes to find new shores, new lands to explore.

702 **Feuerwagen** The time is at dawn on Easter Sunday, and what Faust sees is the radiance of the rising sun. This he thinks of as a fiery chariot, such as that which was driven between Elijah and Elisha (II Kings 2.11) or such as Milton describes (PARADISE LOST VI, 748 ff.):

> "And the third sacred Morn began to shine,
> Dawning through Heav'n: forth rushed with whirlwind sound
> The Chariot of Paternal Deity,
> Flashing thick flames . . ."

705 Faust thinks of death as the avenue to new spheres of activity, uninhibited by the presence of the earthly *Stoff* of which he complained at 635, and thus 'pure.'

710 **Vermesse** A weak imperative form instead of the normal *vermiß*. Forms of this kind are not unusual in Goethe's verse. — **Pforten** The gates of death (Job 38.17).

712–713 Suicide is spoken of as a deed which will prove the dignity of man to be sufficient to stand in the exalted presence of God. The demonstration will show the power of man to defy the divine commandment which forbids man to kill (Deuteronomy 5.17).

714 **Höhle** Perhaps the cavern into which the souls of the departed go, the place where fancy condemns itself to its own torment. — In Dante's *Inferno* the punishments meted out represent allegorically the sins themselves, in accordance with the Wisdom of Solomon 11.17: ". . . wherewithal a man sinneth, by the same also shall he be punished." Faust attributes such ideas to the imagination. He does not expect to arrive in any such place; rather he expects to enter new spheres of higher activity.

716 **Durchgang** The passageway from this life to the next. To deter men from voluntarily attempting to go through this passage, the fires of hell burn brightly about its entrance. The penalty for suicide, according to Christian belief, is hell-fire. — **hinzustreben** Depends upon *Hier ist es Zeit* 712.

718 **diesem Schritt** Suicide, the drinking of the death-potion. — **zu entschließen** Depends upon *Hier ist es Zeit* 712.

719 Faust believes that he will pass through his death into new spheres of pure activity (705). But he recognizes the risk he runs: he knows that he may destroy himself completely.

720 **Schale** A costly goblet on which various groups of figures or scenes are engraved or embossed (726).

723 **Freudenfeste** A dative singular rather than the plural form which one might expect, since many such festivities are remembered; see 729.

725 **zugebracht** Supply *hatte.* — *zubringen* is used in the technical sense of proposing a toast while holding out the cup toward the person in whose honor the toast is given. At these banquets the person who proposed the toast and who then drank from the goblet was obligated (727) first to explain one of the scenes thereon in verses (as Keats did in his *Ode on a Grecian Urn*), and having done so, to drink the cup at a single draught.

736 **Morgen** Of the new day (701), which is also Easter Sunday morning, whose sun is now rising.

SD 737 **Chor** In the following lines Faust, in his study, hears the Easter morning service in a nearby church. This service is in the form of a cantata of Easter antiphons, with three choruses: the angels, the women with spices, and the eleven disciples. The songs they sing, however, are Goethe's own, and not the traditional Easter songs of the church.

738 **dem Sterblichen** Mortal man, who was caught in the toils of deadly, insidious, hereditary sin, is offered a means of release therefrom in the resurrection of Christ.

742 **Summen** The low-pitched reverberations of the sounds of the bells (SD 737). The bright *Ton* is that of the choral song which the angels sing.

747 **einst** Reference is to the dawn of the first day of the week after the crucifixion of Christ. No chorus of angels is described in the gospel narratives of this scene; but an angel did say to Mary Magdalene and the women who were with her: "He is not here; for he is risen, even as he said." (Matthew 28.6).

748 **Gewißheit** 'making certain' (a new covenant). The resurrection of Christ was to be the guaranty of the covenant which Jesus made with his disciples (John 14.3): "And if I go and prepare a place for you, I come again and will receive you unto myself, that where I am, there ye may be also."

SD 749 **Chor der Weiber** These are the women who came to visit the sepulchre of Christ and found it empty: Matthew 28.1, Mark 16.1, Luke 24.10, John 20.1.

749 **Spezereien** See Mark 16.1: "And when the Sabbath was past Mary Magdalene, and Mary the mother of James, and Salome, brought spices that they might come and anoint him." John 19.39: "And there came also Nicodemus . . . bringing a mixture of myrrh and aloes, about a hundred pounds. So they took the body of

Jesus, and bound it in linen cloths with the spices, as the custom of the Jews is to bury."

758 **der Liebende** Christ, who has withstood the test of mortal life. Human life is spoken of as a trial, a test, which is distressing but beneficial, since it provides training for the life after death, for those who pass the test.

763 **am Staube** 'earth-bound,' not *im Staube* 'in the dust.' 'Why do you seek me among the earth-bound? Proclaim your message among more easily persuaded (*weiche*) people.'

765 **Botschaft** The news of the resurrection of Christ.

771 **sonst** In earlier years, while the faith of his youth was still alive.

780 One rite of Spring, Easter Sunday, brings joy to many, as is shown in the next scene: *Vor dem Tor*. The 'free joy' is more fully set forth in lines 903–940.

787 **lebend Erhabene** In apposition to *der Begrabene*: 'he who in this life was exalted.'

789 **Werdelust** 'joy of becoming,' becoming again something which he has not recently been: the Creator, one with the Creator.

790 **schaffender Freude** Dative with *nah*. Christ is thought of as passing through a change from his mortal condition to that of the godhead, where he will have the joy of creating, and will be again one with God the Father and the Holy Ghost.

793 **die Seinen** = *uns* 794.

795–796 The apostles weep at the departure of Christ from their midst, even though this departure means happiness to Christ in Heaven.

799 **Banden** The bonds of earthly cares and the fear of death.

801–805 The weak participles are used absolutely, as would be the case if Goethe had written: "*ihr tätig ihn preisenden,*" 'you who praise him with your deeds, you who do all these things . . . to you the Master is near.' — In substance, the two great commandments of Christ to his disciples are here represented: (1) "This is my commandment, that ye love one another, even as I have loved you." John 15.12. (2) "Go ye into all the world and preach the gospel to the whole creation." Mark 16.15.

4. Vor dem Tor

Concerning the genesis of this scene there is some uncertainty, although it is clear that it got its present form in the period between 1797 and 1801. Concerning the function of the scene in the economy of the play there is no doubt. It forms the necessary contrast or relief in the long sequence of discourses in Faust's study (354–807), (1178–1529), (1530–2072). More importantly, it motivates the change in Faust's behavior. Held back from suicide by the return of memories of youthful religious fervor, Faust finds among the simple folk of the village the kind of credulity and faith of which he himself is no longer capable. His doubts and his yearning for truth amidst the error of the world return to him, and his mind goes back to thoughts of spirits, with whom he may ascend to fuller and brighter life. As he thinks of these spirits, a poodle appears, which presently reveals itself as indeed a spirit.

The scene is difficult theatrically. Proper effects can best be approximated by means of a revolving stage, since the action moves without stop from the crossroads just outside the town gate, to the nearby village, thence to an adjacent hill, and then back to town again. The characters are types rather than individuals, as the naming of the *personae loquentes* indicates; and much of the scene is operatic rather than dramatic. There are, finally, a few inconsistencies and contradictions which may be observed, but which are of no importance in the over-all understanding of the poem.

SD 808 **Vor dem Tor** The scene lies outside the wall of a small medieval fortified town.

809 **Jägerhaus** Goethe, as he wrote this scene, remembered pretty accurately a similar terrain near his native Frankfurt. But it is clear that he did not mean to permit his readers to recognize the place. This could be any university town in central Germany (Franconia or Thuringia). The forester's lodge was a favorite place to which to walk, because it usually was beautifully situated. One may think of benches and perhaps tables under the trees, where people might picnic.

810 **Mühle** Old mills were favorite dancing places because their floors were made very smooth by the constant dragging of sacks of grain and meal across them. The millers made capital of this asset by operating their properties as resorts on holidays.

811 **Wasserhof** Probably an inn beside a river.

814 **Burgdorf** Probably a village atop a hill; it seems to have an unsavory reputation.

818 **das Fell** We say in English: "I'll tan your hide!" German: "*Ich gerbe dir das Fell! Ich komme dir aufs Fell!*" 'I'll let you have it.' Hence this line means: 'Are you itching for a third tanning?' It appears that the Fourth Apprentice has already had a couple of unsuccessful encounters at *Burgdorf*.

SD 821 **Andre** The feminine form with natural gender, instead of *Andres* (*Dienstmädchen*) with grammatical gender. So also *Erste* instead of *Erstes*.

824 **Plan** A hardwood floor set up out of doors for dancing. This word, used in the sense of *Tanzplatz*, is Franconian, which indicates that the town is in Central Germany.

827 **sagt** Present tense. Lively interest in what one is reporting often induces a shift from a past to the present tense.

SD 828 **Schüler** Used instead of *Student*. This is a calculated adaptation of the language to the time of the action. When Goethe wrote his first Faust scenes he used *Student*, but in 1790 he changed all these forms to *Schüler*, which is the older term and which is still used in translating *vagans scholasticus, der fahrende Schüler*.

832 **mir** The dative indicates the person to whose advantage, or at any rate in accordance with whose wish, the action is done. See note to line 320.

842 **geniert** 'restrained by the fear of committing a social error.' The First Student prefers the laxer social code of the servant girls to the stricter etiquette of the middle-class young ladies.

846 **Burgemeister** A colloquial form, used instead of *Bürgermeister*. Although the word now has the effect of an archaic expression, it was not so felt in Goethe's time, but was a well-known word in the spoken, colloquial language.

852 **guten, schönen** Weak adjective forms, as is usual in the vocative case after the pronoun.

856 **leiern** The beggar has some kind of a mechanical music box which he operates by turning a crank. Probably it is a hurdy-gurdy (*Drehleier*), which has the general shape of a lute and the strings of which are made to vibrate by a rotating rosined wheel. Or it may be a barrel-organ (*Leierkasten*).

862 In the sixteenth and seventeenth centuries the Turks repeatedly disturbed European peace of mind. In 1529 they laid unsuccessful siege to Vienna, and thoroughly frightened everyone in Europe. In 1570 they drove the Venetians out of Cyprus. But from this time on their power declined, although they again laid siege to Vienna in 1683. The probable parties to the war here alluded to are Russia and Turkey, which were remote enough from this little German town to permit comfortable discussions of tactics and of the latest news by people of limited, philistine insight.

863 **Völker** is probably to be taken in its older sense, 'armies.'

871 **bleib's** = *bleibe es* 'may it remain' (optative).

872 **Das junge Blut** Equivalent to *der junge Mensch*, who may be either male or female; or *Blut* may be collective, referring to several young persons. The reference here is to the young *Bürgermädchen* of 832, who have apparently remained at the crossroads, waiting for escorts.

874 The girls evidently show their distaste for the old woman, who reacts thereto by saying first that they need not be so proud, second that they must not be offended, and that she will say no more.

875 The Old Woman seems to be something of a procuress.

876 **Agathe** The name of one of the *Bürgermädchen*; it has an "upper-class" flavor.

878 **Sankt Andreas' Nacht** The night of November 29–30. Popular superstition had it that if on this night a girl recited the proper verses and looked in the right kind of a crystal ball, sword, or mirror, she would see her future husband. The assistance of a fortune teller was deemed helpful.

881 **soldatenhaft** 'in soldier's uniform.'

883 **will** This verb does not say anything about the willingness of the future lover to meet the lady. It personifies the chance which stubbornly refuses to bring the two lovers together. Translate: 'But it seems I'm never to find him.'

892 **werben** 'We let the trumpet summon us, both for the joy and for the destruction of a soldier's life.'

893–894 The soldiers sing of two conquests which seem to them similar. Both bring pleasure to the victor and ruin to the vanquished.

905 **Hoffnungsglück** A neologism, like *Hoffnungsdunst, Hoffnungsfülle, Hoffnungsglut, Hoffnungsgrün;* as Jean Paul wrote: "Mancher Schnee ist geschmolzen, und wir sehen das Hoffnungsgrün des teuern Bodens." The word implies: 'The early plants of Spring, with their promise of happiness to come, are showing green in the valley.'

912 **Bildung und Streben** Things in nature are taking shape and beginning to grow.

914 **Revier** Since this is indeed a river-landscape, the word *Revier*, Italian *riviera*, perhaps still had its more literal meaning of 'a district along a river's bank.' Otherwise, the word may be taken to mean simply 'countryside.'

915 The sun, as the painter of this scene, is said to abhor white and to have used people in their bright Sunday clothes instead of flowers (which were not yet in bloom) to give color to the whole. — Goethe was an unusually acute observer of color and other phenomena of light. In the years from 1790 until his death these problems occupied him more continuously and more completely than any other of his interests. His FARBENLEHRE (1810) was a source of greater pride to Goethe than any of his poetic creations.

937 **schon** The strollers, Faust and Wagner, are approaching a country village some distance from the university city from which they have come.

952 **Linde** The village linden tree was the center of social functions in Spring and Summer.

954–955 **Juchhe, Juchheisa, Heisa** These are interjections, of long literary tradition, which connote noisy jubilation. They are roughly equivalent to our "Hurrah!" or "Whoopee!"

964 This line is part of the girl's remonstrance, spoken to the shepherd, as are also lines 973–975. — According to another view, these lines are spoken by the author of the song to the characters in it.

984 **Hochgelahrter** This form, rather than *Hochgelehrter,* is the form natural for the old peasant.

987 **bring' . . . zu** 'I present it to you with this toast.'

995 **doch** 'indeed, as everyone will testify.'

996 **bösen** The reference is to the evil days of the great plague.

998 In the Faust Chapbook, Faust's father is a peasant. Goethe makes him a physician, the predecessor and teacher of his son (as was the father of Paracelsus); see lines 676–677. The whole incident of the plague and Faust's part in it was introduced into the story by Goethe, to whom it was perhaps suggested by a somewhat similar incident reported in accounts of the life of Nostradamus, a contemporary of the sixteenth century historical Dr. Faustus.

1000 **gesetzt** Supply *hatte.*

1009–1010 Faust judiciously replies to the peasants in stereotyped language which they can understand. He realizes that his own philosophical doubts have no place in these circles.

SD 1010 **Wagnern** An inflected form of the name, no longer in use.

1014 **Vorteil** The advantage, as Wagner sees things, of being revered by these people.

1021 **das Venerabile** The Holy Host, the sacred wafer of the sacrament in its monstrance. When the Holy Host was carried through the streets, the people were expected to kneel as it was carried past them. This practice is still observed in those parts of Germany which are strongly Roman Catholic in their faith.

1034 **ein dunkler Ehrenmann** A man of honor who shunned the public eye, or an honest man of solitary habits.

1035 **Kreise** A property of a circle is that if one follows its line one arrives finally at the place from which one started. The obvious cyclical nature of some natural phenomena is here attributed to all life.

1037 **grillenhafter** Here 'capricious,' without steady, rational control.

1038 **Adepten** The technical title given to the most advanced practitioners of the art of alchemy.

1039 The alchemist's laboratory is called a kitchen because fire and heat (in ovens) were its basic means of effecting changes in materials. It was called 'black' because alchemy was a 'black art,' from the Latin name, *nigromantia*.

1042–1047 There seems to be no point in attempting to identify the technical jargon of these lines with passages in the works of alchemists, though this is to some extent possible. — The theory on which these men proceeded was that the elixir, the great panacea, would be produced, in the form of a bright-colored precipitate, by mixing two substances in a tepid medium and then treating the mixture in heated retorts. The fancy of the alchemists conceived this chemical union as a marriage, and the production of a new substance as a birth. So here the red suitor-lion (reddish mercuric oxide) is 'wed' with the white bride-lily (hydrochloric acid), and the offspring (the sublimate, a solid substance) is called the young queen, the sought-for panacea. Inasmuch as mercury was a favorite substance for these alchemistic experiments, it is easy to understand that many of the products of these black kitchens were indeed deadly poisons.

1053 **Gift** Here masculine, though usually it is neuter.

1056–1063 Wagner's attitude is by no means contemptible, as is sometimes alleged. But he is no genius, — just the hard-working, intelligent scholar, content to make progress in his field when he can, and not disposed to suicide if he can't. He will never reach the top bracket of his profession, though he does come close to it, as Faust's successor. He will not be in the lower brackets at all.

1064–1067 Faust's words are related to Wagner's argument but not a direct reply to it. He is back at the point of pessimism from which he started in line 354.

1073 The sun is earth's source of energy and as it moves along to shine upon other quarters of the earth it fosters new life and growth there. Faust wishes he might fly aloft (*Flügel*) to follow the sun, so that he might see more of the beauty of nature in the evening light. In his study (392–397) he had been moved by the sight of the moon to wish to fly aloft in its soft light. These impulses are symbols of a strong drive to escape, and suggest frustration.

1078 After the light of the setting sun leaves the valleys it still gilds the tops of the adjacent mountains. What follows is reported as if it were seen by Faust in his flight toward the light.

1079 **Silberbach** Some take this word as the name of some particular stream. Since Faust is imagining all mountain heights and every valley, it is more likely that this is a generic singular form, meaning every silvery brook. — From his great elevation Faust sees the brooks flowing into golden rivers far away.

1084 **Göttin** The sun, the symbol of the divine. For a moment it seems that the flight over the sea has deterred Faust. The sun appears about to sink from his sight after all.

1085 **der neue Trieb** The impulse to fly after the sun, to seek divine truth, regardless of the horizon, or sea, or land, always to fly towards the day, leaving night forever behind.

1100 **grillenhafte** Here equivalent to *wunderliche* 'strange, fantasy-filled.'

1110–1117 Mephistopheles described these two driving forces in lines 304–305. The one requires the satisfaction of the highest ambitions and desires of the individual among his fellows; the other, which Wagner is said not to know, requires the satisfaction of the highest aspirations of the human spirit for universal truth, transcending the world of the senses. Faust feels these two driving forces to be incompatible: the one clings with primitive passion to this earth, while the other seeks to rise to a new and richer life beyond this earth.

However, it must not be believed that Goethe here was thinking of anything so simple as a dichotomy between sensuous and intellectual impulses. There is, first of all, the basic fact that Faust has both of these driving forces, Wagner only one. It is not possible to say that Wagner has only sensuous impulses (944–948), and it will not do to identify his intellectual interests with the spiritual flights of Faust. Wagner says, in fact, that he has never had such an impulse (1101).

The drive which Faust has in common with Wagner is the thoroughly respectable, earth-centered drive which seeks the highest satisfactions and the greatest successes for the individual man among men (305).

The drive which Faust has and Wagner lacks is the drive toward universal knowledge and insight, the drive to be "like God." This drive rests upon Faust's capacity to imagine the indescribable, the reality behind phenomenal things and events, the achievement of the humanly impossible. It is the drive of the genius and it is frustrated by the earth-bound nature of man. It reveals itself in the desire to fly, which Faust several times feels: it puts the cup of poison into his hand (735), that he may shake off this burden of his earthly nature, and it is frustrated then by the symbol of the most celebrated case of *caritas*, *Menschenliebe*. See also the *Chorus mysticus* (lines 12 104–12 111) of Part II. In the present passage, this drive toward the humanly impossible is symbolized by the urge to fly *zu den Gefilden hoher Ahnen*, the abodes of great departed spirits, who have achieved some insight or knowledge denied to their more average fellow mortals.

1118 **Geister** Not to be identified with the great departed spirits, the exalted forebears of line 1117. These are the intermediary, elemental spirits who intervene in the affairs of men with magic carpets, magic cloaks, and the like. The sphere beneath the cavity of the sky was believed to be ruled over by the moon. This sphere was looked upon as the abode of these elemental spirits. Faust reverts to his hope that such spirits might transport him out of this world into the higher realm to which he again aspires, or that they might at any rate provide him an escape from his present earthly limitations. — The Faust of the legend and Chapbook made frequent use of a magic cloak (1122).

1120 **steiget** The two parts of this sentence do not fit the normal pattern. *gibt es* 'if there are,' would usually be followed by a third person appeal, 'then let them descend.' Instead, we have the direct, second person, imperative addressed to these spirits. This is another case of anacoluthon, used by Goethe to indicate that Faust's excitement is rising; see note to line 542.

1125 **nicht feil** To be taken with both *um die köstlichsten Gewänder* and *um einen Königsmantel.* This is a trope called "apo koinou."

1126–1127 Wagner deprecates Faust's impulse to invoke these elemental spirits. Everyone, he reminds Faust, knows the evil spirits who on the slightest hint bring biting winds with sleet and hail from the north, drought from the east, scorching heat from the south, and deluging downpours from the west. In western and central Europe, wet weather is often accompanied by west winds, bringing moist air from the Atlantic; east winds, from the Eurasian landmass, often bring dry air. — Wagner has no insight into Faust's purpose in summoning a spirit to transport him to another world, but thinks only of the numerous evil spirits which plague mankind.

1140 Take *sich* with *stellen* and read: *sie stellen sich, als ob sie vom Himmel gesandt wären.*

1141 **englisch** 'like angels,' not 'like Englishmen.'

1147 **Saat und Stoppel** A field in which the fresh young grain has begun to show green amidst the stubble of the former season's crop.

1150 **Pudel** A French poodle, with dense curly hair tightly crimped.

1154 **Feuerstrudel** Faust, who is sensitive to spirit manifestations, perceives the phosphorescence left in the air behind the circling poodle. In the path taken by the dog he sees a figure, drawn according to the rules of magic, intended to involve the two men.

1167 **pudelnärrisch** *Pudel* is used as an intensive prefix in words like *pudelnackt* 'stark naked,' *pudelnaß,* 'wet as a drowned rat.' So here, with a Wagnerian pun, it may mean 'very droll, very amusing,' or simply 'as amusing as a trained poodle.'

1177 Wagner guesses that the poodle has been well trained by a group of students. The form *Skolar* here, and *Skolast* in line 1324, are medieval Latin forms characteristic of the learned speech of the sixteenth and seventeenth centuries.

5. Studierzimmer (I)

This is the first of two scenes called *Studierzimmer*. The room is the *gotisches Zimmer* of the scene *Nacht* (354–807), and the action follows immediately after that of the scene *Vor dem Tor*.

The function of the scene is to introduce Mephistopheles into the life of Faust, so that the attempt to lead this servant of God (299) away from his spiritual heritage (324–329) may begin.

The germ of the idea which leads to the compact between Faust and Mephistopheles is put into Faust's mind in this scene (1414), but the actual agreement and with it the initial impulse to the dramatic action of this conflict between Faust and Mephistopheles is left to the second *Studierzimmer* scene.

1180–1181 The subject of *weckt* is *eine tiefe Nacht* (1179), but the connection between the two clauses is not expressed. The night is covering the fields and meadows; and, as it does so, it arouses the better soul of the human observer. — **mit ahnungsvollem, heil'gem Grauen** 'with awed and sacred dread.'

1184–1185 With the coming of night we see the transition from the active life of the preceding scene to the contemplative mood of Faust as he sits down in his study. His thoughts turn to the love of his fellow men and the love of God.

1187 Faust will discover later (1395) why the poodle is sniffing at the threshold.

1197 **sich . . . kennt** This is the heart of a philosopher. Socrates said: 'Know thyself!' and regarded this imperative as the sum of all philosophy.

1198–1201 The feeling is that of deeply religious contemplation and reflects the thought of Spinoza, for whom the highest good was the *amor intellectualis Dei*, man's knowledge and love of God: reason is the instrument, hope the support, and the love of God the motive power of philosophy. — **Vernunft** (1198) may be understood to mean the intellectual power of arriving at truth by reflection, without the assistance of empirical proof.

1200–1201 **Bächen . . . Quelle** There is a progression here. From the stream of life one longs to move toward the source, upstream into the feeder brooks, indeed into the very springs which feed these feeder brooks. The phrase *des Lebens Bächen* is not Biblical, but was widely used by the religious poets of Goethe's day. The phrase *des Lebens Quelle* is Biblical in origin. Both phrases were favorites with the mystic and pietist poets of the seventeenth and eighteenth centuries. Hence there is some reason to believe that the phrases here refer to the revelations of truth in the Bible.

1204 **will** This verb does not attribute volition to the animal noise which is its subject. *will nicht passen* means no more than 'just isn't suited to.'

1212 **der Strom** The feeling of satisfaction with which he has returned from his afternoon walk, and which welled up from his heart as a stream wells up from a spring. This metaphor continues that of *des Lebens Bächen, des Lebens Quelle* in lines 1200–1201.

1215 **dieser Mangel** The lack of the spontaneous flow of the feeling of satisfaction. This can be made up for by turning to divine revelation as this is found in the Bible.

1220 **Grundtext** The theologian turns to the Greek text of the New Testament. What troubles Faust is the meaning of "logos" in the first verse of the first chapter of the Gospel of John.

1237 **Tat** Faust's reasoning has brought him back to the position of the Old Testament, where we read (Genesis 1.1): "In the beginning God *created* the heavens and the earth."

1238 The dog, who has shown signs of distress each time God was mentioned or implied, is thrown into paroxysms of protest by this translation of the Biblical text.

1247 'What's this I see?'

1257 **halbe** Not a full-fledged demon, direct from hell, but some sort of witch or wizard or semi-infernal creature.

1258 **Salomonis Schlüssel** The *Clavicula Salomonis,* a conjurer's book of spells and incantations for the holding, evoking, or exorcising of spirits. This book was widely circulated in the sixteenth, seventeenth, and eighteenth centuries.

SD 1259 **Geister** Subordinate spirits, rallying to the aid of their captive master. They do not enter the study, lest they be trapped as he has been. At line 1447 they sing the song which lulls Faust to sleep and allows Mephistopheles to depart. Faust appears not to hear what these spirits say (1259–1270).

1262 **Höllenluchs** = Mephistopheles. There is irony in this designation: the lynx is the symbol of keenness of vision; yet Mephistopheles is trapped because he failed to see clearly the form of a pentagram on the threshold.

1272 **Spruch der Viere** Against the four spirits of the four elements of Paracelsus, designed to force each to appear in its proper form, revealing its true nature. Faust now reads, or recites, from the conjurer's book (1258).

1273–1276 **Salamander** Fire, because this animal is supposed not to be harmed by fire. It is conjured to glow, thus revealing its nature. — **Undene** Water, a generic name for water nymphs (also *Undinen* 10 712). This spirit is to show its true nature by swimming. — **Sylphe** Air, since the sylphs, according to Paracelsus, dwell in the air, either invisible to man, or glowing like meteors. This one is bidden to vanish (into the air). — **Kobold** Earth. The earth spirits are either kindly or inimical to man, as the mood strikes them. They are *Kobolde, Wichtelmännchen, Pygmäen, Gnomen,* or *Incubi.* One of the latter is called upon in line 1290. This one is told to show its true nature by working (1276).

1291 **Tritt hervor** The imperative is addressed to whichever one of the four spirits may be hiding within the poodle.

1300 **Zeichen** The symbol of Christ. This is a conjurer's diagram in Faust's book, perhaps a picture of a crucifix, perhaps a monogram of the letters J.N.R.J. representing the sign set by Pilate at the head of Christ's cross (John 19.19). These initials come from the Latin text: *Jesus Nazarenus Rex Judaeorum* 'Jesus of Nazareth, King of the Jews.'

1302 **die schwarzen Scharen** The black hosts of Hell.

1305 **ihn** By synecdoche, the name of Christ, who is spoken of as being never born, never described, omnipresent, and wickedly transfixed (see John 19.34).

1319 **Licht** A symbol of the Trinity, possibly an equilateral triangle with the flaming eye of God in the center. — **dreimal glühend** Because it derives light from a threefold source, the Trinity.

1326 **machen** 'made.' Since this verb is here treated as an auxiliary, synonymous with *lassen,* it is put in the infinitive form, as *lassen* would be.

1328 An allusion to line 1226.

1330 **Tiefe** Accusative, the goal which Faust's spirit strives to reach. — This is an ironical reference to Faust's efforts to attain to an understanding of the nature of things by turning away from the world of appearance (*Schein*).

1331 **Herrn** Plural; spirits, who may and sometimes do assume human form as this one has done.

1334 **Fliegengott** This is a translation of "Beelzebub." — **Verderber** is a translation of Greek "Apollyon," Hebrew "Abaddon," of Revelation 9.11. In Exodus 12.23 the Destroyer is spoken of as a spirit whom Jehovah controls. Probably the same spirit is referred to in Job 15.21 and I Corinthians 10.10. — **Lügner** John 8.44 refers to the Devil as a liar. — There is no evidence to show just what Goethe intended by the two words *Verderber* and *Lügner*. The most likely guess is that he used the two words as designations of evil spirits.

1335–1378 Mephistopheles' problem now is to work his way into the good graces of Faust. He endeavors to awaken Faust's interest in dealing with him, first by posing riddles as to his identity. He begins by describing himself (1335–1336) as a devil in the sense of the optimistic philosophy, let us say, of Leibnitz. Then he describes himself (1338) as the spirit of negation in the sense of an active pessimism. Then he depicts himself (1349–1354) as the son of Chaos and the opponent of order, in the sense of a dualistic philosophy. Finally, by way of reducing himself to Faust's level, and even exciting some measure of sympathy in the heart of one also foiled and frustrated, Mephistopheles (1362–1378) tells of the futility of his efforts.

The first proposition (1335–1336) implies that there are two forces: the force of evil, of which Mephistopheles says he is a part, and the opposition to this force, presumably the force of good. It further implies that out of the conflict between these two forces only good results. This is not exactly the same thing as was said in lines 342–343, but both statements are compatible with Leibnitz' optimistic doctrine that ours is the best possible world.

1338 In the Prologue in Heaven, God refers to Mephistopheles as *one* of the spirits of negation (338), the crafty knave. Here, Mephistopheles says he is *the* spirit of negation. Here the two principles of good and evil are thought of as the force of affirmation and the force of negation, and these are then identified with creation and destruction, respectively. The pessimistic judgment expressed by Mephistopheles is designed to appeal to the pessimistic Faust. Mephistopheles is always primarily concerned with the effect of his words on others, never with the truth as truth.

1347 **Wenn** = *während*, or perhaps *wenn auch* 'although.' — **die kleine Narrenwelt** Mephistopheles parodies the phrase: *Der Mensch — die kleine Welt*, in which the view is expressed that each man's spirit is a microcosm, a living mirror of the macrocosm, or universe. This microcosm, or *kleine Welt*, as Mephistopheles sees it, is a 'silly microcosm.'

1350–1358 The doctrine that a dark chaos was the source, by separation, of fire, and hence of light, was taught by Paracelsus. — The argument of these lines is that light is effective only as a property of bodies and hence has no more permanence than they.

Mephistopheles says that he is a part of the force of darkness and, as such, engaged in a conflict with the force of light. This force of light, however, is able to operate only through 'bodies.' Mephistopheles hopes that, when all bodies are destroyed, chaos will be restored (1358).

1359–1361 Faust scorns Mephistopheles' duties of allegiance to the cause of destruction — *würd'gen* is to be taken as ironical. He taunts this evil spirit with the derogatory slur that Mephistopheles can do nothing against the created universe on a major scale, or wholesale, and is therefore obliged to operate only on the individual item — at retail, so to speak — by attacking a single *Körper*. Mephistopheles concedes (1362–1378) that his job seems hopeless at times.

1364 **Etwas** The earth, a 'something' created by the force of affirmation. The *Nichts*, to which this *Etwas* is opposed, is Chaos, — the non-corporeal, non-organic, formless state in which no thing can exist. — **diese plumpe Welt** suggests woodcuts of the seventeenth century, in which the terrestrial globe is represented as a being with pudgy little legs, and in which reference is made to the "crooked and tortuous ways of the world."

1369 **Zeug** Mephistopheles refers to the amazing pertinacity of living species, with their fantastic capacities for the reproduction of their kind.

1374–1378 In the philosophy of Paracelsus there were four elements (see line 1272), one of which, fire, Mephistopheles claims as his own. The four elements, fire, water, air, and earth, were recognized by ancient philosophers (Empedocles, Aristotle) long before Paracelsus. — Mephistopheles claims fire as his own element, since it is the one which destroys all forms of organic life. Yet no life can exist without some heat.

1376 The four qualities of the four elements: air = warmth + moistness; water = cold + moistness; fire = warmth + dryness; earth = cold + dryness.

1381 **kalte Teufelsfaust** 'Cold,' because it is the fist of death, of negation. This is a good example of the aesthetic value of the adjective. Despite Mephistopheles' immediately foregoing assertion that fire is his peculiar element, the poet's choice of attribute is 'cold' rather than 'hot,' because of the association of 'cold' with death, and of 'warm' or 'hot' with life.

1383 **suche** Optative, not imperative. — Faust is not interested in Mephistopheles' account of his failures. If he is to listen to this spirit, it will have to offer something more than pessimistic talk.

1386 At this point we have another of the joints in the composition of the poem. Mephistopheles makes the unmotivated assumption that there will be other interviews between himself and Faust, and the poet permits him to excuse himself now without telling us why he does so. To be sure, we can find a reason in the situation: It is clear that Mephistopheles has maneuvered Faust into a positive, superior frame of mind (1379–1384) and that it would be disadvantageous to try to deal further with him while he is in this mood. In the Chapbook, the contract between Faust and Mephistopheles is signed after the third "disputation" between the two parties.

1395 **Drudenfuß** The five-pointed star was a symbol credited with the power to keep out evil spirits. This one had failed to keep out Mephistopheles, because it had been imperfectly drawn. — The figure occurs on old Greek coins, was used as a symbol of perfection, or of the universe, by the Pythagoreans and others.

1406 **hereingesprungen** Supply *ist.* See 1187, where the poodle becomes aware of his predicament after he has entered.

1418 **das** The business of arranging a compact between a man and the Devil is not a simple business and requires discussion.

1439 **Geister** These spirits begin to sing now at their master's command. Faust sinks into a trance during which he will see what the spirits suggest in their song.

1441 **leeres** Devoid of tangible, physical effect upon the spectator. These images, which are *nicht leer,* not only appeal to the imagination, they also stimulate the senses, the sense of smell, the sense of taste, so that in the end Faust is enraptured.

1448 **Wölbungen** In the imagination of the sleeping Faust the Gothic arches of the walls and ceiling of the study are to melt away, revealing the sky — at first clouded, then clearing to reveal the stars and the entrancing spectacle of angels hovering and bending over the sleeper as he floats past. The singing spirits give orders (imperative *schwindet*) to the Gothic walls, and more politely request, even suggest, the changes in the heavenly scene (optative *schaue,* potential *wären zerronnen*). Thereafter they narrate (present indicative).

1461 **Neigung** With longing the sleeper follows the angels through the sky, and the fluttering ribbons of angelic robes spread out over the landscape as he floats past the rows of bowers, each with its pair of embracing lovers. These bowers are covered with heavily laden vines, the grapes of which fall into wine presses, from which brooks of bubbling wine, trickling through beds of jewels, flow into the valley, where they become lakes at the feet of the hills.

1482–1483 **Genügen grünender Hügel** A violent metaphor which has been variously understood, according to the meaning attributed to *Genügen.* Some take this to mean 'sufficiency,' others take it to mean 'satisfaction.' Probably the orthodox solution is that which understands *Genügen* to refer to the feelings of the observer and takes the whole to mean: 'at the feet of pleasant hills turning green with spring.' Others take *Genügen* to be the satisfaction of the hills which are washed by the waves of these lakes of wine: 'spread themselves into lakes to the quiet satisfaction of the newly green hills.'

1484 **das Geflügel** The birds sip this flowing wine and fly jubilantly toward the sun and the bright isles of the blest, toward which the eyes of the dreamer turn. There he hears people far away joyously shouting and dancing all over the rustic scene. Some even hover in the air, as the scene fades into the more remote distance of those stars which provide them life, love, and protection, and the dreamer drops into a deeper slumber.

1516 Mephistopheles calls himself Lord of rats and mice and various other vermin; see also lines 6592 ff. The Devil is associated with pestiferous, ugly, or uncanny animals, particularly with those of nocturnal habits.

1520 The pentagram which guards the threshold has to be opened by cutting through one of the points on the room side of the figure. By applying oil to the appropriate portion of the lines Mephistopheles induces the rat to gnaw the figure so that a break will release him. The most likely way in which Mephistopheles could get the oil he uses is to dip his finger into the oil of Faust's study lamp.

1525 **Fauste** A vocative, and in the Latin form, as is appropriate in university conversations and as is usual in the chapbook versions of the story.

1526 **abermals** The first disappointment was his encounter with the Earth Spirit.

1527 **der geisterreiche Drang** The throng of spirits which he has just seen in the vision induced by the song.

1528 **daß** 'so that,' in such a way that he must conclude that all this has been a dream and that nothing has really happened except that the poodle has escaped from his study.

6. Studierzimmer (ii)

The latter part of this scene (from line 1770 onward) was incorporated into the Fragment of 1790. The first part was written around 1800, and first printed in 1808. Old and new materials have been fused into the present form of the scene and the process has left a number of inconsistencies.

The primary reason for separating this scene from the preceding scene in the study is the fact that for some time Goethe planned to write a *Disputation*, or Ph.D. Examination scene, in which Faust and Mephistopheles were to match wits. It was to have come between the two *Studierzimmer* scenes and is alluded to indirectly in line 1712. In the first Study scene Mephistopheles appears as a wandering scholar (1324); here he appears as a young nobleman.

The departure of Mephistopheles from the preceding scene has only the inner motivation — too subtle for theatrical purposes — that Mephistopheles has maneuvered Faust into a proud, positive frame of mind and can make no further progress in his negotiations with him until this attitude is destroyed. The dramatic reason for separating the two *Studierzimmer* scenes, as the text now stands, is therefore the need to throw Faust into a state of depression.

There is no indication of the length of time which may be supposed to have elapsed between Mephistopheles' escape from the study (1525) and his return at line 1530. His first words to Faust (1533–1543) seem to imply intervening meetings between the two with some talk of a "deal" or agreement and some talk about what 'life,' as Mephistopheles sees it, might do for Faust. Yet this is only an implication, not a clearly defined fact of motivation.

The discussion between Mephistopheles and the new student is one of the oldest parts of the Faust play. Yet it is episodic and without external relation to the action of the play. It is an interlude of acid satire directed at the less likable aspects of university life in Goethe's own day. It is internally related to the Faust problem insofar as the student is analogous to Faust in his natural make-up, a potential Faust about to begin his career.

The major dramatic function of the second *Studierzimmer* scene is to bring about the conclusion of the pact between Faust and Mephistopheles, which sets the terms of this contest for the soul of Faust and establishes the framework of motives for the subsequent adventures of the two great adversaries.

1530 **wieder** Faust is in a somewhat petulant mood as a result of having been disturbed by someone in some way or ways not indicated. Usually he is thought of as sitting at his desk, deep in thought.

1531 Mephistopheles makes Faust repeat his invitation to come in. He is pleased to find Faust not unwilling to join in his hocus-pocus.

1534 **Grillen** 'cares, melancholy thoughts.' Mephistopheles knows that Faust is depressed. How he knows this can be guessed from lines 1581–1582, but not answered on the basis of the current text. Probably he refers to Faust's whole way of life as 'melancholy.' At any rate his first problem as he sees it is to get Faust out of the environment of his discontent. See Introduction pp. 74–75.

1535 **Junker** A cavalier in court dress of Spain. This was a favorite form of incarnation attributed to Satan. In this guise he had ready entrée into the best social circles.

1541 Faust is urged to put aside his professor's garb and with it his professor's way of life and to take on the raiment and the way of life of a gay cavalier.

1549 **Entbehren** There are two points of view open to an individual who finds the fulfilment of a wish impossible. He may revolt against the forces which, as he sees it, deprive him of this thing he desires; or he may renounce the desire. — Faust at this point is on the verge of revolt.

1566 The God within him, who rules his entire being, is unable to change anything outside him. His God is an entirely subjective experience.

1573 **er** = *der Tod.*

1577 **des hohen Geistes** Of the Earth Spirit, lines 482–513.

1580 A direct reference to the events described in lines 737–784.

1583–1587 **Wenn . . . so** 'If . . . still.' The meaning is, substantially: 'Granted that I was deluded, still I curse . . .' — **Gewühle** The tumult of his emotions (354–736).

1584 The form *süß* is ambiguous. Either this is an adjective with the omission of case ending from the first of two or more correlative attributes = *ein süßer, bekannter Ton,* or the form is an adverb, limiting *bekannter.* Either this is a 'sweet (and) well-known tone' or it is a 'sweetly well-known tone.' One can decide such questions only on the basis of the relative appropriateness of the two possible meanings. The reference here is to the Easter music of lines 737–807.

1587–1606 The following tirade is well organized. Faust curses and reviles the physical body which limits the soul, man's overweening pride of intellect, the blinding effect of phenomena which obscure ideas, the illusory hopes of fame, the transitory world of possessions with which man surrounds himself, the solace of wine, the ecstasy of love, and, finally, the qualities which make this life possible to live: hope, faith, and patience to endure. As he reaches the conclusion of this bitter denunciation of things as they are, Faust has reached the pinnacle of his confusion.

1588 **Lock- und Gaukelwerk** Hendiadys for *lockendes Gaukelwerk* 'alluring jugglery.' Similarly, 1590 *Blend- und Schmeichelkräften* for *blendenden Schmeichelkräften* 'deluding powers of flattering persuasion.'

1589 Among the religious poets of the seventeenth and eighteenth centuries, *Trauerhöhle* was a standard metaphor for "body," just as *Jammertal* and *Tränental* were metaphors for "earth." This, therefore, is the body in which Faust's soul is confined.

1591 **Verflucht** Supply *sei.* — **voraus** 'first and foremost.' Man's confidence in the power of the intellect to solve the world's problems appears to Faust to be the first source of evil.

1593 The world of phenomena which occupies our senses blinds us to the reality which transcends that world.

1607 These spirits do two things: (1) they lament the fact that Faust by his renunciation of patience, faith, and hope has destroyed beyond repair the foundations upon which the beauty of this world once rested; (2) they exhort Faust to build with a clear head a more stately world in his own heart, a new world in which he can start on a new course in life. That is, these spirits appeal to Faust's will. Mephistopheles 1627–1630 claims that these voices are those of his own minions, presumably the same spirits who sang Faust to sleep (1447–1505). Some critics believe Mephistopheles; others think that, with his usual crafty guile, he is turning to his own uses the utterances of spirits which might represent Faust's guardian genius, or his better self. The poet's intention is by no means clear.

1616 **die Schöne** = *die Schönheit.* See note to line 345.

1617 These spirits speak of Faust as a 'demigod' (1612), and as a 'mighty one among the sons of earth.' This appears to mark them as earth-spirits, in a friendly rather than an inimical mood.

1619 **prächtiger** Comparative adverb with *baue*, or a predicate adjective correlative with *sie*.

1633 **Säfte** 'humors,' vital juices. — In medieval physiology four fluids were conceived as entering into the constitution of the body and determining by their relative proportions a person's health and temperament. Abundance of blood conduced to sanguine temperament, predominance of phlegm made a man phlegmatic, too much yellow bile made a man choleric, too much black bile made him melancholy.

1635–1638 Faust is urged to put aside his solitary grief and to seek the company of other men. Even the least distinguished of such associations will, he is assured, restore his sense of human values. Mephistopheles' use of *spielen* is an allusion to the "joy of grief," which was a topic of interest in Goethe's Weimar. Literary reflexes of the idea can be seen in Karl Philipp Moritz' novel ANTON REISER (1785 ff.). — The vulture (1636) is an allusion to the story of Prometheus.

1641 Mephistopheles' description of himself here as a lesser familiar spirit, rather than as Satan himself, accords with the tradition of the chapbook Faust story rather than with Goethe's later conception of his character.

1652 **um Gottes willen** 'as a matter of charity, without recompense.' The choice of this form of expression produces a secondary antithesis, or an antithetical overtone, because of the word *Teufel* in 1651.

1656–1659 The contrast between this world and the next is in the Christian tradition. Faust immediately says that the life after death (1660) does not interest him. His joys arise in *this* life, his sufferings are lighted by the sun he knows. Only if this world were to be destroyed would he perhaps be interested in another. This does not imply skepticism concerning the reality of the world beyond.

1665 **kann** 'If I find it possible sometime to give up these joys and sufferings, then . . .'

1669 **jenen Sphären** This is *das Drüben* of 1660. Faust has said that only if this world is destroyed or if sometime he finds it possible to renounce this world will he concern himself about another. He does not now wish to listen to a discussion of the putative conditions in that other world, whether it knows emotions or differences of degree or rank, whether it contains a Heaven and a Hell.

1672 **in diesen Tagen** Probably implies 'right away,' 'in the immediate future'; possibly it implies 'in the days you live on earth.'

1677 **gefaßt** 'understood.' *fassen* echoes *erfassen* of 325. What the Lord called (328) 'the obscure striving of a good man,' Faust calls 'the lofty striving of a human spirit.'

1678 Food which does not satisfy, red gold which melts away like quicksilver, a game one cannot win, love which is not true, honor which is not lasting — Faust concedes (*doch* = 'indeed') that Mephistopheles can produce these things. But they cannot afford satisfaction to a striving human spirit. They are as unsatisfactory as fruit which rots before it can be picked or as trees which daily burst into leaf, but never get beyond that stage. After Faust has enjoyed some of the things Mephistopheles can provide, he repeats with greater definiteness the thought which underlies these lines (3240–3246): the conviction that nothing perfect is accessible to man. Hence nothing which Mephistopheles could give him would satisfy Faust's striving for the perfect realization of his powers.

1688 Mephistopheles, as Faust has said, fails to understand that anyone could regard these sensual satisfactions with contempt. He knows that their enjoyment is exhausting and he seeks to suggest, as the best thing he can offer, the luxurious indolent repose of idle 'retirement' as an ultimate delight. This is the one thing Faust is sure he will never wish to enjoy.

1698 **die Wette** Faust wagers his life that Mephistopheles cannot persuade him to give up his striving. One of the essential qualities of the human spirit is its drive to higher things, its aspiration toward perfection. Faust knows that if this drive is lost, all is lost. Faust's wager is by no means identical with the bargain proposed by Mephistopheles (1656–1659), although if Faust loses, he expects to become Mephistopheles' servant (1710–1711). — When Faust says "Die Wette biet' ich . . .," he holds out his right hand toward Mephistopheles, who, with the interjection "Topp!" claps his own right hand into that of Faust. Thereupon Faust claps his left hand upon the two right hands thus joined, with the words: "Und Schlag auf Schlag!" which represent an unusually strong confirmation of the bargain thus sealed.

1699 The agreement here made is a contract pursuant to the wager. Mephistopheles is bound to serve Faust until such time as Faust concedes his wager to be lost. If that time comes, then Faust is bound to be the captive of Mephistopheles. The form of Faust's admission of defeat is to be the expression of satisfaction with a condition which he would wish to have continue (see line 11 582). It is quite possible for Faust to enjoy the services of Mephistopheles without surrendering to him.

1705 **Uhr . . . Zeiger** Various explanations of the falling of the pointer have been suggested. If the *Zeiger* is part of the *Uhr* here mentioned, it would seem likely that the clock in question was a water clock. These clocks had a single pointer which rose along a scale, usually for a period of twenty-four hours. At the end of this rise, the mechanism dropped the hand to the bottom of the scale and the rise began again. If at any time the lifting pressure of the water in the clock failed, the pointer at once fell back to zero.

1707 **wir** Mephistopheles, the party of the first part in the contract.

1710 **wie ich beharre** 'as I am living now,' or 'no matter how persistently I strive,' or 'as soon as I cease to strive.' The interpretation hinges on the meaning assigned to *beharre:* 'persist' or 'stagnate.' *beharren* usually means 'to persist.' The meaning 'to stagnate,' although not documented elsewhere, is required for the usual interpretation of this passage. — In the word *Knecht* some critics see an ironical echo of line 299.

1712 **Doktorschmaus** The doctoral banquet is the normal sequel to the successful passing of the final oral examination for the doctor's degree. Mephistopheles knows somehow (1582) that one is scheduled for this evening. — We know that Goethe once planned to include a doctoral examination scene in his FAUST. He subsequently gave up that idea, and aside from this reference we have only a draft of his plans plus a small fragment of the planned disputation.

1714 **um Lebens oder Sterbens willen** 'just in case something should happen to you.' A formula used to ask for a written contract without the discourteous implication that the other person's oral word alone was not enough.

1718 The contract entered into is to be binding throughout Faust's entire life. He regards his oral promise as adequate. But the thought of this kind of permanence suggests the basic impermanence of a world in which all things flow (Heraclitus); see lines 1720–1721.

1722–1725 **Wahn** The curious notion of fidelity to one's pledged word. This fidelity is the basis of all social peace and it is a source of great satisfaction to know that one has always kept faith.

1726–1729 These lines reflect the experience that a written and sealed contract very often is the cause of much distress, since the written word loses the benefit of the full level of presupposition which goes with the spoken word. It becomes rigid, or dead, and thus the instrument of parchment, with wax seal, rather than the will of the contracting parties, dominates the execution of the provisions set down.

1731 Faust has no fear of such a contract. He offers a document, engraved with a stylus in bronze, cut with a chisel in marble, or inscribed with a pen upon parchment or paper. He seems to be just a bit violent in his contempt as he makes this offer; see Mephistopheles' reaction, lines 1734–1735.

1737 **Blut** The use of blood of contracting parties to bind a serious bargain is attested as far back as records go. This feature is a part of the Faust story in all the forms known to us before Goethe.

1739 **Fratze** 'If this will satisfy you completely, then I will not balk at such tomfoolery.' Faust, a scholar and a man of reason, regards this use of blood to bind a contract as nonsense. Mephistopheles insists upon the use of blood, because he knows the strength of popular belief in the efficacy of a signature in blood, and he expects this popular superstition to help constrain Faust to abide by the terms of his contract. — Goethe here follows the tradition of the Faustbuch.

1741 **Bündnis** Faust has bound himself (1701) to surrender to Mephistopheles if he ever reaches the point where he is willing to cease striving because he has become satisfied. Evidently he could not resist Mephistopheles' authority, if he ever became subject to it by the terms of this contract. When he accepts Faust's wager (1698), Mephistopheles binds himself to serve Faust (1704) until he can persuade Faust to give up his striving. The contract is not that proposed by Mephistopheles in lines 1656–1659.

1744 Here there is an abrupt transition from the Faust whose character Goethe depicts in the completed poem to the Faust of the old legend and of the URFAUST. Faust says here that his aspiration to associate with the major world-spirits overreached his capacities (compare line 500) and that he is at best capable of converse only with lesser spirits, with whom Mephistopheles has identified himself (1641). The Earth Spirit had scorned him (512–513): he confronts a blank wall in his quest for nature's secrets. He has lost the directing line for his thinking and is sick of his studies.

1750 The difference between Faust's action here and his decision to drink the poison cup (735–736) so that he might escape to another sphere of activity can be attributed to the fact that Faust now has at his disposal the arts of Mephistopheles. Since in the past his contemplative life has brought him no adequate reward, he will now turn to the active life. From the uses of reason he will turn to the uses of the senses. He invites Mephistopheles to produce his full program of miracles, in their inscrutable magic form. He will not try to penetrate their outward guise to learn their inner reality, but will allow them free play on his senses. The point at which the older conception of Faust fuses with the newer and final conception is the *purpose* which is attributed to this attitude of Faust. Originally, Faust's major purpose was escape. Now, he desires most of all to experience to the full the joys and sorrows of the human heart.

1758 **miteinander wechseln, wie es kann** There are two problems here: what is the antecedent of *es;* what dependent infinitive is to be supplied with *kann?* We should expect either (1) *Da mögen denn Schmerz und Genuß, Gelingen und Verdruß miteinander wechseln, wie sie können;* or (2) *Da mag denn Schmerz und Genuß, Gelingen und Verdruß eins mit dem andern wechseln, wie es kann.*

Probably what is actually in the text is to be regarded as a telescoping of these two constructions. In that case, the implied dependent infinitive is *wechseln:* 'Let the pleasant and the painful alternate to the limits of the possible' or 'as may well be possible.' — If *es* refers to *das Wechseln* (suggested in the verb *wechseln*), then the missing infinitive should be something like *geschehen, vorkommen, sein.* — In either case, we should expect *wie es nur kann* 'as much as it can' or *wie es wohl kann* 'as it quite possibly may.' Perhaps the occurrence of *nur* in line 1759 led Goethe to omit it here.

1764 **mir** 'I tell you.' See note to line 320.

1766 **dem schmerzlichsten Genuß** Like *verliebtem Haß, erquickendem Verdruß*, an oxymoron, a figure of speech which brings together two apparently contradictory notions in order to challenge the reader to reconcile them. The essence of *Taumel* is excess, and the excess of any positive emotion easily results in its negative counterpart.

1774 **zu ihrem Selbst** Faust wishes to expand his own being until this comprises the whole of humanity. Such expansion of the self to the proportions of the whole of humanity seems to bring with it an end in disaster, when humanity itself (*sie* 1775) crashes against some unyielding obstacle and is ruined (*zerscheitern*).

1779 **Sauerteig** Humanity, human life on earth, is compared with bread containing an indigestible mass of fermented dough. It is as difficult for any man to know all of human life as it is for anyone to digest a lump of fermented dough.

1780 Infinite light can be endured only by a divine being. Mephistopheles and his group (*uns*) have no light, while human beings like Faust must have light and darkness alternately, and so must lack complete power to apprehend everything all the time.

1785–1802 Mephistopheles replies with irony to Faust's insistence upon the impossible. There is only one little thing, he says, that might keep Faust from achieving his purpose: there may not be time enough at Faust's disposal for him to learn all he wishes to know. Perhaps a poet might help Faust in this undertaking. Poets can create imaginary characters whom they endow with every virtue; possibly one of them might so endow Faust. These noble qualities in real life as a rule are mutually exclusive. The climactic contradiction suggested is that of instinctively falling in love according to plan (1800).

1790 **den Herrn** The poet.

1792 **Ehrenscheitel** 'revered head.' The word is conceivably applicable to the Faust of the scene *Vor dem Tor*, but if the reference is to the effect of the future action of this poet, then *Ehrenscheitel* is a short cut for *auf Euren Scheitel zu Eurer Ehre häufen*, 'to pile upon your head, thereby to honor you.'

1796 **des Nordens** This form is peculiar, if it means what it appears to mean in contrast with *des Italieners. Der Norden, des Nordens* normally means the geographical region 'north,' while *der Norde*, which is used elsewhere by Goethe to mean the inhabitant of these northern regions, should have as its genitive *des Norden*, and this is sometimes printed here.

1801 This gentleman is the creation of the poet, made of all the ingredients just named. He would indeed be Mr. Microcosm, since he would comprise within himself an epitome of the universe of human experience.

1804 **der Menschheit Krone** The goal of Faust's strivings is the perfect realization of human potentialities, to become the perfect human being and thus to comprise all humanity within himself. This is equivalent to becoming "like God." The belief in the perfectibility of the human individual is an important part of Goethe's thought. A notable example is his novel WILHELM MEISTER, which follows the development of the hero from apprenticeship to mastership.

1807 **Perücke** Probably the *Staatsperücke* or *Allonge*, which was most luxurious in its baroque exuberance about 1700.

1808 **Socken** Probably to be taken in the sense of 'shoes.' Goethe uses the word again in line 5546, where it is clearly the German word for the flatsoled, heelless footwear of wool, which was somewhat like what we should today call "loafers." — **ellenhohe** refers to the height or length of these *Socken*, and presumably the wealthier the man, the longer his *Socken*, within natural limits. The intent of the two lines 1807–1808 is clear enough: 'No matter how big a wig you put on; no matter how high your shoes, you are what you are.' Many commentators take this *Socken* to be the 'sock' of ancient comedy. Some even believe that Goethe misused the form here instead of *Kothurnen* (*cothurni*) 'buskins,' which the actors in ancient tragedy wore. These were built up with very thick soles and high heels. It is impossible to believe that Goethe did not know the difference between *soccus* and *cothurnus*, and it is not likely that he had either in mind here.

1816–1817 Mephistopheles recognizes in Faust's despair nothing of its real causes, but sees only the despair itself. Hence he says, in effect, 'Well, good sir, your way of looking at things is that of everyone else, but we have a chance to fix things up, if we get at it before you become quite inaccessible to the joys of life.'

1820 Mephistopheles somewhat drastically points out that a man is more than his physical body. His enjoyments are also a part of him. — Goethe has given no indication of the precise syllables represented by the dashes of line 1821. According to the standards of his day, in any event, the word was vulgar or indecent.

1825 **die meine** Instead of the normal form *die meinen*, in order to rime with *Beine*. A plural *die meine* was permissible in the language of the sixteenth century, but exceptional in that of the eighteenth, although the form without *-n* is regularly used in the Frankfurt dialect.

1828 **Sinnen** The contemplative life, which Mephistopheles cannot comprehend.

1829 **grad mit in die Welt** An imperative verbal idea may be supplied. It is implied in *frisch*, and we may translate: 'Come right along with me into the world.' It has been suggested that *mit* may stand for *mitten*, in which case *grad mit* would mean 'directly into the midst of.'

1835 Mephistopheles regards Faust's study as a place of torture and his occupation as a teacher of the young a frightful bore for one so gifted as Faust. It is a life for someone with embonpoint and without distracting ambitions and driving force, for someone who thrives on the easy life of repetitious rehearsings of things already known — straw from which the grain has been threshed (1839).

1841 Compare here lines 590–593.

1847 The spirit of negation (338–339, 1338) in the garb of the professor presents an incongruity which could be highly amusing, because professors are people who are supposed to be dedicated to the active search for truth.

1851–1867 This soliloquy of Mephistopheles reflects rather the poet's early than his final conception of the Faust problem. In terms of earlier plans, the Mephistopheles who speaks here was a servant of the Earth Spirit, and this Faust is the Faust of the first monologue (354–385). Mephistopheles is pleased to see Faust renounce reason and science and place his reliance in works of magic and in the help of spirits like himself. Faust's incontinent drive to achieve the satisfaction of his great urge for transcendent knowledge will lead him, as Mephistopheles sees things, to disillusionment and ruin. Hence Mephistopheles refers to this drive as Faust's *Lügengeist*.

Efforts to reconcile these lines in detail with the features of the later Faust are more likely to confuse than to clarify the issue. For example, it is not necessary, and probably not permissible, to identify the *übereiltes Streben* of line 1858 with the *Gärung* of line 302, for lines 300–307 were not written until 1797 or 1798, while the monologue of Mephistopheles, lines 1851–1867, was printed in 1790.

1862 The figures are from the bird catcher's trade. The bird is caught in the "lime." It struggles, but the more it flaps and jerks (*zappeln*), the sooner it becomes exhausted and the more firmly it becomes entangled in the glue, until finally it is seized with cramps (*starren*) and sticks fast firmly and helplessly (*kleben*).

1863 **Unersättlichkeit** Dative. Food and drink for his insatiable appetite for experience and knowledge shall dangle before him, but he shall never partake of them.

1868 The scene between Mephistopheles and the Student is one of the oldest parts of FAUST. It underwent drastic revision between the URFAUST and the finished FAUST, Part I. This revision changed the scene from a mere satirical burlesque to a dramatically acceptable interlude after the climax of the scene at line 1867. The *Schülerszene* remains episodic, but it is interesting and pertinent because of the parallels which suggest themselves between this youngster and Faust. We shall meet this fellow again at line 6689, as a *Baccalaureus.*

1873 Mephistopheles' first lie to the student.

1879 **hieraußen** This student when at home would refer to the city in which this university is located as *draußen im Reich.* When he gets there he says he is *hieraußen* (*im Reiche*). This points to the eighteenth century use of the term *Reich* to designate Upper Germany, or even more narrowly the western regions along the Rhine and Main rivers and exclusive of Bavaria and Austria. Probably this student comes from some province in central or northern Germany, whereas the university is located *'im Reich,'* in one or the other of the senses indicated. This student is a boy from a good home, who is away from home for the first time and who takes his mission very seriously.

1881–1887 The halls of learning are not a natural environment. Culture and nature are in many particulars at odds with each other. Too much culture to the exclusion of nature is distressing.

1897 **Fakultät** See note to line 354. In this discussion the fields of Law, Theology, Medicine are mentioned as possible fields of specialization after preliminary courses in logic and metaphysics.

1898–1901 This youth voices the same ideal of knowledge as that which possesses Faust, but he is made of much less stern stuff, as is shown by 1905–1907.

1908 **der Zeit** Genitive object of *gebrauchen,* instead of the more usual accusative, as in line 235.

1911 **Collegium Logicum** *Collegium* is used here in the German sense of *Kolleg,* 'course.' The course in logic was the chief occupation of students in their first semester, even in Goethe's day, and he wrote of this part of his experience in Leipzig [DICHTUNG UND WAHRHEIT, Book VI.]: "Meine Kollegia besuchte ich anfangs emsig und treulich . . . In der Logik kam es mir wunderlich vor, daß ich diejenigen Geistesoperationen, die ich von Jugend auf mit der größten Bequemlichkeit verrichtet, so auseinander zerren, vereinzeln und gleichsam zerstören sollte, um den rechten Gebrauch derselben einzusehen."

1913 **spanische Stiefeln** Instruments of torture used in the Spanish inquisition and designed to squeeze the calves of the victim's legs within iron boot-shafts which could be contracted by means of wedges or screws.

1924 **Tritt** The normal hand-operated loom has two foot-bars or treadles by which the operator lowers and raises the heddles. These guide the longitudinal threads of the warp. When one treadle is up the other is down. Each movement of a treadle raises or lowers half of the total number of longitudinal threads on the loom. The shuttles carry the cross threads of the weft, each of which is ultimately held in place by the alternately raised and lowered threads of the warp. The weft is settled neatly into place by the reed and packed tight by a blow (*Schlag*) of the batten.

1928–1935 The philosopher's ability to analyze a process does not enable him to create a masterpiece.

1929 The first stress is on the third syllable of this line. The second stress falls on *Euch*, or in the pause after *Euch*. The third and fourth stresses fall on *müßt'* and *sein*, respectively.

1930 In our own day logicians speak rather of A, B, C, D than of *das Erste, das Zweite*, and so on. These appear here to be terms of a conjunctive conditional syllogism, perhaps of what was once called a "destructive dilemma."

1936–1941 The phraseology of these lines rests either upon the lectures or on the book, INSTITUTIONES CHEMIAE, 1763, of Professor J. R. Spielmann, who was one of Goethe's teachers in Strassburg in 1770–1771. The chemical study of organic life involves extracting and identifying the components of the living body, but this can only be accomplished by driving out the apparently non-material bond (the spirit) which unites and animates these parts. This bond disappears under analytic procedure and without it no synthesis of the parts to form a living organism is possible.

1940 **Encheiresin naturae** The process of nature by which substances are united into a living organism. The term *encheiresis* is frequent in the chemical literature of the eighteenth century, but the term *encheiresis naturae* is not. Chemists had no *encheiresis* which would permit them to do what nature did in every living organism. By giving a name, 'nature's *encheiresis*,' to something which they could not describe or use, but which is an essential component of that whole they were seeking to explain by their science, chemists put themselves into the ridiculous position of having to concede that they understood everything but the indispensable essence of it all.

1944–1945 **reduzieren, klassifizieren** Two logical procedures: reduction of propositions to their basic terms, and the classification of observed data according to a limited number of characteristic features.

1946 **alle** An uninflected, invariable form, equivalent to *all*.

1949 Metaphysics is that part of philosophic speculation which seeks to transcend experience and to understand the ultimate or the first principles of existence.

1955 **der . . . Ordnung** Genitive object of *wahrnehmen*. Modern usage requires an accusative object.

1956 **habt Ihr** 'you will have,' for such is the prescribed course.

1957 **drinnen** In the lecture hall.

1959 The paragraphs are those of the textbook, which served as the basis for the lectures of each day. Despite the fact that the lecturer is likely to say nothing that is not in the book, the student is advised to be exceedingly industrious in taking notes.

1972 **Gesetz' und Rechte** = *leges et jura* Laws enacted by a legislature (*leges*), and laws which have grown up out of custom and court decisions (*jura*). — Goethe was a student of law at Strassburg, graduating in 1771.

1975 **von Ort zu Ort** As the laws of Rome have become the basis of the laws of Germany, and indeed of all western civilization.

1977 By the changes which come with the lapse of years, and by the transfer of laws from the environment out of which they grew to an environment in which they make little or no sense, the grandson who inherits these laws is made to suffer grave inequities.

1978 The natural law of justice to the individual which inheres in his innate human rights.

1982 The freshman appears to believe that Mephistopheles is professor of theology. He believes him to be Faust, who, at any rate, was qualified in that field (356).

1983 When Goethe (in 1829) was supervising the preparation of a performance of this scene, he directed that a considerable pause be made after line 1982 and before this speech. Then he had his Mephistopheles speak with some show of malice and irony.

1986 **verborgenes Gift** Theology is the science of religion and the pursuit of this science by a young scholar may be damaging (*Gift*) or healing (*Arzenei*): damaging, if it leads him away from religion to heresy; healing, if it helps him to find true religious faith. But the theological doctrines which lead to heresy are not easily distinguished a priori from those which lead to the true faith. Peace of mind comes most readily to those who learn only one doctrine, for a conflict of basic teachings is incompatible with the ideal of a unique truth.

1990–1996 **Worte** A Mephistophelian aspersion of merely verbal learning, which is too strong even for our freshman, who thinks that words must mean something. This Mephistopheles admits, but he adds that frequently, when thinking becomes vague and nebulous, the mere symbols of meanings are bandied about without regard to their appropriateness. The use of *Pforte* in line 1991 is probably an ironic allusion to the "gate that leadeth unto life." Matthew 7.14.

2000 **Jota** 'iota.' The expression is based on Matthew 5.18: "Till heaven and earth pass away, one jot or one tittle shall in no wise pass away from the law till all things be accomplished." There may be an allusion here also to the bitter conflict between the Arian and Athanasian Christians at the Council of Nicaea (325 A.D.), where the debate hinged upon the presence or absence of an iota in the Greek word which was to be used to define the nature of Christ: "*homoousios*," the form without the iota, means 'of the same nature'; "*homoiousios*" means 'of similar nature.' The Athanasians, who introduced the word without the iota, were victorious and their form of the creed has become the orthodox one for the Eastern and Roman communions and for the majority of the Reformed churches. Hence, what Mephistopheles says cannot be done may appear actually to have been done at Nicaea and some critics therefore regard these lines as ironical.

2003 The boy has asked or has been told about philosophy, law, and theology. Medicine is the last of the four faculties and he wishes to be advised about it also.

2005 **Jahr** The uninflected form after a numeral instead of the plural form *Jahre,* which is now required. In FAUST, Goethe uses this monosyllabic form six times after numerals. He uses the normal plural form *Jahre* seven times, but only once (2342) after a numeral.

2009 This aside warns us that what Mephistopheles now says will be in a quite different vein from that of his previous, not wholly flippant comments. He proposes to speak now as the Devil would speak, if he had got into the professor whose role Mephistopheles has been playing. Nevertheless, some of the things he says have very high practical value (2016–2018, 2021–2022).

2012 **die groß' und kleine Welt** The world of organic life (courses in biology and botany) and the world of man (courses in human anatomy and physiology).

2026 **Punkte** Mephistopheles means that the source of most female ills, real or imagined, is the reproductive function of the female body.

2029 **Titel** The *Doktortitel,* or M.D. degree.

2030 **viel** The older uninflected form, now normally *viele.*

2031 The meaning of this line is defined in lines 2033–2036. The word *Siebensachen* means 'things,' usually trifling things, which belong to a person, and then by metaphor it is used to refer to the physical charms of the fair sex.

2042 'To plumb the depths of your wisdom by listening (to you).'

2045 Students of the eighteenth century usually carried an album in which they collected autographs and appropriate comments from people of importance with whom they became acquainted.

2048 The Latin version of the end of Genesis 3.5, except that *Deus* has been substituted for *dii.* These are the words the serpent spoke to Eve in the Garden of Eden, advising the first lady to go ahead and eat of the forbidden fruit, saying: "Ye shall not surely die; for God knoweth that in the day ye eat thereof, then your eyes shall be opened and ye shall be as God (or as Gods), knowing good and evil."

2049–2050 These lines are sometimes scanned as hexameters but may better be taken as somewhat irregular Alexandrines. — The meaning is: 'Go ahead and become like God, and you will surely sooner or later thereby get into a state of anxiety.'

2052 The antithesis here is not that of microcosm to macrocosm nor yet that of line 2012, but rather the practical distinction between the world of the little man and the world of the great, the burgher and the courtier. The trip on which they are about to embark is compared with an academic course (*Cursum*); but in this one, loafing will bring advantages (*Nutzen*), and this course will not cost anything. *Durchschmarutzen* means to enjoy as a parasite, without paying tuition or contributing to the support of the enterprise.

2065 Travel by magic cloak is standard procedure in the Faust legend.

2069 **Feuerluft** Usually taken to allude to the balloon flights of the brothers Montgolfier (first on August 27, 1783), who lifted their balloon with heated air. In the same year, J. A. C. Charles flew a balloon filled with hydrogen. Goethe is known to have been interested in the flights of the Montgolfiers, and it is not probable that he would have referred to hydrogen as *Feuerluft;* hence it is unlikely that this line refers to the flight made by Charles.

2070 **behend** 'expeditiously.'

7. Auerbachs Keller in Leipzig

Auerbach's Keller, in Auerbach's Hof in Leipzig, was a restaurant and wine room in which Goethe frequently sat with friends while he was a student in Leipzig (1765–1768). It has long been associated with the Faust legend and has mural paintings of scenes from the Faust story, painted about 1625.

This scene in all its essentials was part of the Urfaust (1775?). It was revised in the direction of greater politeness and less realism of diction when the prose of the Urfaust was replaced by the verse of the Fragment (1790). Also, the magician's tricks with the wine, which were performed by Faust in the first version, are performed by Mephistopheles in the Fragment and all subsequent editions.

The scene is a very successful and amusing genre picture of one phase of German student life. Its function in the economy of the Faust play is slight. We have to assume that our Faust, the renowned University teacher and physician, was familiar with such scenes as are here depicted. Hence this visit in Auerbach's Keller cannot be a new experience for him. Neither should we charge Mephistopheles with being so stupid as to suppose that this sort of thing would captivate or divert Faust. Faust speaks only twice during the scene, once to greet the assemblage politely, and once to say that he would like to leave. The scene is therefore an episode and an interlude between Faust's decision to try Mephistopheles' plan and the real embarkation upon that journey through the little and the great world as promised in line 2052. The scene begins late in the course of the night's revelry, when things have become dull and some new incitement is needed to stimulate the weary drinkers.

SD 2073 **Frosch** A student nickname for a new freshman (*Fuchs*). So also the name *Brander* suggests *Brandfuchs*, a student in his second semester; and *Altmayer* suggests *alter Herr*, a student of advanced standing. Hence it is presumed that this is a party of students. Although the name *Siebel* has no connotations similar to those of the other names, its bearer must be supposed to belong to the same social group. A mixture of town and gown in such a party is unthinkable.

2078 **Sauerei** May mean either 'swinishness' or 'obscenity' — in either case 'dirtiness.' There is possibly a play on this word in these lines, in that Brander may mean by *Sauerei* a dirty story, while Frosch turns the word to the meaning 'swinishness.'

2079 **Doppelt Schwein** (You are) 'doubly a swine'; once for the *Dummheit*, once for the *Sauerei*.

2082 **Runda** Often the first word of a refrain to be sung by all, while one of the group has to empty his glass at a single draught.

2090 The Holy Roman Empire in Goethe's day was a frequent target for satire because of its lack of unity and because of the disparity between its pomp and its lack of real power. Brander, in lines 2093–2096, is not just indifferent to world affairs; he is aware that the Emperor and his Chancellor are in no enviable position.

2098 Students in the 17th and 18th centuries often amused themselves in drinking bouts by choosing one of their number to be "Pope." The criterion for elevation to this high eminence was the capacity to consume beer. The person chosen was seated on a chair on a table. If he could still talk, he was obliged to answer (in Latin) the questions which other members of the company addressed to him, beginning with the formula: "O lector lectorum, dic mihi . . ." He also was supposed to drink to the health of everyone present until he became incapable of doing so any more. Or, in another version of the game, the "Pope" had to sing a Latin song of twelve stanzas draining a measure of beer after each stanza. The name *Papst* is also given to a mixed drink composed of the finest ingredients, and the preparation of this potion — *einen Papst machen* — is sometimes referred to as *einen Papst wählen*. Just which of these rites Goethe had in mind is not clear.

Some editors suggest that lines 2099–2100 are an obscene allusion to the legend of Pope Joanna and to the procedure of the college of cardinals in subsequent elections to assure themselves that the candidate was not a woman. This view ignores the student custom of choosing a "Pope" as just described, according to which the critical *Qualität* was not masculinity but *Trinkfähigkeit*.

2101 This line is the exact duplicate of the first line of an old folk song of the mid-seventeenth century, and the next line is very much like the last line of many folk songs.

2103 Siebel takes this song to be addressed to a particular person with whom his own affairs of the heart have not been particularly fortunate.

2111 **Kobold** An unpleasant, unlovely, torturing goblin, an imp, a son of Satan.

2112 **Kreuzweg** According to general popular superstition, the intersection of two roads is a favorite meeting place of evil spirits.

2113 **Blocksberg** The popular name of the *Brocken,* in the Harz Mountains. This is a high, flat-topped summit of bare rocks where on Walpurgis Night (the night between April 30 and May 1) witches are said to disport themselves in the company of all manner of evil spirits. Some of these took on the form of goats and galloped up and down the mountain-side.

2118 **die Fenster eingeschmissen** By way of taking revenge for the failure of this damsel to open her window to him in response to his amorous attentions.

2122 **nach Standsgebühr** 'as is due them according to their station' (as lovers).

2123 **zur** 'as a toast to,' or 'to put us all into the spirit of' (a fine, jovial evening).

2124 **vom neusten Schnitt** This statement that the song about to be offered is strictly up to date (it is a coarse satire of love) need not be taken to mean that Goethe intended this song to be like any particular song or songs of the mid-sixteenth century. However, the mention of Dr. Luther, the use of the auxiliary *tät* (2145) and of the old form *genung* (2139) give the song an archaic flavor.

2129 The usual pictures of Dr. Martin Luther show him to be exceedingly well-fed.

2138 **tät** The old preterite indicative form for the first and third persons singular, later replaced by *tat,* by analogy to the plural form *taten. tät schnaufen* (2145) is vernacular for *schnaufte,* with *tät* serving as an auxiliary verb. In this use the plural form is commonly *täten,* by analogy to *tät,* as in line 2781.

2139 **genung** A middle German form of *genug* used by Hans Sachs, Gryphius, and Goethe, but in FAUST only in Part I, and only in rime (five times). The usual form in FAUST is *genug* (fifty times).

2151–2152 Siebel, who is quite as *platt* as the rest, thinks that poisoning rats is a stupid business which should not interest anyone, and the cruel exuberance of his fellows moves him to compassion for the victim: Siebel is already a bit maudlin.

2154 **Schmerbauch** Siebel is meant.

2172 **ein klein Paris** Paris was the center and zenith of style and refinement for European society. Leipzig in Goethe's day prided itself upon its approach to Parisian manners, social refinement, and gallantry.

2174 **Bei einem vollen Glase** When they have drunk one full glass with the party.

2176 The idiom is French: *tirer les vers du nez,* and is an ironic sample of the elegance so hotly emulated in Leipzig.

2179 **Marktschreier** 'advertising agents.' Leipzig has long been the chief German city of fairs. Anyone who appeared "foreign" there was likely to be taken for a person connected with the exhibition and the trade in furs or manufactured articles, for which these fairs were held.

2184 **hinkt** Mephistopheles has one human foot and one horse's hoof, which makes his gait uneven. His *Pferdefuß* is mentioned a number of times, for instance at 2490 and 4065 in Part I.

2188 **verwöhnt** Because of his expressed contempt for the locally obtainable vintages.

2189 **Rippach** A village southwest of Leipzig, and last post station on the route Naumburg-Leipzig. The people of Leipzig in Goethe's day spoke of Rippach as the home of yokels. *Herr Hans von Rippach* is a variant of a widely used Leipzig name for a country bumpkin of uncouth manners. Mephistopheles turns the insult back upon Frosch by calling him and his companions cousins of this yokel (2193).

2205 Since there is no other reference to this trip to Spain, this appears to be one of Mephistopheles' superfluous falsehoods. The Faust of the Chapbook was widely traveled.

2210 'I think a flea is a fine kind of a fellow.'

2211 This song, set to music by M. P. Moussorgski (1879), is a popular concert piece for baritone or bass singers.

2214 **Sohn** In the dialect of Frankfurt am Main the vowel of this word is nasalized and the final *–n* is more or less inaudible. Therefore in that dialect *Sohn* is an endurable, if not attractive, rime with *Floh.*

2222 **die Hosen** 'The hose' (or trousers) of a Spanish cavalier were skin-tight from hip to toe, and absolute freedom from wrinkles was the ideal of the wearer and his tailor.

2225 **Bänder** Perhaps horizontally around the puffed sleeves, perhaps embroidered ribbons used on the margins of the coat, possibly tc be connected with the decorations mentioned in lines 2226–2228.

2226–2228 **Kreuz, Stern** 'decorations.' The highest class decoration is the *Großkreuz*, worn on a broad ribbon running over the left shoulder and down to the right hip, together with a jeweled star (*Stern*) on the left breast.

2230 **Herrn** A plural form, instead of the dissyllabic *Herren.*

2237 **wir** The people who sing the song, or those for whom it is sung.

2246 See line 2186.

2251 Siebel undertakes to mollify the proprietor if he protests.

2255 Since a full mouth makes fine distinctions of taste impossible, this remark brands its maker as a man of no discrimination.

2256 **vom Rheine** Altmayer suspects that the newcomers come from the Rhine, where the finest wines reputedly are grown, and that perhaps they are even wine merchants.

2268 **Champagner** A French wine, from the one-time province Champagne, with its capital at Troyes.

2269 **moussierend** The characteristic quality of champagne, bubbling.

2276 **Tokayer** A golden yellow sweet wine from the region around the town of Tokay, in northern Hungary.

2284 The first lines sound like a children's rime. The incantation begins with statements of facts and proceeds to nonsense.

2293–2294 These lines suggest the bestiality which Mephistopheles wishes to show Faust (2297–2298). They are to be understood also as the refrain of a drinking song, well known to these carousers.

2295 A sarcastic observation made to Faust and referring apparently to some discussion of freedom which the two have had.

2304 **Er** See note to line 548.

2307 Here and in line 2538 *Hokuspokus* is neuter. The noun is now regularly masculine.

2308 **Weinfaß** An allusion to Siebel's corpulence; see 2154.

2313 Another incantation to delude the senses of the party.

2330 An allusion to a different Faust episode, which was depicted on one of the murals in Auerbach's Keller.

2332 **Mein!** Comparable with the English interjection: "My!" from which something like "Goodness," "Lord," or "God" has been left off.

2336 **Nun sag' mir eins** 'now just let someone tell me . . .' *eins* = *einer* = *irgend jemand.*

8. Hexenküche

In this scene witchery is afoot, for the Faust we have come to know has to be made over into the very different Faust of the Gretchen tragedy which follows. The hocus-pocus and the magic potion which make Faust a young and amorous fellow would be completely incredible in any other story. Indeed, except for the rare skill with which it is managed, it would be intolerable here.

No witch's kitchen is complete without a cauldron. The various figures which appear in the steam from this one may be thought of as scorpions, salamanders, and the like. The *Meerkatzen* are monkeys with long tails, who have been given by the Devil to his old sweetheart, the witch, to be her servants. In medieval folklore and art they are often used as symbols of sexual incontinence and lust.

2338 **genesen** The malady from which Faust hopes to recover is described in lines 2055–2060. He cannot enjoy his journey through the world until he is relieved of his reticence and of the burden of his years.

2342 This mention of thirty years makes the Faust of the *Studierzimmer* scenes a man of about fifty.

2345 The hocus-pocus of this witch's kitchen revolts Faust by its irrational nonsense. He suggests that some product of nature or of man's noble intelligence would have a better chance to make him young again than this witchcraft.

2349 **Buch** Not in the book of magic, but in some other book.

2353–2359 This advice is, in sum, to live the life of nature, the simple life with no intellectual effort to expand one's environment. An old couple who have lived this life appear in Part II, Act V, in the persons of Philemon and Baucis.

2361 **auf achtzig Jahr** 'until you are eighty years old.'

2369 Brewing this potion takes a great deal of time, indeed much too much time and patience to suit Mephistopheles. — The Devil is a noted builder of bridges, by means of which he reaches souls he seeks to capture. Many natural bridges and wild arrays of rugged rocks are called *Teufelsbrücke*. See line 10 121.

2376 **sie** = *die Hexe.*

2381–2383 The lady of the house is out for dinner.

2385 Typical nonsense. They cease to toast their toes when the mistress returns.

2392 The essence of a beggar's soup is that it is copious, has no meat, and is easy to digest.

2393 **Publikum** Since this word suggests an audience rather than a group of customers (*Kundschaft*), it is inferred that Goethe intended these two lines as a satirical quip directed against the taste of the great bulk of the public of his day for shallow, "meatless" literature of entertainment (*Unterhaltungsliteratur*).

2394–2399 The papa-ape finds himself distraught by the lack of funds (*schlecht ist's bestellt*), and thinks that if he could win some money by gambling he might be normal again (*bei Sinnen*).

2401 **Lotto** While traveling in Italy (1786–1788), Goethe was impressed by the ruinous effects of the state-supported numbers lottery, which was called in Italian *lotto.*

2402–2415 Attempts of commentators to find deep meaning in nonsense of this kind amused Goethe no little. Line 2410 is probably best taken as a parenthetical exclamation by the ape, as he leaps aside to escape the rolling ball. Having done so, however, he goes to get the sieve, which has nothing whatever to do with the sphere. Another interpretation takes line 2410 to be a statement made by the sphere itself.

2419–2421 **Sieb** Popular belief has it that if you look at a thief through a sieve and say his name, the sieve will turn in your hands.

2427 **Wedel** Something bushy, to be waved back and forth; a fly-brush, a feather duster, a fan. This one has a considerable handle with which Mephistopheles breaks glasses and pots (SD 2475).

2428 **in** = *in'n*, from *in den.* A contraction not unusual in Goethe's early works, especially in Götz von Berlichingen.

2429–2430 What Faust sees is the image of an unidentified beautiful woman, lying on a couch, presumably like the Giorgione or the Titian *Venus.* Because of lines 2601–2604 and 6495–6497 it is often inferred that this was an image of Helen of Troy, but this inference does not have to be drawn. It has also been suggested that the lady was Cressida, and that the scene shows the influence of Shakespeare's Troilus and Cressida, particularly of the scene in Pandarus' orchard (III, 2).

2442 **"Bravo!"** A somewhat brash version of Genesis 1.31: "And God saw everything that he had made, and, behold, it was very good."

SD 2448 While Faust fixes his eyes upon the image of feminine beauty which he sees in the mirror and becomes progressively obsessed with its erotic suggestion until he is driven to propose flight from the scene, Mephistopheles lolls in an armchair, waving a *Wedel*, which he says might well be his scepter, if he had a crown to go with it. He encourages Faust to look his fill at the image, and meanwhile he listens to the young apes who sing their rime about a broken crown. There is no immediately evident connection between this crown and the talk about it and the purposes of this scene. Hence critics have looked for a hidden meaning at this point.

2450–2452 Damaged crowns are commonly restored by the sweat and blood of the subjects thereof. Although it is often held that these lines refer to the French crown and the French Revolution of July 1789, it is clear that this scene was composed in February 1788 in Rome, and it is relatively certain that these lines were written then and not interpolated later.

2453–2455 For no good reason, the little apes now pose as poets, and what they say is a satire on the rimesters who, if by some happy chance they achieve a good rime, pretend that there is a meaning behind their words. Mephistopheles concedes that as poets they are, in any event, honest in thus describing their methods (2464).

2483 Anacoluthon: *Was hält mich ab,* [*daß ich nicht zuschlage*] plus [*wenn du mich nun nicht erkennst,*] *so schlage ich zu.*

2484 **Katzengeister** The *Meerkatzen,* the apes.

2485 See lines 1536–1539. As a badge of their eminence the leading actors of traveling theater troupes used to wear a red waistcoat, called a *Permissionsweste;* and they behaved much as Mephistopheles is behaving, if they thought they dared do so.

2491 **Raben** The two ravens are usually associated with the Germanic god, Wotan (Odin), whom they served as messengers. Here Goethe associates them with Mephistopheles, as he does again at lines 10 664 and 10 717.

2495 **beleckt** 'covers with a thin surface coating or veneer'; *alle Welt* is the object.

2498 The conception of the Devil as a creature with horns, a tail ending in a dart, and vulture-like claws for hands, seems to be peculiar to Northern European mythology, and to rest perhaps on Revelation 12.9, where the devil is called, "the great dragon and the old serpent, he that is called the Devil and Satan."

2500 **bei Leuten** If the Devil is to appear among people (and if he is to be a possible figure in a serious drama) he must be stripped of these wholly nonhuman attributes.

2502 **falsche Waden** Pads worn to simulate large muscles of the lower leg. They can be seen in many of the paintings of the Brueghels.

2504 **Junker Satan** (also 1535), and *Junker Voland* (4023). Mephistopheles does not object so much to the name *Junker* as to the name *Satan.* He prefers to be called (2510) *Herr Baron.*

2507 'The name of Satan and the belief in a Satan have become part of fabulous lore in which men no longer seriously believe.'

SD 2513 The 'indecent gesture' poses a problem for the actor. Goethe taught one actor here to face the witch, with his back to the audience, to raise one leg high, and to slap his thigh as he did so. What gesture Goethe had in mind when he wrote the scene is another matter. There is a problem of the same sort at 3291, and another at lines 5778–5794 in Part II.

2518 **schafft** This use of the verb *schaffen* in the sense of *befehlen* is dialectal and old. Dialectal and old also is the neuter gender of *Saft,* implied by the reference *das älteste* (2520). Standard German has now only *der Saft,* which is Goethe's form in all other unambiguous occurrences in FAUST.

2538 This hocus-pocus with a big book is not unlike the conjuration of the Earth Spirit by Faust himself, SD 481.

2540 The *Hexen-Einmaleins* is sheer nonsense, but with unction. There is a vast body of critical comment on these lines.

2553 **dünken** Used with the accusative more often than with the dative in FAUST. The ratio is approximately three accusative forms to one dative.

2555 **das ganze Buch** This is the book of the witch, SD 2540.

2556 **manche Zeit** The use of *manche,* rather than *viel,* expresses the repetition of the waste of time as well as the quantity of time wasted: 'I have often wasted a great deal of time over it.'

2561 A reference to the numerical difficulty of the doctrine of the Holy Trinity, which Goethe found it impossible to resolve. See Eckermann's report of his conversation of January 4, 1824:

"Ich glaubte an Gott und die Natur und an den Sieg des Edlen über das Schlechte, aber das war den frommen Seelen nicht genug: ich sollte auch glauben, daß Drei Eins sei und Eins Drei. Das aber widerstrebte dem Wahrheitsgefühl meiner Seele; auch sah ich nicht ein, daß mir damit auch nur im mindesten wäre geholfen gewesen."

2564 **den Narrn** A monosyllable for the dative plural *Narren,* people who spread error rather than truth. It is too much trouble to bother to try to stop them. The crowd is against such an effort.

2568 **Wissenschaft** 'The things known,' *das Wissen,* 'knowledge, wisdom.' What the witch says about it is, as Faust observes (2573), nonsense. But it is the kind of nonsense which is particularly seductive to the gullible or the intellectually lazy.

2577 **Sibylle** A general name for a divinely inspired prophetess. It comes from the name of the Cumaean Sibyl of Virgil.

2581 **vielen Graden** The many degrees in the *Bierfehde* or *Bierskandal.* These were drinking bouts, regulated by various *Bierkomments* in the various university communities. They recognized six or seven "degrees" of "insults." A "*Doktor*" was usually a three-glass insult. Or, this may mean that Faust is many times over a D. C. n. e. b., that is, *Doctor Cerevisiae, nunc est bibendum,* the degree "Doctor of Beer, now let us drink." This degree was won in drinking examinations, where the capacity to take on the liquid was the quality which won "promotion."

SD 2582 **sie** = *die Schale.*

2590 **Walpurgis** Walpurgis Night, the night of April 30 to May 1. Then all witches convene on the *Blocksberg* (the Brocken) and receive their due rewards for services rendered the Devil; see note to line 2113. — The name is that of an English nun, Walpurga, who died February 25, 779, as abbess of the Bavarian convent Heidenheim. She became a Saint and her day is May 1. — **darfst** Used here in the sense of 'have to,' 'need to,' as is frequently the case when it is used with a restrictive *nur*, *kaum*, or *nicht*.

2591 **Lied** A song printed on a single sheet of paper and prepared for public distribution. This song was presumably lewd.

9. Strasse

With this scene we enter upon the Gretchen tragedy and the central problem of the earliest FAUST of Goethe. In the ultimate composition of the poem this became an episode, rather than the central problem. Indeed, four scenes which were not part of the URFAUST are now included within the compass of the Gretchen tragedy. These are the scenes: *Wald und Höhle*, *Nacht*, *Walpurgisnacht*, and *Walpurgisnachtstraum*.

The scenes which portray the tragedy of the deserted sweetheart do not stem from the old Faust story. They embody rather the revolt of eighteenth-century individualism against the pedantically harsh treatment of the unfortunate victims of nature's strongest impulse. The catastrophe of the deserted Gretchen is the inevitable resolution of this conflict between nature and a human society which does not dare to permit the free sway of impulses and which has to exact expiation for the transgression of its laws, whether this transgression results from crass lewdness or from yielding to the impulses of purest love.

The desertion of the sweetheart, rather than the socially acceptable justification through wedlock, is the result of a second natural impulse, the drive for individual freedom. To a man of any human dignity, this act of desertion brings the feeling of guilt and the need to perform expiation.

2605 **Fräulein** This form of address in Goethe's day was proper only to persons of the nobility. Commoners were addressed as *Jungfrau* (3018) or *Jungfer*.

2606 **Ihr** Dative of *Sie*, used like *Er* as a pronoun of the second person. See note to line 548.

2611 **sitt- und tugendreich** The hyphen should indicate either *sittreich* or *sittenreich*. Goethe used *sittenreich* at least once in another context; *sittreich* does not occur elsewhere. The usual word is *wohlgesittet*.

2619 **Dirne** Originally without pejorative connotation, this word even before Goethe's day had fallen from good usage except when applied to a girl from the country, *Bauerndirne*. The romantic poets tried to reinstate this old word in its earlier pleasant flavor. Nevertheless, perhaps because of *schaffen*, this line sounds a bit coarse and brutal, and line 2627 is indubitably so. See also line 3174.

2627 **Jahr** For *Jahre;* see note to line 2005.

2628 **Hans Liederlich** *Hans* is used with an adjective or noun, to describe a person who appears to be the incarnation of the quality named. This usage was once widespread. English remnants are Jack Frost, Jack Sprat, Jack-an-apes (*Hans Aff*), jack-ass (*Hans Eselein*). German forms similar to *Hans Liederlich* are *Hans Nimmersatt, Hans Ohnesorge, Hans-im-Glück.*

2630 **dünkelt ihm** The subject is an impersonal *es:* 'in his conceit he imagines . . .'

2633 **Magister Lobesan** 'Worthy Master.' *Lobesan* (or *lobesam*) was sometimes used after titles, e.g. *ein König lobesam* 'a worthy king.' It is here used ironically. The connotation is that of a dogmatic academician, who lays down the law to his listeners.

2634 **Gesetz** Faust understands line 2632 to concern the legal impediment to the fulfillment of his desires. Mephistopheles has merely indicated that some things are beyond his powers to procure (2626), and indeed that some things may even be impossible for Faust.

2638 This threat to dissolve their agreement at midnight reflects the oldest conception of the relationship between Faust and Mephistopheles, but it is also quite in keeping with the wager of lines 1699–1706.

2639 **gehn und stehen** A fixed riming phrase which means 'be done.' — **mag** Here used in its older meaning 'can.'

2645 **Franzos** The French novel of amatory adventure led to the use of *ein Franzos* as a symbol for a roué or rake.

2652 **welsche Geschicht'** Refers to the lubricious Renaissance love romances from France or Italy.

2654 **Schimpf** Here in its older meaning of 'jest,' hence a synonym for *Spaß*.

2674 Mephistopheles' use of the foreign words *reüssieren* and *revidieren* contributes to the impression of sophistication and lubricity he makes here and contrasts with the hot impetuosity of the newly enamored Faust. To complete the French atmosphere, the line is an Alexandrine.

2676 Buried treasure is generally thought to be in the Devil's care.

10. Abend

The function of this scene is to make vivid the basic antagonism between Margarete's simple purity of heart and the baseness of the threat to her peace. Neither Faust's heedless passion nor Mephistopheles' lewd sensuality is compatible with the cleanliness of this room and its occupant.

The atmosphere of the room has its effect upon Faust. His passion is, for the moment, sublimated in a romantic analysis of the objects around him, until he finally realizes the incongruity of his present undertaking with his former standards of conduct (2720). Mephistopheles intervenes before this turn of thought can become effective in a decision which might disrupt his plans.

2683 **keck** Namely in lines 2605–2606.

2694 **Kerker** A clear indication that this lover would regard permanent residence here as imprisonment. — Some critics see in the use of this word a grimly ironic anticipation of the final scene of the Gretchen tragedy (Scene 27).

2706 After the floor has been duly scrubbed, sand is strewn upon it, and fastidious housewives arrange the sand in ornamental patterns, or, at any rate, in undulating lines.

2708 **Hütte** Throughout his works Goethe employs the *Hütte* as a symbol of peace, happiness, and contentment — an ideal state of life, which often becomes the target of the destructive impulses of self-assertion, self-expansion, and desire for power. See lines 3353 and 11 304–11 315 for other instances.

2711 With *bildetest* supply a subject *du.*

2712 The angelic quality of this girl is innate; after her birth, nature has merely developed it. The process is restated in lines 2715–2716.

2714 **den Busen** An accusative absolute.

2715 **Weben** The 'weaving' is probably best understood in the sense of *webe* (503) or of *webt* as this occurs in Luther's translation of Genesis 1.21: "Gott schuf allerlei Tier, das da lebt und webt." In this usage, the noun *Weben* means 'the free movement of a living being.'

2717–2720 Faust recognizes the despicable nature of the intention which brought him here. A conflict seems about to arise within him. But his senses and his lust are too strong, though some change has come over him. The forthright urge to animal indulgence has changed, with the dissolution of his emotions, into a dream of love.

2732 **woanders** He has 'found' it, never mind where.

2736 **eine andere** Mephistopheles says he put jewels into this box to enable Faust (*Euch*) to win a different sort of lady. In the URFAUST this line reads: *Um eine Fürstin zu gewinnen.* When he changed *Fürstin* to *andere*, Goethe, for some reason, wished to remove this reference to a lady of noble rank, but he left the essential situation unchanged. The contents of this casket will assuredly astonish so simple and ingenuous a girl as Gretchen.

2737 The game is the same and the person involved is not important.

2738 **soll ich?** The hesitancy is in the face of the decision whether to seduce or not to seduce this maiden. Mephistopheles, as is frequently the case, fails to understand Faust's motive for hesitation and thinks in terms of his own patterns of behavior.

2740 **Eurer Lüsternheit** 'Your Greediness,' a title like 'Your Highness.'

2744 Gestures of extreme exertion, mental and physical.

2751 The subjects of the lecture Faust seems about to deliver.

2753 The Devil, Mephistopheles, has left an ominous, oppressive atmosphere behind him.

2759 A ballad which has often been set to music, notably by Liszt, Schumann, Gounod, and Berlioz. The melody most frequently heard, however, is that by Zelter (1821). — It is a song about the faithful lover, which the workings of Margarete's subconscious mind have brought to focus.

2761 **Buhle** The emotional value of this word is usually unpleasant or pejorative, either mildly, as in the case of a paramour, or more violently, when used of persons on a lower social level.

2775 **Zecher** The king is so called, because he is at the moment drinking at a gay banquet. It is not necessary to believe that he was a habitual heavy drinker.

2781 **täten . . . sinken** This use of the auxiliary past-tense form of *tät* or *täten* with an infinitive in place of a simple past-tense form is a characteristic feature of the style of the folk song. See note to line 2138.

2786–2787 These lines indicate that Gretchen's family was moderately well-to-do, so that upon occasion the mother could lend money to persons who needed ready cash. It is not likely that Gretchen's mother should be thought of as a professional pawnbroker.

2800 'But people pay no attention to those qualities.' Beauty and youth are not enough; one must be really wealthy in order to attract a fine suitor.

11. Spaziergang

The word *Spaziergang*, which replaced an earlier *Allee* ('tree-lined avenue') at the head of this scene, means 'Promenade,' a place suitable for strolling, perhaps outside the city, perhaps on its walls.

The function of the scene is threefold. It retards the progress of the main action of the Gretchen adventure; it introduces Gretchen's mother as an opposing force in that conflict; and it removes the last uncertainty as to Faust's scruples (2730, 2738), or his determination to have this girl (2857).

2805 **Elemente** A very frequent oath in the literature of Goethe's time. We do not know its origin, but it may be noted that *Element* rimes with *Sakrament* and may be a substitute for this word. If it is one of the four elements, it is fire.

2807 **Was hast?** 'What's the matter? What ails you?'

2808 **So kein Gesicht sah ich** = *So ein Gesicht sah ich nie.*

2812 Irony.

2814 **Pfaff** In this context *Pfaff* has a strongly pejorative connotation of contempt and disgust; compare note to line 367.

2817 **gar einen feinen** = *einen gar feinen.*

2819 **Möbel** Used here in the older meaning of *fahrende Habe*, 'piece of personal property,' 'goods and chattels.'

2823–2824 **ungerechtes Gut** Reflects Proverbs 10.2 "Unrecht Gut hilft nicht," or as the popular version has it: "Unrecht Gut gedeiht nicht."

2828 **geschenkter Gaul** The proverb says: "*Equi donati dentes non inspiciuntur*," or "Einem geschenkten Gaul sieht man nicht ins Maul." 'One doesn't look a gift horse in the mouth.'

2835 Reflects several verses of the second chapter of Revelation, which promise various rewards "to him that overcometh." (Verses 7, 11, 17, and 26), or Chapter 21.7: "He that overcometh shall inherit these things."

2838 **übergessen** The participle of the compound *überessen.*

2843 The subject of *strich . . . ein* is the priest.

2849 **Gretchen** Faust always uses this form of the girl's name. In the stage directions of scenes 9, 10, 12 (except at line 3006), 14, 15, 18, and 27 Goethe writes her name *Margarete.* In scenes 17, 19, 20, 21, 22 he writes it *Gretchen.* No consistent correlation between the use of these two forms of the name and any factor, such as date of composition or dominant emotional tone, has been established.

2851 Faust brought her the jewels, and Gretchen thinks of Faust. Whether or not she suspects him of bringing them is not indicated, but she could hardly fail to make the connection.

2857 **mach** 'Bestir yourself! Do something!'

2859 **Teufel** Has been construed as an expletive, a vocative, or a predicate nominative. *Brei* is thick porridge, which flows sluggishly, like molasses in January. Hence either: 'Confound it, don't be slow about it!' or 'You devil, don't be slow about it!' or 'Be a devil, but just don't be slow about this!'

2861 Faust has asserted his authority with some vehemence and Mephistopheles replies, as a servant would reply, with "gnädiger Herr." If there is irony in his voice it is not sufficient to stop Faust in his departure.

2863 **Euch** Includes each member of the audience among those who are being imposed on by this extravagant lover.

12. Der Nachbarin Haus

The function of this scene is to prepare for the tryst between Faust and Margarete. It is difficult to imagine how Mephistopheles could have arranged a more favorable site for the love affair he is promoting than he finds ready-made in the house and garden of Gretchen's older friend and neighbor, Marthe.

2868 **Stroh** = 'bed' (by metonymy). In olden days it was customary in Germany to fill mattresses with straw. Goethe probably intended an allusion here to the noun *Strohwitwe,* a woman whose husband has gone on a long journey or remains away from home for a long time. The word should not be understood to imply poverty.

2869 **tät** See note to line 2138.

2872 The death certificate would make it possible for Marthe to take another husband.

2873 **Gretelchen** A double diminutive, with somewhat saccharine connotation.

2879 **Sie** See note to line 548.

2880 **tät** Serves equally well as a subjunctive past in these auxiliary forms; hence *tät's tragen* 'would carry.'

2883 **Gassen** An old dative singular form.

2884 **mit** Instead of *damit.*

2889 **gibt's** 'there will be.'

2890 The dative with *sehen läßt* is an old construction with *lassen,* which perhaps was suggested by a synonymous *zeigt,* and accepted because it was not wholly obsolete in Goethe's day. Perhaps also the choice was influenced by the French idiom *faire voir à quelqu'un.*

SD 2896 **Vorhängel** Most old European houses had some kind of arrangement which permitted those inside to see who was at the door before they unlocked it. In this case it is a peep-window with a curtain.

2897 **Bin so frei** The standard reply in accepting a favor offered by a superior, here the request to enter: 'If you don't mind, I'll come right in.'

2902 Mephistopheles pretends to think Margarete a fine lady, because he finds her adorned with a precious necklace and pearl earrings.

2904 **nach Mittage** Here we follow the text of the URFAUST and the edition of 1790. The editions from 1808 onward print *Nachmittage,* which must be construed as an adverb, and should not be capitalized.

2806 **Fräulein** See note to line 2605.

2911 The use of *Sie hat* and *bringt Er* (2913) as second person forms is formal or 'polite' speech for these people. See note to line 548. — **scharf** 'keen.'

2921–2922 Tragic irony: this is precisely what happens to her.

2923 Mephistopheles is not wholly conventional here. The first half of his statement is nearly universal. Proverbs 14.13: "Even in laughter the heart is sorrowful and the end of mirth is heaviness," or Chaucer in the "Nun's Priest's Tale" (line 4395): "For evere the latter ende of joye is wo." What is unusual is the second half of the sentence. He evidently knows that Marthe is not one to pine for a long time over the death of a husband; and, certainly, constancy in Marthe would fit poorly with Mephistopheles' schemes.

2926 The basilica of St. Anthony in Padua is one of the finest structures of its kind. The tomb of the saint is in a splendidly decorated chapel in the basilica, which would be a quite incongruous resting place for the remains of the errant Schwerdtlein.

2927–2928 *an einer Stätte wohlgeweiht zum ewig kühlen Ruhebette* would be the more usual order.

2931 Three hundred masses at the rate of one each weekday, but none on Sundays or holidays, would require practically a whole year. Masses for the dead were usually said at the funeral service and on the third, seventh, and thirtieth days after a person's death, and then on the anniversary of his passing. Three hundred masses in such a sequence would require nearly three centuries.

2943–2950 This brief but important exchange with Margarete is managed while Marthe turns away to quiet her weeping.

2946 **Galan** A high-sounding foreign word (from Spain) for the native *Buhle.*

2948 The *lieb Ding* is the *Galan*, whom Mephistopheles is recommending to Margarete.

2954 **hätte** The subjunctive softens the assertion of Schwerdtlein's turpitude and gives it a cautious and polite tone.

2968 **aller Treu', aller Lieb'** Genitives, objects of *vergessen*, now regularly with the accusative, as in lines 3333, 4114.

2970 **Euch** The so-called ethical dative, indicating the person according to whose desire something is done. See note to line 320.

2974 Naval warfare between Turkish and Christian ships was incessant well down into the eighteenth century. Each party plundered the ships of the other whenever it could do so.

2981 **Ein schönes Fräulein** Here a euphemism for streetwalker. The form of the word *Napel*, instead of the German *Neapel*, suggests the French *mal de Naples*. This was one of the euphemisms used for venereal disease, particularly syphilis. Probably this was the lasting gift the lady gave Mr. Schwerdtlein.

2992 **mein erster** Hints that she is ready to entertain the idea of finding *einen zweiten*.

2998 Marriage with Schwerdtlein was a possible arrangement, provided he overlooked about the same amount and kind of transgression on the lady's part.

3005 **Wort** The conditional promise of 3001–3002.

3007 This aside is an astonishing lapse from the cynicism characteristic of Mephistopheles. It is probably primarily the expression of the attitude of strong sympathy for Gretchen which the poet wished to create in his audience. Even a devil is moved to compassion.

3009 **Zeugnis** Marthe wishes some legally valid evidence that her husband is dead, so that she can publish the fact of his death in the local paper, thereby making her status as a widow legally clear. In the absence of a proper death certificate the facts can be established by the testimony of witnesses in court (3016).

3013 The theory was that if at least two witnesses testified to the same effect, their testimony must be true.

3020 **Fräuleins** A plural in *–s* like *Mädels, Jungens;* here the indirect object of *erweist*.

3024 **der Herrn** Genitive plural, predicate to *warten*.

13. Strasse

This little scene exhibits the state of Faust's emotions, and furnishes motivation for the scene which follows.

3028 Goethe changed the reading of this line from *Nachbars Marthen* in the FRAGMENT of 1790 to *Nachbar' Marthen* in the edition of 1808 and it has remained in that form. The URFAUST had *Nachbaar Marthen*. Neither *Nachbar Marthen* nor *Nachbars Marthen*, that is, *des Nachbars Marthen*, would occasion comment. The use of an apostrophe to indicate the omission of *–s* is odd. Perhaps the two words should be written as one; for compounds like *Nachbarfriedel*,

Nachbarliese are well known, and Goethe may have so intended his *Nachbar Marthen.*

3030 **Kuppler- und Zigeunerwesen** Gypsy women practiced the arts of clairvoyance and divination to predict the future of the love affairs of the young people of the community. From this it is a short step to the business of a procurer. A case in point is found in the *Alte* of lines 872–883.

3031 **was** = *etwas.*

3037 **Sancta Simplicitas** Latin, 'Holy Innocence!' An exclamation said to have been uttered by John Hus when he saw an old woman throw a fagot into the fire to feed the flames by which he was being burned to death in the year 1415.

3040 **Da wärt Ihr's nun!** 'There you are!' or 'Isn't that just like you!'

3050 **Sophiste** The essence of sophistry is the fallaciousness of the sophist's reasoning. The fallacy here is the argument (*secundum quid*) from the proposition that Faust as professor of theology has stated as true many things which he did not know to be true, to the conclusion that he could with equal propriety testify falsely concerning Schwerdtlein's death.

3051–3054 The meaning is: 'Yes, you might call me a liar and a sophist with some justification, if I did not know that very soon you yourself will be just as much a liar and a sophist in your relationship with this girl.'

3057 The incomplete sentence implies the idea: (*wird*) *die Rede sein,* 'there will be talk.'

3059–3066 A good example of the style of Storm and Stress.

3069 If a person is determined to come out on top of an argument all he has to have is a tongue. If his determination and his lungs hold out, he will eventually emerge victorious.

3072 Faust concedes that he means to deceive and betray Gretchen. He says he is being forced to this action by his inability to resist the compelling force of his impulses. It is the poet's task to make this appear credible.

14. Garten

This scene and the next display the first tryst between the two lovers. The chief function of the scenes is to demonstrate the purity of the girl and the genuineness of her attraction to Faust. The contrasts between Gretchen and Marthe and between Faust and Mephistopheles, as the pairs pass alternately before us, are used to emphasize the differences between nature at work and the Devil at play.

When the scene opens, the visit of Faust and Mephistopheles is well along in its course. We have been spared the sight of Faust's perjury concerning Marthe's husband. Also the rather difficult business of Gretchen's first meeting with the dashing gallant, who has twice sent her jewels with obvious intent, has been skipped; and Faust and

Gretchen have reached a comfortable stage in their conversation when we first see them.

3081 **Inkommodiert** A distinguished foreign word to fit a distinguished guest of a higher social level.

3091 **kömmt** The only occurrence in FAUST of this archaic form of the third person singular present indicative of *kommen*.

3094 **weiten** An archaic adverbial form; see note to line 532.

3112 **spat** An old adverbial form beside *spät*, now no longer in use. It occurs in FAUST only in conjunction with *früh* (4958, 11 416) or for the sake of a rime (11 339).

3118 **vor der Stadt** 'just outside the city.' In the older towns with walls the burghers had their gardens outside the limits of these fortifications.

3122 **liebe** Like English 'blessed,' used to indicate a mildly unpleasant connotation.

3146 **wie heut so morgen** 'tomorrow the same as today.'

3147 'Under these circumstances one isn't always fresh and lively, full of courage.'

3153 **nichts** Equivalent to *niemand*.

3155–3156 The proverb says: "Eigner Herd ist Goldes wert," and the virtuous wife is praised in Proverbs 31.10: "Wem ein tugendsam Weib beschert ist, die ist viel edler denn die köstlichsten Perlen." 'To the man who has one, a virtuous wife is more precious than the choicest pearls.' The Devil is citing scripture for his purpose, which at the moment is evasion.

3174 **Dirne** The word is chosen to reflect what Gretchen thought Faust thought she was, at their first encounter.

3176 **hier** In her heart. — **begonnte** An old weak past-tense form of *beginnen*, regularly used by Goethe in his youth but not in the second part of FAUST.

3179 **Was soll das?** 'What is that meant to be?' The answer: *Es soll nur ein Spiel.* 'Only a game is intended. I'm just going to play a little game.'

3198 **niemand nichts** Double negation is frequent in natural, colloquial speech, but has been frowned upon in careful prose by those who accept the heresy that two negatives make an affirmative. Goethe used these double negative forms at times in his most dignified prose. They often give added emphasis or intensity to the utterance, as here.

3204 **der Lauf der Welt** Alludes to the second chapter of Ephesians, which deals with the evils of unredeemed life, with its governing lusts of the flesh and anger, prior to the coming of Christ. The meaning here is simply: 'That is the way things go in this (wicked) world.'

15. EIN GARTENHÄUSCHEN

The scene is the interior of the summer house in the garden. The action is so brief that it is commonly staged as a part of the preceding scene.

3211–3216 There is nothing in the garden scene which would justify these words of Margarete, for up to this point Faust has said almost nothing, while listening to a great deal.

16. Wald und Höhle

In the Urfaust only a small part of this scene (lines 3342–3369) existed, and these lines occurred after the monologue of Valentin, where they followed directly after line 3659. In the Fragment of 1790 this scene was created as it appears now: Faust's monologue (3217–3250) and his dialogue with Mephistopheles (3251–3341) were put first; to them the lines of the Urfaust (present lines 3342–3369) were added, and then finally lines 3370–3373 were added. The scene was then put between *Am Brunnen* and *Zwinger*.

In the Fragment, therefore, what is said about Faust and Gretchen is said after Faust has seduced the girl. In the present sequence of scenes, these things are said before Gretchen's fall, and some of them do not fit the new situation. In the Fragment, however, the whole tone of Faust's monologue was incongruous with the situation in which Faust was supposed to be. Hence Goethe, in 1808, with deep insight into the essential values of this monologue, moved the scene to its present position. He did not revise the text to fit his changed conception of the *Erdgeist* and of Mephistopheles. We cannot reconcile in detail all of the relationships which appear here with the premises set up by the final plan of Faust, Part I. The fact that Goethe allowed these discrepancies to remain is evidence that he did not regard them as vitally important to the effect he sought to produce, provided the text was read, as he wished it to be read, by readers who would take these lines at their face value, understanding them on the basis of the text as it now stands, without trying to search out the history of composition behind this scene.

By putting these lines in their present position after the scene in the Summer House, Goethe produced a symmetrical structure by giving two soul-revealing scenes of self-examination, one devoted to Faust (*Wald und Höhle*) and the other to Gretchen (*Gretchens Stube*), which might be thought of as occurring simultaneously, rather than one after the other, as the exigencies of the theater dictate.

As to the scene itself, we have to think of Faust in a forest glade, to which he has withdrawn to think. The landscape is not gloomy, but it is wild, rocky, mountainous, and, for a lazy fellow like Mephistopheles, arduous and dank. There is a grotto into which Faust could withdraw and before which he stands.

The opening soliloquy of this scene has two parts. The first is a paean of triumphant bliss. Faust is as nearly completely happy in the realization of his intellectual powers as a human being is likely to be. The second part of the soliloquy, however, is the antithesis to this bliss. Faust is reminded of his limitations once more, and particularly of his debasing association with Mephistopheles.

In the dialogue which follows, Mephistopheles brings all his cunning to bear upon the problem of getting Faust out of this mood and back to his amorous adventure with Gretchen, which has not yet reached its culmination. He first reproaches Faust for what he thinks is a return to morbid, solitary speculation about the universe. This once had led Faust to the brink of suicide and will again exhaust and ruin him, if he persists in it. Then Mephistopheles ridicules the incongruity between this great intellectual ambition (as he conceives Faust to feel it) and Faust's overpowering sexual drive, which has been aroused in the Witch's Kitchen and by Gretchen. And then Mephistopheles turns to sheer sensuous incitement, until Faust has been whipped into a frenzy of emotion.

3217–3239 Faust's thanksgiving for the granting of all his prayers. The items granted are referred to one by one: (1) knowledge of the world about him, (2) knowledge of himself, (3) the peace of contemplative living.

3223 **ihre** Nature's.

3225 **die Reihe der Lebendigen** The series of phyla of animate creatures, from the single-cell protozoa through the invertebrates to the mollusca, thence to the vertebrates, from the fishes to man (in the order: pisces, amphibia, reptilia, aves, mammalia).

3231 'The hill reverberates upon its (*der Riesenfichte*) fall with the dull and hollow sound of thunder.'

3232–3239 When the storm interrupts his contemplation of the world of nature outside himself, his thoughts are turned inward upon his own being. And when the clear moon rising above him stimulates his imagination, this brings before his inner eye shadowy figures from the past. The desire for these experiences was expressed in lines 392–397.

3240–3250 The relation between Faust and Mephistopheles is laid before the spirit to whom Faust speaks. Calmly the case is put, and but for the interruption, some solution would certainly have been prayed for.

3241 **zu** 'along with' the bliss of this all-embracing insight into the works of creation.

3243 Mephistopheles is meant.

3245 **erniedrigt** Mephistopheles has introduced Faust to the juvenile doings in *Auerbachs Keller*, to the revolting irrationality of the *Hexenküche*, and has lately enticed him into perjury as to Schwerdtlein's alleged death and burial in Padua.

3248 **Bild** The symbol of sexual attraction; see lines 2599–2600.

3249–3250 **Genuß** As the scene now stands, before the seduction of Gretchen, these lines must be read in a general sense, expressing the turmoil of a striving human spirit which cannot be satisfied with mere enjoyment of any sort.

3254 **Neuen** A weak form instead of the usual strong form *Neuem,* chosen here for the sake of rime. — Mephistopheles is trying to get his program (of lines 1860–1864) started again.

3256 The implication is that Faust also has his bad days, when he is much less at peace with himself. One such bad day is revealed in lines 1544–1571.

3258 **darfst . . . nicht** 'You really have no grounds' (for complaining).

3268 **Kribskrabs der Imagination** The frustration and confusion of the Faust of lines 354–736. Mephistopheles had indeed induced Faust to turn his back on this kind of "nonsense" *auf Zeiten lang* 'for quite some time.'

3271 Mephistopheles claims that if he had not appeared Faust would have 'left this world.' The only plan for suicide which we know Faust to have entertained is that of the Easter night of lines 686–736. Mephistopheles knows about this (see lines 1579–1580), but he had nothing at all to do with preventing its fulfillment. Moreover, when Goethe added these lines 3266–3277, neither lines 720–736 nor lines 1579–1580 were in the text of the Faust play. Yet we can accept it as quite probable that Faust's earlier confusion and feeling of frustration would have led him to attempt suicide if there had been no change in his way of life. It is easier for us to understand this than it was for the readers of the FRAGMENT, for we have seen Faust once (720–736) on the brink of suicide, and again (1570–1571) in a proper mood for it.

3274–3277 Faust has apparently been drinking from springs and small streams and eating water cress and similar delicacies. This is abhorrent to Mephistopheles, who implies that only toads, very despicable beasties, do this. He can imagine a Ph.D. doing something of this kind, but not a proper human being. — The reason for Mephistopheles' antipathy to Faust's communion with nature becomes clear from a letter which Goethe wrote to Herder, August 9, 1776. He said: "Ich führe mein Leben in Klüften, Höhlen, Wäldern, in Teichen, unter Wasserfällen, bei den Unterirdischen, und weide mich aus in Gottes Welt." This also throws light on lines 3278–3281, for such retirement into nature was a normal procedure for Goethe.

3278–3279 Goethe reveals how invigorating this kind of experience was for him in the letter of May 10, 1771 at the beginning of his novel: DIE LEIDEN DES JUNGEN WERTHERS (1774).

3282–3292 In these lines Mephistopheles satirizes the overweening desire for knowledge of the Faust of the *Erdgeist* scene, and the Faust of lines 1770–1775. He thinks (3277) that Faust's withdrawal into the forest and cave shows a return of this intellectual ambition. — Lines 614–622 provide parallels to the substance of lines 3283–3290. Yet Mephistopheles clothes his satire in erotic imagery calculated, even as brutally sardonic overtones, to incite the passion of Faust and to prepare for more overt appeals to his lust.

3287 The allusion is to the first chapter of Genesis, which tells of God's work of creation.

3291–3292 'And then to bring this lofty intuitive insight to a close — I dare not say how.' The gesture of SD 3292 presumably indicates copulation.

3293 **will . . . behagen** 'You find that difficult to accept.'

3294 Bitterly ironical.

3298 **vorzulügen** The allusion is to Faust's conviction that he can intuitively or rationally know everything (3220–3234) and penetrate the central secrets of the universe (3285–3287). The *Vergnügen* of line 3297 is the same as that of line 3282.

3300 **abgetrieben** 'worn out' by the days in the forest (3272–3277), as Mephistopheles thinks of them. According to another view, *abgetrieben* is used in the naûtical sense, 'drifted off course.' — The shift of pronouns of address reflects a shift in attitude from distant politeness (*Euch, Ihr*), to irritated contempt (*Ihm, Er*), to cajoling intimacy (*du*).

3303 **dadrinne** = *dadrinnen*, with a gesture pointing toward the town: 'in yonder.'

3307–3310 The metaphor is that of a spring torrent in a mountain brook. Faust's wooing is compared with the torrent of a mountain stream swollen with melted snow. Such torrents last but a short while, after which the brook becomes a shallow stream.

3318 A well-known folksong begins:

"Wenn ich ein Vöglein wär'
und auch zwei Flügel hätt',
flög' ich zu dir . . ."

3324 **Schlange** The serpent, according to Genesis 3, was the first and a very successful tempter of human beings.

3325 **Gelt** 'I'll wager (that I capture you),' (in the sense of lines 312–314). This remark indicates Mephistopheles' satisfaction with the effect of his suggestions upon his intended victim. Since the words are spoken to no one in particular, the expression: 'I'll wager,' is not a proposal, but an expression of confidence.

3326 **Hebe dich** The phrase is reminiscent of Christ's words to the Devil, Matthew 4.10, which Luther rendered: "Heb dich weg von mir, Satan!" There is an analogy between the temptation of Christ in the wilderness and Mephistopheles' incitement of Faust in this scene.

3329 **halbverrückten Sinnen** Having once put his desire away, Faust protests against its being brought again to his senses, distraught by the conflict between his conscience and his lust.

3334 The 'Body of the Lord' is either the image of Christ on the Crucifix or the bread of the Holy Sacrament.

3335 **indes** While Faust is not with her.

3337 **Zwillingspaar** A direct allusion to the Song of Songs 4.5, which Luther rendered: "Deine zwei Brüste sind wie zwei junge Rehzwillinge, die unter den Rosen weiden."

3339 **Bub'** = *Buben*. This kind of contraction in pairs of words joined by *und* is frequent in FAUST.

3339–3341 A scurrilous interpretation of Genesis 1.27–28: "And God created man in his own image, in the image of God created he him; male and female created he them. And God blessed them; and God said to them: 'Be fruitful, and multiply, and replenish the earth, and subdue it' . . ." — **Beruf** Alludes to *Kuppler* (3338) and *Gelegenheit machen* means *kuppeln* 'act as procurer.' — Faust has called Mephistopheles a pander; Mephistopheles maintains that God recognized this as the noblest calling and practiced it Himself by bringing Adam and Eve together.

3349 **Unmensch** 'brute." In contrast to the composed and purposeful *Mensch* 'human being' he ought to be.

3350–3360 These lines symbolize the ruin brought about by irresistible natural forces.

3352 **mit kindlich dumpfen Sinnen** 'childlike, with senses half-aroused.'

3353 **Hüttchen** See note to line 2708.

3362 In the present sequence of scenes the reference must be to the conflict within himself and within the girl's heart, whether or not to yield to their passion.

3369 **er** The man with the *Köpfchen*, or with the *Kopf*, which is implied in *das Köpfchen.* Goethe changed *es* of the URFAUST to *er* in this line in the FRAGMENT of 1790.

3372–3373 Since a devil has nothing for which to hope, despair on his part is a silly waste of time and a complete lack of realism.

17. GRETCHENS STUBE

Since this scene was composed with no reference to the content of the scene *Wald und Höhle*, which now precedes it, there are several difficulties of reference in the text as it is now constituted.

Gretchen's distress is not at all based on the belief that Faust has deserted her (3330–3331), though lines 3315–3319 fit her condition well enough. She is in love and this alone robs her of her peace.

The scene is a necessary antecedent and motivation to the discussion of religion in Marthe's garden. Also, without this scene *Am Spinnrade* we could not understand Gretchen's acceptance of the sleeping potion for her mother.

SD 3374 **Gretchen am Spinnrade** The women of Goethe's day, both of peasant and of small town circles, were likely to spend any leisure moments they could find at their spinning wheels.

3378 **Wo** Any place where he is not with me.

3390 **Nach ihm** 'Hoping to see him.'

3392 **nach ihm** 'hoping to meet him.' Lines 3390–3393 stress Gretchen's longing for Faust; whether she stands looking from her window, or goes out to do her errands (3145), always she longs for him.

18. MARTHENS GARTEN

Having shown us the emotional state of the two young people, the poet brings them together again in the garden. Here, as in the first

Garden Scene (3073–3204), we are plunged into the middle of a conversation during one of a number of such meetings between the lovers in this convenient trysting spot.

The function of this scene is to exhibit the conquest of Gretchen by Faust (3502–3520) and to provide the motivation which makes tragedy inescapable in this case (3511).

3414 **Heinrich** The Faust of the legend before Goethe was *Johann.* In order to exclude the vulgar associations connected with the name *Johann Faustus,* particularly in the puppet plays, Goethe selected a different given name. The reasons for his choice of the name *Heinrich* are not certainly known.

3415 **wie hast du's mit . . .** 'just how *do* you feel about . . . ?'

3422 **auf dich könnte** = *über dich vermöchte* 'had any influence on you'

3428 **Magst . . . fragen** 'Ask, if you wish . . .'

3429–3430 **Spott über den Frager** Because the answer of theologians and philosophers is in terms of names (3457), which mock the real seeker after truth and conceal the true divinity rather than reveal it.

3432 The declaration of faith which Faust here gives is usually viewed as the most eloquent expression of Goethe's pantheistic belief in God. Insofar as the utterance is pantheistic, it is most like Spinoza's pantheistic philosophy. In the main, however, it is the expression of the impatience of the men of the Storm and Stress with the inadequacy of mere names, and of the intuitive belief in love as the central principle of the universe.

3447 'Does not the divinity, all these things — you and I, the sky above, and the earth below, life — crowd in upon your senses and your feelings, forever mysteriously visible in the invisible close beside you?'

3451 **so groß es ist** 'to its full capacity.'

3456–3458 'Feeling is the all-important thing; a name is noise and smoke, which beclouds the glowing light of heaven.' In sum, the mere confession by His name: *Ich glaube an Gott,* may well enough be completely empty. But the person whose heart is full of God's all-pervasive spirit cannot help but confess his faith in that spirit.

3460 The priest, too, tells her that God is a mysterious presence and that He is present in all things — that God is love, and that she must love God.

3463 **unter dem himmlischen Tage** 'wherever the light of heaven shines.'

3470 **der** Has demonstrative force, 'that.'

3475 **widrig** Here probably in its older meaning: 'hostile.'

3480 **dem** Demonstrative 'that.'

3481 **Schelm** Here with its older unpleasant meaning: 'scoundrel,' 'wretch.' In line 2515 (*Hexe* to Mephistopheles) and in line 3205 (Faust to Margarete) the word is used playfully, hence with a pleasant meaning, such as attaches to 'rogue' or 'rascal' in some uses.

3488 The double negative gives added emphasis. See note to line 3198.

3490 **mag** = *vermag* 'he is (not) able.'

3492 **hingegeben warm** 'warm in my surrender.'

3494 Faust recognizes and appreciates this girl's intuitive perception of evil.

3496 **wo . . . nur** 'wherever.'

3498 'I just couldn't pray at all.'

3501 'This is just a case of natural antipathy,' the opposite of a "natural affinity."

3505–3506 In order to understand the character of this girl, it is necessary to understand the customs of her country and her day. It was not at all unusual for a respectable girl to admit her suitor to her bed before wedlock. Gretchen's fault is that she, with her *kindlich dumpfen Sinnen,* fails to make a clear distinction between a lover and a suitor, although she is at times aware of the reality of the case, and although she knows that her mother would not regard Faust as a proper person to be her companion. Church and society placed severe penalties on young women who were deserted by their lovers. See the scene *Am Brunnen,* 3544–3586.

3511 One may assume that this situation has been foreseen by Faust. Gretchen's mother ultimately dies from taking this sleeping draught. Some see in this merely the result of Gretchen's anxiety and fear of being apprehended by her mother, a fear which led her to give to her mother an overdose of the potion. Others see in this the evil treachery of Mephistopheles, who gives Faust a slow-working, deadly poison in the guise of a harmless sleeping draught, and thereby places the onus of murder on Faust if Gretchen's mother dies. A similar act of treachery towards Faust is the act of Mephistopheles in destroying Philemon and Baucis in Part II.

3512 **in ihren Trank** Supply *gegossen.*

3523 **wurden** The so-called plural of majesty, used in particularly formal speech to lofty personages; hence *Ihnen* in the next line.

3527 Girls, says Mephistopheles, believe that wholly orthodox religious belief on the part of a husband-to-be is a good omen for their future ability to control the man of the house.

3531–3532 'Which in her sight is absolutely the only way to salvation.'

3534 **übersinnlicher sinnlicher** Two attributes of this suitor which alternately dominate him: at one time he is above all sensuous motives, at another he is all amorous desire. In sum, he is befuddled. — The trope which puts two contradictory attributes together in this way is called oxymoron; see note to line 1766.

3536 Plato said (*Protagoras,* 320, c/d = § 30) that the Gods had made all mortal creatures out of earth and fire. Faust alleges that the dirtiest of dirt must be a constituent part of Mephistopheles.

19. Am Brunnen

The function of this scene is to reveal the fact of Faust's betrayal of Gretchen. The time of the action is some days or weeks after her seduction and before her condition becomes known.

The village well was the usual place for neighborly gossip among young women. Beside the *Brunnen* was the *Brunnensäule,* where notices of social disgrace were usually published. In Tyrol, and elsewhere also, the hair of a girl who had associated with soldiers or with men from other regions was cut off and nailed to the *Brunnensäule.*

3544 **Bärbelchen** Diminutive of *Barbara,* the name of one of the four great virgin saints of the third century: Agnes, Barbara, Catharine, and Margaret.

3546 **Sibylle** A woman's name, presumably that of a neighbor.

3548 **Es stinkt** 'Something is rotten.'

3560 **Gekos' und Geschleck'** Both words have a strong connotation of vulgarity.

3561 **Blümchen** The symbol of maidenhood.

3569 **Sünderhemdchen** The law required a girl found guilty of fornication to appear in public in the church, dressed in a sinner's smock, or shift, and to confess the transgression and receive a public reprimand (*deprecatio publica in templo*). Fear of this ordeal led many unwed mothers to kill their illegitimate offspring in an attempt to conceal their guilt. The situation was quite serious in Goethe's day, and he had a hand in the abolition of this public expiation in the churches of Weimar by a decree of May 15, 1786.

3572 **anderwärts** In another district the young man would not be made to suffer for his wrongdoing, as he would if he remained on the scene.

3575 **Kränzel** A young woman who bore an illegitimate child was forbidden to appear before the altar for her wedding wearing a bridal wreath, and candles before the altar could not be lighted. If she appeared with a bridal wreath it was snatched from her head and torn up by her neighbors.

3576 **Häckerling** 'Chopped straw, or sawdust, will be scattered before her door.' Indeed, a trail of chopped straw was often made from the girl's door to that of her lover.

3579 **andrer** Genitive plural of the pronoun: 'other people's.'

3580 **der Zunge** Dative, 'for my tongue to say.'

3581 **schwärzt's** = *ich schwärzte es* 'I made it blacker.'

20. Zwinger

Like the preceding and the following scenes this is a brief picture which reveals Gretchen's soul as her suffering progresses. Several weeks must be assumed to have elapsed. There is no single English word which translates *Zwinger.* This is the narrow space between the town wall and the nearest houses. There is a niche in the town wall of this scene, where a shrine with an image of the Holy Virgin at the cross has been set up.

3587–3588 **neige: Schmerzenreiche** Strictly speaking, this is a case of assonance rather than a pure rime. However, Goethe pronounced intervocalic *-g-* without voice and as a spirant, like the *ch* of *mache* or *reiche.* See Introduction, p. 144 f.

3590–3592 These lines refer to the image of the Holy Virgin at the foot of the Cross of Christ. — Some medieval paintings of the Mater Dolorosa depict the Holy Virgin with a sword piercing her heart.

3599–3600 **banget, zittert, verlanget** Best taken as intransitives, and *was* as equivalent to *wie*.

3605–3606 The moment she is left alone, she begins to weep.

3608 Outside her windows she keeps potted plants. From these she has picked the bouquet which she has placed in the vases on the shrine.

21. Nacht. Strasse vor Gretchens Türe

Gretchen's brother has learned of his sister's disgrace. He is lying in wait for her lover, to avenge her betrayal. The dramatic function of this scene is to break off the Gretchen affair by forcing Faust to flee from her town. It also adds one more murder to the guilt of the two lovers.

3621 **mag** Implies the plausibility of such an occurrence, hence: 'Where, as is quite to be expected, many a man speaks boastfully.'

3623 **gepriesen** Supply *haben.*

3624 **Mit vollem Glas** 'With a toast' (to the lady). — **verschwemmt** Supply *haben.*

3625 Valentin did not participate; he was an observer of these boastful harangues.

3633 Like our own: "Hold a candle to," the idiom "das Wasser reichen" implies a worthiness to serve another person. The same idea is seen in Mark 1.7: "The latchet of whose shoes I am not worthy to stoop down and unloose."

3637 **stumm** Because they could not produce anything to surpass the praise of Gretchen.

3638 'It is enough to make one . . .'

3648 **er** The betrayer of Valentin's sister.

3650 **Sakristei** The vestry is usually located immediately adjacent to the choir of the church and not far from the main altar. Conceivably — though it is certainly not usually the case — the altar lamp, which is kept lighted day and night, might cast some light from a window of the vestry. It is to be thought of here as a weak shaft of flickering light coming from below upward and casting no light upon the street below the window.

3654–3655 Faust is depressed; Mephistopheles is gleeful. — **sieht's** = *sieht's aus* 'things look.'

3656 Villagers and farmers usually kept a ladder handy to permit them quickly to reach their roofs to extinguish fires which might be set by sparks. Cats used these ladders to reach the thatched roofs which were choice hunting and trysting places for feline society.

3658 **tugendlich** To feel 'virtuous' is to feel that one is doing what one should do: that is, that one is *tüchtig.* This is a comfortable feeling, and the comfort is really what Mephistopheles means to express: 'I'm quite satisfied with myself.'

3661 **Walpurgisnacht** The night of April 30 to May 1; see note to line 2590. — **übermorgen** in line 3662 indicates that this scene occurs on the night of April 28.

3664–3665 According to popular superstition, a buried treasure is revealed to a spirit seer by a phosphorescent glow above its resting place. This one is being elevated to the surface by mysterious unnatural powers. Such a treasure is said to "bloom" (*der Schatz blüht*). This one is a kettle full of silver coins with the Lion of Bohemia embossed on them.

3673 Pearls are associated in popular superstition with tears.

3679 **Kunststück** Not merely the song that is to be heard, but the cynical trick of using a truly moral song for the accomplishment of quite immoral purposes.

3682–3697 This song has many points of similarity with the Schlegel translation of Ophelia's song in HAMLET IV, 5. The borrowings were cheerfully conceded by Goethe in a conversation with Eckermann, January 18, 1825: "So singt mein Mephistopheles ein Lied von Shakespeare, und warum sollte er das nicht?"

3684 **Kathrinchen** Catharine was the name of one of the four virgin saints; see note to line 3544.

3693 **Dinger** This form of the plural is often used to refer to small helpless human beings, or to inexperienced young girls, as here.

3698 **Element** See note to line 2805.

3699 **Rattenfänger** Either an allusion to the Pied Piper of Hameln or a reminiscence of Shakespeare's ROMEO AND JULIET III, 1, where Mercutio calls Tybalt a rat-catcher. Some suggest that both Shakespeare and the Pied Piper are reflected here.

3703 Supply a verb of motion: *Nun soll es . . . gehen.* 'Now we proceed . . .'

3704 **gewichen** Like *zugestoßen* (3707), a past participle used in a command. This usage is most frequent in short sharp commands or warnings.

3711 **zahm** 'no longer dangerous.'

3714–3715 **Polizei : Blutbann** With the former, which deals with crimes other than murder, Mephistopheles can deal. With the latter, which deals with matters of life and death, he cannot. The most likely reason would appear to be that this court requires imperial sanction and the Emperor is looked on as the instrument of God. Mephistopheles says he has no means of controlling decrees arrived at in the Emperor's name or in his behalf.

3720 By calling Valentin 'Your mother's son,' rather than 'Your brother,' the crowd indicates its abhorrence of the fallen Gretchen. Stage directors usually make the crowd show their revulsion by turning away from Gretchen.

3731 **sei** Probably best taken as imperative, second person, with *'s* = *eine Hure* as predicate.

3732 **Was soll mir das?** 'Such words to me?' or 'What's all this going to come to?'

3737 **mehre** An inflected form of *mehr*. In older German this word was occasionally inflected when used as a pronoun, but it is now invariable: *mehr.*

3740–3744 These lines prefigure the birth and destruction of Gretchen's child.

3752 **Leichen** An old dative singular form in *-n,* like *Erden* (1374); see also 3763.

3754 **soll** Expresses the will of the speaker.

3756 Valentin lists a few of the penalties his sister is to suffer, all of them in accordance with the laws and customs of the time. Young women of ill repute were forbidden by local or church law to wear golden jewelry, to participate in church services, or to wear fine clothes in public places.

3757 **Altar** This word occurs twice in Part I of FAUST and has the stress on the first syllable (3757, 3778). In Part II it occurs three times and has the stress on the second syllable (4788, 9433, 10 959).

3760 **Jammerecken** An archaic accusative singular.

3765 **Lästrung** The blasphemy is implied in his cursing Gretchen despite the possibility that God forgives her (3762–3763).

3766 Supply *kommen*: 'If I could only get . . .'

3767 This is a direct accusation of Marthe's complicity in Gretchen's fall.

3769 **reiche Maß** This is the only feminine form of this noun in FAUST. The other forms are either clearly or presumably neuter.

3772 **der Ehre** Genitive singular with *lossprechen.*

22. DOM

Originally this was the last of three short scenes revealing in consecutive pictures the growing anguish of the desperate girl. The insertion of the Valentin scene between the second and the third of these scenes (between *Zwinger* and *Dom*) interrupted the continuity which these scenes had in the URFAUST, where the sequence was unbroken.

As the scene was first planned, Gretchen is in the cathedral to attend the funeral services of her mother, who has been killed by the sleeping potion given her by her daughter. Gretchen's disgrace was not yet a matter of public knowledge.

After the introduction of the Valentin scene, it is impossible to explain the presence of Gretchen in the cathedral except on the grounds that the authorities have not yet acted on what must, after lines 3726–3763, be regarded as a notorious situation. On the whole, it is more satisfactory simply to concede that there are in FAUST, as we have it, certain irreconcilable discrepancies, due principally to Goethe's only partially carrying out a late intention to lighten the weight of guilt on Gretchen by making it appear that she had sinned but once. (See lines 12 065–12 068.)

The evil spirit of this scene is Gretchen's own consciousness of sin, her bad conscience, personified as a demon, probably analogous to the evil spirit of Jehovah (I Samuel 16.14), who plagued Saul.

3779 **Büchelchen** Her prayerbook, handed down from generation to generation and hence well-worn.

3788 **Pein** In purgatory, because she died unshriven in her sleep and without benefit of extreme unction. According to Roman Catholic belief, the souls of persons who die in the grace and love of God expiate in purgatory such sins as do not merit eternal damnation.

3795 **Gedanken** Genitive plural with *los.* Modern usage requires the accusative, as at line 2509.

3797 **wider mich** 'in spite of all I can do.'

3798 This famous Latin hymn (a sequence) is often incorporated in masses for the dead. Its author is unknown, and its attribution to Thomas of Celano (ca. 1250) is uncertain. The hymn can be found with a German translation in Karl Simrock's LAUDA SION, 2nd ed., Stuttgart, 1863, p. 333, or Friedrich Wolters, HYMNEN UND SEQUENZEN, 2nd ed., Berlin, 1922, pp. 136–138. Goethe quotes directly from the first, sixth, and seventh of the seventeen stanzas, and alludes to the content of the third and fourth. The first two lines go: 'Day of wrath — that day will change the world into cinders.'

3800 **Grimm** The wrath of the Day of Judgment (*dies irae*).

3801 The trumpet of I Corinthians 15.52: ". . . at the last trump: for the trumpet shall sound, and the dead shall be raised incorruptible . . ." In the hymn:

"Tuba mirum spargens sonum
per sepulcra regionum
coget omnes ante thronum."

'The war-trumpet, casting its astonishing sound
through the sepulchres of the lands,
summons everyone (to appear) before the throne (of God).'

3803–3807 Gretchen's Evil Spirit tells her that instead of being raised up incorruptible to dwell forever with God, as St. Paul promised the Corinthians and the Thessalonians, she will rise from her grave to suffer the torments of flaming Hell. Even such peace as her heart will meanwhile find in the grave is described as a 'peace of ashes,' *Aschenruh.*

3811 'As if the song would break my heart.'

3813 'For when the judge shall hold court,
whatever is hidden will appear publicly;
nothing will remain unavenged.'

3821 **Verbirg dich!** This imperative form is best taken ironically: "Hide yourself, indeed!" The more direct utterance from the *Böser Geist* would be a question: *Verbirgst du dich?* 'Do you think you can hide?' The URFAUST has: *Verbirgst du dich! Blieben verborgen dein Sünd' und Schand'!* These are exclamatory questions with ironic tone. — Gretchen's Evil Spirit is telling her what she has thought to herself all the while as the answer to her perplexed query: "What can I do?"

3822 **bleibt** A singular verb with a compound subject (*Sünd' und Schande*) which is thought of as a single unit.

3825 'What then am I, wretched one, to say?
What patron am I then to implore,
when scarcely the just man is secure?'

3829 **Verklärte** Transfigured souls (see I Corinthians 15.49–54), who have risen from their graves (see I Thessalonians 4.16–17). These turn away from the sinful soul.

3834 This *Fläschchen* contained smelling salts. — In the days when women fainted frequently, most of them carried a little bottle containing an aromatic preparation of carbonate of ammonia, usually with some perfume added, the vapor from which they inhaled when they felt faint.

23. Walpurgisnacht

The *Walpurgisnacht* scene, plus the *Walpurgisnachtstraum*, plus a third scene, planned but never written, were to have presented Faust's adventures between the slaying of Valentin and Faust's unsuccessful attempt to rescue Gretchen from prison. Since the third scene was not written, the subtitle *Intermezzo* does not fit the *Walpurgisnachtstraum* too well.

Dramatically these scenes are important; theatrically they are well-nigh impossible. Mephistopheles, in his campaign to win Faust's soul, has snatched him from his intellectual pursuits, has transformed him into a young man, has involved him in a tragic love-affair and in two murders; but he has never been able to stifle the essential nobility of Faust's soul completely. In his love for Gretchen there was something more than mere bestiality and lust, something still of the true God-given urge of love. To drag Faust still lower, Mephistopheles now takes him to this witches' holiday on the Brocken, where he can bring to bear the strongest of his wiles to captivate Faust's soul.

The scene is geographically accurate. Schierke and Elend are two little towns on the slopes of the mountain, whose summit is called the Brocken. Schierke is at the southern foot of the mountain, 650 meters above sea level. Elend (508 meters above sea level) is a bit farther south and somewhat lower than Schierke. The top of the Brocken is 1142 meters above sea level. The two usual footpaths from Schierke to the top of the mountain are respectively 7 and 9.2 kilometers long, requiring a walk of two or two and a half hours. A shorter path of 6 kilometers takes about two hours.

One has to imagine a constant change of scenery as the action moves along until we reach line 4117. Since the festivities are to begin at midnight, the time of the beginning of this scene is perhaps 9:30 or 10 P.M.

3835 Standard transportation for witches and sorcerers calls for either a broomstick or a male goat.

3841 **hinzuschleichen** 'to stroll at a comfortable pace.'

3845 **Frühling** It is the night of April 30, a little more than a year from the time of the monologue in Faust's study with which Part I begins.

3849 Since Mephistopheles is eternal, he feels no seasonal changes with the passage of time. He is also lazy and vexed at the labors of this climb. He would prefer to ride to his destination; hence he feels *winterlich.*

3851 **die unvollkommne Scheibe** Probably a gibbous moon, with the bright part greater than a semicircle and less than a circle. A gibbous moon can rise only after sundown. The later it rises the less of its surface is visible and the more it has waned. We hear that this one is rising late, with its light diffused to a reddish glow by the dense lower air through which its rays must travel from the horizon to the observer, thus giving just the right kind of light for the ghostly scene which is to come. Goethe was an unusually keen observer of nature and this kind of minute accuracy is not unusual in his writings.

3855 Since the usual occupation of an *Irrlicht* (*ignis fatuus*) is to lead travelers astray and to their destruction, these creatures are thought of as servants of the Devil.

3857 **fodern** Instead of *fordern;* used only here and at 11 314 in FAUST. Although *fodern* was the newer of the two forms, it was used chiefly in poetry in Goethe's day and has not survived.

3861 **leichtes Naturell** A pun: *leicht* in the sense of 'irresponsible' and in the sense of 'airy.' The *ignis fatuus* is a gaseous phenomenon, not a solid body.

3862–3863 With impatient irony Mephistopheles compares the normal zigzag course of the *Irrlicht* with normal human conduct. Human behavior is as devious and unsteady as the will-o'-the-wisp's course.

3870 From here on the problem of staging this scene is almost insoluble. A revolving stage and a backdrop of moving pictures help, but the result is much less satisfactory than a reader's imagination.

3871–3911 Goethe did not indicate the distribution of the roles for this colloquy in song. It is clear that the third stanza belongs to Faust, the fourth to Mephistopheles. The fifth should probably be assigned to Faust and the second to the *Irrlicht.* Whether Faust or Mephistopheles sings the first stanza is problematical. The most satisfactory arrangement is to assign it to Faust.

3876 **Seh'** For *ich sehe.*

3880 There are two great blocks of rock between Schierke and Elend, called the *Schnarcherklippen.* One of them is said to contain a large natural magnet. The name is said to have been given them because a strong wind blowing over the rocks produces sounds similar to the sound of snoring.

3885 Voices of those divine days when love's dear lament, songs, the rustling of a brook, still found his heart full of hope and full of love, — a state of which Faust speaks in elegiac tone as of something gone but not forgotten. This personal past suggests to him the comparison of the echo with the memory of ancient days.

3886 'What things we hope for! What things we love!'

3889 **Uhu! Schuhu!** Mephistopheles imitates the cry of the night-owl. Both of these words are current as names of this bird.

3890 These are all birds which are usually quiet at night.

3893 This line is troublesome, since one could attribute the fat bellies to salamanders, but certainly not the long legs. Probably one has to think of lizard-like creatures (*Molche*) which are still not lizards, or at any rate not normal ones — possibly overgrown toads crossed with fire-salamanders.

3898 **Masern** These are large erratic growths on trees, particularly on oak trees. Here the protuberances from the tree trunks are said to seem to be living creatures thrusting out arms like the tentacles of an octopus to seize the passing traveler.

3908 **drehen** Used intransitively instead of *sich drehen.*

3916–3931 Mammon, the ninth prince of Hell, the demon of earthly riches, puts on a show for his lord and master, with special illumination of the deep abyss in which his treasure house of gold is hid.

3919 **er** = *der Schein.*

3921 **Dunst und Flor** Hendiadys, 'the veil of vapor, the hazy veil.'

3923 **sie** = *die Glut.*

3935 **die ungestümen Gäste** The boisterous witches and sorcerers en route to their revel on the mountain top. They ride on the wings of the gale.

3939 **sie** = *die Windsbraut.*

3943–3944 **Säulen** The trunks of great trees are thought of as the columns which support eternally-verdant palaces.

3955 **Zaubergesang** The song of the witches, which follows.

3959 **obenauf** 'uppermost,' 'in first place.' Hence, 'Herr Urian is sitting (or will sit) in first place,' or 'be in command.' But *oben auf*, as the text is printed in the editions published under Goethe's supervision, may be taken to mean: 'Herr Urian will mount (his throne) up there' (to preside over the revels and bestow his rewards). The first interpretation is probably now the usual one.

3961 A coarse line usually disguised in this way, as Goethe himself caused it to be printed.

3962 **Baubo** Demeter's lewd nurse, — a classic figure astray in a Teutonic-romantic revel.

3964 **Ehre** St. Paul's Epistle to the Romans, 13.7: "Render . . . honor to whom honor (is due)."

3965 **angeführt** A participle for an imperative: 'Let Frau Baubo come forward (*vor*) and let her lead (us) on.'

3966 This line appears to have a double meaning. Baubo is mounted on a *Mutterschwein*, and she is herself a swine, and a mother also. The story has it that she is so evil because her daughter was stolen from her.

3968 **Ilsenstein** Now called *Ilsestein* (near Ilsenburg), a granite block which towers 150 meters above the surrounding valley floor. Ilsenburg is on the edge of the Harz, northeast of the Brocken.

3972 **sie** The same incontinent hag who has just been invited to go to hell because of her great hurry (3970–3971).

3976 The pitchforks and brooms, on which the crowding witches ride, inflict injury on those who are jammed into them by the throng.

3977 This is a very dense crowd. An unborn child is crushed and its mother squeezed until she bursts, like a rubber balloon.

3980 **des Bösen** The Devil's.

3986 **Felsensee** This place name, unlike the others in this scene, has not been identified with any real lake or town in the Harz.

3986–4015 Take these speeches at face value as satirical hocus-pocus. None of the proposed explanations or interpretations of these lines has been generally accepted. Still further impish playfulness on the part of Goethe is evidenced in these voices from above and from below. A half-witch evidently isn't a whole witch: she cannot catch up with the crowd, and she can't stand it at home.

4008 **Salbe** = *Hexensalbe* A magic unction which, being spread on a broomstick and on the person, permits the witch to fly.

4010 A trough with a sail for aerial navigation.

4015 **Hexenheit** A parody of the then current fashion of making new words with *–heit,* such as *Griechheit* for *Griechentum, Deutschheit* for *Deutschtum.*

4023 **Junker Voland** The Devil was called *vâlant* in the twelfth and thirteenth centuries; this name has become *Voland.* We do not know its origin.

4030 The contradictory nature of Mephistopheles' proposal is ironically stated (4032–4033). They have come to the mountain for the very party from which they are now withdrawing.

4035 The club is composed of a general, a minister of state, a parvenu, and an author. These persons are joined together by their common annoyance with things as they are and their preference for the 'good old days.' See note to lines 4076–4091.

4036–4040 **Kleinen** In this little world (4045) there are things and people to see, flames and gay revelers. Faust, however, wishes to push on to the summit where he may find answers to some of his questions about the nature of things.

4039 **zu dem Bösen** 'To the throne of Satan,' where, according to Goethe's earlier plan, the Devil was to discourse cynically with goats, male and female.

4045 An allusion perhaps to the creation of little cliques in the society of eighteenth-century courts.

4050 Mephistopheles is annoyed by any music but his own, but especially by such as implies the harmonious endeavors of a number of people. — These people are probably playing horns of some kind.

4054 By introducing Faust into this circle, Mephistopheles will put him under renewed obligation of gratitude.

4058 Faust and Mephistopheles have entered a cavern filled with picnicking, dancing, carousing witches in various groups. The sad little club of oldsters is also here.

4064 **Knieband** An allusion to the Order of the Garter, the highest distinction of this kind in Great Britain.

4065 **Pferdefuß** The Devil's hoof; see note to 2184.

4069 So many of these persons are intimately acquainted with him.

4071 This line has to do with the relation of Faust and Mephistopheles to the witches at their dancing. First, however, they overhear the club of discontented old men.

4076–4091 The general has been retired, by popular demand. The minister, once all-important in the public eye, laments the passing of the old generation. The parvenu would have liked to preserve the status quo, in which he had worked his way to the top by shrewd but dishonest maneuvers. The author finds no admiring readers but plenty of young hostile critics for his works of moderate and wise content. — In sum, we have a group of caricatures of the reactionaries of Goethe's day.

4089 **mäßig** A pun: 'moderate and moderately.'

SD 4092 Mephistopheles parodies these old and gloomy gentlemen.

4094 When the wine cask has been almost completely emptied, the dregs begin to be drawn out with the wine, making it cloudy. When a glass of such wine has been almost drained, the sediment at the bottom is disturbed and runs out with the rest. Hence *auf der Neige* (4095), applied to the world as well as to a glass of wine, means 'about finished,' 'down to the dregs.'

SD 4096 **Trödelhexe** Every fair and folk festival has booths in which all sorts of things are offered for sale. The items specifically offered here reflect and suggest the Valentin-Gretchen outrages of the pair who pass by.

4110–4113 Mephistopheles does not approve these suggestions of the past. He needs something new to lure Faust to his doom.

4114–4115 Faust, meanwhile, has been pushed about by the throng until he hardly knows which way he is going. He thoroughly approves this great fair.

4119 **Lilith** Rabbinical tradition teaches that the woman created with man (Genesis 1.27) was Lilith, but that she proved unsatisfactory and that therefore another woman, Eve, was subsequently created from one of Adam's ribs (Genesis 2.21–22). Lilith was reputed to have become a spirit, who specializes in seducing men and in injuring little children. At Isaiah 34.14 Luther translated the Hebrew word "*lilith*" by 'der Kobold,' 'the goblin.' The American revised version of the year 1901 translates it 'the night-monster.'*

4121 **einzig** She is otherwise unadorned.

4124 **zwei** Two witches: they have been dancing wildly. A new round is about to begin. Faust and Mephistopheles join in the dance.

*The Revised Standard Version of 1952 translates *lilith* as 'the night hag.'

Die Alte may well be the witch from the *Hexenküche* (2590 ff.). In one sketch of this scene she is tagged: "*Hexe aus der Küche.*"

4126 **Das** Probably best taken to refer to the wild goings-on.

4130 The allusion is to the witch's breasts.

4132 **ihr** 'all you men.'

4138 The dashes here and in the witch's reply represent some sort of abysmal indecency which Goethe chose not to print. — At this point Faust has sunk as low into sheer sensual lust as he can well go. The question is: will he stay there?

SD 4144 **Proktophantasmist** Derived from Greek *prōktós*, 'buttocks.' See note to line 4161. — The first of a considerable number of personal caricatures aimed at Goethe's contemporaries. This one is directed at Friedrich Nicolai (1773–1811), a Berlin publisher and writer, who satirized Goethe's novel, DIE LEIDEN DES JUNGEN WERTHERS (1774), in a parody which he called DIE FREUDEN DES JUNGEN WERTHERS. The rationalist Nicolai was opposed to the uncontrolled or excessive play of emotions which marked the works of Storm and Stress.

4150 **schätzen** The allusion is to the critical activity of Nicolai.

4155 **Mühle** The place where he produces his own literary works and those of others of his kind — his publishing house, where these things are 'ground out' in great quantities. One very extensive publication of this house was the *Allgemeine deutsche Bibliothek* (1765–1806).

4157 **begrüßen** 'ask politely for it as a favor.'

4160 **Regel** These are the geniuses who heed no rules of composition or of aesthetics.

4161 **Tegel** A little town near Berlin. The story is that Nicolai, the great enemy of supernatural spirits in literature, in 1791 himself suffered hallucinations and saw visions. To relieve him thereof, leeches were applied to his posterior, and with some success (hence *Proktophantasmist*). In 1799 he discussed this ghost business in an essay which he called "*Beispiel einer Erscheinung mehrerer Phantasmen.*" Here he included the report of a ghostly visitation in the home of a Mr. Schulz in Tegel.

4166–4167 An intentional pun. Nicolai revolted not only against the despotism of *Geister* ('ghosts') but, according to this thrust, against the supremacy of other peoples' *Geist* ('intelligence'). See line 4175. His own intelligence isn't able to force these leading spirits through standardized drills. There may even be a suggestion of *exorzisieren* ('exorcise') in *exerzieren.*

4169 **Reise** An allusion to the very dull and very long (twelve large volumes) BESCHREIBUNG EINER REISE DURCH DEUTSCHLAND UND DIE SCHWEIZ IM JAHRE 1781, which Nicolai published in the thirteen years from 1783 to 1796. Nicolai is again referred to as the 'Traveler' at lines 4267 and 4319. He says here that he will at least take home with him this trip to the Brocken, presumably to add it to the REISE.

4170 **vor meinem letzten Schritt** 'before my death.'

4171 **bezwingen** He hopes to overcome the devils by means of leeches, applied as indicated; he hopes to overcome the poets through his literary attacks on their works.

4172 **Pfütze** The source of the leeches.

SD 4176 Something has given Faust pause in his sensuous revels.

4179 The significance of the red mouse is mysterious, but the effect of its appearance is revulsion. After all, the lady is a witch. Mephistopheles points out that it wasn't a real (gray) mouse anyway (4181).

4184–4205 The illusion by which Faust here sees the figure of Gretchen is a clairvoyant dream in which Faust's knowledge of the girl's condition lets him see, as it were in a vision, her future fate: her arrest (4186), her death (4195) by the executioner's axe (4203–4205). In the revels on the Brocken Mephistopheles has produced the most powerfully sensuous diversions at his command. His object is to beguile Faust and perhaps to win his wager at once. To succeed he needs first of all to erase from Faust's mind the memory of Gretchen's pure love for him and of Faust's love for this girl. That Faust should see in this phantom on the Blocksberg the form of Gretchen is precisely opposite to Mephistopheles' plans. He hastens to assure Faust that it is not Gretchen but sheer hocus-pocus; the figure is a witch. Nevertheless Faust is not diverted from thoughts of Gretchen, and his last words in the Walpurgis Night presage with tragic irony the discovery he is about to make about Gretchen — a discovery which drives him to furious reproaches against Mephistopheles (in the scene *Trüber Tag*) and to a futile attempt to liberate Gretchen from prison.

4194 The Gorgon Medusa, a terrible monster in Greek mythology, who was laying waste the country of Polydectes. This monster had once been a very beautiful maiden whose chief glory was her hair. But Minerva, who found the girl's beauty troublesome, transformed the curls of her hair into hissing serpents and made her so horrible to look upon that any living thing which did so was turned into stone.

4207 The most noted of the dead who are thus able to walk about with their heads severed from their bodies is probably Bertrand de Born, described in Dante's Inferno. Another is Anne Boleyn.

4208 Perseus was sent out by Polydectes to attempt to destroy the Medusa. He skillfully used his shining shield as a mirror, so that he might approach the monster without looking at her. When he found her, either asleep or in prayer — one is not certain which — he chopped off her head. The image of the Medusa's head was embossed on the shield of Minerva (Pallas Athena).

4209 Faust is still fascinated by this vision which looks to him like Gretchen and which Mephistopheles calls a delusion (*Wahn*). The Devil's purpose is ill suited by a return of Faust's thoughts to the kind of love represented by his experience with Gretchen.

4211 **Prater** An intentionally anachronistic reference to a famous sylvan park in Vienna, with great open-air cafés. It was dedicated to the public in 1766. Mephistopheles is thinking of something like the *Volksprater* or *Wurstelprater* (from *Hanswurst*), with merry-go-rounds, swings, grottoes, puppet theaters, shooting galleries and refreshment booths.

SD 4214 **Servibilis** A name created by Goethe for the dilettante manager of a dilettante theater. The word means apparently 'the one eager to serve.' Just which of Goethe's acquaintances is here satirized we do not know, and he would interest us little if he could be identified.

4217 **Dilettant** After the death of Schiller in 1805, Goethe took a hand in the direction of the court theater in Weimar. He had a great deal of difficulty with people who had no liking for the great works of the theater, but who demanded something new and something flashy. — The essential mark of the dilettante is his delight in a smattering of knowledge and his lack of powers of concentration and of the ability to do hard work.

4220 **mich dilettiert's** An expression coined by Goethe on the model of Italian *mi diletta* 'it delights me.'

4221–4222 Dilettantism belongs with the creatures of the Devil and their hocus-pocus.

24. Walpurgisnachtstraum

The title of this scene is a direct allusion to Shakespeare's play 'A Midsummer-Night's Dream. The names Oberon, Titania, and Puck are directly from Shakespeare's play. The fairy story of this drama had been used by Wieland in his Oberon; and an operetta, by one of the Wranitzky brothers, dealing with the reconciliation of Oberon and Titania, had been produced in Weimar under Goethe's direction in 1796.

This celebration of the golden wedding of Oberon and Titania was intended originally as a separate little entertainment, bringing together a continuation of the satirical criticism of the contemporary scene which Goethe and Schiller had begun in the *Xenien* (1796–1797). Indeed, some of these stanzas were offered for publication in Schiller's *Musenalmanach* (Summer, 1797). That is to say, in its original conception much of the content of this scene had nothing at all to do with Faust.

As the *Walpurgisnacht* scenes were first sketched, the *Walpurgisnachtstraum* was to have come between two other scenes as an entr'acte entertainment. As it now stands, it is not, properly speaking, an intermezzo in that series, although it may be taken as an interlude in the sequence of scenes in which Faust participates.

The scene belongs in the category of the romantic *Märchendrama*. The director of the play, the leader of the orchestra, the audience, all intervene in the progress of the dialogue. There is no plot and nothing happens. The characters step forward one by one and tell who they are and what they represent, or one of them marches past while some of the others make remarks about him. In the main, each character is a caricature of some contemporary figure in whom we now have very little interest.

Various types of literary figures and critics are satirized 4255–4290; then individual critics 4295–4330; representatives of various schools of philosophy 4343–4362; finally, types of politicians 4367–4390.

4224 **Mieding** Johann Martin Mieding, the court theater's master carpenter and scene builder in Weimar, whose title was *Hofebenist und Theatermeister*. He died in 1782 and was immortalized by Goethe's poem *Auf Miedings Tod*. *Miedings Söhne* are therefore the successors of Mieding, or the carpenter's crew, who have but little to do for this performance, since the scenery is very simple.

4229–4230 The reconciliation of Oberon and Titania, rather than the fifty years, is the real cause for jubilation. This royal pair long quarreled over Titania's boy attendant, stolen from an Indian potentate, and the alleged too great promiscuity of the king. Finally, by magic means, Titania is made to see the error of her ways and peace is restored.

4235 **Puck** Robin Goodfellow, the jester of King Oberon. He leads the dance of the comic figures.

4239 **Ariel** An airy spirit, whose name is taken from Shakespeare's THE TEMPEST. He leads the nobler figures of this ballet-like scene.

4241 The heavenly song of noble poetry attracts the beautiful souls (*die Schönen*) as well as many caricatures thereof (*Fratzen*).

4247–4250 Titania repeats Oberon's advice.

4251–4254 The first group enters. The Orchestra, all playing (*tutti*) very loudly (*fortissimo*) to accompany the procession, also steps up and identifies itself and its members. What follows is playful fantasy.

SD 4255 **Solo** The soap bubble speaks alone and says he is the bagpipe. At least the two have this in common: each is full of wind.

4259 Just who was meant to be caricatured here and how this caricature is to be understood is not clear. The elements of this person's creation are quite incongruous, but if too unnatural for nature, they suffice for his poem. It is also not clear whether this *Geist* speaks thus about himself or whether, while he is taking form, someone else speaks about him. Anything can happen here.

4263–4266 No plausible interpretation of this pair has been found. They appear to be poets whose "flights" of fancy are but hops, whose enthusiasms outrun their powers.

4267–4270 This traveler is Nicolai, who disliked phantoms, but was troubled by them. See notes to SD 4144 and to 4161, 4169.

4271 This orthodox person, who judges everything from the standpoint of Christian theology, finds that Oberon is a devil, despite his lack of appropriate claws and tail. As the reference to Schiller's *Die Götter Griechenlands* reveals, Goethe aimed this shaft at Count Friedrich Leopold von Stolberg, who had found blasphemy in Schiller's poem.

4275 The idea is that the northern artist needs to go to Italy to learn how to give his materials that classic form which will transform them from mere sketches into an artistic whole.

4279–4282 This purist is an academician of the old, stiff, narrow-minded, pedantic school. What this purist sees on the Brocken is the precise opposite of what he can approve. Hence he characterizes the behavior of these naked witches as *ludern*.

4282 The allusion in *gepudert* is to the hair or wig which was customarily very heavily powdered. Even so, two properly powdered persons have succeeded in getting into this bad company. Who they are no one knows.

4283–4290 The purist gets an answer to his allusion from one of the party of witches, and she in turn gets a nasty wish from one of the elderly dames to whom she alludes. One may surmise that the young witch may represent erotic frankness for its own sake while the matron may represent prudery in art or letters.

4291–4294 The orchestra again, this time reproved by the director. They have been looking at the young witch to the detriment of their playing. Some indeed have left their places for a more immediate inspection of the lady. Now comes the second group of persons.

4295–4302 The weather vane points with the wind, has no opinion of its own. This one reacts first to the point of view of the young witch. This is a good party. Then he reacts to the opposed point of view and concedes that these are all creatures of Hell, or he'll be damned. There are a number of candidates for the distinction of being immortalized in this character, but no identification is certain.

4303 The *Xenien* are the satirical epigrams published by Goethe and Schiller in the *Musenalmanach* of 1797. These brief stanzas had dealt very severely with most of the contemporary literary products in Germany.

4307 August von Hennings, publisher of a literary journal called *Genius der Zeit*, had attacked Schiller's *Horen* (1795–1797) and his *Musenalmanach für 1797*. — **sie** = the *Xenien*, those insects!

4311–4314 **Musaget** The name of a collection of poems published by Hennings. The name means 'Leader of the Muses' and was applied by the Greeks to Apollo in that capacity. It seems, however, that this person is better fitted to lead witches than muses.

4315 **Ci-devant Genius der Zeit** In 1800 Hennings changed the name of his journal *Genius der Zeit* to *Genius des neunzehnten Jahrhunderts*, and so Goethe pokes fun at the new name by calling it 'Erstwhile Genius of the Age.' This one invites all to join him and foresees for them all plenty of room on the broad top of the German mountain of muses. (Parnassus was a mountain in Greece sacred to Apollo and the nine muses.) The implication of the broad top is that there is no high standard of exclusion in the choice of candidates for artistic eminence in Germany.

4319–4322 It is not clear who speaks these lines. The best guess is that two speakers are involved, each commenting on the figure of the traveler (Nicolai) which passes near by. Nicolai was a very active enemy of the Jesuit order in Germany.

4323 The crane is Johann Kaspar Lavater (1741–1801), a pious religious poet (4325) and an "expert in physiognomy." Goethe at one time was a very close friend of this man, but later turned away from him. There is no doubt about this identification, as Goethe himself confirmed it in conversation with Eckermann (February 17, 1829). — To fish in troubled waters is to seek advantage from the agitation and difficulties of others. This trait of character is thus imputed to Lavater by Goethe and qualifies the author of 100 CHRISTLICHE LIEDER (1776) for a place among these devils.

4327–4330 This *Weltkind* is Goethe himself. A youthful occasional lyric poem, *Zwischen Lavater und Basedow* (1774), by Goethe concludes:

"Und wie nach Emmaus, weiter ging's
mit Geist- und Feuerschritten,
Prophete rechts, Prophete links,
das Weltkind in der Mitten."

Here too, as in FAUST, Goethe is the Weltkind, between Lavater, the theologian, and Basedow, the educator. The latter failed to find a place in FAUST, although one was planned for him.

4331 Transition to the third group of persons. This dancer hears a monotonous drumming and thinks it is the bitterns drumming in unison in the swamp. The dancing master (4335) sees the next group advancing.

SD 4339 **Fiedler** This word appeared in all of the editions published under Goethe's supervision as *Fideler*. The whole group of lines (4335–4342) was first put into the text in the edition of 1828. There has been a great deal of discussion about the name without an indisputable conclusion having been reached. We choose the form *Fiedler* as the more appropriate to the meaning of the lines. The fiddler belongs with the dancer and the dancing master, all of whom comment on the approach of the philosophers.

4339 **sich** Here, as in 4340, the reciprocal pronoun 'one another' rather than the reflexive.

4341–4342 Alluding to the power of Orpheus with his lyre to quiet the animosities of savage beasts. Orpheus was the son of Apollo and the muse, Calliope. He was one of the Argonauts. — **Bestjen,** with two syllables, rather than *Bestien* with three. One of Goethe's manuscripts has the form *Bestjen*, and we have retained it to suggest the pronunciation required by the rime with *Restchen*.

4343–4346 The dogmatist argues (4345–4346) that since there are devils, the Devil must have a real existence. One characteristic of a dogmatic philosopher is his unconditional belief in the correlation of his thinking with reality. If he can by thinking arrive at "*der Teufel*," then "*der Teufel*" must correspond to reality.

4347 The idealist, in the philosophical sense, regards himself, his own ego, as the creator of everything he experiences. All existence to him is merely the representation of his own mind. This one thinks that if all of the wild goings-on on the Brocken are products of his own mind, then he must be crazy.

4351 The realist (this one seems to be a naive rather than a critical realist) accepts as real all objects of his perception. These are so manifold and so insane this evening that he is befuddled by what his senses tell him.

4355 The supernaturalist believes in reality transcending our powers to perceive. He believes in "supernatural" events, and in the divine revelations thereof. He feels himself able, on the evidence of the demoniac existence he observes, to conclude that there must be good spirits, even though he hasn't seen any.

4359 The skeptic regards all perception as delusive and denies the possibility of arriving at any generally valid truth. This skeptic compares his fellow philosophers with seekers after buried treasure (see note to 3664–3665). Such a negative spirit belongs with the devils on the Brocken and knows it.

4363 The orchestra is out of hand again, this time because of the incompetence of the dilettantes and the negligence of the professional musicians among them. A brief transition to the fourth group of persons.

4367 This group of adept political opportunists call themselves *Sans Souci*, 'Without a care.' They have no principles to bother them. They get along — if not one way, then another.

4371 These clumsy fellows are the so-called *Hofschranzen*, hangers-on at court and bootlickers generally. Unlike the skilled ones, when the administration changes these fellows are helpless and suffer the consequences of their previous favor-seeking.

4375 The will-o'-the-wisps are the parvenus, newly made in the confusion of political upheaval, who fall at once into the dance as resplendent courtiers.

4379 The shooting star may represent those gentry of ephemeral fame, who disappear from the public eye as suddenly as they have appeared. Just why this one is lying askew in the grass is not apparent, except that this indicates that he is on the way out.

4383 The massive ones are the proletarian and lower middle classes, whose rise in European politics so distressed the aristocrats. Even as ghosts they trample everything under foot with their ponderous bulk. They are out of place here, where everything should be light and airy. Hence Puck reproaches them.

4391 Ariel leads all the participants in this scene upward to the rose-covered hill, where, according to Wieland's *Oberon*, the castle of the fairy king is located.

4395 The orchestra playing its softest brings this intermezzo to an end. This cannot reasonably be the end of the *Walpurgisnacht* revels, for the two adventurers, Faust and Mephistopheles, had not yet reached the top of the mountain and the main ceremonies of the night have not yet taken place. We have therefore to recognize a lacuna between the *Walpurgisnachtstraum* and the next scene, *Trüber Tag.*

25. Trüber Tag.

This is one of the oldest scenes in the Faust poem. It was part of the Urfaust which young Goethe read to his circle of friends at the court of Weimar. It made a deep impression upon them because of the consuming rage of Goethe as he read Faust's attack on Mephistopheles. It is the only scene in the play which has remained in its original prose form. Goethe planned to put it into verse, as he did the prison scene, but it is clear that the elemental passion of Faust here could not be confined to a strict metrical form.

The scene is in harmony with the emotional state of the principal character: dark, lowering clouds in a late evening sky. Why Faust is in an open field is not explained, except that he had to flee from Gretchen's city to escape arrest for the murder of Valentin and that after every great emotional experience he seeks solitude in nature. To be sure, the entire *Walpurgisnacht* episode has been introduced between this scene and its original presuppositions. Yet if we assume that Faust has just been through the wildest of nights on the Brocken it will not appear unreasonable to find him the next evening in a different place.

Faust has somehow learned of the disasters which have befallen Gretchen: she fled from her home, or was driven from it, and wandered about the countryside in misery. She has been captured by officers of the law and is now in prison. Goethe once planned to have this information given Faust in the third Walpurgis Night scene. As things stand, we are plunged immediately into the midst of Faust's tirade against Mephistopheles, and indeed against himself as well. The dramatic function of the scene is to show Faust's return to his nobler self and his determination to risk everything in an attempt to alleviate the suffering he has caused.

TT 2 **lange** The time factor is ambiguous. Presumably Faust fled from Gretchen's neighborhood immediately after the murder of Valentin. Two days intervened between the murder and the *Walpurgisnacht*, but the interval between that and the time of *Trüber Tag* is not indicated.

TT 4 **Bis dahin** (*ist es gekommen!*)

TT 5 **Steh nur** Mephistopheles is trying to walk away from his master.

TT 9 **Bösen Geistern** Such as the one of the cathedral scene; see the introductory note to Scene 22, *Dom*.

TT 15 **Hundsgestalt** When these lines were written, there was as yet no poodle in the scene *Vor dem Tor*, who transformed himself into Mephistopheles. Hence this appeal to the Earth Spirit (the *unendlicher Geist*) to change this lowest form of life (*Wurm*) into a dog has to be understood more generally and not as a specific reference to earlier motivation in the poem as it now stands. Any demon or evil spirit, which for one reason or another had to serve a human being, quite commonly appeared in the form of a dog. Mephistopheles is here said to have so appeared with Faust on many an evening walk. Indeed, it was the favorite form of this spirit. Such a Mephistopheles, of course, is a creature of the Earth Spirit and not the fallen angel of the Prologue in Heaven.

TT 24–26 Faust speaks from the premise that vicarious expiation of sin is just, and he may be assumed still to believe that guilt can be expiated in the sight of God. He cannot understand why the deep misery of the first girl to suffer as Gretchen is suffering should not have expiated the guilt of all other such transgressors in the eyes of God.

TT 31–32 A reference to Faust's necromancy with Nostradamus' book (420). This devil classifies himself as a subordinate spirit of the realm of the *Erdgeist.*

TT 32–33 People who wish to fly should be secure against attacks of dizziness: people who associate with demons should be secure against attacks of conscience.

TT 36–40 The Earth Spirit seems to have attached Mephistopheles to Faust with a bond like that of a forged iron fetter.

TT 44–45 Gretchen has been found guilty of the murder of her infant child. Mephistopheles cannot control the decrees of the court which deals with murder, because the decrees of that court are given "in God's name." See also note to lines 3714–3715.

TT 47 **Donner** An allusion to the god, Jupiter, who hurled thunderbolts at those who displeased him.

TT 53 **Blutschuld** By the murder of Valentin, blood-guilt has been put upon the city or state, which is obliged then by law to remove this blood-guilt by bringing the murderer to his due punishment.

TT 55 **rächende Geister** Analogous to the Furies of ancient Greece.

TT 64 **Zauberpferde** These are a new means of transportation. Usually the magic cloak suffices (2065).

26. Nacht. Offen Feld

The time, presumably, is in the night following *Trüber Tag.* As Faust and Mephistopheles approach their destination they look down and see a group of figures in an open field.

4399 **Rabenstein** The ravens' stone is a block or platform of masonry built beneath a gallows, or used as a platform for the decapitation of convicted criminals. Hence the word often means a place of execution.

4403 The reference is to the gestures of these figures. Mephistopheles says they are witches and most commentators seem to believe him. Others hold that these are favorable spirits preparing to receive Gretchen's soul when she is executed.

27. Kerker

The scene shows Faust first outside the prison, and then in the cell in which Gretchen is chained. The function of the scene is to present the denouement of the Gretchen tragedy and the end of one phase of the Faust drama.

4405 **Schauer** Faust is once more accessible to the sentiment of compassion and love for humankind.

4408 **Verbrechen** Not the murder of her child, but its ultimate cause: her yielding to Faust's urgings of love and to her own natural, and hence good, impulses, in the belief that anything so good and anything so lovely as this love must also be right (3585–3586).

4411 **Fort** 'Forward.'

4412–4420 This song, sung by Gretchen, somewhat as the distraught Ophelia sings in HAMLET (IV, 5), demonstrates the pathological condition of Gretchen's mind. The text of the song suggests the song of the bird in the *Märchen von dem Machandelbaum* (Grimm):

Meine Mutter, die mich umbracht'!
Mein Vater, der mich aß! —
Meine Schwester, die Marlenichen,
sucht alle meine Gebeine,
bind't sie in ein seidenes Tuch,
legt sie unter den Machandelbaum.
Kiwitt, kiwitt! Was für ein schöner Vogel bin ich!

4423 **Sie** As Gretchen thinks, the servants of the executioner, come to take her to be beheaded. She does not recognize Faust until line 4470, and even then only dully.

4436 **Kranz** = *Mädchenkranz, Jungfernkranz* Every bride hoped to appear before the altar for her wedding wearing a bridal wreath to signify her maidenhood. Gretchen's wreath here may be taken as the symbol of the maidenhood she had lost; see 3561 and 3575.

4443 A hallucination. Her child is dead.

4449–4450 'There is an old tale that ends with a girl's killing her own child. Who bids them apply that tale to me?'

4460 There is a popular belief that a sleepwalker will promptly wake up upon hearing his given name spoken. Faust arouses Gretchen from her distraught condition by calling out her name.

4475 Even before she can take a step to escape, Gretchen is overcome by the sweet memories of a happy past. This is a demonstration of the insuperable power of her love impulse.

4493 Faust is no longer driven by his overpowering love for Gretchen but by his sense of guilt and his sense of duty to expiate this guilt. There is no fire of love on his lips now, and Gretchen infers at once that someone has come between them.

4512–4517 Another hallucination. She thinks Faust's hand is wet with the blood of her brother — that he is still there in the street, sword in hand, after slaying Valentin.

4520–4528 In her imagination the tragic events are all brought together in time, so that the burial of all the victims is to be attended to in the morning.

4532 She feels unable to revive this love as it once was.

4538–4541 Gretchen has prepared herself to die in the first hours of the dawn. She cannot accept a change in this idea. She will go with Faust, if to do so is to go to death with him, but not otherwise.

4545 **Sie** The representatives of state and church, the officers of the law.

4551 Another hallucination. Gretchen thinks she is leading Faust to the rescue of the child she had drowned.

4557 **die Planke** 'the board fence.'

4565 Now Gretchen's mind turns to the death of her mother and the condition in which she found her on the morning after she had given her the sleeping potion.

4567 Gretchen thinks she feels something (*es*) seize her by the hair of her head. Such a hallucination is the result of her anticipation of this sensation as a part of her coming execution. The line is parenthetical and probably derived chiefly from the exigencies of rime; yet the very disjuncture of the imagery suits the mental state of distraction here depicted.

4583 For the explanation of the *Kranz*, see note to 4436.

4590 **Glocke** The *Armesünderglocke* tolls while the condemned is being led to the place of execution. — The rod is broken above the head of the condemned as a symbol of the death decree of the court. Before each execution, the court decree which orders it is read. Then either the judge or his representative breaks a small white wand.

4593–4594 An allusion to the fact that every witness of an execution by the axe so far identifies himself with the victim as to feel, momentarily at least, that the knife is falling on his own neck.

4595 She thinks the blow has fallen, so that she hears nothing.

4597 **Auf!** 'Up and away!'

4599 These horses will disappear into thin air with the first ray of the dawn or the first crowing of the cock.

4603 **heiligen** Because she has resigned herself to God's judgment and this has brought her here, she calls the place sacred. Then too, any prison is an asylum against pursuers bent on doing harm to a fugitive or prisoner.

4606 Mephistopheles is desperate. He threatens to leave Faust to suffer arrest and execution along with Gretchen, because he cannot himself submit to arrest by human hands.

4609 An allusion to Psalm 34.7: "The angel of Jehovah encampeth round about them that fear him, and delivereth them."

4610 Gretchen's terror of her lover results from her determination to follow God's judgment and her conviction that Faust is not included therein. The conviction crystallizes when she sees Mephistopheles with Faust (see lines 3470–3500).

SD 4611 **Stimme, von oben** This voice of God is part of the traditional folk-drama of Faust, and Goethe uses it effectively to balance the verdict of Mephistopheles. Gretchen is not to be thought of as condemned to Hell: she has cast herself on God's mercy.

4612 Mephistopheles drags the dazed Faust away, but Gretchen's voice still reaches him. It is the voice of love which will not pass away.